CHILDREN COMMUNICATING

THE FIRST 5 YEARS

LEA'S COMMUNICATION SERIES
Jennings Bryant/Dolf Zillmann, General Editors

Selected titles in Language and Discourse (Donald Ellis, Advisory Editor) include:

Haslett/Samter • *Children Communicating: The First 5 Years*

Ramanathan • *Alzheimer Discourse: Some Sociolinguistic Dimensions*

Campbell • *Coherence, Continuity, and Cohesion: Theoretical Foundations for Document Design*

Ellis • *From Language to Communication*

For a complete list of other titles in LEA's Communication Series, please contact Lawrence Erlbaum Associates, Publishers.

CHILDREN COMMUNICATING
THE FIRST 5 YEARS

Beth Bonniwell Haslett
Wendy Samter
University of Delaware

LAWRENCE ERLBAUM ASSOCIATES, PUBLISHERS
1997   Mahwah, New Jersey   London

2\98   # 36086047

Lawrence Erlbaum Associates, Inc., Publishers
10 Industrial Avenue
Mahwah, New Jersey 07430

Cover design by Heidi Haslett Magnuson

Library of Congress Cataloging-in-Publication Data

Haslett, Beth.
Children communicating : the first 5 years / by Beth Bonniwell Haslett & Wendy Samter.
p.   cm.
Includes bibliographical references and index.
ISBN 0-8058-0066-2 (cloth).
1. Interpersonal communication in children.   2. Nonverbal communication in children.   I. Samter, Wendy.   II. Title.
BF723.C57H37   1997
155.42'236—dc21   96-37758
                                                                              CIP

Books published by Lawrence Erlbaum Associates are printed on acid-free paper, and their bindings are chosen for strength and durability.

Printed in the United States of America
10 9 8 7 6 5 4 3 2 1

To our grandparents

Walter and Alma Bonniwell
William and Bertha Stoeckmann
Milton and Alberta Schwartz

and to our parents

Clifford and Edna Bonniwell
Charles and Lois Samter

whose loving support provided a firm foundation for life.

Contents

Preface

This book offers a unique focus on the development of human communication and synthesizes a more comprehensive array of research than do most investigations of communicative development. After incorporating materials dealing with the development of nonverbal communication, language, and cognition, we examine how these abilities are integrated in young children's everyday interaction. We also distill information from various fields including developmental and social psychology, sociolinguistics, psycholinguistics, and, of course, communication into a set of key principles and practices for parents and other adults interested in child development.

We hope that this book is useful for students and scholars alike. Although we do not concentrate on any one area, we do attempt a comprehensive overview of the various components of human communicative development and its significance for children's cognitive and emotional growth.

We also hope this book is the first of many to integrate diverse bodies of research. Developmental processes are constrained by multiple influences whose interactions researchers are just beginning to uncover. Examining the diverse facets of communicative development will produce further insights into the mystery of human communication.

ACKNOWLEDGMENTS

Each of us would like to acknowledge the many individuals who have contributed to this endeavor. The people helping to shape our thoughts are listed in the following paragraphs, but we would also like to thank each other for the mutual intellectual stimulation—and sheer fun—of working on this book. We learned that "even beyond the first 5 years," friendship continues to teach worthwhile lessons.

* * *

James J. Jenkins and Gene Piche contributed intellectual inspiration and guidance: Their concern and passion for developmental research, in addition to their breadth and depth of knowledge, provided ideal exemplars of scholarship and mentorship. The Society for Research on Child Development Summer Institute on Children's Communication, held in 1981, offered an exceptional opportunity to interact with and learn from the leaders in research on children's communicative development. For many years, I have enjoyed discussions on children's communication with Brian Ackerman, Sherry Bowen, Bill Frawley, Roberta Golinkoff, and Cal Izard, and have benefited from our interactions. I am grateful to the children and staff of the Newark Day Nursery for their cooperation in research projects. Finally, I would like to thank Lawrence Erlbaum Associates for their assistance and patience during the publication process and for their permission to use materials from my earlier book. My family has been very supportive during the writing of this book, and I appreciate their understanding. Special thanks to Erik and Heidi, who taught my husband and me a great deal about love, tough times, and looking at the world in new and different ways. Thanks for enriching our lives!

—Beth Bonniwell Haslett

Gary Ladd initially sparked my interest in children's communicative development, and Brant Burleson and Thomas Berndt helped enlarge and refine it. I owe a great deal to Brother Gerry Molyneaux of LaSalle University. His acuity in the classroom and his enthusiasm for the field led me not only to pursue graduate work but, more importantly, to see the richness—and the possibilities—of studying human communication. I share my accomplishment with Jeff Hunter, who was a constant source of motivation and encouragement throughout the project. More than anything else, watching him interact with his daughters, Lisa and Laura, affirmed for me the wonderful things that can happen when parents love and support their children.

—Wendy Samter

1

Basic Concepts: Communication, Cognition, and Language

One of our most intriguing scientific puzzles is trying to understand how children learn to communicate. In what may seem a mysterious fashion, children acquire the rudiments of communication by age 2—without being explicitly taught. So widespread is this developmental phenomenon, in fact, that the age of 2 years is frequently used as a rough benchmark of whether children are developing normally.

How children learn to communicate is the focus of this book. Communicative development has been studied in a wide array of disciplines and from different theoretical perspectives. The role of cognition, social relationships, and language in communication and how they interrelate and influence one another present complex scientific and human puzzles. As we investigate these issues, we confront major debates in social science, including such issues as biological predispositions versus environmental influences, continuity versus discontinuity in development, and the functionality of developmental changes.

Before we begin, however, it is necessary to lay out some fundamental assumptions that underlie our perspective on communicative development and therefore shape the way in which the information in this book is presented. First, we believe that the development of communication is intertwined with the development of language and cognition: Communication is the context in which language and cognition develop. People need support from others to survive, and this compels us to communicate, to learn language to master the environment and interact with others. Through language and social interaction, people express their desires, explore the world, and cooperate with others.

Communication, in turn, becomes more precise, abstract, and complex as a result of both increasing skill and cognitive ability. Communicating with others is also the context in which people integrate their linguistic and cognitive abilities to

1

influence others and to achieve goals. Increasing linguistic knowledge enables people to communicate in many ways, such as asking questions, giving directions, and conducting arguments. As individuals mature cognitively, they are able to recognize and cope with an increasingly complex physical and social world. Cognitive activity (thinking, perceiving, interpreting, and reasoning) is based on information, especially feedback, that we receive from others during interactions with them.

Throughout this book, we emphasize the interplay of language, cognition, and social relationships in the development of communication. No single component alone can account for children's unfolding communicative abilities. Rather, at any given point in time, language, cognition, and social relationships interact and mutually influence one another as well as influencing youngsters' communicative behaviors. The nature of these interactions varies across time. The particular facets of language, cognition, and social relationships that combine to enable children to utter their first words are different from the configuration of linguistic, cognitive, and social factors that influence the ways in which they develop and maintain friendships.

Our review focuses primarily on research conducted in Western countries. Cultures vary in terms of the communicative channels they emphasize, the ways in which they view children, and the interactional behaviors they endorse and sanction. In chapter 9, which deals with parenting principles, we introduce some cross-cultural differences in communication values and parenting styles. Although a full examination of this research is well beyond the scope of our book, a plentiful literature exists concerning cross-cultural variations in family practices and ethnic differences in family styles within the United States.

Finally, a word about our organization is in order. Our chapters are sequenced to reflect the developmental progression in which children's communicative skills emerge. Thus, our discussion of nonverbal communication precedes our chapter on language development because children learn to communicate via nonverbal channels before they understand how to use language to make their intentions clear. This organizational framework, however, is not meant to imply that the areas we cover develop in isolation from one another. For example, youngsters acquire reciprocity and turn taking largely through the nonverbal interactions they experience with caretakers during the first 12 months of life. In this way, early exchanges not only facilitate the development of nonverbal behaviors that promote interaction throughout a child's first year but simultaneously lay the foundation for verbal skills children employ in their later conversations. Nor do we intend for our organizational framework to suggest that the communicative elements we discuss are actually used separately. In the real world, communication occurs on many levels and uses multiple cues simultaneously. With these caveats in mind, let us turn to a brief survey of the chapters in this book.

The book begins with an overview of our basic assumptions about communication, language, and cognition. We also highlight the implications of these assumptions for the study of communicative development. The next four chapters cover the major communication systems. In chapter 2, we discuss nonverbal communication, infants' earliest form of communication. Babies are born with well-developed visual and auditory perceptual systems. These biological capacities "prewire" them for interaction with adults and, therefore, help ensure their survival. As language develops, it enables greater clarity in young children's communication and allows them to talk about past and future events. Relevant stages in children's acquisition of language are presented in chapter 3. As both the nonverbal and linguistic systems mature, they enhance children's communicative abilities as well as their capacity to achieve goals and develop relationships with others: Two chapters cover the development of communication skills and the underlying knowledge that makes these skills possible. In chapter 4, we examine youngsters' increasing mastery of conversations and their growing ability to introduce and sustain topics, enter ongoing activities of their peer group, engage others in play, and manage conflict. Chapter 5 explores how children's increasingly sophisticated knowledge of self, others, and social relationships allows them to use this knowledge and these skills appropriately in context. For developing children, both skill and knowledge are necessary for effective communication.

Whereas the early chapters survey the basic elements of communication and how they develop, the following chapters deal with the critical contexts in which development emerges. Two major developmental contexts include family and friends. We explore the family as a developmental context in chapter 6. Mothers, fathers, and siblings provide important models for communicative behaviors, shape youngsters' social and emotional development, and impart significant lessons about self and others. The family is also a key context for learning the values of the larger culture as well as appropriate sex-role behaviors. As discussed in chapters 7 and 8, different but equally important lessons are acquired from peers. Although adults can adapt and accommodate to children's perspectives, peers typically cannot. Thus, friendship is a meeting ground for equals who, together, must negotiate the terms of their interactions and their relationships. Friendship also provides a context in which children can compare themselves with similar others as well as develop and refine important communication skills such as conflict management.

In our final chapter, "Parenting: Principles and Practices," we try to condense essential lessons for parents from the breadth of social science research covered in this book. The developmental consequences of the first 5 years have lifelong implications, and we hope that our suggestions help parents and other adults navigate this challenge with insight and preparation.

Even this brief overview shows the fascination and complexity of communication. In our coverage of communicative development, we incorporate research from several disciplines, encompass a wide array of methodologies, and discuss many developmental issues and controversies, in both current research and classic studies such as early work on facial expressions and attachment.

Throughout, we emphasize the first 5 years as the time in which critical communication skills are developed. These skills have consequences for people's entire lives in terms of relationships, self-esteem, and interactional competence. The book title should perhaps state "the first 5 years . . . and a whole lot more," for lifelong consequences flow from the communicative patterns and activities established during children's first 5 years.

In what follows, we present our beliefs and assumptions about the nature of communication, language, and cognition and discuss how these assumptions shape our study of children's communicative development.

BASIC CONCEPTS: COMMUNICATION, LANGUAGE, AND COGNITION

Communication

Although everyone communicates, this everyday activity is complex and not easily defined. No single definition or explanatory concept comprehensively captures the complexity of communication, but some conceptualizations are more useful than others. Among the most satisfactory definitions of communication is that of Albert Scheflen (1972, 1974), a noted scholar in nonverbal communication. Scheflen defined communication as an organized, standardized, culturally patterned system of behavior that sustains, regulates, and makes possible human relationships.

Scheflen's view implies several underlying assumptions. First, communication is a socially shared activity that allows humans to develop relationships with each other. Second, communication is multimodal; it incorporates verbal, paralinguistic, and nonverbal channels. Although verbal communication relies on language as its symbolic code, nonverbal communication has many codes, such as proxemics (use of space), movement, posture, facial expression, eye gaze, gesture, touch, smell, and territoriality (personal space). Of special interest are the paralinguistic codes like pitch, stress, intonation, and juncture (pausing) which accompany speech. Because the focus of this book is on communicative growth in the first 5 years of life, we give special attention to facial expression, paralinguistics, eye gaze, touch, gesture, and their development; these appear to be the most significant nonverbal communication systems early in life.

Other assumptions include communication's structured nature, which is not random but purposeful and goal directed. Communication patterns also vary from culture to culture, incorporating both linguistic and nonverbal differences. Finally, communication is generally a conventional (standardized) process: Although human communication varies substantially from person to person, both the formulation and the interpretation of messages rely upon conventionally agreed-upon, socially shared meanings.

Communication is thus an interactive process that requires a message sender (encoder) and a message interpreter (decoder). In order for meaningful interaction to take place, both speakers and hearers must share common interpretive assumptions. For interactants, these common principles of interpretation acknowledge that communication is:

- inferential
- intentional
- conventional
- jointly negotiated between speakers and hearers
- varies according to context and language user
- involves commonsense knowledge
- sequential
- accomplished in real time and space
- systematic
- interpretive, and
- varies according to the participants' social relationships.

These concepts or assumptions are developed later, and we pay particular attention to the ways various research traditions dealt with the study of each concept. Citing different scholars, however, does not imply that researchers used these concepts in identical ways. Rather, we incorporate these views to illustrate some commonalities underlying the concepts and to demonstrate their centrality in various approaches to studying communication and its development.

Inferences

Inferences are the implicit meanings humans assign to objects and events; meanings develop on the basis of what is said (through presuppositions, conversational implicatures, and so on), on the basis of context, and on the basis of commonsense knowledge. Cicourel (1980) defined inferences as the "tacit ways in which we link information from different sources to create coherency and relevance in our speech acts and nonverbal and paralinguistic actions" (p. 117). Interestingly, Cicourel explicitly linked verbal and nonverbal communication as sources of inference making.

Speech act models rely on inferential processes because an utterance's illocutionary force is inferred from the social action accomplished by that spoken utterance. Grice (1975, 1978) suggested that interactants constructed plausible rationales to support one interpretation over another by using conventional meanings, the Cooperative Principle, conversational maxims, and contextual knowledge. Similar views were expressed by Bach and Harnish (1979), who argued that inferences reflected the participants' analysis of a given social context, their assessment of others' intentions, and the specific language used. Dimitracopoulou (1990) suggested that multiple considerations, such as context, intentions, social cognitive knowledge, and linguistic form, interact simultaneously to form one's inferences about what is going on; these inferences change across conversational settings and over time.

Young children appear to develop inferential skills slowly over the first 5 years. Many of their early inferences appear to be based on conventional meanings embedded in situations, and they associate certain actions and behaviors with specific settings or individuals. Later, more complex inferences about others, their behaviors, and rationales for their behavior develop. Over time, as children's egocentrism lessens, they are able to develop inferences reflecting differences among individuals and across varied contexts.

Intentionality

Most communication scholars have agreed that communication, as a social act, is inherently intentional (Berger & Bradac, 1982; Tracy, 1991; van Dijk, 1980). Despite this common view, there is little agreement on how to conceptualize or measure intentionality. Unresolved questions, such as the degree to which individuals consciously plan their communication, the degree of cognitive monitoring humans are capable of, and the degree to which humans can accurately report their intentions, present serious intellectual and theoretical challenges.

Three recent approaches to intentionality appear to have important implications for communication research. One approach, taken by Searle (1983), Shotter (1993), and others, views communicative behavior as motivated by the need for social communion and cooperation. People's intentions, from birth, are driven by these basic social needs. Another approach views communicative purposes as tied to issues of social control and influence, whether over our own behavior (Langer, 1983) or over a relationship (Rogers, 1983).

A third approach, taken by researchers in artificial intelligence, views intentionality as goal seeking; people act to accomplish some goal. Parisi and Castelfranchi (1981) defined a goal as a state that regulates an individual's behavior. Douglas (1970), following in the tradition of Schutz and Husserl, argued that "it is primarily intentions at any time—our purposes at hand—that order human thought, that determine the relevance of information and ideas about the world and ourselves" (p. 26). In conversation, speakers and hearers must adopt at least one common goal: At a minimum, they converse with each other. Some researchers, however, have suggested that communicative encounters are shaped by multiple goals. For example, constructivists have argued that people enter conversation with the purpose of *doing* something; conversational participants have instrumental or task goals they wish to accomplish via their interactions with one another (see Burleson, 1987; Clark & Delia, 1979; O'Keefe & Delia,

1982). Instrumental goals can vary; people enter conversation for any number of purposes including persuading, comforting, regulating another's behavior, or simply "shooting the breeze." Constructivists have also maintained, however, that in addition to these instrumental purposes, interactants have identity needs, image or presentational goals, and relational concerns that they wish to have acknowledged. According to Tracy and Craig (1983), communicative goals involve a listener's acknowledgment and adoption of a specific identity and presentational and relational concerns. (For an excellent discussion of the role of goals in communication and problems with linking goals and discourse, see Tracy, 1991.)

Whatever particular viewpoint they advocate, researchers have acknowledged the fundamental importance of intentionality in any theory of communication. Much greater conceptual clarity is needed in order to delineate assumptions about intentionality and to ascertain "what counts" as evidence of intentionality, especially in early developmental contexts such as infancy. In particular, scholars must differentiate between goals and means or motives and the realization of those motives.

Although intentionality is a taken-for-granted characteristic of communication, there is considerable debate over its conceptualization and measurement. A key assumption in communicative development is that adults or caretakers *assume* that young children's utterances have an intended meaning. The assumption of intended meaning reinforces the importance of communication to children and enhances their recognition of the connection between linguistic forms and their meanings. Early practices such as naming depend upon the implicit assumption of intentionality. Over time, as children's cognitive, communicative, and linguistic skills increase, their ability to precisely frame their intentions increases.

Conventionality

Much interaction, especially conversation, is more routinized than commonly realized; conventional rules and stereotyped patterns of behavior underlie interactional routines. Heritage (1984) noted that utterances are interpreted in light of the normal, conventional patterns of interaction operating in a given setting. Communication behavior, then, can be viewed as conventional; it is guided by shared lexical meanings, shared commonsense knowledge, and shared social rules of behavior (Haslett, 1987; Shotter, 1993).

In the context of communicative development, the conventionality of communication is an important feature of adult–child interaction. Routines such as feeding, bathing, and playing games help establish the patterned nature of interaction. These conventions are both nonverbal and verbal; waving bye-bye and saying bye-bye are both conventional signals attached to leave taking. Eventually, conventional practices may build into action schemas that dictate how something is to be done. Katherine Nelson (1973) has studied these action schemas and has suggested that children develop scripts which are detailed representations of conventional action sequences. In Haslett's videotapes of preschoolers' playtime, it is not uncommon to see children correcting each other. For example, when "playing" eating at McDonalds, children pay before taking the food. Doing something out of order or out of context causes great consternation among children; activity is frequently restarted and performed correctly (i.e., in the conventional way).

Tacit, Commonsense Knowledge

Ethnomethodologists, with their focus on understanding how social order is established, assume a common, largely tacit vocabulary of symbols (Denzin, 1970). Communication is not possible without such shared knowledge, but communication itself also enables people to share knowledge. When interacting, participants assume that they share some common definitions of the situation and act on the basis of these shared definitions. These shared assumptions reflect taken-for-granted, commonsense knowledge about communication behavior and everyday life (von Raffler-Engel, 1977). Douglas (1970) suggested that interpreting messages depends, in part, on commonsense understandings of everyday communicative behavior (pp. 30–31). Cook-Gumperz (1986) suggested that contextual cues contain much commonsense knowledge about interacting and interpreting others' behavior. Although scholars have utilized tacit, commonsense knowledge in varied ways in their accounts of communicative behavior, all agree that its role is vital.

During their preschool years, children acquire an increasing awareness of commonsense knowledge, partially as a function of maturity but also through the learning opportunities available for them in the environment. Adults' willingness to add knowledge to what children observe, in terms of explaining both ongoing action as well as possible feelings and motivations of the participants (e.g., "Johnny is sad because his truck was broken," a comment on the action as well as the feelings of the individual), helps develop children's social knowledge.

Joint Negotiation of Interaction

Interaction requires coordinated communicative behavior between at least two participants. In conversations, taking turns and responding to the talk of other participants require joint management by participants (Brown & Levinson, 1978). Interpreting utterances is also jointly managed; hearers must ratify, disconfirm, or otherwise respond to a speaker's utterance. Speakers must secure a response from their conversational partners (Dore, 1983, 1985; Levinson, 1983). As Kreckel (1981) noted, speakers provide potential sources of information that listeners act upon. In addition, Franck (1981) argued that the jointly negotiated nature of interaction allows for the indeterminacy of utterances; this indeterminacy is necessary for maintaining face and for allowing interaction to flow smoothly. Franck did not deny that literal meanings can be attached to utterances but argued that interpretation relies on both negotiated and literal meanings. The systematic research of the Palo Alto Interactional group, first with its study of disqualification and, more recently, of equivocal or ambiguous utterances, has extended the knowledge of ambiguous messages (Bavelas, Black, Chovel, & Mullett, 1990). This research is of particular value because equivocation is studied in naturally occurring contexts.

Appreciating the joint negotiation of interaction begins early in infancy between adult caretakers and infants. Eye gaze behavior is used to create joint attention and involvement with each other. Over time, this eye gaze behavior is supplemented by other nonverbal actions, such as pointing or gesturing; later, jointly negotiated attention is created and maintained by language. There is increasing evidence that infants and their caretakers share control over joint activities and that infants withdraw when the stimulation is too great. Also of interest are the varied strategies both young children and adults use to establish and maintain joint involvement (Schaffer, 1992).

Variability as a Function of Context and Language User

One of the most widely shared assumptions about communicative behavior is that it varies across different contexts and different language users. Van Dijk (1980) suggested that communicative models need to incorporate multiple levels of context (the cultural level, the organizational level, and the immediate social setting) as well as language-user characteristics such as age, sex, motivation, and personal values. Dascal (1981), after Bar-Hillel, distinguished two types of contextual influences. The co-text refers to the background provided by the utterances themselves, and the context refers to the physical and sociocultural environment surrounding the interaction.

Most communication scholars have agreed that communication varies as a function of context and interactants (Ellis & Donohue, 1986) but have seriously disagreed about how the context and user characteristics are conceptualized and measured. Ethnomethodologists, for example, have focused predominantly on contextual determinants of meaning; others in the communication discipline have focused on how interactants' characteristics influence their communicative behavior.

From a developmental perspective, young children begin to communicate differently to different people at a fairly early age, usually between 2½ and 3 years of age; of course, children make distinctions between family and nonfamily members much earlier. Contextual knowledge emerges later; children may not experience situational differences until they participate in preschool, church, or other well-defined social organizations. Both knowledge of the context and individual differences are critical components of communicative effectiveness (Dimitracopoulou, 1992).

The Sequencing of Communicative Behavior

Communication is both retrospective and prospective (Schutz, 1967; Shotter, 1993). Ongoing talk can retrospectively recast the interpretation of preceding turns as well as prospectively shape opportunities for future interaction. Dore (1985) noted that the sequencing of utterances partly determines what is accomplished in interaction and reflects the planned nature of interactions.

The sequencing of utterances influences the interpretation of utterances as well as the general format of interaction. For example, conversations are sequenced structurally; they begin with greetings, then the conversational topic is introduced, and closing remarks end the conversation. Analytic units within conversations, like questions and responses, may be considered both structural and interpretive units.

Most researchers would agree that communicative behavior is sequenced but would differ about how sequencing units are defined, measured, and interrelated. Some scholars have suggested that sequencing rules are similar to those found in generative grammars. Others have argued that conversations are sequenced by participants' strategies for achieving particular goals (Tracy & Craig, 1983). Still others have suggested that formal sequencing structures do not occur in conversations (Levinson, 1983). Although there appears to be sequencing in conversations, the principles governing such sequencing are not fully understood.

The understanding of how communication is organized, for infants and preschoolers, appears to develop from the interactive routines that they observe and later participate in (Forrester, 1993). Bruner (1977) has referred to this sequencing as "scaffolding" that allows young children to know what is happening in the stream of ongoing behavior. Some linguistic sequencing—for example, the segmentation of sounds—appears to be learned without conscious awareness; other communicative sequences, such as the greeting–information exchange–farewell organization of conversation, seem to be consciously practiced. For developmental research, the nature of sequencing and the multiple levels of simultaneous sequencing pose serious analytic and methodological issues.

Communication Occurs in Real Time and Space

Adequate models of communication must reflect real-world time limitations and spatial references because interactions are limited by humans' ability to process language. Psycholinguists have been particularly concerned with the analysis of language in terms of human perceptual and information processing limitations. For example, in their model of discourse comprehension, van Dijk and Kintsch (1983) emphasized the importance of time constraints on comprehension. In addition, time and spatial constraints have different effects on different mediums. Ricouer (1981) noted that writing is not subject to the time and space considerations of speaking. Any modeling of interaction should acknowledge the time and processing limitations under which interaction occurs.

For young infants, limits on information processing and a focus on the immediate situation are factors influencing their development. Memory limitations seem to be especially important; some researchers have suggested that the move from single words to multiword utterances depends on an expanded memory capacity. Other cognitive developments, such as an appreciation of object permanence and causality, are steps needed to free infants from the here-and-now bias of their earliest communication.

Any explanatory models of information processing need to accommodate the facts known about the way the brain processes information, the limits of speech recognition, and the like. For developing infants, these constraints are even more powerful and less likely to be well understood.

Systematicity

The systematicity of communication reflects both its sequential and its structured nature. We have already noted the sequential aspects of communication, particularly the debate over the most appropriate means for analyzing such sequencing (Goodwin, 1979; Heritage, 1984; Levinson, 1983). Wilson (1970) noted that both normative and interpretive approaches to social behavior (including communicative behavior) have assumed that social behavior is systematic. Normative approaches have stressed people's organized, socially sanctioned expectations about social behavior. In contrast, interpretive approaches have emphasized the cultural patterning of social behavior and individuals' recognition of these patterns.

Many different structural communicative units have been suggested. Discourse analysts have identified overall structural formats that characterize jokes, narratives, conversations, and news reports (Dimitracopoulou, 1990; Forrester, 1993; McTear, 1985; Tracy & Craig, 1983). Scholars have also identified structural pairs within conversations, including compliment–response, greeting–greeting, and question–answer. Still others, such as the Palo Alto Interactional group, view communicative behavior as a cybernetic system, with its structural properties of feedback, redundancy, homeostasis, and equifinality. Thus, the systematicity of human communication appears on many levels of analysis. Depending on a researcher's purposes, different aspects of the systematic nature of communication are of interest.

From a developmental perspective, the acquisition of at least four layers of structure appears critical: The sound, meaning, grammatical and discourse levels of language must all be understood. Within each of these layers, of course, many different potential units of analysis are possible. For example, in the sound system, humans discriminate phonemes, pitch, stress, and juncture. Meaning relies on prefixes, suffixes, words, and words-in-combination. How the child acquires these multiple tiers of structure, and how these structures are simultaneously coordinated in the act of communication, remains one of the most challenging communication puzzles.

Interpretiveness

The text, context, interactants, and their mutual interrelationships determine how communicative behaviors are interpreted. The relative influence of each factor appears to be a function of the task and goals associated with any given interaction. Additional complexity in interpretation is apparent when one considers that a text may have multiple meanings (Franck, 1981; Haslett, 1984; Pinker, 1995).

Ethnomethodologists and phenomenological sociologists have been particularly concerned about the interpretive procedures individuals use to make sense of everyday social behavior. Cicourel (1980), Douglas (1970), and others argue that interpretive procedures must be analyzed independently of the decontextualized (literal) meanings of lexical items. These interpretive procedures are based upon taken-for-granted, commonsense knowledge about everyday life (Giddens, 1983). These interpretive procedures are characterized by (a) the reciprocity of perspectives, (b) the et cetera assumption, (c) the presence of normal forms of interaction, (d) the retrospective-prospective nature of talk, (e) the reflexivity of talk, and (f) the indexicality of talk (Cicourel, 1970).

We can reach several conclusions based on this brief survey of interpretive procedures. First, interpretations of communicative behavior vary as a function of text, context, communicator and/or their interrelationships. Second, contextualized meanings must be analytically separated from decontextualized meanings. And finally, communicator characteristics and the social relationships among participants appear to play a central role in the interpretation of interaction (Haslett, 1987).

Young children seem to use multiple cues to interpret ongoing interaction. Nonverbal cues, such as intonation, pointing, and the characteristics of the environment (for example, a highchair or bathtub) alert children about what might occur. Naming and labeling are important ways in which children identify the environment and share their recognition with others. Throughout these processes, children build interpretations based on particular people, like parents, and particular social situations, like play.

Relational Influences on Communication

The most fundamental purpose of communication is to develop and maintain social relationships among individuals. Only through communication are individuals able to share information and to coordinate their activities. Scholars from a wide range of disciplines have acknowledged the fundamental role of communication in establishing social order, cooperation, and social relations (Goffman, 1974, 1976; Shotter, 1993).

We believe that participants' goals govern their interactions with others. In pursuing their conversational goals, interactants rely on commonsense knowledge relevant to accomplishing their aims. This relevant commonsense knowledge includes knowledge of the appropriate norms of behavior in a particular social situation and expectations about the other interactants and their goals. The text—that is, the utterances of the interactants—expresses the strategies people use to pursue their goals.

Interacting with others causes people to increase the amount of socially shared information among them. Interpretive procedures for assessing ongoing interaction depend on this socially shared knowledge as well as commonsense knowledge. Primary relationships—those with our family and closest friends—reflect collective, mutually understood experiences and knowledge. Frequently, people's ambiguous utterances may be immediately understood by family and friends because of their intimate knowledge of speakers and their goals. As people develop relationships with others, the added depth of relational knowledge they possess about each other becomes an important aspect of how they interpret ongoing interactions.

One of the most critical determinants of attitudes and predispositions toward communication as well as general attitudes toward others is the relationship between infants and adult caretakers. Adult caretaker–infant relationships form the basis for emotional bonding and interactional patterns. Initial relationships form between caretakers and infants, and then expand to include others in the family. Beyond the family, children must negotiate the world of peer relationships and develop friendships. Authority relationships first develop with parents and later extend to others, such as doctors and teachers. From these beginnings, children's fundamental relationships with others begin to form. The role of communication itself is fundamental to learning about others, the environment and how to relate effectively to both.

LANGUAGE

We view language as the symbolic code that underlies verbal communication. The well-known distinction between linguistic knowledge (competence) and linguistic performance (speech) identifies two different components of language. Most agree that what people say (linguistic performance or speech) imperfectly reflects their linguistic competence (the idealized knowledge of language); people speak under conditions of stress, fatigue, memory limitations, and other factors that cause them to make errors. Thus, any theory of language need account only for the idealized knowledge of language rather than its flawed performance. Despite this strong distinction, many psychologists of language have studied speech errors to better understand how humans use and process language.

The study of language as a system (in its idealized form) has focused on three subsystems: grammar (or linguistic structure), semantics (or linguistic meaning), and phonology (the sound system of a language). Linguists have assessed both the universal aspects of development in each linguistic subsystem and the specific features of each language which must be acquired by young children. The learning features general to all languages are viewed as linguistic universals; some have argued that these universals reflect humans' innate predisposition to acquire language.

Studies of grammar focus on the structure of language and its acquisition by young children. Theories of language need to account for the grammaticality of utterances and how different linguistic forms can mean the same thing. For example, the statements 'John hit Sally' and 'Sally was hit by John' have the same meaning, although the former is an active sentence and the latter a passive one.

Semantic research focuses on the meaning of words and utterances and tries to account for young children's mastery of both. Meaning incorporates both referential and expressive functions of language. Referential language refers to the meanings humans assign to concrete objects and things; expressive language refers to the expression of emotion and abstract concepts or ideas. Single words are combined into phrases and sentences that convey meaning; thus, young children need to interpret connected discourse. Part of children's interpretive skill also relies on the conventional meanings embedded in specific social contexts, such as taking a bath, reading bedtime stories, conducting an argument, or preparing supper.

The phonological system of a language consists of the finite set of phonemes used in a particular language. Children need to separate language sounds from nonlanguage sounds and to understand that language sounds form meaningful words and syllables. An understanding of the sound system of a language also involves recognizing intonation patterns and producing appropriate patterns in timing, stress, and pausing.

Communicating appropriately and effectively in specific contexts requires mastering a complex, multilevel language system. The rapidity with which children acquire language and its appropriate use in context is truly amazing. (In chapter 3, language development and acquisition are discussed in more detail.)

COGNITION

Cognition is the study of how people acquire knowledge. As such, cognition incorporates the processes involved in people's representation of knowledge as well as the processes involved in the storage, use, and retrieval of knowledge. Researchers have often discriminated between cognitive and social cognitive development. Cognitive development encompasses knowledge of the world; social cognition refers specifically to knowledge acquired about the social world of humans.

As children grow, they mature cognitively and develop increasingly differentiated cognitive categories, expanded memory capabilities, and increased reasoning ability which depends upon more finely differentiated categories. As Garton (1992) observed, knowledge has been studied from either a product orientation, focusing on the biologically determined aspects of cognition, or from a process orientation, focusing on the socially derived aspects of knowledge. Most recent theorizing has chosen the midposition between these two extreme views: From this perspective, cognition develops as an innate human predisposition triggered by children's interaction with environmental influences. In what follows, we briefly outline the theoretical perspectives of the two foremost developmental cognitive theorists, Jean Piaget and Lev Vygotsky. Although other theorists fall between these two perspectives, the differences between Piaget and Vygotsky outline the terrain of cognitive development.

Piaget

Piaget's insights were developed over several decades of systematic observation and testing of young children's thinking and coping with the world (Piaget, 1959, 1965). His theory suggests universal stages of cognitive development, which are guided by accommodation and assimilation. Accommodation refers to changes made in existing cognitive structures as a result of children's encountering new information. In contrast, assimilation refers to incorporating new information into existing cognitive structures. Thus, accommodation provides for change in existing structures while assimilation allows for acquisition of new information into pre-existing cognitive structures. Equilibration is the self-regulating mechanism that maintains stability between accommodation and assimilation. Or, in other words, equilibration maintains a stable balance between the organism and new information.

Piaget suggested that children move through four major stages of development, each containing several substages. Sensorimotor intelligence, the first stage, occurs from birth through the second year and reflects the developmental stage when babies and toddlers are exploring their world physically, through their senses—hence the term *sensorimotor intelligence*. Several substages play major roles in communicative development. In Stage 4 of sensorimotor intelligence, from 8 to 12 months, young toddlers develop a sense of causality, intentionality and a connection between means and ends. In Stage 5, from 9 to 18 months, they develop a sense of self as an independent object; at Stage 6, from 18 to 24 months, children are able to represent causal relationships and use language to influence others' actions. These cognitive developments are important foundations for communication because children can now communicate their goals intentionally and understand their effects on others. Other advances during this period, especially the development of imitation and symbolic play, are also important for language development (Owens, 1992).

Other major stages include *preoperational thought*, from 2 to 7 years, the period of children's physical exploration of the world through concrete actions (or operations) that they perform. The *concrete operational thought* stage, from 7 to 11 years, reflects children's use of concrete mental operations like negation, reversibility, or conservation, to solve problems mentally rather than physically. The final developmental stage, *formal operational thought*, reflects the use of language on an abstract, systematic level to solve problems. It is at this stage that Piaget argues that language (as an abstract representational system) begins to strongly influence thinking. Through language children can perform operations conceptually rather than through physical manipulation, and increasingly complex levels of abstraction and reasoning are possible.

Subsequent scholarship on Piaget's theories suggests that the stages children go through cannot be reversed or skipped; however, children appear to vary in terms of how rapidly they progress through these stages. There may also be critical environmental influences and individual differences which affect cognitive development that are largely ignored by Piaget. In contrast to Piaget, Vygotsky's work focuses on the connection between the environment and a child's development.

Vygotsky

Vygotsky (1962, 1978) suggested that language and cognition emerge through social interaction. He argued that language and thought develop independently but that at 2 years of age, children exhibit "verbal thought" in which speech becomes rational and thought becomes verbal. The fact that some children talk to help them work through a problem is often cited as support for Vygotsky's views. Vygotsky also believed that children's social and cultural environment was critical; he saw social interaction as the means through which children can participate in the environment. Mental development thus occurs as a result of sociocultural influences; social interactions are made possible by language and by children's practical intelligence (like tool use and concrete, trial-and-error problem solving; Wertsch, 1985).

Vygotsky argued that speech becomes more decontextualized (i.e., less dependent on the immediate environment for interpretation) as children mature. Decontextualized, abstract language enables more flexible thinking and problem solving. Egocentric speech is used to control the child's own behaviors and derived from social speech. For Vygotsky, "language develops from the social dimension (language as communication) through egocentric language (largely intelligible language used explicitly to guide and monitor behavior) to inner speech. Inner speech . . . can be regarded as an abstract manifestation of a conceptualising of real-world relations" (Garton, 1992, pp. 92–93).

Inner speech facilitates complex, abstract intellectual activity. Over time, as children mature, the function and structure of language also evolves. For Vygotsky, both egocentric language and social speech are necessary to solve complex problems. As the complexity of problems increases, the role of social speech becomes increasingly important because children may request assistance or clarification. Social interaction enables the integration of practical intelligence and social speech. Although language may accompany early actions, language has an important planning function for children as they grow older. As Garton (1992) has pointed out, for Vygotsky, both the cognitive (intrapersonal) function of language and the communicative (interpersonal) function are necessary for complex mental activity.

Vygotsky also proposed a zone of proximal development for children in which learning opportunities are maximized. As Garton (1992) noted: "The zone of proximal development is thus a measure of learning potential. It represents the region wherein cognitive development takes place. It is important that the zone of proximal development be accorded a central position in the theory since it implies that the social environment, and the support and assistance it can offer, is crucial for development" (p. 95). Garton also pointed out that these learning opportunities help children establish intersubjectivity (shared meanings) with others. As noted earlier, mutually shared meanings are necessary for communication.

In summary, language plays an important role in cognitive development for both Piaget and Vygotsky. Although Piaget focused primarily on cognitive development, language played an important role in thought at the formal operations stage because it permitted more abstract, complex thought. Social interaction played a role in cognitive development at earlier ages, primarily through conflict and conflict resolution. In contrast, Vygotsky suggested that language directed cognitive development. Both language and cognition emerged through social interaction, which allowed children to interact with their environment. The zone of proximal development also facilitated cognitive development, and, more broadly, learning, through collaborative interaction with others.

Psycholinguists have vigorously debated the mutual interaction between language and thought. Some have taken the position, compatible with Piaget's view, that thought influences language. Others, like Vygotsky, have argued that language influences thought. Still others (and this is the position we take in this book) suggest that thought and language mutually influence one another. Whatever particular view is adopted, the role of social interaction is crucial in both language and thought. For Piaget, social interaction influenced language and thought, especially in conflict situations. For Vygotsky, social interaction was fundamental for learning, cognition, and language. Our view is that communication, language, and thought all interact and mutually influence one another; these complex interactions, and their development, are the focus of this book.

According to Forrester (1993), the most important social cognitive skill is the ability to understand and participate in conversation. He advocated an ecological approach to communicative and cognitive development and suggested that other perspectives could not capture the dynamic, participatory nature of conversation and communication. For example, one major approach to cognition, the constructivist-representational views (reflected in Piaget and others), does not model the unexpected paths conversations can take; Forrester argued that formalisms in this approach focus on closure, not on flexibility and on being able to react to unanticipated events. The information processing models that dominate this perspective also conflate theory and data.

A second major view, the social interactional approach (as represented by Vygotsky or Mead), focuses on conflict and confrontation as triggering cognitive development, but the explanatory processes are neo-Piagetian. Relatively little is known about the underlying processes that account for social cognitive changes. A final mainstream view, that of language and social cognition, focuses on developmental issues in acquiring language and cognition. In this view, the social world is a linguistic world (Durkin, 1988), but as Forrester (1993) noted, language is but one of the systems by which individuals interact with their environments.

To overcome some of these theoretical deficiencies, Forrester (1993) has developed an ecological model, in which young children learn from "overhearing" interaction, both as participants and as observers. His model is partially based on Gibson's ecological work (1979), which stressed the relationship of an organism to an environment. As Forrester stated, "One resonates with the environment and the environment 'affords' sets of actions and events" (p. 49). Young children need to recognize invariant as well as transformational aspects of action. Forrester's model suggests that young children, through observation and direct interaction, are able to extract social information. In addition, children recognize that conversation is an intentional activity; as Forrester pointed out, communication involves speaking with displays of intention. In conversations, young children notice invariant processes, like taking turns, as well as transformational processes, such as interruptions or questions that may take a conversation in unanticipated directions. Overhearing allows young children the opportunity to extract social cues or to process social information via linguistic means. Overhearing also focuses children's attention, especially in naming, whether they actively participate in a conversation or merely observe. Finally, overhearing allows conversational monitoring or tracking; young infants can learn conversational implicature (i.e., the intentions behind a particular communicative act).

Overhearing, then, affords infants the opportunity to extract social information, to discern communicative intentions, and to monitor conversations. Forrester argued that the overhearing model allows us to specify the relationship between various social-cognitive dimensions and language use. This framework needs more careful articulation especially, as Forrester noted, in the area of distinguishing between social-functional and formal linguistic aspects of overhearing contexts.

SUMMARY

In this chapter, we have outlined our fundamental, underlying assumptions concerning the nature of communication, our beliefs regarding the fundamental nature of language as a symbolic system, and our views on the major competing views on cognition. Finally, we have developed our views on the interrelationships among communication, language, and cognition.

Communication is a necessary foundation for language and cognition. As language develops, cognition becomes more complex and abstract. With increasing cognitive development, more complex problem solving and learning take place. As opportunities to socially interact expand for growing children, their language and cognitive development are enhanced. Communication skills are important for the expression of feelings, for opportunities to interact with others, and for cooperative activities.

In the following chapters, we explore different aspects of early communicative development, such as nonverbal communication and its relationship to verbal communication. We then assess language development and its relationship to verbal communication. In addition, we examine important relational contexts in which communicative development occurs; these contexts include adult–child interaction, peer interaction, and friendship development. Finally, we offer suggestions for parenting practices that facilitate the young child's ability to communicate in a complex, ever-changing social world.

2

Nonverbal Communication:
Its Origins and Development

Nonverbal communication is a basic dimension of human communication. The earliest form of human communication is nonverbal while verbal communication emerges in the latter part of the infant's first year. Because nonverbal and verbal communication are integrated with one another, it is important to understand how nonverbal communication develops and its subsequent relation to verbal communication (Birdwhistell, 1970; Haslett, 1987; Knapp, 1980; Scheflen, 1972, 1974).

We take an approach to nonverbal communication consistent with a functionalist perspective (Barrett, 1993; Patterson, 1983, 1991). Nonverbal communication performs several functions: It regulates behavior and social interaction, provides mechanisms for internal (self) regulation, and expresses emotions. Nonverbal communication is always embedded within a context, and it varies across cultures, as in, for example, the length of eye gaze and the interpretation of gestures. Inconsistent, ambiguous messages can be conveyed via nonverbal means, and a single nonverbal behavior may be interpreted in different ways.

Nonverbal communication occurs on many different channels. The major channels of nonverbal communication include facial expressions, kinesics (body movements), paralinguistics (pitch, loudness, pausing, and timing of speech), proxemics (space), olfactics (smells), eye gaze, gestures, and artifacts (like clothing and jewelry).

CHARACTERISTICS OF VERBAL AND NONVERBAL
COMMUNICATION CHANNELS

Some characteristics define both verbal and nonverbal channels of communication (Burgoon, Buller, & Goodall, 1989). Both dimensions have cues or units that are discrete and arbitrary, such as gestures or words. Both dimensions appear to follow sequencing rules; for example, greeting rituals involve eye contact before a handshake rather than the reverse, and word order determines a sentence's meaning (e.g., 'John hit Mary' as opposed to 'Mary hit John'). Both verbal and nonverbal dimensions rely on culture and context for interpretation. Although both verbal and nonverbal channels are flexible and varied and help participants make sense of what is going on, they can also be used to deceive or mislead others. Finally, both channels have rules about public displays, for example, norms governing the use of cursing or the display of intimate touching behaviors. While similar in many respects, the verbal and nonverbal channels of communication also have some important differences as well. For example, verbal channels are self-reflexive and not bound to the here and now, unlike most nonverbal cues.

Properties unique to nonverbal channels include its analogic coding, in which behaviors form a natural continuum, such as in interpersonal distance or eye gaze behavior. For example, intimate interpersonal distance is approximately 0 to 18 inches; personal distance between people is approximately 18 inches to 4 feet, and so forth. Some nonverbal channels are iconic; there is a one-to-one correspondence between the object and its representation (e.g., an illustrative hand–arm gesture indicating the size of an object, etc.). Other qualities include the universality of some nonverbal codes such as facial expressions of fear or interest and the simultaneous occurrence of multiple nonverbal signals across nonverbal channels. For example, people can display an angry face simultaneously with a threatening fist–arm gesture. Finally, the directness and spontaneity of nonverbal communication are believed to accurately express true feelings (Burgoon et al., 1989), but people do learn to conceal their feelings. As we shall see later in this chapter, preschoolers acquire the ability to "mask" some of their facial expressions and thus can limit the directness and spontaneity of their nonverbal communication.

Exploring infants' development across the range of nonverbal communication is well beyond the scope of this book. Thus, we have chosen to focus on the development of nonverbal systems that are significantly integrated with verbal communication, including eye gaze, gesture and touch, facial expression, and paralinguistics. In what follows, we briefly characterize the perceptual capacities of infants, especially during the first year of life; these capabilities underlie infants' ability to send and interpret messages. Next we outline the development of each nonverbal system closely related to verbal communication and conclude with a brief note about the developing integration of verbal and nonverbal communication in childhood.

PERCEPTUAL BASIS OF COMMUNICATION

Perception refers to our awareness of events immediately outside ourselves, relying on sensations produced by sensory systems like the skin, auditory and visual systems. Perceptual processes involve the processing of incoming sensory stimulation, during which the brain compares incoming stimuli to referents stored in memory. Differences in the muscular and neuromuscular organization of perception account for developmental differences across different nonverbal channels. For example, infants' control of their voluntary muscles generally flows from the top of the body to the body's extremities; thus, infants gain control of head movement, then of sitting, and finally of standing and movement. Children's use of facial expressions should develop before their use of gestural communication (Rinn, 1984, 1991).

The Developing Visual System

Shortly after birth, the infant's most accurate visual perception is at a distance of approximately 8 inches, roughly approximating the distance between the infant and the mother's face during feeding (Owens, 1992). By 1 month, infants gaze and vocalize at their caretakers (Bullowa, 1976) and by 3 months, prefer to gaze at more complex rather than simpler stimuli. When compared to other stimuli, infants prefer to look at a face (Fantz & Yeh, 1979) and prefer to look at a live human face over an inanimate object with irregular facial features (Langsdorf, Izard, Rayias & Hembree, 1983). Infants appear to compare actual faces to their internal schema (model) of a human face (Stern, 1985).

Controversy exists over whether infants process human faces by particular features only or by utilizing a gestalt or holistic view of faces (Fogel & Reimers, 1989); possibly they first process particular features and then develop a gestalt representation of faces. Infants' gazing behavior and their ability to focus visual attention develop according to their increasing perceptual and processing skills. Infants' focus on human faces facilitates their communicative development because they are monitoring others' eye gaze, facial expression, and mouth movement—all key features in human communication.

Although, as noted previously, researchers have verified infants' discrimination of facial expressions, they do not know how this discrimination occurs. Some scholars have suggested that visual experience with facial expressions is necessary for the ability to discriminate (Ludemann & Nelson, 1988). Meltzoff and Moore (1977) found that infants perceive some aspects of facial expressions soon after birth. Others have questioned whether infants can perceive faces as a gestalt or discriminate only a few features (Fogel & Reimers, 1989; Younger, 1992). Further evidence has indicated that infants do not begin to have the capacities for gestalt facial judgments (i.e., integrated scanning, differential response to feature versus gesture) until 5 to 7 months of age (Zivin, 1989). Thus, how and when perceptual processes operate in infants' assessment of facial expressiveness remain unclear, yet infants demonstrate a high level of sophistication in their monitoring of human faces.

Perception and Processing of Vocal Stimuli

The vocal quality of speech conveys information through intonation patterns, which can signal different meanings in a sentence (for example, '**John** is giving the money to Dave,' where who is giving the money is emphasized, as opposed to 'John is **giving** the money to Dave,' where John's giving the money rather than loaning it to Dave, is emphasized [Knapp, 1980]). Pitch level, loudness, vocal qualities like harshness or thinness, and timing of speech (e.g., pauses, hesitations, etc.) also can signal emotions and confidence (Siegman & Boyle, 1993).

Adults adjust their speech in many ways to make it easier for infants to recognize and to interpret speech. Prosodic characteristics of adult language addressed to children consist of higher-pitched voices, wider pitch variation, longer pauses, shorter utterances, and more prosodic repetition than does adult-to-adult speech (Fernald & Simon, 1984). Infants appear to discriminate affective vocal qualities (approval versus disapproval in adult voices) and to respond more to infant-directed speech (adult–child language) than to adult-like language use (Fernald, 1993). At 9 months, infants prefer listening to prosodic features emphasized in their native language; this fact suggests that stress patterns play an important role in children's segmentation and learning of language (Jusczyk, Cutler, & Redanz, 1993).

At birth, infants have a unique orienting response to human voices and appear sensitive to differences in loudness, pitch, and duration of voices. Within a month, infants can discriminate different phonemes, and at 2 months, infants discriminate their mothers' voices from the voices of others. Infants can also imitate or produce adultlike intonation patterns at 2 months of age (Beebe, Alson, Jaffe, Feldstein, & Crown, 1988; Lieberman, 1967). This unique infant responsiveness to the human voice predisposes infants to pay attention to human speech; perhaps this has survival value for the infant and facilitates language development (Lenneberg, 1967; Stern, 1977; Trevarthen & Hubley, 1978).

At 3 months, infants revocalize when caregivers vocalize in response to infants' initial vocalization. Over the next several months, infants discriminate frequency differences, and by 7 months of age, they recognize intonational patterns. Infants encode five different tones at birth and gradually discriminate approximately ten by age 7 (Sheppard & Lane, 1968). And at 5 and 6 months, infants vocalize in response to different attitudes displayed by others and to indicate their interest in different objects. At approximately 7 to 9 months, infants demonstrate understanding of single words and sequences of arbitrary sounds (such as train sounds). Use of pauses, hesitations, tempo, and loudness patterns are stable and follow adult-like patterns by 6 years (B. Wood, 1981).

As children mature, the pitch of their voices lowers. Pitch levels of girls are higher than those of boys; researchers have suggested that this difference is due to socialization as well as to physiological differences in the vocal systems of men and women. People judge others' social class, personality, confidence, and persuasiveness on the basis of vocal qualities. People with more rapid rates of speech and more vocal modulation are generally judged as more extroverted and persuasive (Siegman, 1987). Young children also learn how to moderate their voices in communication. Even 3-year-olds are aware of the need to speak with greater loudness as listeners move away (Johnson, Pick, Siegel, Cicciarelli, & Garber, 1981). Children also adjust their vocal behavior in different contexts, such as whispering when telling a secret or speaking more loudly and slowly when telling a story to others.

In summary, as infants mature, they are able to hear more vocal distinctions and subsequently to reproduce these in their own speech. Young children demonstrate considerable skill in picking up subtleties in vocal qualities and eye gaze. Adults also adjust their speech so that vocal qualities are emphasized in simple messages.

Gaze and Gesture Interaction

When communicating, individuals coordinate their gaze and gestures with their speech. For example, we may raise our voice, make a gesture and gaze intensely at another when we emphasize a point. Much of this behavior is patterned, unconscious imitation of the speech patterns heard in the environment.

Early finger movement, tongue protrusion, and finger sucking begin around 1 month, and newborns modeled tongue protrusion when displayed by a model (Kaitz, Meschulach-Sarfaty, Auerbach, & Eidelman, 1988). Gaze and vocalization gradually become coordinated, and gaze and gesture also become coordinated with infants' early pointing and reaching gestures. Taken together, gaze, body orientation, and vocalization appear to signal infants' readiness to interact (Fehr & Exline, 1987). Infants' control of their visual systems, when combined with a caretaker's exaggerated expressions, close distance, and baby talk (behaviors elicited by infants) facilitate infant–caretaker interaction (Stern, 1983). For example, a baby's smile and arm waving may elicit a broad smile and light tickling from his or her caretaker; these tightly interwoven behaviors establish synchrony and bonding between infant and adult.

Gestures also accompany phonetically consistent forms, even though it may not be clear what infants are referring to. At Stage 5 in Piaget's sensorimotor intelligence, infants intentionally use objects, and by Stage 6, they intentionally use object and person interactions (e.g., showing and giving a toy to their parent). According to Bijou (1993), gestures develop in three phases. Random motor acts first change into skills involving body managment, movement, and hand dexterity. Then infants use these motor skills to actively explore the environment through activities like touching, pointing, and rolling over. Finally, these motor skills emerge as gestural communication.

To use gestural communication, infants must display behaviors appropriate for both speaking and listening. As "speakers," infants must respond both to a referent (e.g., reach out their hands to receive a toy) and to another listener (e.g., by gazing or pulling at another's arm or clothing). As "listeners," infants must be able to respond appropriately to another's gesture, perhaps by looking away, turning away, or reaching eagerly for something. Bijou (1993) concluded that children who have developed some gestural communication are "at an advantage in acquiring verbal-vocal referential behavior, since their new modality can supplement their developed skills in nonverbal activities" (p. 227).

Special Perceptual Processing for Social Cognition Information

To coordinate all these nonverbal communication channels (e.g., gaze and gesture), some mechanisms for control and coordination must be available to infants. Locke (1993) suggested that humans possess a specialization in social cognition, or SSC, that integrates perceptions and behaviors around social interaction. As he stated, the SSC

> is domain-specific, since certain kinds of social interactions evoke behaviors that are not otherwise displayed. It is heavily influenced by genetic factors and its activation requires no more than a minimal role for experience. It contains some hardwiring: there are brain cells that fire mainly to faces or to specific facial expressions, and different parts of the brain are responsible for linguistic and nonlinguistic prosody. And it is arguably autonomous. (p. 353)

Locke (1993) not only argued for specialization in social cognition but also supported a "specialized information processing system with specific responsibilities that pertain to language" (p. 352). He suggested that this dual specialization hypothesis (specialized information processing and specialized social cognition) enabled children to rapidly acquire language and communication skills that facilitate their survival. As Locke humorously noted, these rapid perceptual, interpretive processes ensure survival; with lengthier processing times, "We could die before deciding whether an approaching individual was friend or foe" (p. 353).

In a similar vein, Steven Pinker (1995) has also supported an innate, prewired language capacity (discussed in chapter 3). Locke (1993), however, also posited an innate predisposition for social cognition (social interaction being an important aspect of this) which relies on nonverbal, perceptual, interpretive processes such as face and voice recognition.

As already noted, infants possess a range of sophisticated perceptual abilities that facilitate their communication. The rapid development of the visual system, coupled with a well-developed auditory system, enables infants to focus on speech and its varied, related nonverbal behaviors such as eye gaze, gestures, and body orientation. Although researchers have demonstrated the sophistication of infants' perceptual abilities, they are less certain about how these abilities are executed. For example, are there special coordination centers in the brain that facilitate social cognitive processes?

We turn next to a detailed overview of nonverbal dimensions of communication and focus on facial expressions, eye gaze, gesture, and paralinguistics, the nonverbal dimensions centrally integrated with verbal communication.

NONVERBAL SYSTEMS OF COMMUNICATION

Facial Expression

An important nonverbal communicative dimension is facial expression, one of the earliest nonverbal forms of communication, and used primarily to express emotions. A fundamental purpose of human communication is to express emotions; expressing emotion is a major way in which attachment develops between infant and caretaker (Izard, 1971; Malatesta, Culver, Tesman, & Shepard, 1989). During infancy and preschool years, children learn a range of behaviors that express emotions. Some scholars have suggested that certain emotional expressions are present at birth and later become more varied, blended, and complex. During preschool years, children develop increasing control over facial expressions and can dampen negative affect as well as substitute one facial expression for another. These changes reflect children's socialization by parents and others as well as their innate perceptual and cognitive capacities.

Current Theoretical Debates. Theoretical controversy exists over the nature of emotions and how they are expressed. At present, three alternative theoretical positions are advocated (Malatesta et al., 1989). From one viewpoint, innate, discrete emotions are present at birth and are signaled by specific facial displays; these behaviors reliably reflect infants' feeling states until they acquire the ability to control or mask them (Izard & Malatesta, 1987). According to a second position, developed by Bowlby (1973, 1980) and generally called attachment theory, nonverbal affective signals are activated by a biologically based, goal-directed motivational system. Certain behaviors, like crying, gazing, or clinging, elicit supportive behaviors from caretakers who are predisposed to respond to them. Attachment between infants and caretakers develops because of caretakers' consistent responses to infant behaviors. A third position, developed by Sroufe (1979, 1988, 1989), maintains that early emotional states signal distress or nondistress, and by 2 to 3 months of age, infants signal more specific emotions. Sroufe and others have argued that emotional expression relies on a minimal level of cognitive development (some elementary cognitive activity and consciousness) (Urban, Carlson, Egeland & Sroufe, 1991). This position has been labeled the *cognitive-constructivist* position.

All these views agree that emotional expressiveness is a fundamental aspect of infant behavior but differ in how emotional expressiveness develops and what it conveys. Do facial expressions signal a specific emotional-cognitive state like interest or just a general state like distress versus nondistress?

Fogel and Thelen (1987) have developed a lesser known alternative view, a systems perspective for early expressive and communicative action. They have suggested that expressive and communicative actions are organized and integrated with aspects of infants' physiology, cognition, behavior, and social environment. Change occurs asynchronously as a result of interactions among these cooperating systems (e.g., expressive actions, cognition). According to Fogel and Thelen, a central control mechanism drives developmental changes as infants mature and deal with different tasks and in different environments. Fogel and Thelen have thus proposed a more broadly integrated system of emotional development than have the three theorists previously discussed.

These perspectives all suggest that infants' affective feeling states can be reliably detected early in infancy through facial expressions. Caretakers seem to reliably identify, and react differently to, different affective signals. These alternative theoretical positions differ on what levels of skill, intentionality, and consciousness infants are assumed to have with regard to affective states and their expressions of them. For our purposes here, we are assuming that infants' facial expressions signal their emotional states, that different expressions signal different affective states, and that caretakers can reliably and appropriately respond to different signals. Increasing cognitive development and motor control enable preschoolers to mask their facial expressions so that their expressions do not necessarily accurately reflect feeling states. For example, preschoolers are able to smile and thank someone for a gift they do not like.

Understanding facial expression is important because humans express their emotions and thus share feelings through their facial expressions. In early infancy, affective communication signals allow infants and caretakers to bond. These attachments form the basis for early social and emotional development, and in turn, the security and comfort of early socioemotional development profoundly influence children's subsequent growth and development. Other social influences, such as the physical and social settings, the cultural practices surrounding child care and rearing, and the psychology of the caretakers, also shape subsequent socioemotional development (Harkness & Super, 1985). (These influences are discussed more thoroughly in chapter 6.) It is also important to note, however, that deviant expressive behavior may disrupt basic developmental processes such as the synchrony between mother and infant (Izard, Haynes, Chisholm, & Baak, 1991).

With this broad overview of socioemotional development in mind, we turn to a more detailed examination of infant expressiveness and changes in emotional expression during the preschool years. As we shall see, the infant moves from limited emotional expressiveness to masking emotional states as a preschooler.

Universal Facial Expressions. Substantial research suggests that the earliest facial expressions are innate: Humans are prewired to express certain emotional states such as fear and anger, which appear to be universal. Ekman and Izard have been primarily responsible for suggesting the innateness and universality of certain facial expressions. As Izard (1994) noted, "A substantial body of language-independent evidence supports the hypothesis of the innateness and universality of at least some of the patterns of facial movements that signal emotion states in human and nonhuman primates" (p. 288). Both Izard (1994) and Ekman (1994) have argued that expressive behaviors can be modified and changed as a result of socialization and culture. As humans mature, they increasingly exercise voluntary control over innate emotional expressions as a way of influencing others' impressions of them (Halberstadt, 1993; Wintre & Vallance, 1994).

Ekman's neuro-cultural model suggested that some emotional expressions are universal while others are culture specific. For example, facial expressions to illustrate speech or the use of symbolic gestures or emblems vary across cultures (Ekman & Friesen, 1969). Different evoking stimuli, affective states, display rules for emotional expression, and behavioral consequences are all sources for cross-cultural variation in facial expressiveness.

Words used to represent and describe emotions are also influenced by culture (Ekman, 1993). As Ekman noted, "Each emotion term, I believe, refers to a different set of organized, integrated processes. They include the antecedent events, the physiological and motor responses, the memories, thoughts, images, and information processing, and the mobilization of efforts to cope with the source of emotion. All or any of these may be implied when someone says 'he looks angry' " (p. 159). Some words may include references not only to a specific emotion but also to antecedent situations, metaphors, attitudes, and the like.

In both preliterate and literate cultures, infants and adults are able to identify facial expressions of *happiness, interest, surprise, sadness, fear, disgust,* and *anger.* Finding agreement in identifying facial expressions across preliterate cultures is especially important because people would not have access to shared visual information, such as through the mass media. There is higher agreement on identification of happy facial expressions (like interest or surprise) as opposed to negative facial expressions (like anger; Ekman, 1994). In most studies subjects identified or labeled a facial expression; in a rare study that measured spontaneous facial expressions of emotion, however, "Strikingly similar facial responses in these two cultures" (Japanese and North American) were found (Ekman, 1982, p. 259). Subjects identified similar meanings for facial expressions, whether displayed by Japanese or North American subjects.

Differential Emotions Theory (DET).   In this book, we focus on Izard and his colleagues, whose work has emphasized the development of infants' facial expressions and their impact on caretakers. Differential emotions theory (DET), as proposed by Izard (1992), argued that each discrete emotion has a unique organizational and motivational character. A physiological, neuromuscular basis, which provides patterned feedback, underlies facial expressions. Facial expressiveness is functionally preadapted for infants' survival because it signals the need for caregiver intervention and underlies the way that people experience emotion. Thus, facial expressiveness enhances preverbal infants' ability to communicate and develop relationships with others. As Izard (1994) noted:

> Although all developmental psychologists do not agree on the time of emergence of discrete facial expressions, few doubt their significance in socioemotional development. It has been well documented that discrete facial expressions of human mothers have predictable and differential effects in regulating their infants' behavior in happy circumstances and what can be perceived as a dangerous situation. (p. 291)

Emotions come under increasing self-regulation by children through increasing cognitive development and socialization. For people to accomplish their goals and enjoy harmonious relationships with others, emotions must be regulated. With age, emotions become more varied in their frequency, range, discreteness, and integrity (Izard, 1991; Izard & Malatesta, 1987). According to the DET model, discrete emotions can vary in intensity, from subtle to very strong feeling. Discrete emotions can also be independent of cognition and vary in their expression through differences in socialization, culture, and experience.

A distinction must also be made between facial expressions that reflect discrete emotional states (like anger in response to pain) and facial expressions that reflect affective-cognitive structures. Izard (1994) termed the latter phenomenon the "expression–feeling link" because feelings are associated with particular facial expressions. These expression–feeling links rely on some cognitive processing of information; they develop over time and are influenced by culture and socialization. In everyday interaction, humans use facial expressions to infer the feelings, intentions, character, and personality of others.

Developing Facial Expressiveness in Infancy.   Infants quickly develop their abilities to encode and decode facial expressions. At 2½ months, infants encoded full-face and partial expressions of interest, joy, sadness, and anger; expressions of surprise, disgust, and fear were also encoded, but less frequently. Infants imitate others' facial expressions soon after birth; over time, parents' expressive style may influence infants' repertoire of facial behaviors (Field, Woodson, Greenberg, & Cohen, 1982; Halberstadt, 1991). As Halberstadt noted, the relationship between parents' and children's expressiveness begins in infancy and is maintained into adulthood. However, individual differences in facial expressiveness also are apparent at birth (Field et al., 1982).

When infants' expressions paralleled adult facial expressions, adults could reliably identify these emotions (Izard et al., 1995). Japanese and North American infants encoded anatomically identical expressions of anger, enjoyment, fear, and sad anger (Camras, Oster, Campos, Miyake, & Bradshaw, 1992); this study provided additional support for the notion of universal facial expressions. In a study using both adult and infant facial expressions, adult expressions were more accurately identified than were infant expressions. Positive expressions were more accurately identified than were negative expressions, and recognition was higher for adult, rather than infant, negative expressions (Izard et al., 1995).

Face-to-face play, which peaks in infants from 3 to 6 months of age, provides ample opportunities for affective expressiveness by infants and responses to their signals by caregivers (Malatesta & Haviland, 1982). In early infancy, infants' expressiveness is elicited primarily by their mothers; at 3 months, more reciprocal interchanges between mother and infant are observed (Kaye & Fogel, 1980). Infants first smile at people between 2 and 6 weeks of age (Tennes, Emde, Kisley, & Metcalf, 1972) and later respond by smiling at others' actions (Hayes & Watson, 1981). Infants' involvement with and interest in others increases from 3 to 6 months, especially when caretakers or strangers exhibit playful rather than nonresponsive faces, and then subsequently declines (Lamb, Morrison, & Malkin, 1987). At 6 months, infants begin to initiate interaction sequences. At 10 months, infants change their smiling behavior depending upon whether the mother or a stranger was present (Fox & Davidson, 1988). Early infancy thus provides many opportunities for infants' responsive facial expressiveness, which facilitates attachment with adult caretakers (Biringen, 1994a, 1994b).

Emotional recognition by infants occurs around 3 months of age, when they discriminate between positive and negative expressions. Emotional expressions appear to be perceived categorically and decoded rapidly (Izard, 1994). At 3 months, infants preferred faces that were either still or displayed emotion, both of which were salient to them (Biringen, 1987). Anger, fear, and surprise are reliably discriminated by infants at 4 to 6 months (Ludemann & Nelson, 1988; Serrano, Iglesias, & Loeches, 1992). Infants distinguish different negative facial expressions around 6 to 7 months of age. Termine and Izard (1988) found that 9-month-old infants responded with more gazing and expressions of joy when their mothers displayed happy faces and showed more sadness and averted gazes when their mothers were sad. From 7 to 10 months, infants undergo a developmental transition: At 7 months, they appear to identify specific facial features, and at 10 months, they are sensitive to a pattern of correlation across facial features (like widely spaced eyes with a high forehead; Younger, 1992). Thus, infants' ability to recognize different facial expressions apparently develops rapidly from 3 to 10 months. In addition, infants seem to identify specific facial features as well as a pattern of co-occuring facial features by 10 months. Four negative affect signals (pressed lips, sadness, knit brow, and anger) were consistent and stable from 7½ to 22 months. Negative affect expressive patterns appeared more stable over time and across situations than did positive affect expressions (Malatesta et al., 1989).

To voluntarily modify their affective expression (by intensifiying, minimizing, neutralizing, or substituting affective expressions), infants must be at Piaget's Stage 5 in sensorimotor intelligence (Malatesta et al., 1989). Stage 5 is characterized by the emergence of intentional behaviors (Bruner, 1975a, 1975b; Dore, 1983). Malatesta and Haviland (1982) also suggested that infants' ability to modify their affective expression depends upon the stabilization of emotional states (occurring between 3 to 6 months) and some symbolic representation of affect.

Influences on Infants' Emotional Development. Socialization, especially through interactions with parents, appears to influence how children recognize and respond to emotions. For example, when a child is upset, some parents directly intervene and can help their children resume ongoing activities (Cassidy, 1994; Thompson, 1990). Other adult caretakers use reinforcement techniques (Malatesta & Haviland, 1982) or verbal comments (Halberstadt, 1991; Saarni, 1987, 1988) to help children regulate their emotions. Parents can also model appropriate emotional responses. Social referencing, in which children observe their parents' interpretation of a situation to form their own understanding of the situation, occurs many times throughout childhood. For instance, infants crossed a visual cliff when their mothers showed a happy expression but avoided the situation when they displayed fear (Campos, 1981; Sorce, Emde, Campos, & Klinnert, 1985).

Infants learn appropriate display rules (rules governing the expression of emotion) through contingent learning, observational learning, and their own self-regulation. Emotional development also appears related to subsequent personality development. Through repeated expressions and experiences, infants build up certain responses from others; these interactions, over time, enable distinct personality characteristics to develop (Malatesta et al., 1989). Stifter and Grant (1993) found that infants responded with more anger when an object of interest was removed than when objects of little interest were removed. Thus, over time and different contexts, emotions (affective-cognitive structures) become motivators; they direct subsequent behavior and guide the interpretation of social experiences (Boyatzis, Chazen, & Ting, 1993; Bretherton, 1995).

Early Interactional Influences. Attachment theory research, by Bowlby (1969/1982, 1973, 1980), Ainsworth (1973), and others, has dealt with interactions between infants and caretakers and the implications for emotional expressiveness and bonding. Briefly, the crying, clinging, and other such behavior of infants elicit caretaker interventions so that infants' distress (for example, crying because of hunger) is taken care of. Three signals—crying, orientation (gaze and body position), and smiling—are viewed as innate signals with emotional overtones.

During the first year, caretakers' consistent, contingent, and caring responses lead to infants' feeling secure and loved (Isabella & Belsky, 1991). These feelings, when in the physical presence or proximity of the caretaker, create a tension between the need to remain close and the need to explore (Malatesta et al., 1989). Mothers' responses, in combination with infant characteristics, lead to infants that are secure, insecure-avoidant, or insecure-anxious in their attachment. Each attachment pattern fosters different types of emotional expressivity (Bretherton, Biringen, Ridgeway, Maslin, et al., 1989). (Refer also to the discussion of attachment and its influence on children's communicative and social skills in chapter 6.)

Mothers' responses have been characterized as accepting, cooperative, or interfering. Accepting mothers accept their infants' positive and negative behaviors; cooperative mothers guide their infants, and interfering mothers "train" their infants. Maternal sensitivity to infants is important to develop secure attachment: Sensitive mothers are aware of their infants' signals, interpret them accurately, and respond appropriately and promptly (Ainsworth, 1973; Ainsworth, Bell, & Stayton, 1971; Ainsworth, Blehar, Waters, & Wall, 1978; Bretherton, 1995).

Maternal sensitivity is closely linked to the security of infants' attachment. Mothers of 1-year-old secure infants were more sensitive, responsive, and less rejecting than mothers of insecure infants. For insecure infants, the mothers of resistant infants become less rejecting over time and mothers of avoidant infants became more rejecting over time, when compared to other mothers (Isabella, 1993). Another study linked the security of attachment to specific interactive behaviors between mothers and infants. Isabella and Belsky (1991) found that mother–infant dyads developing secure attachments interacted with well-timed, reciprocal, and mutually rewarding interactions. In contrast, insecurely attached dyads were characterized by mothers who were intrusive, minimally responsive, or unresponsive to their children. Infants who were insecure-avoidant had mothers who were intrusive and overstimulating whereas insecure-resistant dyads had poorly coordinated interactions in which mothers were uninvolved, inconsistent, or both. A study by Sroufe, Fox, and Pancake (1983) found a relationship between quality of early attachment and children's dependency on others: Preschoolers with secure attachment were less dependent on adults (see also Waters & Sroufe, 1983). Consistent attachment behaviors have been found whether infants were observed at home or in the laboratory (Vaughn & Waters, 1981).

In a major study of maternal behavior and infant affective signals, by the second year infants were consistently regulating their own expressions, especially dampening negative affect (shown by compressed lips, knit brow, and lip biting). Interactions between 2-year-olds and their mothers were primarily positive, and toddlers recovered quickly from their distress at being separated from their mothers. Mothers who displayed low to moderate levels of contingent facial expressions may be more sensitive: These mothers maintained more eye contact with their children (Malatesta et al., 1989). Secure children also demonstrated higher levels and longer periods of symbolic play than did insecure children (Slade, 1987a, 1987b).

Infants also receive a wide range of stimuli. One study showed that mothers displayed greater expressivity with girls than with boys; thus, girls experienced a greater range of emotional expressions and social smiling (J. Robinson & Biringen, 1995). As infants matured, maternal affect displays decreased (J. Robinson, Little, & Biringen, 1993). Gender differences in infant–mother dyads are apparent, with less maternal matching of infant affect in infant–mother dyads. Maternal sensitivity is associated with maternal matching of their sons' affect in contrast to their creation of a shared affective state with their daughters. In other words, mothers appear to mirror their sons' affective states while they co-create shared affective states with their daughters. In a follow-up investigation, mother–daughter and mother–son dyads displayed no significant differences in balance of control in the interactions between mothers and their children, but gender-specific stylistic differences were found across the dyads with mother–daughter dyads displaying more emotional expressiveness (Biringen, Robinson, & Emde, 1994).

In addition, more securely attached children received more maternal expressivity, more positive emotions during play and looked more at their mothers than did insecure children. Insecure children showed more interest expressions (believed to reflect greater monitoring and wariness about the environment) than did secure children (Malatesta et al., 1989). Malatesta et al. (1989) suggested that maternal affective responses alter children's expressive development: Both maternal contingency and their specific responses predicted children's subsequent development. As they noted, "Displays of interest to early infant affect predicted positive affect, whereas tendencies to ignore sadness and pain (but not anger) were associated with more sadness and anger following separation at age 2 years" (p. 71). Over time, girls dampened negative affect more than boys, and girls received a wider range of emotional expressions directed to them. Infant expressive behavior does appear to be "coherently integrated" with their feeling states.

The security of mothers' attachment to their children influenced the children's subsequent social and communicative development. Secure attachment predicted more social engagement and acceptance by others (Booth, Rose-Krasnor, McKinnon & Rubin, 1994; Rubin, Caplan, Fox & Calkins, 1995) and more healthy socioemotional development (Rubin, Booth, Rose-Krasnor & Mills, 1995).

As infants mature, mothers spend less time acknowledging their infants' affect and make fewer comments encouraging affective displays. This observation appears consistent with cultural norms about increasing suppression of negative affect as infants mature (J. Robinson, Little, & Biringen, 1993). That is, displays of negative affect, like anger, decline with age. Being able to regulate emotions is viewed as a sign of increasing maturity. From 3 to 6 months, infants produced fewer knit brows and expressions of pain, and their expressions of pain reflected less distress. Over time, mothers displayed a more restricted yet stable range of facial expressions and responded quickly to infants' expressiveness (on average, a half-second delay in responding). Mothers reinforced positivity in their infants' expressiveness (and did not reinforce negative facial expressions). In addition, mothers also responded with more variable expressions to female infants. As Malatesta (1982) noted, although mothers responded verbally to their infants, it was "the mothers' facial expressions, their tone of voice, and the infants' feeling states that comprise the most salient aspects of the interchange for preverbal infants" (p. 21).

In a rare test of infant responsiveness to mothers or fathers, Hirschberg and Svejda (1990) found that infants showed more positive affect with happy as opposed to fearful signals by parents. No differences were found between maternal and paternal signals, except that infants looked more to mothers when no signals were given.

Mothers present full-face expressions to their infants, and infants imitate their mothers' pitch and facial expressiveness as early as 2 to 3 months (Stern, 1977; Trevarthen, 1979a, 1979b). In addition, mothers model various facial expressions for their infants, respond contingently to their expressions, and selectively reinforce some emotional expressions. Three-month-old infants express anger, pain, interest, surprise, joy, sadness, knit brow and brow flashes (of greeting or agreement). Conscious, voluntary control over facial expressiveness develops over time, and at the age of 2, toddlers can intentionally plan and use display rules (Malatesta & Haviland, 1982; Malatesta et al., 1989).

Modifying Emotional Expressiveness. Gradually, young children learn to control their own emotional expressiveness; the expressive displays characteristic of early infancy become transformed into variable forms of social communication. For example, spontaneous expressions of fear, interest, or surprise become blended into indirect, "soft" signals. These soft signals (like pouting) are more flexible and fluid than earlier expressions and may reflect imitation or instrumental learning, rather than reliably indicating children's emotional states (Malatesta, Culver, Tesman, & Shepard, 1989; Malatesta & Haviland, 1982; Zivin, 1986, 1989).

According to Izard (1994), efforts to modify emotional expressions and expression–feeling relations begin in early infancy and can be measured by 4 to 6 months. Humans learn display rules (rules about the degree and concealment of emotions) in infancy and childhood; such rules reflect culture, gender, and personal norms. Families play an important role in the development of personal display rules; they influence *what* emotions can be expressed as well as *how* the face conveys facial expressions (Malatesta, 1982). In an investigation of preschoolers' understanding of display rules, Josephs (1994) found that 6-year-olds were better than 4- to 5-year-olds at identifying a story protagonist's real and apparent emotions. In a subsequent task, both groups of subjects were able to control their negative emotion upon receiving an unattractive gift. Josephs concluded that even younger preschoolers were able to follow display rules in their behavior before completely understanding the difference between real and apparent emotions.

Preschoolers can modulate their emotional expressiveness and display neutral affect in their facial expression (Lewis & Michaelson, 1983). Gender differences also occur, with girls displaying a greater range of facial expressiveness. People also act to minimize negative affect, and some researchers suggest that minimizing it may lessen its impact (Malatesta et al., 1989). For instance, smiling when unhappy is one way to minimize negative affect (Ekman & Friesen, 1975). As Malatesta et al. (1989) pointed out:

> . . . the earliest forms of expressive control involve intensification and deintensification (miniaturization) of expressive behavior related to ongoing states. Some degree of skill in this area is achieved during the first year of life. When deintensification of affect is taken to the limit, it results in neutralization, a behavior that can be observed in preschoolers. Developmentally, the most difficult feat appears to be masking . . . expressive behavior should remain a fairly reliable index of feeling state until the third year, although the intensity of felt emotion may be somewhat exaggerated or minimized. (p. 8)

With age, children's encoding (sending messages) and decoding (interpreting messages) skills increase. Yet children are better at decoding than at encoding, a fact suggesting that nonverbal comprehension precedes production. In one study, children were more accurate at facial emotion skills than at gesture skills. Their overall nonverbal skills correlated significantly with peer popularity. This observation suggests that preschoolers may possess an encoding skill that generalizes across nonverbal channels. Finally, children's ability to interpret and to send gestural messages was also related; thus gestures may be interpreted in terms of "nonverbal styles" (Boyatzis & Satyaprasad, 1994).

What emotions are most readily identified? Do tasks children were doing influence their ability to recognize emotions? Task type (situation discrimination, matching discrimination, forced choice labeling, or free labeling) had no effect on emotional recognition; all age groups (either 4, 6, or 8 years of age) most accurately identified happiness, followed by sadness, anger, and fear. Surprise was least recognized by 4-year-olds and most identified by 8-year-olds (Markham & Adams, 1992).

The underlying dimensions that preschoolers use to interpret facial expressions appear to be based on judgments of pleasure, degree of arousal, and degree of assertiveness versus being taken aback (Russell & Bullock, 1986). During middle childhood, children's knowledge of how and when to control emotions increases, but they are still sometimes unaware of situations in which people might want to control their emotions. In addition, verbal control of emotional display is understood more than is facial control (Gnepp & Hess, 1986). Finally, as children mature, they can accurately identify a discrepancy between verbal comments and nonverbal displays in order to detect lying (Rotenberg, Simourd, & Moore, 1989). Thus, over time, preschoolers gradually increase their ability to control their own expressiveness and become more accurate at identifying others' emotional expressions.

Children begin to learn multiple functions for nonverbal behaviors as well. For preschoolers, smiling appears to have both an expressive function (to express joy) and a communicative function (to excuse failure) (Lutkenhaus, Grossman, & Grossman, 1985). Joy is expressed by a smile, straight posture, and hands thrown up; failure is displayed by smiles and an oblique head posture with lowered eyes and head. According to Schneider and Josephs' (1991) study, failure smiles are true smiles, frequently intense smiles. Preschoolers who failed a task looked at the experimenter and smiled more than did successful subjects. A second study, in which there was no face-to-face contact with the experimenter, found that children smiled less. Thus the earlier smiling with failure may be a type of social referencing (Schneider & Josephs, 1991). Although preschoolers appear to tacitly understand display rules and behave in a manner consistent with them (e.g., smiling when receiving an undesirable gift), it may not be until late childhood that such rules are conceptually understood (Saarni, 1988, 1989).

Interpersonal communication skills rely on children's being able to decode and encode nonverbal messages; these interpersonal skills influence popularity and social competence. Four- to 6-year-old girls' expressiveness was positively related to their sociability and number of friends; although this relationship was positive for boys, it was not significant (Buck, 1975). Another study linked preschoolers' social status positively with their expressiveness but not with their performance on an encoding task (Field & Walden, 1982). In addition, preschoolers' identification of emotion was also related to their peer popularity (Denham, McKinley, Couchoud, & Holt, 1990) and their social competence (Philippott & Feldman, 1990). (The interrelationships between communication skills and peer acceptance are more thoroughly explored in chapter 8.)

Three major strategies are used to control affective facial expressions: inhibition, in which subjects display no feeling when they really have an emotional response; simulation, in which subjects show feelings when they feel none; and masking, in which subjects display false facial expressions to cover other feelings (Ekman & Friesen, 1969, 1975). Although some minimizing of negative affect occurs during infancy and preschool years, preschoolers do not develop much skill at masking feeling. As mentioned previously, at around 6 years of age, children recognize some disparity between a facial expression and what that person really feels, and from 6 to 10 years, they begin to openly discuss display rules (Saarni, 1979, 1984, 1988; Saarni & Crowley, 1990). A study by Halberstadt et al. (1992) found that second- and fourth-grade children were skilled at managing facial displays when they were asked to inhibit, simulate, and mask feelings, but the older children used more complex strategies to manage affective displays.

Display rules also characterize the ways in which people manage nonverbal impressions. For instance, prosocial rules protect others' feelings ("Don't point at the lady with the crutches"); self-protective rules protect people's own feelings ("Don't cry because kids will tease you"), and self-centered display rules help people gain advantages or avoid disadvantages ("Be quiet so we can concentrate") (Josephs, 1994). Josephs' study demonstrated that 4- to 6-year-old children consistently knew when real and apparent emotions did not coincide in prosocial and self-centered stories. Furthermore, the children could regulate their responses appropriately when receiving either a liked or a disliked gift.

Recognizing Emotions and Situational Constraints on Emotional Expressiveness

Young children are able to identify the emotional implications of situations (Fabes, Eisenberg, McCormick, & Wilson, 1988). In a study comparing situational versus vocal cues for identifying emotions, children's emotional identification improved with age (5 to 11 years) and relied more on channels depicting anger or happiness than on a channel displaying neutrality. Vocal cues were used to judge happiness and contextual cues to detect anger (Hortacsu & Birsen, 1992).

Recognition of emotion from vocal, contextual, and facial cues usually improves with age; but children differ in their ability to recognize different emotions, and neutral emotions are especially difficult to label (Gross & Ballif, 1991; Matsumoto & Kishimoto, 1983). Hoffner and Badzinski (1989) concluded that, with increasing age, children can interpret situational cues and are cautious about taking facial displays as genuine. They also appear to simultaneously process situational and facial cues (Gross & Ballif, 1991). By 5 years of age, children can interpret emotions in adult strangers' vocal tones and distinguish between different emotional tones in infant vocalizations (Papousek, 1989; Sincoff & Rosenthal, 1985). They also appear to be more skilled at identifying anger than happiness from vocal cues (Berk, Doehring, & Bryans, 1983).

In a major review of children's understanding of emotion from facial expressions and situations, Gross and Ballif (1991) developed the following set of consistent research findings:

1. Young children could detect similarities and differences in facial expressions of emotion as early as 2 years of age.

2. Children's ability to detect and identify facial expressions of emotion increased with age and varied according to the emotions conveyed. Children correctly identified happiness more than they did other emotional expressions.

3. Children made systematic errors in identifying facial expressions of emotion and at times confused eyes and mouth expression in different drawings or confused emotions which have similar facial features (e.g., confusing anger and sadness). Sometimes errors occurred because of insufficient information.

4. When multiple cues of information were available, children used facial expressions of emotion to infer what others' subsequent actions might be and to guide their own responses.

5. Children's identification of facial expressions of emotion was influenced by their ongoing social environment, such as the degree of maternal expressiveness.

6. Social rules about gender and the expression of negative emotions appeared to influence children's recognition of facial expressions of emotion.

7. The evidence was conflicting about the influence of the decoder's race on identification of facial emotional expressions; these findings might be confounded by differences in verbal ability.

8. Verbal ability influenced children's recognition of emotion from facial expressions. The responses required in studies influenced children's recognition scores.

9. With increasing age, children's understanding of display rules increased. (Display rules govern the overt expression of emotions; children may hide true feelings to protect themselves, to avoid trouble, etc.)

10. Children were able to offer reasons for people's emotional reactions in different situations.

11. Gender influenced children's explanation of a story character's responses to various situations.

12. When past behaviors of protagonists were used to explain their emotional responses to situations presented to them, preschoolers and kindergartners often ignored information based on past experience and just responded to the situation. School-age children understood that the same situation could create different emotional responses in people. Preschoolers could often suggest ways to mitigate a negative emotional response to a situation, such as changing the circumstances or changing the way in which a person thought about the situation. Preschoolers thus combine situational as well as personal cues in responding to circumstances.

13. Children with disabilities, such as emotionally disturbed children, were less accurate in recognizing facial expressions of emotion and used less situational information in judging emotional expressions.

14. Western and non-Western children were similar in their ability to recognize facial expressions of emotions and in their use of situational cues to explain emotional responses.

15. With increasing age, children could identify and explain more complex emotional reactions.

(For the interested reader, Gross and Ballif's review is excellent and also includes methodological assessments of various studies).

Influences on Emotional Expressiveness
in Early Childhood

Family environment continues to influence a young child's emotional expressiveness. For instance, parental talk about emotions facilitates their children's social and emotional abilities by allowing them to learn how others think and feel (Denham, 1992; Dunn, Brown, & Beardsall, 1991). The family's emotional climate and maternal socialization also influence children's nonverbal communication skills (Halberstadt, 1986, 1991). A series of studies by Biringen and his associates (Biringen, 1990; Biringen & Robinson, 1991) found maternal sensitivity and emotional availability related to security of mother–infant attachment. Gender differences in mother–toddler attachment were also found; mothers with sons mirrored their sons' affect whereas mothers with daughters co-created a shared affective state (Biringen, Robinson, & Emde, 1994; Robinson, Little, & Biringen, 1993). Gender influences emotional expressiveness, with males displaying less emotion, and different emotions, than do girls (Buck, 1984; Buck, Miller, & Caul, 1974; Strayer, 1985). Some gender differences may arise because parents expect different nonverbal behavior from boys and girls (Brody & Hall, 1993).

Mothers try to regulate their children's emotional expressiveness in different ways, depending upon the particular emotion being expressed. According to Casey and Fuller (1994), mothers' most frequently used strategy was to match children's emotional reaction and make a brief verbal comment. A family's climate primarily expressing either negative or positive emotions also influenced maternal regulation. Negatively expressive mothers regulated their children's responses in happy situations. Mothers were more accurate at predicting their daughters' and their older children's responses. Mothers often predicted verbal responses while their children frequently indicated that their responses would be nonverbal. Overall, mothers regulated their children at a relatively high level over time. Casey and Fuller concluded that families may reinforce children's expressive styles that are similar to the overall family style.

Another study linked preschoolers' patterns of emotional expressiveness and their reactions to others' emotional display with their mothers' patterns of emotional expressivity. Maternal expressiveness, especially the management of negative affect, is an important learning context for children. As Denham and Grout (1993) noted, "Mothers' actual display of negative emotion during interaction is dysregulating for children, but mothers' **experience** of negative emotion, paired with less tension displayed during interaction, appears to expose the child to potentially useful socialization." (p. 224). That is, when mothers experience some negative emotion, they should do so without creating additional stress for their children by venting their emotions at them. Children whose mothers externalized (overtly displayed) emotionality displayed greater overall emotionality in preschool and were less effective interacting with their peers. In contrast, mothers responding with calm, task-oriented behaviors appeared to facilitate their children's positive interactions with peers.

Social regulation of preschoolers' emotions has been related to their social interaction skills. Being able to regulate emotions means being able to control their overt expression. For instance, children may feel anger when someone takes their toy, but they do not "beat them up" as a response. Based on parent temperament ratings and observations of children during free play sessions, children were classified as either low, average, or high social interactors and as poor, average, or good emotion regulators. Results indicated that low social interactors with poor emotional regulation were more wary and anxious during interaction than were low social interactors with average or good emotional regulation. High social interactors with poor emotional regulation were judged as having interpersonal problems because they displayed their emotions in un-controlled ways. For example, such children would refuse to continue playing when a peer wanted to change their game. Rubin, Caplan, Fox, and Calkins (1995) noted that "the dynamics of emotional experience, expression and regu-lation can influence the quality of children's social interactions and relationships" (p. 49). (For an excellent review and analysis of emotional regulation, see Garber & Dodge, 1991. Peer social competence and communication skills are more thoroughly discussed in chapter 8.)

As language develops, further changes in emotional expressiveness and ex-perience might be anticipated. Some emotions are hypercognized (referred to by many linguistic terms), and others are hypocognized (referred to by few terms) (Levy, 1980). Language itself may reflect the significance of certain emotions within a culture and also helps draw attention to the emotional dimension of interaction (Malatesta & Haviland, 1982). Finally, language is used to build conceptual categories and labels for emotions. For example, a study by Camras, Pristo, and Brown (1985) found that children associated less polite directives with speakers who were labeled as angry. These linguistic aspects further socialize children's emotional expressiveness.

Calkins (1994) developed a model for the development of emotion regulation. This model incorporates many aspects of emotional expressiveness discussed in this chapter. Internal components include children's neuroregulatory mechanisms, behavioral traits, and regulatory style. External components include caregiving, training, and peer interactions. Calkins argued that caregivers influence emotional development in three ways. First, caregivers influence children's immediate emotional response in a situation, an influence exemplified in the studies of attachment presented in this chapter. Second, caregivers influence children's beliefs and perceptions about the world and about how to respond to events. For instance, parental talk about emotions has been found to influence their children's emotional expressiveness. Finally, caregivers may directly affect the regulatory styles that children develop to control their emotional expressiveness. As we have previously noted, children frequently mirror their parents' styles of emo-tional expressivity.

In summary, some aspects of facial expressiveness are believed to be innate but are also shaped by culture and socialization. Infants can recognize emotional states at around 2 to 3 months of age, and they identify positive emotions more readily than they do negative ones. Through joint activity with primary caretakers, typically an infant's mother, infants develop their repertoire of facial expressiveness and associate predictable consequences with certain expressive behaviors. With increasing maturity, young children begin to exercise more control over their emotional expressiveness and use different channels to interpret ongoing behavior. By the end of the preschool years, children use situational cues as well as facial expressiveness to detect others' affective states. Children learn to mask their facial expressions but find the process difficult.

While facial expressiveness is a significant indicator of one's emotions, eye gaze facilitates social interaction. Eye gaze serves to gain attention, to maintain and regulate interaction, and to indicate interest. How eye gaze functions in a particular encounter may vary as a result of social characteristics, such as age, gender, social status and culture. We now turn to a discussion of eye gaze.

Eye Gaze

Face-to-face communication relies heavily on mutual eye gaze between interactants. Gazing behavior can signal attentiveness, threat, or affect and is important as a source of feedback about the interaction. Infant–mother interaction has been likened to a dance in which the participants engage and disengage with each other: Much of this synchrony is governed by eye gaze behavior (Stern, 1977). Finally, the preverbal infant signals feelings, involvement, and attention through gaze behavior.

Eye contact begins at about 6 weeks, peaks at 8 to 12 weeks as social smiling begins, and lessens at about 3 months when children become interested in inanimate objects (Fogel, 1982). Mothers time their gazes to accommodate the natural cycles of infants. When infants gaze at their mothers, mothers increase their facial expressiveness; and when infants gaze elsewhere or break the gaze, mothers reduce their affect (Fogel, 1982).

According to Field (1981), mothers try to maintain a level of stimulation which maintains infants' optimal level of stimulation, during which regular cycles of gazing and smiling occur (Brazelton, Koslowski, & Main, 1974). When mothers stopped interacting with their babies (e.g., displayed a neutral face as in the still-face procedure), their infants looked and smiled; when infants were, however, unable to engage their mothers' attention, they averted gaze and displayed less positive affect (Tronick, Als, & Brazelton, 1977, 1980; Tronick, Ricks, & Cohn, 1982).

The relationship between maternal behavior and infant responses plays a significant role in determining how infants interact with others (Bretherton, 1985). At 3 months, infants are establishing their interaction patterns with their mothers, and by 6 months, they have sufficient experience so that their competence and sense of personal effectiveness is stabilized. When 1-year-old toddlers were given conflicting signals by their parents, they monitored both sets of signals and displayed increased negative affect (such as agitated sucking and rocking) and decreased positive affect (Hirschberg, 1990). With infants' increasing age, their ability to simultaneously initiate and terminate gaze with their adult caretakers increases. By 36 months, children have adult-like gaze patterns (Farren, Hirschbiel, & Jay, 1980).

Researchers examined three different maternal styles—elaboration, overcontrolling, and undercontrolling—for their effects on infants' interaction patterns. Mothers displaying the elaboration style (responsive, exaggerated their expressions and "backed off" when infants were not responding) elicited positive affect from infants. When mothers were asked to flatten or depress their behaviors (as if very tired), infants tended to look away and to express wariness or protests. When infants were presented with a stressful situation (the Still-Face procedure in which the mother's face is neutral and expressionless), they displayed more negative affect behaviors (Gusella, Muir, & Tronick, 1988). The Still-Face procedure is one way to assess how infants regulate their own emotional state when their mothers are not responding. Isabella and Belsky (1991) found that securely attached mother–child dyads displayed well-timed, mutual and reciprocal exchanges when interacting.

Eye gaze behavior continues to be an important dimension of nonverbal communication. Preschoolers accurately interpreted gaze and proximity as indicating affiliation, although older girls were more accurate than older boys in their judgments (Post & Hetherington, 1974). Social rank was also reliably indicated by gaze behavior; both boys and girls looked more at high-ranking peers. The gaze measure, or "attention rank," was also positively correlated with sociometric choice, interactive play, and interaction with that peer (Vaughn & Waters, 1981). Furthermore, eye gaze behavior differs between males and females: Girls gaze longer than boys, and this difference is maintained by older children and adults (Hittelman & Dickes, 1979). Fehr and Exline (1987), however, suggested that some of these effects might be artifacts of the experimental situations (e.g., boys might be more accurate at decoding conflict situations). With increasing age, preschoolers completing a puzzle-solving task with their mothers looked less at them and more at the model they were to follow. This finding suggests that, as preschoolers mature, they can self-regulate their own activities and emotional states (Wertsch, McNamee, McLane, & Budwig, 1980).

In summary, eye gaze is an important way for infants to gain attention and maintain joint regard. Coordinated eye gaze and joint attention between mother and infant foster secure attachment and effective interaction; caretakers appear to regulate eye gaze behavior with infants so as to maintain optimal stimulation for the infant. Gaze behavior is also associated with social competence and self-regulation among preschoolers.

We turn now to a discussion of gesture and touch as nonverbal communication channels. Gestures play a role in directly communicating a desire for an object by pointing or reaching for it. These early uses of gestures evolves into the use of gestures to specify to dimensions of something, to represent something or to directly signal meaning as in a "thumbs up" gesture. Gestures also begin to accompany speech, typically emphasizing an idea being expressed.

Gesture

There is very little research on the development of gestures, although research on gestural communication is increasing. The lack of research may be partly due to the dominance of facial channels in conveying emotion. Generally, facial messages are decoded more accurately than are body messages (Amady & Rosenthal, 1992). In addition, emotions tend to be conveyed by facial expressions, while gestures convey specific meanings (like emblems) or intensity of emotion.

Gestures are difficult to define; they cover a broad range of movements, some of which have communicative value and others which are random. Gestures are often integrated with gaze behavior, posture, and head orientation, as in, for example, pointing while gazing at an object. In general, speech and gestures seem to interact: Speech qualities influence gestures. For example, speakers typically time their gestures to occur at the end of sentences. Gesture and posture also convey information about emotions and socioaffective attitudes (Feyereisen & deLannoy, 1991).

Ekman (1977), following the work of Efron, distinguished eight categories of gestures, each functioning in a distinct manner: *batons*—gestures that emphasize specific words; *underliners*—gestures that emphasize a clause or a sentence; *ideographs*—gestures that highlight a direction of thought; *kinetographs*—gestures that outline a bodily or nonhuman action; *pictographs*—gestures that draw the shape of an object; *rhythmics*—gestures that detail the rhythm or pacing of an event; *spatials*—gestures that outline spatial relationships; and *deictics*—gestures that point out a referent. Other categorical systems subdivide gestures into simpler systems: *emblems*—gestures that have direct verbal equivalents, such as a hitchhiking signal; *illustrators*—gestures that accompany speech; *regulators*—nonverbal behaviors that help regulate interaction; and *adaptors*—movements that comfort or help regulate an internal state, like tapping fingers when a person is bored or in a hurry.

Developmental Basis for Gestures. Considerable debate surrounds the issue of how gestures develop and what accounts for their development. Because speech and gestures can express the same thought, some have argued that both systems have the same conceptual underpinning (McNeill, 1985). For example, Werner and Kaplan (1963) maintained that symbolic representation develops when infants understand the world in terms of action and construct affective-sensory-motor patterns. Others have suggested that language develops from specific processes distinct from those that control gestural development (Feyereisen & deLannoy, 1991).

Still other researchers (Bates, Benigni, Bretherton, Camaioni, & Volterra, 1979) have stated that gesture and speech reflect separate systems ("local homologies") that relate differently to each other depending on the task and the age of the subject. (See Rime, Mesquita, Philipott, & Boca, 1991, for an excellent discussion of these alternative theoretical positions.) It is difficult to argue convincingly that gestural communication leads to a later, more complex linguistic system, but infants are clearly presented with multiple learning contexts in which linguistic and gestural communication are both present. For instance, playing "patty-cake" requires both speaking and gesturing to complete the game.

Early Gestural Communication.   By 2 to 3 months of age, infants' hand movements appear to be coordinated with their prespeech facial movements, like lip contraction and tongue protrusion (Trevarthen, 1977a, 1977b). These facial movements are also accompanied by foot and trunk movement. For example, when gazing at a favorite toy, infants might widen their eyes, elevate their eyebrows, and wiggle their bodies. Hand waving, finger pointing, and fingertip clasping are closely synchronized with prespeech movements, within a time frame of 0.1 seconds (Trevarthen, 1977a, 1977b).

In a study of infant behavior, pointing gestures and mouthing were related to one another. Fogel and Hannan (1985) suggested that later gestures develop from these early manual movements, which are initially noncommunicative but are increasingly used in communication. Feyereisen and deLannoy (1991) maintained that this reflects an innate basis for coordination of oral and manual movements, although subsequent cultural influences shapes their interaction.

Early coordinated behaviors, like tongue protrusion and hand waving or sucking and gazing, occur in "runs" or a string of similar states. These coordinated runs are closely tied to mothers' behaviors: Mothers try to respond in a way that encourages the optimal level of infant arousal, as discussed previously in this chapter. Thus, infants and mothers appear to "co-act" before they take turns. Both appear to share control of their coordinated activities, but it is difficult to discern who exerts more control (Stevenson, Roach, VerHoeve, & Leavitt, 1990). Mothers' gestures seem to play an important role in maintaining their toddlers' attention and sustaining interaction with them (Schnur & Shatz, 1984).

Infants' early gestures consist of physical exploration of the environment: Infants look at, orient to, and then try to reach for objects. They focus on objects that they perceive to be within their reach. Bates and her colleagues (1979) concluded that infants' pointing gestures are the precursors of later verbal demands for the object and also facilitate children's labeling of their environment. Word comprehension and production increased and gestural production decreased in infants 13 to 20 months of age (Bretherton et al., 1981). Bretherton and her colleagues stated that a switch in preferred modality of communication occurred during that time and that abstraction of terms and gestures increased with age. In a similar vein, during the second year, Carter (1978a, 1978b) found that infant vocalization became more differentiated and gestures became optional.

In contrast, however, others argue that such continuity between nonverbal and verbal behavior is not supported by research (Fogel, 1992a; Fogel & Thelen, 1987). Some have argued that hand gestures, in coordination with facial and vocal actions, displayed particular affective states in infants (Fogel & Hannan, 1985; Trevarthen, 1977a, 1977b). Legerstee, Corter, and Kienapple (1990), however, found that pointing was associated with both positive and negative affective states. Smiles, gazes, and open-handed arm extensions were associated with positive affective states while closed hands accompanied distressed facial expressions, averted gazes, and arms extended down at the infants' sides. Rather than supporting continuity between gestures and subsequent linguistic behavior, these scholars have suggested that early nonverbal and vocal behaviors signal specific feeling states.

In addition, Trevarthen and his colleagues (Trevarthen, 1979a, 1979b, 1980b, 1982; Trevarthen & Hubley, 1978) observed a shift, during 8 to 12 months, from only social or only physical (nonverbal) interactions to interactions involving both a partner and object manipulation. As children's first words emerge, interactions appear to integrate the physical and social dimensions of behavior.

Feyereisen and deLannoy (1991) theorized that caregivers' consistent responses to infants' gestures attach meaning to their gestures. Through these interactions, infants develop ways to communicate and anticipate responses from caregivers (Fogel & Thelen, 1987). Over the first years, language becomes separated from preverbal communication; the early coordination of gesture and speech becomes differentiated in function. As Feyereisen and deLannoy (1991) have noted, "As a general rule, infants have to use what they know to learn more. Gestures, in particular, enable them to elicit verbal utterances from adults and, thus, to obtain the material that is necessary for the acquisition of a native language and to associate word meaning with environmental features" (p. 125).

Gestural Use From 1 to 5 Years of Age. During the first 2 years, babies develop a range of gestures. Masur (1983), when studying gestures of 9- to 18-month-old infants, noted that pointing developed last, around 12 to 14 months. Instrumental gestures, like offering objects and reaching, were shown before pointing and showing (Zinobar & Martlew, 1985). Reaching and pointing appear to have two distinct functions: Reaching is viewed as a request for something while pointing is naming or identifying something. Caregivers respond verbally to pointing rather than to a reaching gesture (Lempert & Kinsbourne, 1985). At around 14 months, babies use pointing with vocalization and gaze to clearly identify a referent; about 70% of their deictic expressions include both gestures and vocalization (Feyereisen & deLannoy, 1991). At 15 months, babies are able to use gaze and hand movement to indicate two different directions, one referring to the social partner and the other referring to the referent (Lempers, 1979; Lock, Service, Brito, & Chandler, 1989). This ability to refer to two objects simultaneously is a considerable accomplishment for toddlers.

During the second year, toddlers substitute hand movements for objects, actions, or agents; the use of single words is usually accompanied by a gesture.

Early utterances depend heavily on the immediate context for interpretation. Interactional routines, like saying hello or goodbye, are well developed and frequently employ gestures, like waving goodbye. Some gestures, such as pretending to stir in an empty bowl, are referred to as manual names and designate known actions and objects (Bates, Bretherton, Shore, & McNew, 1983).

Some researchers have suggested that gestures are related to the acquisition of first words. (This issue is somewhat related to our earlier discussion about whether gestures and language share the same conceptual basis.) In infants observed at 9 and 13 months, Bates et al. (1979) found that different gestures had distinct meanings. Gestures associated with gaze in a social context had communicative value while noncommunicative gestures referred to themselves. Both types of gestures correlated with the number of words toddlers understood or produced, and this correlation increased over time. At around 12 months, children used either a word or gesture to identify a particular referent (Bates, Thal, Whitesell, Fenson, & Oakes, 1989). Adult speech also helped infants when they were imitating modeled gestures, but gestures were also connected to the infants' expressive vocabulary. The researchers concluded that both comprehension mediation (the adult speech) and parallelism (the modeled gesture) aided infants in reproducing gestures (Bates et al., 1989).

In a similar vein, Acredolo and Goodwyn (1988) suggested that symbolic gestures (representing objects or needs) developed in conjunction with early words. Their experiments found that girls relied on gestures more than did boys and that gestures reflected the functions that objects performed. The researchers concluded that patterned parent–child interaction provided an important learning context for the development of gestures.

In a longitudinal study, Blake and Dolgoy (1993) observed four infants biweekly from 9 to 14 months, around the period when first words emerge. Their study is noteworthy for the range of gestures analyzed; their analysis included comments (like pointing), object exchanges, requests (e.g., arms raised upward), protests (e.g., body stiffening), and emotive gestures (e.g., vigorous arm flapping). They found that comment gestures increased after 11 months and request gestures (addressed to adults) increased after 13 months. Reach requests and emotive gestures decreased after 11 months. Their results paralleled those of a study by Blake, McConnell, Horton, and Benson (1992), with English Canadian infants: Both groups showed an increase in give–request gestures after 12 months and a significant decrease in emotive gestures. These results are compatible with other findings suggesting that infants begin to dampen their expressions of negative affect around this time.

From 10 to 16 months, children imitated toy manipulation more than they did meaningful gestures, and meaningful gestures more than nonmeaningful gestures. At 13 months, toddlers found gestures easier to imitate than vocalizations, but by 20 months, vocalizations were imitated more successfully. At 20 months, utterance length correlated with the ability to sequence gestures, but this was no longer the case at 28 months. These findings suggest that distinct competencies, rather than a single symbolic capacity, underlie gestural and vocal communication (Feyereisen & deLannoy, 1991).

Research appears to support the presence of different developmental trajectories for language and gestures in children older than 24 months. Subsequent language development is not correlated with either an increase or decrease in gestures. Children between 2 and 4 years used fewer gestures and more verbal commands to request an object from a doll (Read & Cherry, 1978). Beyond age 4, gestures appear to increase (Van Heugten & Van Meel, 1980), but gestural frequency seems to decrease around 3 to 4 years and between 8 and 9 years of age (Evans & Rubin, 1979).

Gradually, batonic gestures (which appear at age 4) increase, and representational gestures decrease (McNeill, 1985). Children use more expansive gestures and sometimes mime actions, and they may also use gestures such as counting by hand to solve problems successfully (Saxe & Kaplan, 1981). More movements occurred at the end rather than at the beginning of utterances among 4- and 5-year-old children (DeLong, 1974). With increasing age, preschoolers moved from using parts of the body to gesture (e.g., using a finger as a toothbrush or comb) to being able to use imaginary object gestures (e.g., pretending to hold an imaginary toothbrush; Boyatzis & Watson, 1993). When asked to imitate a gesture that was being demonstrated, 3-year-olds had difficulty imitating imaginary object gestures as well as body part gestures. Boyatzis and Watson suggested that gestural communication may develop from using concrete body parts to using imaginary object representations for gesturing during the preschool years.

Studies of preschoolers' gestures found that they can decode gestures more skillfully than they can encode them; older preschoolers are better at decoding and encoding gestures than younger preschoolers (Kumin & Lazar, 1974; Michael & Willis, 1968). In a referential communication task, children improved their decoding skills and were able to change their own gestures to communicate more clearly (Boyatzis & Watson, 1993). By 4, some of children's gestural meanings are understood, especially when these gestures conform to their childhood culture, like waving hello (Boyatzis & Satyaprasad, 1994).

Gestures remain coordinated with speech pacing and speech content. DeLong (1981) found that preschoolers' body movements and hand gestures accompanied their pauses and hesitations. Other gestures have been found to precede speech, especially when the material to be described is difficult. Complex behavior such as explaining geometric figures was also accompanied by lengthy gestures (Van Heugten & VanMeel, 1980).

With increasing age, the use of gestures increases. As Kendon (1987) noted, the early pantomines and substitution of gestures for speech give way to gestures coordinated with speech. Gradually, gestures, vocal tones, and speech are increasingly coordinated to accurately signal the meanings of utterances, and gestures grow more finely differentiated to describe, amplify, or substitute for other objects.

Some gestures also involve touching. A gesture to attract attention might involve touching someone's arm or hand. The somesthetic system (skin and sensory system) is the earliest and largest sensory system to develop. Tactile stimulation is important during normal development in many species; in humans, touch serves to soothe (Barrera & Maurer, 1981; Korner & Thoman, 1972) and to gain attention during interaction (Carter, Mayes, & Pajer, 1990; Roggman & Woodson, 1989). It is to this area we now turn.

Touching Behavior. Touch is an important part of early mother–infant interaction. In fact, maternal touch appears to occur during 33% to 61% of brief interactions with infants (T. Field, 1981, 1984). Another study by Hill and Smith (1984) indicated that the more contact between infant and mother, the more synchronization and coordination of mother–infant behaviors. Thus, touch seems to play an important role in early synchrony between mother and infant. As previously mentioned, synchrony fosters effective communication and is central in the development of secure attachment between mother and infant. Maternal touch also helps focus the infant's attention (Schur & Shatz, 1984).

The interaction abilities of young infants are frequently tested using the Still-Face procedure, which consists of three brief periods of interaction: First, the mother acts normally and uses her typical facial expression, voice, and touch; second, the mother assumes a neutral, nonresponsive, "still" face without vocal or tactile stimulation; finally, the mother resumes normal interaction. Typically, infants decrease gazing and smiling at mothers during the Still-Face period. Stack and Muir (1990) found that mothers touch their infants (from 3 to 9 months) over 65% of the time during normal interaction. A follow-up study by Stack and Muir (1992) found that an adult's touch (whether a stranger's or the mother's touch) drew an infant's gaze and fostered positive affect, even under the Still-Face condition. A second experiment found that active touching initiated by adults elicited infants' positive affect; a third experiment found that active touching alone elicited positive affect. A study by Fogel, Dedo, and McEwen (1992) found that babies who reached less looked at their mothers more. When babies try to reach objects, they gaze at them, and gaze directed toward the mother decreases.

Reaching and Touching Objects. Touching behaviors are a specific hand gesture, frequently accompanied by leaning and shifts in body posture. Toy manipulation, for example, requires infants to have the toy. Young infants show sensitivity to different distances: J. Field (1976) found that infants' reaching behavior lessened as their distance from the object became greater. Gordon and Yonas (1976) also found that 5-month-old infants attempted to reach closer objects and leaned toward more distant objects. Another study found that 5-month-old infants behaved differently when an object was within or outside their reach: Nonleaning infants decreased their reaching behaviors when the within-reach boundary was crossed, and leaning infants leaned forward. Thus, 5-month-old infants appeared to be aware of an object's absolute distance as well as the effect of leaning on their ability to make contact with a distant object (Yonas & Hartman, 1993). Older infants seem to develop their sense of reaching and recognize that leaning extends their reach. At 8 months, infants realize that leaning extends their reaching space; by 10 months, they appreciate the limits of leaning and by 12 months, begin to perceive how mechanical aids can extend their effective reaching distance (McKenzie, Skouteris, Day, Hartman, & Yonas, 1993).

Other studies have related reaching behavior to factors such as body position or early walking. For example, Biringen, Emde, Campos, & Appelbaum (1995) found that infants who were early walkers displayed more reaching. In addition, Fogel (1992a, 1992b) argued that infants' movement skills, as in reaching, vary as a function of body position (e.g., reclining, sitting).

A rare naturalistic study of family interaction showed that as children's ages and as the number of children in the family increased, parent–child distance increased and touching decreased (Sigelman & Adams, 1990). Infants and toddlers were touched more than older children. Whether they were alone or accompanied by their spouses, parents interacted with their children in similar ways. Other studies have found that same-sex parent–child dyads maintain closer distances and touch more than do opposite-sex parent–child pairs (Belsky, 1979).

In summary, gestures appear to be coordinated with prespeech behavior and to occur in runs. Infants use gestures to indicate their affective state, to make requests, to gain attention, or to refer to or play with objects; they also use gestures to show objects and then point to them. By 1 year, gestures are related to the number of first words; by 4, children have a wide range of gestures available. During the preschool years, children are able to decode gestures better than they can produce them. Touching is used to soothe and to gain attention; it appears to play an important role in early comforting. Touching is also instrumental in facilitating interactional synchrony between mother and infant.

As we have seen, nonverbal behaviors between adult caretakers and infants are closely coordinated. This coordination is frequently likened to a dance: Just as dancers adjust their steps to one another, infants and adult caretakers adjust their actions to one another. As we have previously noted, this synchrony fosters secure attachment between caretakers and infants, and enhances the infants' developing communication skills. Because this interpersonal synchrony plays such a significant role in the child's early development, we will explore this area in more detail.

Coordinated Attention and Activity

Infants and caretakers frequently appear to coordinate their behavior, and this coordination, which seems to have survival value for infants, is used to maintain attention. In early infancy, these coordinated or mutually negotiated episodes are accomplished nonverbally. Infants appear to participate in routines and gradually associate their actions with consequences. Their coordinated behaviors include eye gaze, vocalization, and body movement. Such coordination reflects infants' coordination of their own nonverbal behaviors as well as the ability to synchronize their behaviors with those of their interactional partners. Intentionality, an important aspect of this coordinated behavior, emerges around 9 months.

As they mature, infants develop increasing complexity in their understanding of the communication process itself and of the effects of particular communicative acts. This preverbal understanding occurs in two substages: preverbal routines and communicative intentionality. Many preverbal routines, as jointly negotiated activity between infants and mothers, combine vocalization, gestures, and alternating turns in interaction. Although early preverbal routines revolve around everyday activities such as bathing, feeding, and playing, later preverbal routines build on infants' acts such as initiating play sequences or requesting objects. (These preverbal routines are also discussed in chapter 4 as a part of the emerging communication skills of young children.) Here, we focus on its importance as an instance of coordinated attention and joint activity.

Preverbal Routines. Two scholars, Elizabeth Bates and Jerome Bruner, are most often associated with the study of preverbal routines and their importance as precursors to linguistic communication. Bates and Bruner suggested that preverbal routines, with their repetition, alternating roles, and closure, act in effect as "early" or prototypical conversations, albeit primarily nonverbal conversations.

Aspects of interactional synchrony, the coordinated movements of infant and caretaker, can be observed within 20 minutes of birth. Infants move in response to patterned, connected speech; they orient to human voices and search for the sources of vocalization. As noted earlier, infants prefer looking at faces or facial patterns rather than at other stimuli (Stern, 1977). By 2 weeks of age, infants respond differently to their mothers than to other adults. By 1 month, infants and caretakers exchange gaze and vocalizations (Bullowa, 1976) and infants begin to imitate vocal pitch and duration in their vocalizations.

A longitudinal study tracking infants from 12 to 24 months reported that infants actively structured their interactions by the end of the second year. Children's gazing followed an adult pattern by 18 months. There was considerable individual variation in the ways children structured their interactions (Kutter & Durkin, 1987). Thus, from early infancy, over a variety of communication channels, infants and caretakers attempt to coordinate their attention and joint activity.

Infant emotional self-regulation also develops in the context of jointly negotiated, mother–infant interactions. According to T. Field (1994), because infants spend most of the time with primary caregivers, typically mothers, this interactional context can be viewed as the "primary learning environment for the development of emotion regulation" (p. 209). It is also the major context in which communication between infant and adult develops. As mentioned previously, mothers interpret their infants' signals and try to provide them with optimal stimulation, which in turn enables infants to remain alert, attentive, and receptive to the mothers' signals. For example, Stern (1983) has found that 48% of mothers' behaviors mirror or echo infants' visual or vocal behavior. Maternal absence, prolonged in the case of maternal depression, affected infants' play behavior, affect, activity level, and a number of physiological responses (T. Field, 1994). Thus, early interaction between mothers and infants critically influences infants' emotional, social, and communicative development. *Attunement* is the term used to refer to the coordinated behaviors of mothers and infants; other terms include *synchrony, behavior meshing,* or *entrailment.*

By the age of 3 to 4 months, infants and caregivers participate in rituals and games. Such protoconversations consist of initiation, mutual orientation, greeting, alternating dialogue, and then disengagement (Bruner, 1975b). In a study of mother–infant play, mothers and infants matched switching pauses (when one speaker stops and another begins) at 4 months; the degree of matching by a single speaker reflected positive affective engagement between participants (Beebe, Alston, Jaffe, Feldstein, & Crown, 1988). Among adult speakers, attentive interactions are reflected in synchrony, when speakers begin to converge their style differences: A rapid speaker may slow down and a slow speaker speed up so that their styles converge to a rate comfortable for both speakers. By 5 months, infants can deliberately imitate others' movement and vocalization. With increasing maturity, infants exert more control and respond differently to varied partners. By 9 or 10 months, infants respond to requests, visually orient to their mothers when they mention the infants' names, and clearly signal their intentions to others (Sugarman, 1984). When playing with their mothers, infants' responsiveness is directly related to their mothers' affect and responsiveness (Brazelton, Koslowski, & Main, 1974; Stern, 1977). Mothers' responsiveness also elicited longer gazes from their infants (Fogel, 1982).

Preverbal routines provide a basis for later verbal interactions because both joint reference and joint action are provided in such interactions. Infants are able to focus their attention and to follow caregivers' gazes. The repetition, variety, and exchange of responses foreshadow the later structure of verbal conversations. Infants also understand they can initiate as well as respond in such exchanges, and their partners help complete these interactions. Gestures, vocalization, gaze, and body–head orientation all help infants communicate their intentions. It is important to note that these activities occur in well-defined contexts (Bruner, 1977; Ross & Lollis, 1987) and help to establish intentionality because both infant and caretaker treat each other's responses as meaningful and necessary to complete the interaction.

Communicative Intentionality.   As we have discussed earlier in this chapter, intentional behaviors appear to develop during Stage 5 of sensorimotor intelligence. Bates et al. (1979) viewed intentionality as behavior in which "the sender is aware a priori of the effect a signal will have on his listener, and he persists in that behavior until the effect is obtained or failure clearly indicated" (p. 36).

Intentional behavior involves infants visually checking adults for feedback; altering their signals upon changes in adult behavior; and making their signaling shorter and ritualized (i.e., conventionalized). As these signals become conventionalized, regular and predictable communication between adult and child can occur.

Dore (1983) extended Stern's analysis of the affective nature of the mother–child dyad. During the transitional period from babbling to words, when babies express a marked affect, mothers respond by *matching* it (i.e., "analoguing" the affect), by *complementing* it (i.e., responding with a different state), or by *imitating* it. Thus Dore linked the affective relationship between mothers and infants to infants' intentional signaling of emotional states. These emotional states are signaled by conventional means (i.e., by socially recognized means of expressing emotion).

Those cases in which the mother's responses contravene the infant's affect state rather than model it are critical for their relationship. As Dore (1983) pointed out, if the infant's affect is breached rather than attuned to, the conflict threatens their communion, and anxiety arises. Being able to express their affective state intentionally allows infants to match positive affect, to deny negative matches, and to test the state of their relationship with their mothers (p. 169).

Dore's work placed the development of communicative intentionality and conventional communicative signals in the context of the mother–child affective relationship and, more important, began to explain how the dual nature of human communication, in which utterances express both propositional and relational content, is established. Finally, and in our view accurately, Dore emphasized the importance of the relational element in human communication. As both Dore and Trevarthen pointed out, communication is, at heart, the way people establish relationships with others. Trevarthen's (1992) work and that of Shotter (1984, 1993) demonstrated that the human need to establish relationships with others is a fundamental motivation for acquiring communicative skills. Dore's research recognized that testing and expressing relational states are fundamental aspects of the communicative process.

Researchers in communicative development have focused on intentionality as expressed in infants' communicative behavior. Dore's work (1983) emphasized mothers' use of accountability procedures in helping children achieve a desired goal. Bruner (1977), however, focused on the routinized nature of formats in helping children accomplish an expected or desired goal. Ryan (1974) identified cues adults use to interpret children's communicative behavior. Finally, Bates's discussion of intentionality dealt with its cognitive bases and with children's ability to alter their communicative behavior in response to adult feedback.

These varying approaches reflect two important points about intentional communicative behavior. First, communicative intentionality is accomplished in an interpersonal context (Carpenter, Mastergeorge, & Coggins, 1983). Whether through formats, accountability procedures, interpreting cues, or giving feedback, others' responses to infants' messages are critical. These responses by adult caretakers appear to help infants recognize the conventions by which they can signal their steps in accomplishing a specific goal. According to Bruner, such reciprocal fine-tuning requires an interplay between contextual and linguistic factors, an interplay that also reflects the social cognitive knowledge of self, others, and relations with others, discussed in chapter 1.

Second, intentionality is related to the concept of control over message-sending or encoding abilities. In early infancy, control over communication may consist only in infants' recognition of the value of communication in establishing relationships with others (i.e., Trevarthen's concept of intersubjectivity). As infants mature, they participate in routines and develop an appreciation of what is necessary to complete these routines. Particular routines take on specific meanings, and infants become "accountable" for completing these routines. Finally, infants alter their messages as a result of feedback from adults (i.e., Bates's idea of intentionality). Over time, children become increasingly adept at altering messages in response to feedback and at encoding messages in light of their anticipated consequences. The earliest developments of intentionality, then, are experienced in interpersonal contexts and reflect increasing control over communication, both in terms of understanding and performing communicative acts. Although researchers have taken varying approaches to try to account for intentionality, all approaches view intentionality in terms of altering behavior. This emphasis on the infant's ability to alter his or her communicative behavior also highlights the interactive nature of communicative intentionality.

Our final consideration will focus on the degree of communicative control expressed by the infant during the nonverbal (preverbal) period. Considerable attention has been given to the control infants exert over their coordinated activity with caretakers. In the past, scholars have suggested that caretakers are primarily in control of infant–caretaker interaction, but recently, scholars have demonstrated the degree to which infants themselves orchestrate their own involvement and attempt to maintain optimal levels of stimulation.

Sharing Communicative Control. Infants' abilities to initiate interaction develop during many interactional opportunities with their parents and other caretakers. Infants have internally and externally directed regulatory mechanisms. External mechanisms are behaviors, such as gaze and smiling, that elicit responses from adults. Internal mechanisms reflect infants' capabilities to soothe themselves, and are used to maintain attention and reduce tension. Both internal and external mechanisms are vital for social interaction and subsequent social development. Tronick and Gianino (1986) suggested that when mothers are unable to respond or miss infants' bids for interaction, infants become frustrated and try to initiate interaction. If parents and caretakers consistently do not respond, infants turn inward for comfort.

The still-face procedure, where a mother initiates interaction with the child and then displays a neutral face, is one way to assess infants' capabilities to restart interaction. Tronick, Als, and Brazelton (1977, 1980) found that infants tried to regain their mother's attention during the still-face situation. When mothers were asked to display a depressed look, although they could talk and touch their infants if they wished, their infants behaved more negatively, protested, and acted wary; they showed only brief positive behaviors (Cohn & Tronick, 1983).

Employing the still-face procedure, Mayes and Carter (1990) found that 3- to 4-month-old infants responded with neutral affect and looked away from their mothers. Girls displayed more intense negative responses, although other studies have not reported this reaction. Infants who gazed longer at their mothers, early in the still-face situation, showed lengthier early positive responses.

Another study, by Carter, Mayes, and Pajer (1990), looked at infants' affect and sex and their reactions to the still-face situation. Infants who displayed negative affect also responded with negative displays during the still-face situation. Maternal positivity during play was associated with longer gazes by infants. In addition, positive maternal behaviors were associated with decreased expressivity for girls, and with early positive bids, then negative bids, and negative affect for boys. Thus, infant girls and boys may experience maternal positivity in different ways.

Joint involvement is also found in other activities. By 1 year of age, babies follow their mothers' gaze; mothers lean forward to monitor their babies' focus of attention. During reading, 9-month-old babies follow their mothers' naming and pointing; at 20 to 24 months, babies follow their mothers' pointing and naming objects (Murphy, 1978).

Overall, then, preverbal infants, using a variety of nonverbal means, sustain very rich communication with their caretakers. Through interaction, infants exert increasing control over the environment and over others; they become increasingly skilled at expressing their intentions to others. As they begin verbal communication, infants build on an extensive repertoire of interactions with others, primarily their caretakers. These influences continue to shape children's communication and subsequent development.

SUMMARY

Nonverbal communication is a system of considerable complexity and sophistication. The rapid development of nonverbal channels of communication depends upon infants' visual and auditory systems and their increasing motor control. There appears to be considerable prewiring for human communication, including infants' orientations toward human voices and faces. Some researchers have also suggested that there are special centers in the brain for processing social cognitive information. During the first year, infants' perceptual skills become even more finely tuned with increasing recognition of familiar faces, the sounds of language, and the tones and gestures used to refine messages.

Our overview focused on four major nonverbal channels—facial expression, gaze, gesture, and touch—which are most closely tied to verbal communication. In addition, we devoted special attention to the interactional synchrony achieved in adult caretaker and infant interactions. Facial expressiveness conveys our affective states to others. People signal emotions and their intensity by means of facial expressions. Over time, infants can identify "blended" emotions like pouting. By age 3, toddlers have learned to dampen negative affect and to mask their emotional state, although they may not be adept at doing so. Children appear to mirror their parents' nonverbal styles of facial expressiveness.

Through eye gaze, infants establish their interest in what is going on. To act in concert with others, infants must learn to jointly focus their attention with others and to coordinate their actions. They must control their actions as well as coordinate them with another—quite an accomplishment! The timing and synchrony of eye gaze behavior are very precise, and their management reflects considerable skill at managing interaction. Infants can self-regulate their involvement by gazing or averting gaze. Gaze behavior can also vary as a function of gender and activity.

Gestures help to clarify infants' requests and to gain attention. The early pointing and reaching of infants are regarded as precursors to verbal requests and statements. Gestures substitute for vocalization in early infancy but later accompany vocalizations. During the preschool years, children coordinate their gestures with the content of what they are saying, for example, by raising a hand to emphasize a particular point. Although infants' gestures may not be easily understood in early childhood, they become increasingly precise and well understood. Touch, as a component of gestural communication, helps gain attention and is also important in comforting infants and children. Through experience, infants learn to coordinate their touching behavior with judgments of reach and distance to a desired object.

These nonverbal systems interact with each other during joint attention and activity between infants and caretakers. The importance of interactional synchrony between adult caretakers and infants cannot be emphasized strongly enough. Such synchrony lies at the heart of infants' secure attachment to adult caretakers; the attachment has long-lasting consequences for an infant's self-esteem, trust, ability to interact, and a host of related behavioral and emotional issues. Such exchanges also foreshadow the conversational exchanges people use as a basic system for verbal communication.[1]

As language begins, at around 2 years of age, infants are already fairly sophisticated communicators and bring well-established nonverbal communication patterns to bear when learning language. Interactions between young children and others provide the necessary input for language acquisition.

NOTE

1. Some final comments on methods of assessing nonverbal communication are in order. From the range of studies and behaviors measured here, it is easy to see that nonverbal channels are difficult to measure, and controversy surrounds various techniques, their accuracy, and their reliability.

One of the most heavily studied nonverbal dimensions, facial expressive behavior, has generated many measurement tools including ethologically based systems or descriptive systems like FACS or MAX. Ekman (1982) outlined some concerns about reliability, and others (Unzner & Schneider, 1990) expressed concern about normative data. Capella (1981) noted that baseline measures for nonverbal behaviors need to be developed. In determining interactional synchrony, for instance, there are so many varied discrete behaviors that some are undoubtedly random rather than synchronized. Unzner and Schneider (1990) found that using the FACS coding system established reliable measures of facial movements which were stable up to 18 months of age.

Yet others have noted that sensitive timing issues are involved, especially in measuring interactional synchrony. Because nonverbal behaviors are analogic, it is often difficult to ascertain a beginning or ending point, as in the case of paralinguistic behaviors or gestures. Through the use of videotaping, filming, and computer analysis, a much more fine-grained analysis is possible.

With reference to research on facial expressions of emotions, many have found that it is difficult to isolate specific emotional displays. Frequently, similar emotional expressions may co-occur or blend and form what Barrett (1993) called emotional "families." These emotional families, for example, fear, anger, and shame–embarrassment, share crucial features with one another and often appear in similar contexts. Controversy exists as to what degree specific emotions can be detected, when emotional states may blend, whether it makes theoretical or analytic sense to separate various emotional states, and other questions. Barrett suggested that it is appropriate to look for patterns of facial expressions and related judgments of emotion, but these patterns may not represent emotions, in contrast to the positions outlined by Izard, Ekman, and others. Camras, Sullivan, and Michel (1993) proposed, for example, that infants give general signals of distress rather than specific emotions, like anger or fear.

Burgoon and Baesler (1991) raised issues about whether micro or macro nonverbal measurements should be used. They suggested that in choosing measurement units, researchers should be concerned about reliability, concurrent and predictive validity, and isomorphism between the measurement and the phenomenological experience of interactants. In their opinion, a more molecular coding might be most useful for dynamic, "objective" behaviors and a more molar coding might be preferred for static behaviors and perceptual judgments.

All these methodological concerns, in addition to the obvious complexity of the preverbal developmental period, suggest that researchers should advance their claims modestly and test them rigorously. The present picture depicts infants as gaining increasing control over the available means of communication, including multiple nonverbal channels. See also Chandler and Chapman (1991) for a full discussion of general issues in measuring children's competence.

3

The Development of Language

Children's nonverbal communication skills, especially those developed through interactional synchrony with adult caretakers, foreshadow the conversational exchanges that typify interpersonal communication. Language builds upon these preverbal communicative skills and adds more precision and specificity to communication. It also enables children to talk about past events and future possibilities.

The interaction between infants, caretakers, and others is rich and expressive, and with the onset of language, becomes more precise and informative. A reaching or pointing gesture, for example, can be much more explicit when accompanied by the words "Want ball." In addition, events which have occurred as well as those about to occur can be discussed between interactants. Thus, language enables young children to explore their world in more depth.

Language, like nonverbal channels of communication, is believed to have an innate component, and we will thoroughly explore the biological and linguistic evidence that supports innate language-specific mechanisms. Yet scholars also acknowledge the importance of the social environment in stimulating language development. The scholarly debate about language acquisition focuses on the contributions of both innate and environmental factors and their interaction. In what follows, we examine the biological basis for language, some proposals about the universal structure of language, and, finally, environmental factors, such as the language directed toward the child, that influence the development of language. For purposes of analytic clarity, we discuss each component of language—phonology, semantics, and syntax—separately, but readers should keep in mind that youngsters learning language acquire these three components simultaneously.

Although we focus explicitly on language development in this chapter, it is difficult to separate communication from language because language is acquired in the context of communication. Our distinction is the traditional one of viewing language as the symbolic code that underlies communication and communication as the use of language to express thoughts and feelings to others and to achieve goals.

PREVERBAL TO VERBAL COMMUNICATION

The controversy over the relationship between preverbal communication and linguistic development has guided research in these areas and provides important background information about the connections between language and communication development. A key question arises when turning from preverbal (nonverbal) development to the emergence of language: What, if any, relationship exists between preverbal communication and the subsequent development of language? Some theorists have suggested that preverbal communication is a necessary prerequisite for language development, and others have proposed that the preverbal and linguistic stages are separate, with no continuity between them. Still others have maintained that some aspects of preverbal communication may be linked with subsequent language development while other aspects are unrelated. Investigating these alternative views and understanding the controversy among various scholarly positions provide important information for assessing the research.

Continuity and Discontinuity in Language Development

Bruner (1975b) has presented one of the strongest claims for continuity in language development. He discussed four major preverbal precursors to language: (1) mothers' interpretations of children's communicative intent; (2) the shift of prespeech topic–comment organization to linguistic predication; (3) joint reference as a precursor to deixis; and (4) children's strategies in accomplishing a task with another. Bruner argued that support for continuity rests on demonstrating that a specific precursor is "an instrumental prerequisite to a more involved utterance" and on recognizing the social, meaningful nature of speech (p. 260). It is this latter sense of continuity that Bruner is most concerned with: If children know communicative conventions acquired during the preverbal period, like reciprocity of roles, then they are better equipped to learn language. Bruner thought that *formats* (a routine that specifies actions) frame an interaction so that children discover communicative conventions and can use them to accomplish social goals. Formats limit the range of available interpretations and actions so that children can coordinate their actions with others to achieve a specific goal. For example, feeding requires coordinated actions between infants and adult caretakers; everyone knows how difficult it is to feed an uncooperative infant, and even with cooperation, such events are usually "grubby" events! Such reciprocal fine tuning, suggested Bruner, requires an interplay between pragmatic and linguistic factors. (This interplay reflects the knowledge of self, others, and relationships with others discussed in chapters 1 and 2 [Damon, 1977].)

While Bruner has emphasized instrumental connections between preverbal and verbal communication, others have stressed their shared cognitive bases. Bates (1979) emphasized cognitive prerequisites for language and claimed that homologous relationships exist between language and protodialogues (e.g., preverbal routines that reflect postural synchrony, patterns of turn taking) because of their shared cognitive base (pp. 15–36). A correlational study of 25 U.S. and Italian children by Bates, Benigni, Bretherton, Camaioni, and Volterra (1979) found that symbolic play, imitation, tool use, and combinatorial play appeared to have a homologous relationship with language. In addition, the same cognitive capacities that relate to language development were associated with some preverbal communicative behaviors that correlate with language (p. 316). Other studies have found correlations between aspects of cognitive development and various communicative skills (Harding & Golinkoff, 1979; Sugarman, 1973). Bates (1979) thus concluded that a neo-Piagetian approach, identifying specific language–cognition relationships, has been supported (p. 15).

More recently, Bates, Bretherton, and Snyder (1988) completed a series of studies that confirm more specific connections between cognitive and linguistic development. They noted that three underlying assumptions are widely held about language development: (1) that language is creative; (2) that there are predispositions or learning constraints that enable language to be acquired; and (3) that there are biological bases for language shared by all humans. Some of these biological predispositions were discussed in chapter 2. However, not everyone appears to learn language in the same manner. There do not appear to be any universal patterns of language acquisition; the ways children acquire first words and their strategies for interpreting sentences differ strongly (Bates et al., 1988).

Theories about linguistic universals have been reformulated in light of such evidence. Linguistic universals are now believed to be processing mechanisms that allow children to discover the specifics of their native language. Bates and MacWhinney (1982), for example, suggested that these universal processing mechanisms are strategies that govern frequency of linguistic structures, their perceivability, their memory load, and their semantic transparency (clarity) for language users. In contrast, Chomsky (1980, 1981) argued that these parameters set the range of structural possibilities for a specific language. These parameters are "implicational universals," such that one language feature indicates the presence of another linguistic feature (i.e., If 'x,' then 'y.'). From this perspective, language acquisition becomes a process of "setting successive parameters and living with their preordained consequences" (Chomsky, 1981, p. 6).

Even if universal general strategies exist for language learning, children's acquisition rates and strategies still vary substantially. According to Bates et al. (1988), at the earliest stages of language development, four processes—*rote reproduction, segmentation, analysis,* and *mechanisms for comprehension or production*—create individual variation in language acquisition. Individual differences occur because of the different strengths, different timing, or both, of two or more of these underlying language acquisition mechanisms. (As noted in chapter 1, comprehension refers to the knowledge of language that enables us to interpret utterances [decoding] while production refers to the ability to speak [encoding].)

These general processes cut across the traditional, vertical categories of language (i.e., phonology, morphology, and syntax). Rather than focus on vertical modules or components such as syntax or phonology, Bates et al. (1988) emphasized horizontal modules, like segmentation processes, that encompass all aspects of language. In other words, language has a *componential* structure, consisting of "identifiable and partially dissociable mechanisms for perceiving, learning, and using a natural language" (p. 10).

Yet other contemporary views have considered language a set of cognitive modules. Each module has processes and representational capacities that allow for developing a specific content domain, such as intonational patterns in language, recognition of facial features, or identification of spatial relations. Interactionism is the view that language depends on processes and representations from a variety of cognitive domains. As Bates, Bretherton, and Snyder (1988) noted, the debate between modularists and interactionists focuses on the nature of the components (i.e., are they vertical or horizontal?), their interactions, and the timing of such interactions. Scholars' views of these issues determine how they view language as being acquired: What learning strategies, for example, would children have available? Such issues also determine what, if any, continuity exists across preverbal communication and language. These issues, therefore, strike at the heart of the controversy over *how* language is acquired.

The series of studies conducted by Bates et al. (1988) indicated that language is acquired by "partially dissociable mechanisms" (p. 277). Analytic versus rote processing and comprehension versus production are two process mechanisms that differ across the content areas of language. Bates et al. (1988) found a noticeable increasing separation between comprehension and production among infants at 10 months. Some aspects of comprehension and production, such as the use of object names, appear to operate in synchrony, but in other aspects, language production appears rote or routinized rather than involving comprehension and analysis of words. There was strong evidence that lexical and grammatical development are closely intertwined in the early stages of language acquisition, an observation suggesting that vertical cognitive modules, like lexicon and grammar, are not separate cognitive modules, although they may appear relatively independent later in development. At 20 months, there is a strong link between nominal multiword speech and the ability to combine two gestures into a meaningful symbol. Bates et al. (1988) offered this observation as an example of a "local homology" that links language development with nonlinguistic areas of cognitive development.

In contrast to other views emphasizing either continuity or discontinuity, Sugarman (1983) considered communication, as it moves from preverbal to linguistic form, as both continuous and discontinuous. Communication is continuous, but the means of communication are discontinuous. Researchers must look for the points of continuity and discontinuity in communication and specify the units of analysis (i.e., dimensions) being assessed. Focusing on language as a purposive communicative system allows people to notice more continuity than if they focus on language as a formal, symbolic rule system.

Along similar lines, Snow and Gilbreath (1983) also pointed out that both cognitive factors and social interaction influence communicative development. They claimed that "any hypothesis about the social environment implies a hypothesis about the cognitive mechanisms the child uses in language acquisition" (p. 18). For example, if certain types of social information are most beneficial, so too are the cognitive mechanisms needed to process that information. (Recall proposals discussed in chapter 2 that outline specific centers in the brain for processing social cognitive information.) Snow and Gilbreath argued for an interactional, integrated view of language acquisition which includes both continuity and discontinuity across different dimensions of language.

Different language acquisition processes exist in different cultures. Social variables relevant in some cultures are irrelevant in others (LeVine, 1977; Schieffelin & Ochs, 1983). In fact, communicative development is "highly buffered" (Snow & Gilbreath, 1983). Children have a variety of cognitive and interactive abilities available for developing communication skills, and if some abilities are not present, others may be used. This feature of communicative development—its emergence in a wide variety of diverse contexts and at differing cognitive levels—may account for both continuity and discontinuity in communicative development, as well as for individual developmental differences. Bates (1979) reached a somewhat similar conclusion when she argued that social interaction may affect language development by providing a minimal "threshold level" of interaction which can be achieved in several different ways.

This discussion of continuity and discontinuity leads to some tentative conclusions. First, some achievements viewed in the past as representing new developments (i.e., transitions) now appear to be the result of more gradual shifts in development (Haslett, 1987). Second, although a sharp distinction is generally drawn between cognitive and social interactive explanations of development, theorists are now beginning to acknowledge their interactive effects (Bates, 1979; Bruner, 1983; Golinkoff & Hirsch-Pasek, 1990; Golinkoff, Mervis, & Hirsch-Pasek, 1994; Nelson, 1973; Pinker, 1995). Both vertical cognitive modules and horizontal processes may be critical in language acquisition. Third, variables must be more carefully specified and linked to specific outcomes. In particular, multiple pathways apparently can achieve linguistic and communicative competence, and cultural and individual differences influence this process.

If language is innate, does this fact influence the continuity–discontinuity issue? An innate ability to acquire language would appear to support continuity between preverbal communication and language development. Would this continuity limit the possibility of important social interaction influences on language development? These questions are addressed in the next section.

The Innateness Hypothesis:
Are We Prewired for Language?

The innateness hypothesis implies that humans are predisposed to develop language and that environmental influences are of negligible significance for language development. Many theorists, however, have claimed that the innateness hypothesis is a separate issue from environmental influences (Bates, 1979; Bruner, 1977; Snow, 1978; Sugarman, 1983). As Sugarman stated, "That we are somehow constrained to develop the language that we do does not say how we do it" (p. 4). Chomsky (1965) did not rule out the possibility of considerable environmental "fine tuning" for communicative development. Bates et al. (1988) noted that universality or innateness has been reframed so that we are now focusing on universal *processes*, rather than universal *content,* as was emphasized previously (i.e., a speaker-hearer's ideal knowledge or linguistic competence). Trying to detail the innate basis for language acquisition and development, as well note the influence of environmental factors on language development, is a point of continuing controversy. Below, we sketch the major positions in this ongoing debate.

Nativism. The *nativist* position argues that language is innate. Chomsky (1965, 1981) argues that universal principles, referred to as a *universal grammar*, limit the form of any possible human language. These principles are innate, an aspect of children's genetic make-up, that allow them to develop language as rapidly as they do. These innate principles can be generalized as follows. First, children are able to distinguish language sounds from all other sounds; that is, they are able to identify sounds that belong to language as opposed to other sounds, like coughs or burps. Second, they have some conceptualization of the universal structural form of languages; that is, children recognize that all languages have a sound system (phonology), a meaning system (morphology or semantics) and a structural system (grammar or syntax). Third, the child has an innate appreciation of the nature of formal rules of language; for example, that linguistic rules may be obligatory or sequential. Fourth, the child has an appreciation of the rules that allow one to move from universal principles that apply to all languages to construct the particular rules that apply to a given language. That is, a child needs to be able to apply the principles of the universal grammar to the specific structures found in a particular language. For instance, every language has a way of expressing pluralization (referring to more than one object) but not every language does so in the same way. This principle allows for language diversity. Finally, children have a set of discovery procedures that allow them to develop the optimal grammar (the simplest, most efficient grammar) at any given point. As children grow and mature, so, too, does their language. There must be mechanisms to allow the grammar to change over time, as, for example, when acquiring new grammatical structures. Chomsky suggested that a universal grammar, an innate component for language, must exist because children's utterances are often entirely new combinations and therefore cannot be behaviorally programmed or reinforced. The speed with which children acquire language without any formal instruction also suggests that humans are prewired for language development.

For any given language, Chomsky maintained, there are two levels of representation, a surface structure and a deep structure. The surface structure is language as it is spoken and thus reflects performance. The deep structure, or meaning level, reflects children's competence or knowledge of language. Children's ideas are formed and represented in the deep structure, and then, using transformational rules, expressed in an utterance's surface structure.

Two levels of representation are thus needed to explain both linguistic ambiguity and linguistic interpretation. For example, the sentence "They are flying airplanes" has more than one meaning; explanatory principles must demonstrate how a sentence's surface structure can have two distinct meanings. On the other hand, sentences with two different surface structures ("John hit Mary," and "Mary was hit by John") have the same meaning. Transformational rules—the formal rules included in Chomsky's universal grammar—allow people to move from ideas to utterances and to derive interpretations (ideas) from utterances.

In more recent formulations of transformational grammars, scholars have de-emphasized the role of the deep structure or d-structure and have suggested that sentences are made up of different types of phrases. For example, the sentence 'The old lady sat in the park' has the phrase structure of NP (noun phrase) + VP (verb phrase). 'The old lady' is the NP, and 'sat in the park' is the VP. The VP can be subdivided into V (verb) + PP (prepositional phrase) as follows: 'sat' (V) + 'in the park' (PP).

When diagrammed, the structure looks like this:

$$S \rightarrow NP + VP$$
$$NP \rightarrow Article + Adjective + Noun$$
$$VP \rightarrow Verb + PP$$
$$PP \rightarrow Preposition + Article + Noun$$

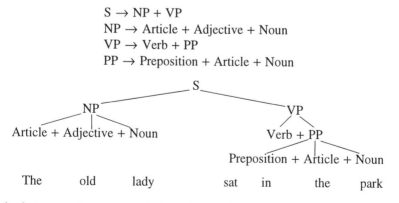

Such phrase structures appear to be universal in all human languages. The head word in a phrase (like 'lady' or 'park') in this example is what the phrase is about; in sentences, such phrases also relate to each other in particular ways. For example, phrases can be noun phrases, verb phrases, or even a sentence embedded in another sentence ('The cat the dog bit died').

Rules explain the consistent ways in which phrases function as well as their potential internal structure (e.g., if a phrase contains a modifier). These rules are called super-rules; information about how these super-rules operate differently in different languages is called a parameter. In Japanese, for example, verbs follow objects rather than preceding them as in English. Thus, the super-rule for the phrase would be the same, but in Japanese, one would specify the parameter (order of verb-object) as "head last" whereas the parameter in English would be "head first" (Pinker, 1995). As Pinker notes:

> [T]he super-rule is beginning to look less like an exact blue-print for a particular phrase and more like a general guideline or principle for what phrases must look like. The principle is usable only after you combine it with a language's particular setting for the order parameter. . . . Chomsky suggests that the unordered super-rules (principles) are universal and innate, and when children learn a particular language . . . all they have to learn is whether their particular language has the parameter value head-first, as in English, or head-last, as in Japanese. (pp. 111–112)

Children learn these parameter values through observation of the language spoken around them. Learning a few parameter values, rather than lists of rules, obviously makes language acquisition much more rapid.

Pinker (1995) argued that there is strong support for an innate basis for language, or a universal grammar, because of the basic design features found in all languages. Support for a universal grammar is also significantly strengthened by the correlations among characteristics of linguistic units that are similar for all languages. For example, subjects of sentences, in all languages, act as agents of verbs and agree with the verb in number and person. As Pinker stated, all languages seem to have the same underlying symbolic mechanism: "There seems to be a common plan of syntactic, morphological, and phonological rules and principles, with a small set of varying parameters, like a checklist of options" (p. 239).

In addition to the super-rules, there must be a lexicon, or set of words, with notations about how these words can be used in sentences. These notations or case markers allow speakers to combine words appropriately in a language. Pinker (1995) gave an example of how these markers might work with the verb 'put.' According to him, our mental dictionary may include something like this:

> 'put'
>   verb
>   means "to cause something to go some place"
>   putter = subject
>   thing put = object
>   place = prepositional object (p. 113)

These case markers allow noun phrases to be coordinated with related roles as defined in a verb's entry in our mental dictionary. Thus, the word 'put' can be appropriately used with subjects capable of performing actions, direct objects (things that can be moved), and nouns specifying location (areas where things can be placed).

These case markers also account for why some sentences are not produced, even though the super-rules would allow them to be produced. Speakers of English do not say, 'Ask if the barn is burning Jane' because the noun 'Jane' needs to be adjacent to the verb 'ask,' consistent with its case marking. Thus people would say, 'Ask Jane if the barn is burning.' Pinker (1995) concluded that "The phrase structure . . . defined by the super-rules, is the deep structure. Deep structure is the interface between the mental dictionary and phrase structure" (p. 121). Finally, transformational operations can move phrases around in sentences while still maintaining their specific roles in the sentence (e.g., as an object or subject).

Humans also rely on their commonsense knowledge of the world in using language. Mental concepts reflect real-world events, actions, and experiences. Particular categories of events, like actions, are represented by certain types of words, namely verbs; nouns typically reflect actors or objects. As discussed in chapter 1, people interpret sentences in light of the context, the interactants, potential actions, and the like. Tacit or commonsense knowledge helps people interpret sentences in terms of what they know about the world and the people in it. As Sperber and Wilson (1986) noted, we are driven to look for the relevance of what is said to what is going on around us; this process relies heavily on tacit knowledge and conversational practices.

Explanations of languages based on structural rules are referred to as transformational grammars, or more generally as the Standard Theory (ST). One variation of the ST is Chomsky's government and binding theory (1981). Binding theory places restrictions on co-references of sentence elements, such as pronouns that refer to a specific noun, and the traces that indicate movement, as in passive sentences. Binding theory accounts for hierarchical relationships within a sentence; for example, a "bound" element is one that is co-referenced with another element in a sentence. In the sentence "While *Barry* was singing, Chris hit *him*," the noun *Barry* is co-referenced with *him*. Golinkoff and Hirsch-Pasek (1995) pointed out, with regard to language acquisition, that it is still undetermined whether the parameters are found in the universal grammar (UG) or whether the UG interacts with other learning.

Such grammars emphasize the structure or syntax of a language and view the structure of a language as its key feature. Various transformational grammars can be written to account for the linguistic properties of a particular language, and there is a considerable debate about which transformational grammar might best account for linguistic data.

Alternative theories have suggested that the semantic foundation of a language is more important than its structure; some theories have even maintained that semantic features *determine* the structural features of a language. Studies of how people process sentences (i.e., studies of derivational complexity of sentences in the 1970's) showed that structurally complex sentences are generally more difficult and time consuming to interpret. However, in situations where semantic cues were available to aid interpretation, cued sentences were easier to process even though they were more structurally complex than other experimental sentences. In short, when interpreting sentences, people appear to be guided more by semantic features of sentences than by syntactic or structural features.

Several types of semantic-based language grammars have been proposed, an example of which is case grammar. In case grammars, fundamental relationships between parts of sentences are determined by their semantic relationships to one another. For example, a sentence like "John hit Jane" would be explained by the semantic or case relationships between elements of that sentence. "John" is the actor or agent, "hit" is the action, and "Jane" is the recipient of the action or its object. Thus, the sentence would be interpreted (and learned) as Agent + Action + Object. In this case, universals internalized by children would be universal semantic relations found in everyday life, such as *agents* performing *actions*.

Considerable research and theorizing have focused on the innate aspects of language acquisition. Structural models have proposed elements of a universal grammar, and other models have emphasized universal semantic features, such as the expression of action. Language thus appears to have some universal features on both the structural and semantic levels. Another basis for universality is the biological evidence, amassed since the 1960s, regarding humans' unique predisposition for language. It is to this issue we now turn.

Biological Foundations of Language. In the 1960s, Eric Lenneberg wrote a pioneering, two-volume work titled *The Biological Foundations of Language* (1967). In it, Lenneberg reported the results of his studies of patients with aphasia, individuals with a brain injury who had experienced some resulting language loss. Lenneberg discovered that those patients whose injuries occurred before puberty had a much better probability of regaining their language functions than did patients whose injuries occurred after puberty. He therefore hypothesized that there must be a critical period for language acquisition; when injuries occurred during this critical period, more language remediation was possible. Lenneberg also pointed out that the universal age of onset for language (defined as the production of two-word utterances) was 2 years of age. Mylenation, the coating of the neural pathways in the brain, is complete at approximately 2 years and allows for more rapid, error-free transmission of neural messages. Finally, he noted that specific brain areas, such as the left hemisphere and specifically Broca's area and Wernicke's area, are involved in language. All this led Lenneberg to conclude that language ability is innate, although environmental stimuli were necessary for its emergence.

Since Lenneberg's studies, the empirical evidence for an innate language predisposition has been significantly strengthened. Cognitive scientists and neurolinguists have advanced the knowledge of brain functions, especially those involving language. Language, in fact, is widely studied primarily because of its capacity to illustrate the workings of the human mind. The critical language learning period is now believed to be in early childhood, probably within the first 3 years of life; children exposed to language after this period apparently do not acquire a full range of normal language functions. The left perisylvian region of the brain, near Broca's area and Wernicke's area, appears to be a region for language functions. Positron emission tomography scans (PET), magnetic resonance imaging scans (MRI), and computed tomography scans (CAT) have greatly increased the ability to observe the electrochemical activity of the brain and the blood flow during language processing. Information culled from these procedures confirms that specialized areas in the brain are used in language processing. (A detailed report of these findings appears in a special issue of the journal *Discussions in Neuroscience*, titled "Evolution and Neurology of Language" [April, 1994].)

Neurolinguistic studies have thus helped pinpoint specific anatomical regions involved in language processing as well as the component functional processes that enable language behavior to occur (Caplan, 1991; Fox, Calkins, & Bell, 1994; Gajdusek, McKhann, & Bolis, 1994). Such studies have contributed significantly to the understanding of the different roles played by the left and right brain hemispheres in language processing and of the language deficits that occur as a result of brain injury.

Specialized brain centers for language processing speed up the interpretation and production of language. Pinker (1995) noted that Wernicke's area (important in hearing and interpreting language) is located near the intersection of three lobes of the brain which integrate sensory data and spatial relations. He argued that multiple learning modules, located throughout the brain and connected by complex neural circuitry, may be utilized in learning and processing language. Taken together, the neurological evidence suggests that many areas in the brain are responsible for language processing and production.

Considerable attention has been focused on whether innate language abilities were the result of natural selection or from other biological processes. Some researchers have suggested that innate language capacities are simply a byproduct of general, universal learning principles, but the bulk of evidence seems to support the notion of specific language mechanisms that are distinct from other innate abilities, such as perceptual or cognitive capabilities. Some aspects of language are indeed "prewired," and these language mechanisms appear to be unique to the human species. Although attempts to teach language to other primates, such as gorillas and chimpanzees, have had limited, mixed results, their level of language functioning seems to be around the level of an average 2-year-old child.

We began this section by asking two questions: (1) whether the progression from preverbal communication to language is best characterized by continuity or discontinuity and (2) whether language development is best described by innate predispositions or environmental influences. Pinker (1995) suggested that the entire nature–nurture, continuity–discontinuity issue is inappropriately framed. Rather, he has proposed the idea that the environment provides input to innate psychological mechanisms that in turn cause certain behaviors. Heredity contributes to the innate mechanisms as do the skills, knowledge, and values that are acquired. As he stated, "Learning is not an alternative to innateness; without an innate mechanism to do the learning, it could not happen at all" (p. 408). We agree: Evidence supports an innate language capability that is stimulated and enriched by the surrounding environment of social interaction and shared knowledge. Although the precise relationships between innate capacities and environmental influences may not be fully known, there are clearly powerful interactive effects.

In the remainder of this chapter, we discuss the general course of language development. Our treatment of language development is descriptive and outlines the normal achievements in phonology, semantics, and syntax occurring during the preschool years. Environmental influences, especially those dealing with sources of individual variation in achievement, such as socioeconomic status, are explored in subsequent chapters. (The role of environmental influences is significant for both language and communication development and thus receives separate attention in chapter 6.)

STAGES IN LANGUAGE DEVELOPMENT

In the following discussion, we use the term 'stage' to refer to qualitatively different and distinct developmental periods. Stages also index the sequencing of behaviors: Behaviors in the first stage precede those in the second stage. Relationships across stages, however, are specified for each area.

Most agree that language begins when children produce two-word utterances: The use of two words implies a syntax or underlying grammatical structure. For example, 'Daddy bye-bye' is interpreted as, 'Daddy is leaving or going away.' One-word utterances, like 'ball' or 'Mama,' do not imply a grammatical structure. Some authorities have suggested that single-word statements function like sentences because there is an implied action, such as 'Bring me the ball' or 'Come here, Mama.' But for our purposes, we use the more rigorous requirement and place the onset of language at the beginning of two-word utterances. Before the onset of language, however, significant prelinguistic developments like the acquisition of phonology, which begins early in the first year, enable language to emerge.

Prelinguistic Development

One of the unique aspects of innate language capacity is the ability to identify and recognize the sounds of language with speed and accuracy, despite differences in speech rate and despite the speaker's accent. No machines have been able to emulate this remarkable skill. Voice recognition devices such as a telephone directory that identifies a few basic sounds specifying the name of a city are programmed to identify a few possibilities, such as Detroit or Ann Arbor, or to recognize more sounds, but spoken by only one individual.

Babies orient uniquely to a human voice almost immediately after birth. Of course, babies have been listening to their mothers' voices in utero for many months. Four-month-old infants detected a signal modeled after adult–child language (ACL) rather than a pure tone or a signal modeled after adult–adult language (Colombo, Frick, Ryther, Coldren, & Mitchell, 1995). In addition, the quality of a human voice is distinct from that of any other sound produced; human voices have a fundamental frequency and at least 50 harmonics. People are uniquely responsive to human speech—apparently another aspect of our prewired language capacity.

Humans hear sounds in a range of approximately 20 to 20,000 cycles per second (cps); the shape of the human ear canal amplifies sounds between 3,000 to 4,000 cps. Because people are binaural, they can judge the speed of an approaching object and the direction it is coming from by the time delay of the sound entering one ear as compared to when it enters the other ear. For example, a sound coming from the right reaches the right ear slightly before it reaches the left ear.

Speech Perception.   Controversy exists over how infants perceive speech. Supporters of a universal theory have argued that infants' speech perception is excellent at birth, but proponents of attunement theory have suggested that infants' initial skills, although excellent, develop further. Disagreements center on the role of experience in speech perception, on accounting for the loss of some discrimination of speech sounds (i.e., some sounds perceived early on are not discriminated at a later time), and on detailing the relationship between physical maturation and speech perception. As Ingram (1991) noted, infants' perception of speech is more complex and sophisticated than was previously thought.

To perceive speech, infants must divide or segment the acoustic stream of speech (Gleitman & Wanner, 1988). Because acoustic information exists at multiple levels and in overlapping units, segmenting speech is fairly complex. Infants must also analyze the world into categories of events and experiences; these cognitive categories must be marked linguistically as well. Subsequently, infants need to correlate language with the meaningful events they observe. Most researchers have argued this mapping must be done on the lexical (word) and syntactic (structural) levels. Infants are thought to use acoustic cues to help identify lexical and syntactic units.

Different acoustic cues in speech enable infants to identify and interpret different linguistic units (Golinkoff & Hirsch-Pasek, 1990; Hirsch-Pasek & Golinkoff, 1993). Segmental features include limits on how phonemes and allophones (nonmeaningful variations of a phoneme, like /b/ in 'bit' and 'bat') are distributed. For instance, successive stop consonants like /kt/ cannot occur at the beginnings of words in English. Suprasegmental features include intonation, stress, pausing, and duration. Some of these features, such as higher patterns of intonation and more exaggerated stress in sentences, are marked in adult–child language (ACL). Infants also prefer to listen to ACL which stresses prosodic and intonational features (Fernald, 1984). Clauses are set off by vocal stress and by longer pauses and shifts in pitch at clause boundaries. Bertoncini, Bijeljac-Babic, Jusczyk, Kennedy, & Mehler (1988) found that newborns and 2-month-olds were able to detect phonetic differences between syllables. In fact, infants can identify their native language from other languages by using prosodic and intonational patterns (Mehler et al., 1988). As is readily apparent, evidence supporting the categorical nature of speech perception is plentiful (Fenson et al., 1994).

Infants can also ignore variations in acoustic signals. For example, Kuhl (1987) found that infants ignored speech variations that were produced by changes in intonation or a change in a speaker's voice. Infants can also readily identify a familiar syllable in multisyllabic contexts, but more successfully if the context is redundant (i.e., if the familiar syllable is surrounded by redundant syllables, such as /ko ba ko/) (Goodsitt, Morse, Ver Hoeve, & Cowan, 1984).

Finally, infants can readily detect subtle acoustic distinctions as well as larger units such as sentences. For instance, Hirsch-Pasek and Golinkoff (1993) found that infants as young as 4.5 months were sensitive to acoustic cues that mark clausal units. Infants also focused more attention on discriminating phonetic cues in their native language than on discriminating phonetic cues for other languages. Five and nine-month-old infants were not sensitive to segmental cues for word units, but 11-month-old infants were. These physical acoustic cues enable children to begin to relate words to meanings. Even even though infants can detect the relevant linguistic units, however, the features or bundle of features they use to identify these units remain unknown. Further studies by Golinkoff and Hirsch-Pasek (1995) using the Preferential Looking Paradigm, found that one-word speakers (toddlers ranging from 13 to 15 months) were sensitive to phrase structure, the sequencing of words, and their meanings. That is, very young children expect words to link together to convey meaning, and they recognize that word order is important in conveying this meaning.

Toddlers also use acoustic signals to convey their meanings. Galligan (1987) found that children in the one-word stage used rising tones to indicate interest and name objects. Youngsters 15 months old used intonation to mark meaningful grammatical distinctions as well. Similarly, Marslen-Wilson and Zwitserlood (1989) found that voice onset time was important in identifying words.

Speech Production. Humans possess vocal tracts that allow them to produce the sounds of any natural language as well as burps, grunts, and belches. (Natural languages are those langues used by social groups to communicate as opposed to invented languages, such as computer programming languages.) During speech, people alter their breathing rhythm and inhale and exhale approximately 15% and 85% of the time, respectively, rather than producing the normal, at-rest breathing pattern of 50% inhalation, 50% exhalation. Because we speak during exhalation, our voices project outward and can be heard by others.

Articulation refers to the production of specific sounds found in a natural language. The physical structures used to articulate include the teeth, tongue, lips, hard and soft palates, nasal passage, jaws, and velum, a flap of soft tissue portruding from the roof of the mouth near the throat opening. When people form nasal sounds (/m/, /ng/, or /n/), the velum remains stationary while air comes up the throat and is exhaled partially through the nose. This process creates the nasal resonance characteristic of the nasal sounds. For all other English sounds, the velum moves back against the wall of the throat and seals off the nasal passages; thus, other sounds have very little nasal resonance. Vowels are discriminated by the height and location of the tongue at its highest position in the mouth. For example, if the tongue assumes a high position in the front of the mouth, a small resonating cavity is formed, and the vowel /i/ as in 'sit' may be produced. The brain interprets these distinct acoustic qualities as different vowels and consonants.

Voicing is another important quality of speech production. Voiced sounds are produced by using vocal fold vibration. The larynx is a set of cartilages suspended in the throat; the opening across the larynx is referred to as the glottis. The glottis is covered by a set of muscular tissues called the vocal folds. Some human sounds produce no vocal fold vibration; others, such as vowels, are produced with vocal fold vibration. When people speak and produce voiced sounds, the vocal folds vibrate and the stream of air exhaled from the lungs is interrupted to form puffs of air. These puffs of air, called laryngeal tones, constitute the air used to speak. Each laryngeal tone consists of a fundamental frequency, set by the rate of vibration of the vocal folds, and at least 50 harmonics or overtones. This rate of vibration varies according to the tension in the vocal folds, the air pressure in the glottal opening, and the length and massiveness of the vocal fold. People perceive the vibrating frequency of the vocal folds as the pitch of someone's voice. Men generally have lower-pitched voices than do women because the larger size of their laryngeal systems produces slower vibrations, which are perceived as lower in pitch. When people speak, they constantly change the pitch of their voices. These intonation patterns are some of the earliest to be recognized by infants; they are one of the acoustic cues babies use to interpret different sounds.

Resonance refers to the quality of sound produced; for instance, a voice may be mellow, harsh, or raspy. Air passing through a chamber (like the throat, lungs, and mouth) is modified by the structure it passes through. Resonance is the process by which air is modified by an enclosure, with some elements of the sound wave being amplified and others canceled. The shape of the lungs, throat, nose, and mouth all determine what sound waves are amplified or canceled, and thus each sound produced has a distinctive acoustic pattern identified with it. In addition, because people share similar genetic pools with their families, they tend to sound more like their families than they do other people. In fact, it may be quite easy to mistake one sister's voice for another's or for their mother's; similar errors may occur with brothers and fathers (sometimes a source of great embarrassment). Voices sound different to the speakers themselves than they do to others because people "hear" the bone conduction produced when they speak and others hear the external air waves the speakers produce.

Each sound is the result of a unique combination of articulatory movements that shape the resonating properties of the mouth cavity. These coordinated movements are called co-articulation, which means that every sound produced is partially shaped by the sounds surrounding it because speech is a continuously changing stream of air. The /t/ sound in "bit" is somewhat different from the /t/ in "ten" because the /t/ is surrounded by different phonemes in each word. However, our brains still identify this sound as the phoneme /t/ in both words. These slight, nonmeaningful sound changes are a natural result of co-articulation. As people speak, they also prepare their articulators for what is about to be said—all of which occurs unconsciously and with rapid, precise timing so as to produce a smooth, continuous sound.

Each language determines the combinations of phonemes possible in that language. Phonemes cluster together; the term *onset* refers to a consonant group at the beginning of a syllable, and *rime* refers the vowel and consonants that may follow it. For example, consonant + vowel + consonant (CVC) clusters are common in English, such as in the word 'bat.' Similarly, as native speakers of English we know that consonant clusters like 'tvzh' are unlikely. Phonemes cluster into *syllables,* which cluster into *feet.* Pronunciation is governed by rules that recognize the features of phonemes, like voicing or stops or fricatives. These pronunciation rules apparently allow speakers the most efficient production of sounds—rapid articulation with minimal physiological effort.

Children learning language recognize and produce countless phonological distinctions as well as ignore minor sound variations, such as the variations of the phoneme /i/ in 'bit' and 'hit.' Underlying this seemingly effortless process of language recognition and production are complex, sophisticated neural networks and interpretive processes that are only partially understood. Most of what is known, however, suggests that considerable 'prewiring' underscores this language function as well.

The work of Roman Jakobson (1971, 1980; Jakobson & Halle, 1956) has focused on establishing a developmental sequence for acquiring phonemes. Three principles support his work. First, all children follow the same phonological principles in acquiring sounds; second, phonemes are learned in terms of contrasts; and third, these contrasts are built on universality, implication, and rarity. Contrasts that occur in almost all languages, like oral (primarily produced in the mouth or oral cavity) versus nasal consonants, are acquired first. The term *implication* refers to the idea that the presence of some consonants implies the presence of other consonants; however, the reverse is not true. For example, if a language has affricates, it has fricatives, but not all languages with fricatives have affricates. The term *rarity* refers to the idea that contrasts present in only a few languages are acquired later.

According to Reich (1986), the developmental sequence predicted by Jakobson is generally accurate, but some specific predictions are reversed. There is a relationship between the order of acquisition of phonemes and their occurrence in natural languages. Roug, Landberg, and Lundberg (1989) found five distinct stages in the development of early vocalizations: the glottal, velar/uvular, vocalic, reduplicated consonant babbling, and variegated consonant babbling stages. Each stage is defined by a production feature that infants master (i.e., vowels in the vocalic stage), a phonological feature (i.e., reduplication of consonants in the babbling stage), or both. Well-formed syllable production is established for hearing children within the first 10 months. Hearing sounds plays an instrumental role in phonological acquisition; infants who are deaf do not develop similarly, especially when their vocalizations are observed from the range of articulatory-acoustic patterns of speech sounds (Oller & Eilers, 1988).

In any given language, the specific order of acquisition of sounds is similar for everyone and mastery of sounds does not occur until 5 or 6 years of age. Mastery of sounds implies that children are able to produce a phoneme correctly **wherever** the phoneme occurs in a word. Children master phonemes first in initial positions of words, then in final position, and last in the middle of words. This order seems reasonable in light of the co-articulation feature, in which sounds influence the pronunciation of other surrounding sounds: A sound in an initial position would be least affected by co-articulation because only subsequent sounds influence its production; in middle positions, sounds before and after the target phoneme influence production.

Oller (1980) suggested that infants are active participants in acquiring the sounds of language. Some sounds are not produced until around 6 months, when the infant's articulatory system is more developed. Infants appear to vocalize with adults and to engage in cycles of vocal play. In addition, some linguistic experience seems necessary to produce sounds. For example, infants imitating sounds they hear try to approximate the sounds as closely as possible, and without feedback, accurate self-corrections may not be possible. Yet newborns appear to have good discrimination of phonemes and to recognize intonation and stress patterns (Morse, 1979).

As noted earlier, infants appear to go through several distinct phases in their speech production (Owens, 1992). From 2 to 6 months, infants "goo" or are able to vocalize quasi-resonant nuclei. Fully resonant nuclei are vowel-like sounds similar to a broad *a* sound, like the "a" in "babe." These sounds require more controlled, mature movements of the tongue and lips; babbling and production of full resonant nuclei occur at approximately 4 to 6 months. Reduplicated babbling occurs from 6 to 10 months, with infants producing repetitive syllables and imitating the vocal qualities of their native language. Evidence is mixed as to whether babbling and subsequent speech are connected developmentally or are relatively discontinuous. Menyuk (1977) noted that the most frequently babbled consonants appear earliest in toddlers' subsequent speech sounds. The vocable stage, from 11 to 14 months, is characterized by variegated babbling in which different syllables are spoken successively and with intonational patterns that approximate adult speech. These vocables, sometimes called phonetically consistent forms, appear to signal an awareness of a sound–meaning link in speech.

On the basis of the work of Olmsted (1971), Sander (1972), and Ingram (1976), reported in Reich (1986), the order of acquisition of English consonants is as follows:

Phonemes	Age (in Years) of General Usage
p, m, n, h, w, b	1
t, k, g, d, ng	2
f, j	2½
s, r, l	3
c	3½
z, j, v	4
θ	4½
ð	5
ʒ	6

Children follow several practices in acquiring sound. Youngsters tend to avoid sounds that they cannot produce. However, children also understand words that are too complex for them to produce and may try to imitate these words as accurately as they can. Other strategies youngsters use to acquire and master sounds are syllable deletion (especially unstressed sounds), syllable reduplication, syllable addition, substitution of sounds, sound assimilation, and reversal of sounds (Reich, 1986). Many times children employ multiple strategies as they attempt to produce a word.

As we have seen, speech perception and production are complex tasks requiring both innate perceptual skills and environmental stimulation. Infants' well-developed perceptual systems enable them to recognize and produce sound distinctions. Interaction with members of the surrounding linguistic community seems to be critical for the acquisition and production of sounds; the necessary links between sound and meaning are built up as infants interact with others in their social environment. As we turn our attention to the child's first words, we focus on the semantic system as it is reflected in his or her growing vocabulary, syntax and knowledge of the world.

Semantic Development

Semantic development is intimately related to cognitive development. Meaning develops through people's experiences with the world, their innate predispositions, and the developmental opportunities made available to them. During prelinguistic development, infants build up meanings for events that they experience and from the feedback they receive from others. During play routines and other instances of shared, joint attention, meaningful linkages between actions, objects, and vocalizations are established.

Understanding language not only presupposes that infants can understand aspects of language, like intonation and timing that help identify words and clauses, but that they can also link the meanings of words in their native language with events in the environment (Veneziano, 1989; Veneziano, Sinclair, & Berthoud, 1990). Linguistic signs are arbitrary and conventionally agreed upon; for example, the long thin object containing lead that is used to write with is called a 'pencil.' We could just have as easily called it 'goo'—however, we all must agree to call it 'goo.'

The relationship between the sign and its signifier is also abstract. Some objects, such as pencils and rocks, are concrete, but other concepts, like freedom and love, are abstract. Piaget suggested that three schemas set up during sensorimotor intelligence—prevision (the ability to anticipate the next event during an ongoing activity), intentionality, and recognition of causal relationships—help children use symbolic systems. When adult caretakers react to infants' vocalizations, they convey to infants that their vocalizations have meaning, whether or not infants actually have an intention in mind. Infants are thus aware of the importance and meaning attached to their vocalizations.

The speech addressed to infants may also signal the communicative and social significance of language. Adult–child language (ACL or "motherese") has distinct characteristics differing from those of adult–adult language. Generally, ACL is characterized by higher pitch, more varied frequencies, slower rate of speech, more varied intonation, shorter utterances, repetition, simple sentence structure, talk focused on the present, and use of special terms, like *teddy*. ACL is oriented toward children's interests and levels of awareness and plays an important role in youngsters' linguistic and communicative development. (In chapter 6, we examine other environmental influences such as parenting style and the role of siblings in development.)

At around 9 months, infants begin to name familiar others, typically their parents. Shortly thereafter, infants use idiomorphs (Werner & Kaplan, 1963). Idiomorphs (vocables or phonetically consistent forms) are unique sounds that infants consistently attribute to an object or action. Although these idiomorphs are not words and are not recognizable as such, they act as words that are idiosyncratic to that infant. Some idiomorphs may be based on imitation, like "rrr" for a car or dog. Typically, caretakers can readily identify the meaning of the idiomorph, although others may not understand it. The phonetic consistency of the form and its meaning are the important features of idiomorphs. The range of meanings associated with an idiomorph can expand, a process referred to as chain association (Vygotsky, 1962). Idiomorphs also reflect children's creativity with language. Frequently, idiomorphs are combined and intermingled with children's first words (Reich, 1986).

Private Speech. As noted in chapter 1, Vygotsky's developmental theory proposed that social speech becomes internalized thought and aids in problem solving and reasoning. Between 2 and 4 years, private speech increases and then declines as it is converted into inner speech. Furrow (1984) suggested that private speech serves self-regulatory, descriptive, and expressive functions. In line with this reasoning, Berk found that first- and third-grade children had greater task attention and fewer extraneous motor behaviors when they used task-relevant private speech (Berk, 1986; Berk & Garvin, 1984). Frauenglass and Diaz (1985) noted that task failure was associated with increased production of self-regulatory speech, a fact suggesting that private speech may not facilitate problem solving. Frawley and Lantolf (1986), however, stressed that all forms of private speech are self-regulatory and speech's appearance with failure at a task does not invalidate its functioning. Although findings are mixed, there is some support for Vygotsky's view that private speech is a cognitively self-guiding function. These findings also suggest that the functions speech performs are in transition during this time.

A collection of essays on private speech edited by Diaz and Berk (1992) has focused on extending and testing Vygotsky's theoretical perspective. According to the editors, the two major strands of Vygotsky's work—the importance of private speech as an intermediary cognitive state between children's collaboration with others and their own mental activity and the self-regulatory nature of private speech—have received empirical support. In addition, Vygotsky's work also provides insight into children's own sociocultural history and their cognitive development so that linkages between the environment and children's growth and development can be examined more precisely (Behrend, Rosengren, & Perlmutter, 1989; Smolucha & Smolucha, 1992).

First Words. Typically, first words appear between 9 and 12 months and represent important people (Mama or Dada) or objects. Words for objects that move (like cars) or that can be manipulated (like juice) are more common than are action words (like bye-bye). Common functions associated with first words include naming, asserting, and requesting. Infants' labels also seem to reflect names for categories, like "doggie," rather than for a specific entity (Baldwin & Markman, 1989). Children appear to have preferences for the types of words they first acquire; children who acquire many common nouns are described as referential, and those who acquire other types of words are called expressive. In a landmark study by Nelson (1973), expressive children were found to have fewer general nominals (words including all members of a category, like 'dogs'), but more personal-social words than did referential children. In contrast, referential children had a faster rate of development and more extensive vocabularies, but by 2½ years these differences have disappeared. During the use of first words, children use words consistently, both in their phonetic form and with reference to their meaning. At this point, youngsters view words as part of the language system and recognize their communicative value.

A study by Snyder, Bates, and Bretherton (1981) replicated Nelson's (1973) finding of a style difference between referential and expressive children at the beginning of first-word acquisition. Interestingly, referential children also appeared to be more advanced in lexical development in both comprehension and production and were more likely to use words in multiple contexts. Although expressive youngsters had some formulaic expressions and a heterogeneous vocabulary, referential children focused on object naming and the use of nouns and adjectives. As we discuss in chapter 6, children's preferences for first words are partly due to their mothers' interactional styles.

Children use multiple strategies to acquire first words; one important principle is the principle of contrast. According to this position, children assume that a new term does not refer to an already named object in the environment (Markman & Wachtel, 1988). Another assumption is the expectation that a new term includes the entire object and not just a part of it; this is the principle of object scope (Taylor & Gelman, 1988). Another study by Taylor and Gelman (1989) found that 2-year-olds used both linguistic form class (e.g., whether a noun or an adjective) as well as lexical contrast to interpret new words. A third strategy, fast mapping, gains information about the meaning of a word by how it is used in a sentence and what words it is contrasted with; this strategy gives quick partial information about new words. Heibeck and Markman (1987) showed that 2-year-olds can quickly narrow down the meaning of words by using this strategy. In addition, children often incorporate new words into their lexicon by forming language hierarchies in which new words are subordinate to an already known category (Taylor & Gelman, 1989).

Other investigations have linked semantic and cognitive development during the one-word stage. Gopnick and Meltzoff (1986) formulated the specificity hypothesis, which suggests specific connections between particular linguistic terms and particular cognitive developments during the one-word stage. Their study demonstrated that children acquired disappearance words shortly after they solved a complex object–permanence task. Similarly, children acquired success–failure words after their solution of complex means–ends tasks. Gopnick (1984) also found children acquired the word 'gone' after they solved invisible displacement tasks, during the period they developed the 'object' concept. A further study by Gopnik and Meltzoff (1987) revealed strong relations between the highest-level categorization behavior (two-category grouping) and the naming explosion in children from approximately 15 to 21 months of age. These findings suggest that children appear to initially acquire words that relate to specific cognitive problems of interest to them.

Meanings for first words, although consistent, can overextend or underextend categorical usage. Underextension occurs when children's range of meaning for a word is much more restricted than is adults'. For example, a child's meaning for *ball* might be restricted to his or her favorite fuzzy ball, not to balls in general and not to tennis balls, baseballs, and basketballs. In contrast, overextension occurs when youngsters overapply a word, when for example, they call all older men 'grandpa.' Overextension appears to be more common in both speech production and comprehension, although the earliest uses of words appear to be underextensions.

There is some controversy about whether first words are primarily symbolic or are mere statements of children's intention. That is, do words reflect underlying concepts or do they serve as an alternative means to an end? Piaget suggested that first words are not symbolic but rather support the development of new action schemas to provide new means for attaining goals. This process occurs in Stages 5 and 6 of sensorimotor intelligence (from 12 to 18 months). Some language scholars have agreed and have maintained that these vocalizations serve as performatives that directly reflect children's intentions. Performatives are usually protodeclaratives (informative comments) or protoimperatives (commands), terms we introduced in our discussion of intentionality in the opening chapter. In order to understand more clearly what underlies the child's first words, we now examine in detail some of the alternative theoretical explanations for first words and their usage.

Alternative Explanations for Concepts and First Words

According to Owens (1992), semantics refers to the system of rules governing the content of words and word combinations. Words do not reflect reality but only people's concepts and beliefs about reality. Cognitive knowledge reflects the knowledge of reality—how people categorize their experiences and perceptions. People store information about experiences (episodic memory) and also about symbols, rules, and their interrelationships (semantic memory). Semantic and episodic memory share a common base of information and experience; as Owens noted, concept formation appears to be the most important cognitive process. When a concept is related to a word, then we have semantic knowledge and this forms the basis for linguistic meaning.

But what features or criteria form the bases for human semantic knowledge? Several alternative explanations have been suggested: the semantic feature hypothesis, the functional core hypothesis, and prototypic learning. Each perspective suggests that different characteristics of the referent are acquired by children, but no one knows what is in the mind of another; people can only infer meanings from the word and the surrounding context. (Although this overview highlights some major approaches to how children form categories and link words or utterances to categories, the process of conceptualization is much more complex. For excellent discussions of these issues, see Nelson, 1985, and Keil, 1989.)

A. The Semantic Feature Hypothesis. Eve Clark (1973a, 1973b) argued that children learn a set of universal features that define all referents, such as being human/nonhuman or inanimate/animate. Children acquire meanings through identifying the salient perceptual features of a referent. For example, a ball might be characterized by roundness, an ability to bounce and to be thrown. As the child grows, criteria may change and some features added or deleted. Categorization by these features proceeds from the most general features to more specific features (Ingram, 1991). For some terms, such as antonyms like 'more' vs. 'less,' one of the terms is considered the more basic, underlying semantic dimension. For example, with the antonyms 'tall' and 'short,' the underlying semantic dimension is the concept of 'tallness.' When asking for someone's height, one typically asks how tall they are; thus, tallness is the most basic underlying semantic dimension. The underlying dimension is considered *unmarked* and its meaning is acquired first (Clark, 1973a, 1973b). More salient categories like movement or taste are acquired first. For example, Backscheider, Shatz and Gelman (1993) found that 3- and 4-year-olds understood the idea of ontological kind; they realized that plants and animals could regrow, but that artifacts could not regrow. Some critics have suggested that the semantic feature hypothesis does not specify *which* features are most critical for defining a referent. They further argue that abstract referents or those involving relative judgments, like 'more,' are not readily explained by this hypothesis.

B. The Functional Core Hypothesis. In contrast, Kathryn Nelson (1974) suggested that the functional features of a referent, not its static properties, characterize a referent's meaning. Children begin by naming objects that involve action; Nelson suggests children define objects by their functional qualities and add relevant perceptual features later. Thus, the core of an object's meaning is its functional usage. The concept is acquired; functional features are then added, and finally, a referent's core features are differentiated from other relationships. For example, apples are something you eat, you can throw them, and they are usually red and round. At some point, the fact that you can throw an apple is discarded as an important functional quality. Although Nelson has accrued some empirical evidence, the functional core hypothesis has not been widely supported.

C. Prototypic Learning. Bowerman (1978) criticized both the semantic-feature hypothesis and the functional-core hypothesis as being too limited with respect to children's ability to detect consistencies across referents. She argued that children have a central exemplar or prototype that they associate with a word; usually this is the referent employed most frequently by adults and for which the specific word was first used. Prototypic learning allows for continual expansion and adjustment of concepts. For example, the word 'chair' may primarily refer to Dad's large sofa chair but gradually comes to include chairs for tables, as well as a stool used by a child. Gradually the stool becomes a 'stool,' separate from the category of 'chairs' because it does not share enough of the core identity of 'chairness.' All shaggy, four-legged animals might initially be called 'doggie,' but gradually dogs, cats, horses, and squirrels become distinct creatures, although all are 'animals.' According to Rosch (1975), this adjustment of concepts can account for word meanings for adults as well. The notion of prototypes has been based on Wittgenstein's (1958) ideas that lexical meanings are not invariant features but rather family resemblances or a cluster of features. Referents sharing the most defining features of a concept or object will become the prototype for that concept or object or its most characteristic exemplar.

According to the semantic feature hypothesis, children develop meanings by adding features; words tend to be overextended at first and then eventually become correctly applied. In contrast, the functional core hypothesis suggests that there is a conceptual level between the referent and the word. Both hypotheses are similar in that they consider meaning to be built up through invariant features (Ingram, 1991). Prototypic learning, by contrast, suggests that a central prototype defines the essential meaning for a word, and other referents are judged in reference to the prototype. There seems no clearcut way to decide which of these major alternative hypotheses is most useful; they both rely on poorly understood underlying cognitive mechanisms so that the balance between innate capabilities and experience is difficult to discern. But a primary underlying capacity does appear to be the ability to categorize experiences, to recognize similarities and differences, and to apply new knowledge to familiar situations and familiar rules to new situations.

   D. Lexical Principles Framework.   In a model discussing the general acquisition of word meaning (as opposed to just the acquisition of first words), Golinkoff, Mervis, and Hirsh-Pasek (1994) proposed a two-tier set of lexical principles to reduce the amount of information that language-learning children must consider in learning new object labels. The first tier, involving reference, extendability, and object scope, consists of word identification and extension. The second tier, involving categorical scope, novel names, and conventionality, allows children to rapidly acquire new words. Principles in the first tier provide the output that the second-tier principles work on. Of these principles, the principle of reference is the most fundamental. Extendability enables a word to be used for other exemplars; shape, sound, smell, taste, and other factors serve as a basis of extension. Object scope applies the word to the whole object rather than to just a part. At the second tier, categorical scope limits extendability and firms up categorical hierarchies. Novel names are applied to whole objects as soon as a novel term is heard. Conventionality restricts reference so that a label is conventionally (i.e., communicatively) effective.

Golinkoff et al. (1994) argued that the first tier is present at the beginning of the second year; the second tier appears by the middle of the second year. They suggested that these principles, tied together developmentally, allow more powerful learning. The issue remains as to whether these principles are domain specific to language, or may be principles of more general cognitive functioning.

Acquisition of Selected Semantic Features. A variety of studies have been produced to test these competing theories, so that it is possible to make a few generalizations about the acquisition of early word meaning. In what follows, we briefly characterize some general conclusions and discuss some words that are acquired late in the preschool years; children may take several years to fully master these terms.

As already noted, early words are typically nominals, especially those that refer to common objects in the environment, favorite objects, or people. Action words are common but less frequent. Nominals also appear to be acquired earliest at the intermediate level of generalization. For example, at the intermediate level, the word 'dog' can become more abstract and general and can be replaced by the word 'animal,' or it can become much more specific and be replaced by 'Norwegian Elkhound.' The intermediate level is probably the most generic and useful for categorization so it seems reasonable that this level should be the earliest acquired.

The wh-words used in questions are acquired in order of their apparent abstractness. *What, who,* and *where* are first acquired; these usually refer to concrete referents in daily interactions and thus are not as abstract as questions using *how, why,* or *when.* 'How' may be somewhat concrete in that it is possible to see how something is done, but 'why' and 'when' appear to be the most abstract. Other factors contributing to this order of **wh** acquisition are the syntactic functions of different **wh**-forms, verbs in **wh**-questions, and the use of **wh**-questions in discourse (Bloom, Merkin, & Wootten, 1982). Earlier studies of **wh**-word acquisition indicated that preschoolers lacked bidirectional reasoning and were thus limited to forward order (e.g., answering questions like "What happened *after* x" more correctly than questions like "What happened *before* x."), More recently, however, French (1989) reported that preschoolers showed a strong response for giving 'after' responses to questions about 'when' something occurred. His results further indicated that if an appropriate context was given, bidirectional responses were possible and relevant in the circumstances.

These findings suggest that cognitive complexity (or the degree of cognitive conceptualization) influences the acquisition of meaning, a hypothesis especially plausible for the acquisition of *relational* words (like 'big' or 'little'), *shifters* (like 'this' or 'that,' which judge a referent's distance from the speaker), and kinship terms (like 'uncle' or 'cousin'). Coley and Gelman (1989) found that the use of 'big' depended upon contextual factors as well as the interplay of cognitive and semantic factors. In their study, older children relied on height in making judgments of which was the bigger object; 3-year-olds depended upon height when judging people but not rectangles, and all subjects relied on area in making judgments of which object was bigger when objects were placed in horizontal positions.

According to Johnston (1979; Johnston & Slobin, 1979), if cognitive development is linked to semantic development, several conditions need to be met. First, cognitive capacity needs to precede linguistic ability. Second, performance on nonverbal measures of cognitive skill and performance on linguistic tasks should be correlated. Finally, concept attainment and its linguistic representations should be parallel. For example, children who use the expression 'in front of' appropriately should pass nonverbal tests for the concepts of proximity and object feature and show mastery of the concepts of proximity and object feature before they use the linguistic form 'in front of'; they should also demonstrate the acquisition of the various meanings of 'in front of' in the same order as the acquisition of the related nonverbal concepts. That is, the order of cognitive conceptual development should precede and subsequently be mirrored by the same order of the related linguistic forms. Johnston and Slobin (1979) found support for their predicted acquisition order, which is as follows: for the relational terms 'in,' 'on,' and 'under' were the earliest acquired; 'beside' and 'between' were next; and finally, 'front' and 'back' in their complete range of application with reference to speaker, referent object, and located object emerged last. A subsequent review by Johnston (1986) indicated that linguistic complexity, frequency of use, and semantic complexity may also influence the order in which relational terms are acquired. Along similar lines, E. Clark (1980) found that children use 'top' correctly first, then master 'bottom,' and finally use 'front' and 'back' as well. She argued that these meanings are acquired in an order determined by children's previous nonlinguistic strategies for using these terms appropriately.

Shifters are terms whose referents change depending upon who is speaking and where or when she or he is speaking. Words like kinship terms, pronouns, and 'this' or 'that' shift referents depending upon the speaker. First- and second-person pronouns are mastered around the age of 3½ years; third-person pronouns are not mastered until after the preschool years (Reich, 1986). Anaphoric references, in which a pronoun can be attached to more than one noun, as in the sentence 'John told Bill that he knew Batman,' are resolved more accurately over time as children can shift perspectives (Smyth, 1995). Distinctions between here and there and this and that are not mastered by the majority of children at the age of 7 (Wales, 1979). Thus shifters and relationals are apparently acquired over a long time, on a case-by-case basis. Tfouni and Klatzky (1983) reported that 'this' and 'here' are more difficult to comprehend than are 'that' and 'there' because they are marked terms. Understanding these terms requires children to locate objects with reference to themselves or with reference to the speaker's point of view.

Mental terms, such as 'think' or 'know,' begin to be used between 2 and 3 years of age. Wellman and Estes (1987) found that mental terms were first employed for conversational functions and that most were used for distinct, explicit mental references. Children could correctly distinguish between real and mental items. By 4 to 5 years of age, youngsters understood the use of mental terms like 'know' or 'think' to express certainty (Moore & Davidge, 1989). By 4, children differentiated 'know' from 'think' and 'guess' and viewed 'know' as a more certain judgment (Moore, Bryant, & Furrow, 1989).

Semantic development, especially the development of first words, is a complex task that depends upon cognitive maturity and complexity, the frequency of word usage, and developmental opportunities. A wide array of linguistic knowledge, ranging from referential terms to abstract, shifting references, is being developed. Children appear to use a varied range of linguistic and nonlinguistic strategies to acquire word meanings. Semantic properties also play a role in children's transition utterances. Two-word utterances frequently build upon semantic connections before more fully formed syntactic relationships develop.

Semantic-Syntactic Two-Word Utterances

During the transition to two-word utterances, children try a range of utterances. Some children add *dummy forms* (forms with variable phonology and no obvious referents) to words; a dummy form adds no new meaning or information, beyond making one word into a two-word utterance. *Empty forms* have a consistent phonological or spoken form but no obvious, consistent meaning. *Reduplications* are a duplication of one word, such as 'doggy doggy.' *Pseudophrases* refer to two-word utterances that children appear to have learned as a single meaningful unit. At times, two words appear together but can be interpreted as two distinct sentences rather than a single combined sentence. The interpretation is determined by whether there are pauses between words, whether they share an overall intonation pattern with falling intonation on the final word, and whether nonfinal words are shortened relative to final words (Reich, 1986, p. 71).

In the early 1970s, a series of longitudinal studies assessed the two-word utterances of children and attempted to explain their underlying development. The semantic relations and sample sentences are listed below (these examples are taken from studies by Bloom, 1970, 1973; R. Brown, 1973; Schlesinger, 1971, and Reich, 1986).

Semantic Relationship	Sample Sentence
Agent + action	Mommy eat.
Action + object	Drink milk.
Agent + object	Mommy shoe.
Entity + attribute	Big doggie.
Possessor + possession	Daddy car.
Recurrence	More juice.
Nonexistence	No milk.
Entity + locative	Doggie bed.
Action + locative	Throw me.

Two-word utterances involving verbs vary in word order, depending upon the semantic relationships of the words. Reflexive relational expansions, such as 'more milk,' develop early and are followed by action expansions, possessives, and locatives (Bloom, 1973). Expressions used mainly for reference include nomination (e.g., 'this hat'), recurrence ('more milk'), and nonexistence ('allgone juice') (Brown, 1973).

Some two-word utterances can be interpreted in more than one way. Stress on words usually indicates their meaning; typically, new information is stressed. The surrounding context is also useful in interpreting children's utterances. When half of the utterances contain two words, children begin to expand to three-word utterances, such as agent + action + object ('John hit ball') and then to four-word utterances, expanded along similar lines. We now turn our attention to syntactic development, the child's use of structural rules to produce his or her two-utterances.

SYNTACTIC DEVELOPMENT

In looking at the earliest stages of grammatical development, Bloom (1970) noted that telegraphic speech (two-word utterances built from content words) and pivot-open class grammars (an utterance composed of a function word, like 'no' or 'more,' + a content word) may reflect two different language acquisition strategies. An empirical study in 1975 (Bloom, Lightbown, & Hood, 1975) found that children followed one of two strategies for composing multiword sentences: A pronominal style, using nonspecific pronominal forms, such as 'I finish,' or a nominal style, consisting of nouns and other content words, like 'Daddy go.' However, these differences disappeared by the time MLU (*mean length of utterances*) was 2.5.

Further research explored differences in pronominal versus nominal approaches in acquiring syntax. Non-nominal approaches to grammar were associated with the use of dummy terms (Bloom, 1973). Braine (1976) also reported that pronominal-expressive children used more frozen forms (formulaic terms such as 'bye-bye'), pronouns and had more rules for using a single lexical item.

In another study of syntactic development, Bretherton, Bates, McNew, Shore, Williamson, and Beeghly-Smith (1981) noted that four different styles appeared among 20-month-old children: the nominal referential style, the grammatical morpheme style (the expressive-pronominal style), and two new styles—a dialogue style (reflecting both labeling and imitation rates as well as conversational interactions) and a semantic-cognitive style (reflecting decontextualized language). A follow-up series of studies by Bates, Bretherton, and Snyder (1988) indicated that children emphasize verbs, not nouns, during the transition from first words to grammar. In English, "verbiness" appears to be an important bridge to grammar because verbs carry inflectional morphology (such as the progressive, 'ing') that needs to be acquired and also convey semantic relationships among nouns (p. 111).

Bates et al. (1988) suggested, after Bloom, Lightbown and Hood (1975), that nominal children focus on word-order aspects of language and thus should excel at early stages of grammatical development. In contrast, pronominal children, focusing on meaning, should excel at morphology. Other mechanisms, however, could explain these style differences. Nominal children may have an information-sensitive mode of processing while expressive children may focus on frequency of occurrence. Alternatively, because expressive children appear to interact more with others, they may develop their interactional skills via imitation, whereas nominal children analyze language and its meaning. Although the explanation of why these two styles occur is unclear, many studies have replicated these distinct styles.

According to Bates et al. (1988), early lexical and grammatical development occur through the same learning mechanisms. During the transition stage from single to multiword utterances, they found that variation in lexical development strongly predicted variation in structural development at 28 months. As they noted: "Lexical style from first words to grammar runs from flexible use of nouns at 13 months, to expansion of the open class as a whole at 20 months, to mastery of closed-class morphology at 28 months" (p. 265). The development of grammatical morphemes thus appears to be continuous with lexical development at every age level. Nevertheless they concluded that individual differences in early language development result from the dissociation between at least two learning mechanisms: an analytic mechanism which serves to break down the incoming language stream into relevant components and a rote mechanism which serves to store and reproduce whole linguistic forms. In addition, such differences could result from differences in maturation, differences in termperament or memory, and differences in linguistic input or interaction style (p. 260). In support of this view, Ninio (1985, 1993) argued that children's first word meanings may reflect differences in interaction style and linguistic input. More complex, three-word constructions may be acquired in order of the complexity of their dependency structures; early sentences usually had dependency pairs adjacent to each other (Ninio, 1994).

Syntactic development emerges as the child's two-word semantic/syntactic utterances become longer and more complex. Roger Brown's (1973) pioneering, longitudinal study of Adam, Eve and Sara enabled an in-depth portrait of this period. We will present his basic findings of early grammatical development and supplement these with the findings of others.

Brown's Stages of Early Syntactic Development

Brown noted that syntactic development changed with increases in children's mean length of utterance (MLU). MLU is a measurement of the length of a child's average utterance; this reflects an average, not the upper or lower limits of the range of words in a child's utterance. Morphemes are used to calculate the MLU. For example, a plural word like 'doggies' is counted as two morphemes—one for the noun 'doggie' and one for the plural 's.' (Morphemes are the smallest meaningful units of sound, and prefixes, suffixes, plurals and the like count as morphemes.)

Brown proposed the following major developmental stages:

Stage	MLU	Approximate Age (Months)
I	1–2	12–26
II	2–2.5	27–30
III	2.5–3	31–34
IV	3–3.75	35–40
V	3.75–4.5	41–46
V+	4.5+	47+

Stage I reflects the stage of single-word utterances and the transitional semantic-syntactic two-word utterances previously discussed. Grammatical morphemes, marking some of the relations expressed by word order in Stage I, appear in Stage II. In Stage III, children use simple sentence forms as well as negatives, imperatives, and some questions. Stage IV is characterized by the beginning of embedded phrases and clauses within a sentence ('The girl who jumped is tired.'). In Stage V, compound and conjoined sentences are produced ('John ran and Mary skipped.').

Stage II. As noted, in Stage II, Stage I relations that were marked by word order, like possessor + possession, are now marked by the possessive ('s'). Fourteen morphemes appear during this stage, but some are not fully mastered (that is, used appropriately in all contexts) until Stage V. The morphemes are, in order of their acquisition:

Morphemes	Example
1. Present progressive—'ing'	Teddy crying.
2. 'In'	Doggie in bed.
3. 'On'	Bell on chair.
4. Plural—'s'	Cars going bye-bye.
5. Irregular past tense	'came,' 'sat'
6. Possessive—' 's'	Daddy's hat.
7. Uncontractible copula	Verb 'to be' as the main verb: 'She is.'
8. Articles	'a' and 'the'
9. Regular past tense—'ed'	John cried.
10. Regular third person—'s'	Mommy sings.
11. Irregular third person	'does,' 'has'
12. Uncontractible auxiliary	Who's leaving now? He is.
13. Contractible copula	Mommy's fat.
14. Contractible auxiliary	Daddy's sleeping.

Kuczaj (1978) argued that children are able to distinguish between verbs that define states of mind (verbs like 'need' and 'know') so that errors are not made in applying the present progressive (as in 'I needing'). Pluralization appears to go through four phases (Miller & Erwin-Tripp, 1964). The word 'more' initially marks the plural; then the plural 's' is used in a few instances; next, more forms are pluralized (sometimes inappropriately like 'foots' or 'hairs'); and finally, regular and irregular plurals are distinguished. Mastery of irregular past tense verbs begins in Stage II, but only for a few forms. Some irregular forms are not learned until the school years. The possessive is used earliest with singular animate nouns and subsequently mastered during Stage III (Owens, 1992).

The verb 'to be' may be used as a main or auxiliary verb. Children acquire the uncontractible copula earliest (i.e., verb forms that cannot be contracted such as in the utterance 'She is'). Full understanding of the contractible and uncontractible copula is complete by Stage V, but it requires considerable time for children to master all the variations of 'to be.' The auxiliary form appears to develop more slowly and is not mastered in all forms until after Stage V.

The articles, 'a' and 'the,' show considerable variation in their acquisition. In their earliest usage, it is difficult to know whether children are differentiating between a nonspecific reference ('a') or a specific reference ('the'). The indefinite article predominates in early usage for naming; then the definite article becomes commonly employed as articles are used for reference. By the age of 3, children distinguish between definite and indefinite reference, although the definite article is overused (Emslie & Stevenson, 1981).

Third person singular markers on verbs (as in the utterance 'Gwendola sings'), both in regular and irregular forms, appear during Stage II but are not mastered until Stage V. There is considerable inconsistency in the ways these forms are used (Tranthan & Pedersen, 1978).

Other morphemes emerging during this period include pronouns, auxiliary verbs, and noun and adjective suffixes, such as 'est' and 'er.' In a pointing task asking them to identify who owned some paintboxes, preschoolers had difficulty using plural possessive pronouns; second-person possessive pronouns were also difficult, and third-person possessive pronouns were the easiest (Wilkins & Rogers, 1987). In production tasks, the first person is understood earliest ('my'); in comprehension tasks, the second person is acquired earliest ('your'). As utterances become more complex, early morphological rules appear to be replaced by morphophonemic rules. Morphophonemic rules help children recognize that earlier forms have more alternative forms than previously recognized—for example, in phonemes changing when a noun is pluralized. Wells (1981) suggested that semantic and cognitive distinctions also affect the acquisition order of syntactic structures. In particular, children's development progresses from the concrete to the abstract.

Stages III to V.   These stages mark the emergence of simple sentence forms and their elaboration into different functions, such as asking questions or giving commands, and into increasing complexity, such as self-embedded clauses and conjoined sentences. Helping verbs, such as 'can' and 'will,' begin to appear in Stage III, and by Stage IV the auxiliary 'do' is used in negatives and questions (Owens, 1992). The regular past tense 'ed' is beginning to be overgeneralized to irregular forms, but mastery is achieved by Stage V. We will now look in more detail at certain sentence forms as they emerge during these stages.

A. Negation. As every parent knows, the earliest negative to appear is the word 'no,' followed by 'no' + utterance. During late Stage II and early Stage III, contractions like 'can't' and 'don't' are used; and 'won't' appears later in Stage III. In Stage V, negative forms like 'wasn't,' 'shouldn't,' and 'couldn't' emerge. Throughout this period, negation functions to express rejection, non-presence, or denial.

B. Questions. Questions require some complex processing when they involve auxiliary verb forms and restrictions about words used in the question. Questions can also be signaled by intonation alone. Reich (1986) classified questions into three types: yes–no questions, wh-questions, and quoted questions. Wh-questions involve what, why, when, whose, whom, who, and how questions. Quoted questions are forms such as 'Ask him *what needs to be done?*'

Children are asked questions quite frequently; estimates of the percentage of questions in the total amount of talk they receive range from 25% to 60% (Snow, 1978). The order of question acquisition is as follows: 'what,' 'where' and 'who' are acquired first, followed by 'why,' 'how' and 'when', and finally, 'which' and 'whose' emerged. Youngsters begin asking questions at around two, peak at five years of age, and then questions decline. Many early questions are referential, asking for names or locations of objects. Full mastery of questions frequently extends into the elementary school years.

C. Passive Sentences. Passive sentences are of particular interest because of their prominent role in transformational grammars. In **short passives**, only the action is stated, as in 'My hat was stolen,' whereas **full passives** specify both action and agent, as in 'My hat was stolen by Myrna.' Short passives usually use stative verbs (that describe states of objects or individuals, such as 'got lost'); full passives typically use action verbs (Reich, 1986). Stative passives appear first, followed by full passives. A **reversible passive** is one in which the roles of both participants can be reversed and still make sense, as in 'Mary was hit by John.' **Irreversible passives,** in contrast, make no sense if the participants' roles are interchanged, as in 'John was broken by the lamp.' Between 2 and 4 years of age, children produce mainly reversible passives. In Stage I, children do not appear to understand passives although they differentiate active from passive sentences and recognize their syntactic difference (deVilliers & deVilliers, 1979).

Children take both syntactic and semantic factors into account when comprehending passives; apparently most children first focus on the semantic differences (e.g., identifying irreversible passives). Animacy, as a characteristic of subjects, aids children in processing passive sentences (Lempert, 1989). DeVilliers and deVilliers (1979) found that children develop an understanding of word order in reversible active sentences late in Stage I. As Ingram (1991) pointed out, when children do not comprehend a sentence, they may use a "Child as Agent" as a strategy for understanding unknown forms, particularly for interpreting passives.

D. Complex Sentences. Complex sentences, which have more than one verb, such as sentences with embedded clauses or conjoined sentences, occur when an utterance's MLU is approximately 3.5–4. Various types of complex sentences can occur (Reich, 1986): object complement structures, as in 'I see you draw pictures'; conjunctions, as in 'You fell down and I helped you'; wh-clauses, as in 'Can I do it when we get home?' 'And' is one of the first conjunctions used, rapidly followed by 'because,' 'so,' and 'if.' Wh-clauses are difficult to understand as well as to produce, and experimental results show inconsistent performance by young children (Reich, 1986).

Children appear to use the **minimum distance principle** (MDP) in interpreting object complement sentences, which allows the noun phrase most closely preceding the complement verb to be taken as the subject when a verb in a complement clause lacks a subject. The sentence 'John is eager to please' is correctly interpreted using the **MDP**. However, consider the following example from a study by Carol Chomsky (1969). Children were shown a doll wearing a blindfold, and asked 'Will you make her easy to see?' Approximately 25 % of the subjects, aged five to ten years, removed the blindfold and said that doing so made her easier to see. These children were interpreting the sentence to mean that the doll was to do the seeing. Generally, by seven years of age, children can correctly respond when the **MDP** is violated. Other studies have replicated this finding. For instance, Cromer (1970) used the following sentence, 'Bozo promises Donald to hop up and down. Make him hop:' Young children made Donald hop while older children made Bozo hop. Although children appear to rely on the **MDP** for sentence interpretation, other factors, like whether or not an addressee is specified, come into play (Reich, 1986).

Although syntactic development grows rapidly in complexity during preschool years, syntactic constructions develop further during elementary school years. Sentences expand internally and have more elaborated noun and verb phrases. New constructions as well as new words are also learned during this time.

As in the case of explaining semantic acquisition, there are alternative theoretical accounts for how children acquire syntax as well. Before taking a closer look at some of these alternatives, we want to raise some general issues about the acquisition of syntax that reflect some of the critical underlying debates among researchers in language acquisition. Ingram (1991) noted, first, the disagreement about whether semantics or syntax drives language acquisition. Do children acquire semantic distinctions that build into grammatical distinctions, or do they focus on syntactic features predicted by the Universal Grammar and use them to build up meanings? The semantic and syntactic components clearly interact, but what is the nature of this interplay? Second, several different learning mechanisms have been proposed, from an innate universal grammar to distribution-learning models. Third, which theory best accounts for linguistic productivity—children's capacity to produce new, creative utterances? Finally, there is the continuity–discontinuity issue previously discussed. Do children develop increasingly adultlike grammars (the continuity model) or do they acquire language in stages which bear no close resemblance to adult grammars (the discontinuity hypothesis)? According to Ingram (1991), these core issues—and the theoretical positions taken on them—articulate the differences among alternative explanations for the acquisition of syntax. We turn now to a closer examination of some basic alternative theories about how children acquire syntax.

Alternative Models of Syntactic Acquisition

The four general models we will discuss are semantic based, functionalist, distributional learning, and parameter setting approaches, each of which represents a distinct set of assumptions and emphases (Ingram, 1991).

Semantic Approaches. These approaches argue for the centrality of *semantic primes* in constructing language. Primes are related to concepts acquired during the period of sensorimotor intelligence and include such basic concepts as agent (objects that can act on other objects with volition) or action. Grammatical categories are derived from these fundamental semantic relationships, such as actors performing actions. An example of this approach would be Fillmore's case grammar (1968) or Brown's analysis of children's early language.

Formal Grammars in Children's Early Language. The other approaches all propose a formal grammar in children's early language, but the amount of this grammar varies (Ingram, 1991). In *functionalism*, children are thought to begin with very limited meanings that gradually evolve into adultlike meanings; there is no assumption of an abstract grammar. According to *distributional theories*, these limited semantic meanings develop into more general grammatical categories. Still other theories assume that children have an initial set of assumptions or procedures for determining syntactic relationships.

In functionalist approaches, as their name implies, the limited meanings children begin with are functional categories, such as topic-comment and agent (Bates & MacWhinney, 1982). *Topic* refers to what is being talked about, and *comment* refers to the point being expressed about the topic. Initially, each function is reflected by a specific surface form. Ingram noted that, if the functional view were valid, there might be a universal set of functions for all children. The cross-linguistic differences in the early languages of children, however, tend to support a distributional theory.

In distributional theories, distributional learning occurs at the earliest times of language acquisition. That is, semantic or syntactic categories do not lead to distributional learning of language units; rather, distributional learning allows semantic and syntactic categories to form. Distributional learning models move from specific to general learning or patterns. MacWhinney (1987) proposed a model based on three general processing mechanisms: rote, analogy, and combination. Rote processing appears to account for early utterances that apparently are internalized imitations of parts of adult language. Analogy is the procedure of splitting up a rote form and replacing one of its parts with another lexical item. Combination incorporates procedures that allow children to order previously unordered strings of lexical items.

Maratsos and Chalkley (1980) presented a distributional learning model in which children first identify individual morphemes and then identify the basic semantic distributional forms (e.g., agent + action, action + object); finally these basic forms are continually reinforced by children's linguistic experience. These basic patterns become overgeneralized and subsequently corrected. Maratsos and Chalkley suggested that adult grammar may be a web of semantic distribution networks. Pinker (1995), however, suggested that people would have to learn a substantial number of patterns and therefore argued that this model is not very efficient. Distributional learning may also require enormous memory demands that are not cognitively available to young children. In addition, there is the difficulty of negative evidence: Children do not hear "errors" that would help them formulate patterns.

Parameter models incorporate abstract, formal grammatical categories in their acquisition models. As Ingram (1991) noted, "The acquisition problem for any theory of abstract syntax is how the child determines the language-specific features of the language being acquired" (p. 315). Ingram proposed semantic bootstrapping, a process by which grammatical categories are triggered by certain semantic properties. As an example, children form categories like subject noun phrases and verb phrases from the early meanings of their utterances. In parameter models, youngsters are assumed to have a universal base or phrase structure grammar that specifies what a possible language is like. The options or parameters of a language are interrelated, so that after learning one parameter, a set of related parameters is seen to be part of the language also. These interrelationships among parameters make learning a language much simpler because the number of patterns is limited rather than infinite.

SUMMARY

In this chapter we have presented an overview of the general course of phonological, semantic, and syntactic development, a picture based on data from studies of young children. We hope to have shown the rich theoretical alternatives available for explaining how language is acquired. Although the understanding of language acquisition has been enhanced by many studies, much remains to be learned. Interactions clearly exist among cognitive ability and complexity, semantic categories and meanings, and linguistic structure and language functions. Whether there is discontinuity, continuity, or both (depending on the area of acquisition being discussed) is unresolved, as is the primacy of semantics versus a universal syntactic base.

All explanatory models of language acquisition presuppose that linguistic input is necessary for language acquisition. Some models even suggest that certain forms of linguistic exposure in the environment influence children's acquisition of both language and communication skills. For example, great linguistic variety in children's language environments may facilitate their development of a more complex and rich grammar. There are many sources of linguistic input in a child's environment. We will discuss the nature and importance of this input—from parents, siblings, peers and a variety of adult caretakers—in chapter 6.

Considerable controversy surrounds children's linguistic data. Both Ingram's *First Language Acquisition* (1991) and Pinker's *The Language Instinct* (1995) are excellent discussions of the methodological issues involved in language acquisition research. Pinker also presents a wide-ranging overview of an innate basis for language which is impressive in its scope of coverage. (Some of these innateness issues were covered in chapter 2 and earlier in this chapter.) These authors have confirmed our belief that more integrative perspectives are needed to make researchers who specialize in particular approaches to language acquisition (such as psycholinguistic or sociolinguistic approaches) aware of findings in other areas relevant to their own specialized interests. Ingram noted the difficulty of reconciling differences in methodology as well as in basic data collection procedures, which range from diary studies to experimental stimuli. For example, how do researchers integrate acquisition data from different children speaking different languages at different ages?

We next turn to an analysis of communicative development, focusing on the use of language to communicate. It is the human need for communication which many believe is the fundamental motivation for language acquisition. Communication skills build upon, as well as further elaborate, nonverbal communication patterns and language skills we have overviewed thus far.

4

Developing Verbal
Communication

As children mature and interact in different situations, their purposes and goals for communication become more varied, and they acquire a wide range of communicative strategies for achieving their goals. Thus, communicative development reflects increasing complexity in both children's communicative goals and their communicative strategies. As we have repeatedly mentioned throughout the prior chapters, communication occurs in different contexts and these contexts help define the appropriateness and effectiveness of various communication strategies. Communicative effectiveness may rely on youngsters' levels of communication skills as well as on their ability to respond appropriately to various settings and to various demands, such as making a request as opposed to giving directions.

As with language development and nonverbal communication, there are many theoretical perspectives used to study communicative development, and no single approach appears to provide an adequate account of developmental processes (Dickson, 1981). Many scholars have recognized that these diverse perspectives must be integrated to accomplish more adequate theory building and research (Ochs & Schieffelin, 1979).

Two competing paradigms explaining communicative development are those using cognitive principles as key explanatory mechanisms and those using principles of social interaction (Garton, 1992). (A third paradigm, nativism, has been used to explain how language itself is acquired but does not concern itself with the appropriate and socially adapted use of language and thus is not relevant to this discussion. Nativism is discussed in chapters 2 and 3.)

The difference between the cognitive and social interaction approaches is one of degree and emphasis rather than of opposition. In both, language and communication are acquired in an interactive context (Dimitracopoulou, 1990; Garton, 1992). Cognitive theorists emphasize people's mental abilities and their role in communication, whereas the social interaction perspective emphasizes the dialogue and developmental opportunities afforded by interaction with others.

Although we do not advocate any particular approach, our sympathies lie with the social interaction perspective, which we believe offers a rich, inclusive perspective from which a unified theory of communicative development may emerge. This perspective focuses on the fundamental nature of human communication—its interpersonal nature. Recall from our discussion in chapter 1 that communication is shared social activity.

In this chapter we outline a model for communicative development based on Haslett's integrative research (1983b, 1987). This view does not imply that previous stages of development are causally related to subsequent stages; for each developmental stage, we discuss the varied communicative and cognitive skills children have acquired and broadly characterize the direction and complexity of communicative development. We will discuss communication skills in this chapter and focus on communication knowledge in chapter 5. Communicative development relies on skills in and knowledge of communication; people must know *how* to do something (like asking a question or interrupting) as well as *when* to do it. Children acquire both skills simultaneously although we discuss each component separately and then explore how the two interact.

Before we begin analyzing the course of development, we need to appreciate what interaction skills involve. Most generally, interaction involves the ability to engage in sustained discourse or conversation. Young children move beyond single words and single sentences to construct discourse aimed at expressing their feelings and achieving desired goals.

THE NATURE OF CONVERSATION

We begin our discussion of how conversations are managed by specifying the characteristics of conversations. We do this for two reasons. First, we view conversations as a primary instance of sustained discourse and the most common context for development, either through direct participation or overhearing (Forrester, 1993). We also believe that conversations are remarkably complex phenomena; understanding their complexity gives an appreciation of the constellation of rules, assumptions, and abilities children must learn in order to be full conversational participants.

Although we do not suggest a specific definition, nevertheless we point out several generally agreed upon features that characterize conversations. First, conversations occur between at least two individuals; although it is possible for three or four people to engage in a conversation, everyone may not focus on the common conversational topic. Goffman (1974, 1976) labeled such interactions as unfocused. Second, participants act so as to maintain a conversational topic. Third, there is role reciprocity because participants exchange speaking and listening roles. Fourth, conversational activity appears to be relatively unplanned; people may enter an extended dialogue with any number of overarching goals in mind but do not generally plan conversations in much detail. Fifth, conversations occur in a wide variety of social settings. Sixth, conversations appear to be relatively informal in the way they are conducted. And finally, conversational meanings are jointly constructed by the participants; listeners respond to a speaker's utterances and thus co-manage the conversation.

A Turn-Taking Model of Conversation

Sacks, Schegloff, and Jefferson (1974) outlined several characteristics of conversations and emphasized turn taking as its basic organizational structure. According to these theorists, conversations are shaped by the following characteristics:

1. Speakers change.
2. Only one speaker talks at a time.
3. Transitions between speakers are usually of short duration.
4. Turn taking is negotiated, not fixed.
5. Turn length varies.
6. The content of turns varies.
7. The length of conversations is flexible.
8. The number of participants in a conversation varies.
9. The number of talking turns a participant takes varies, but generally no single participant dominates talking time.
10. Conversational talk can be continuous or discontinuous.
11. Conversational repair strategies can be used.
12. Talking turns may be allocated.

The turn-taking system allows for the joint management of conversations; each participant's contribution can be coordinated with that of others. Turn taking serves as the basic exchange system that underlies conversations and explains how we develop and share joint attention during speaking. Conversational analysts study these exchange systems and have developed a number of paired exchange sequences, such as question/answer ("What is your name?"/"Wendy") or summons/response ("Hey, John!"/"What's happenin', Dude?").

Conversations can also be examined through the tacit assumptions participants have about them. These assumptions, referred to as conversational maxims (or conversational implicatures), enable participants to evaluate what is going on in the conversation. Although these maxims may not operate in every culture, they appear to be valid in the United States and the United Kingdom. The Cooperative Principle, with its maxims of Quality, Quantity, Manner, and Relevance can thus be viewed as principles that help define conversational activity (Grice, 1975, 1978). It should be noted, however, that conversational maxims provide guidelines for evaluating the on-going exchange. When these maxims are violated, Grice (1975) suggests that they are usually purposefully violated (e.g., to indicate sarcasm, irony, etc.).

Conversational Maxims

Grice's (1975) maxims are rational principles for conducting cooperative exchanges. Although Levinson (1983) suggested that such maxims may apply to any cooperative exchange, such as nonverbal exchanges, here we consider only their conversational implications. These conversational maxims are summarized in the Cooperative Principle. This principle and its underlying conversational maxims are outlined as follows:

Cooperative Principle: Make a conversational contribution as is required, when it is needed, in accordance with the accepted purpose of the conversation in which you are participating.

Maxim of Quality: Make your contribution truthful; do not state falsehoods or inadequately supported claims.

Maxim of Quantity: Give as much information, and only that information, as needed for the purposes of the exchange.

Maxim of Manner: Be perspicuous, avoid ambiguity and obscurity, and be orderly and brief.

Maxim of Relevance: Make relevant remarks.

Grice suggested that communicators assume other participants are either following the maxims or deliberately violating them. For example, intentionally lying or reaching an unwarranted conclusion violates the maxim of Quality. A speaker who gives more information than necessary violates the maxim of Quantity. Violating the maxim of Manner is exemplified by someone who is rude or abrasive. Nofsinger's analysis of indirect answers (1976) contains good examples of violations of the Manner maxim (e.g., "Is it hot out today!" "I always sweat like this on a cold day."). A violation of the Relevance maxim is an irrelevant, "off-the-wall" remark.

The Politeness Maxim.   Other scholars have suggested additional conversational maxims. The most important of these, in our view, is the Politeness maxim (Bach & Harnish, 1979). According to P. Brown and Levinson (1978), face is the "public self-image that every member of a society wants to claim for himself" (p. 66). In general, while interacting, participants try to preserve face for all participants and thus, interactants try to be polite. (Politeness as one of many goals of communication is discussed in chapter 1.)

P. Brown and Levinson (1978) suggested that politeness is the major reason for use of indirect utterances. They argued that interactants avoid face-threatening acts unless the demands for clarity and goal accomplishment are of greater importance. Positive face refers to people's maintenance of a worthy self-image, negative face, to their ability to choose actions without coercion or interference from others. From a speaker's perspective, actions like confessing or apologizing reflect a threat to his or her positive face, while asking for help or accepting an offer reflects a threat to the speaker's negative face. Orders threaten their negative face, accusations and contradictions, their positive face. A voluminous literature exists on face and politeness theory; some scholars have even argued that politeness is a universal consideration in conversation (Levinson & Brown, 1987).

Reciprocal response has been suggested as another conversational maxim. Interactants' communicative behaviors usually parallel each another: Rude speakers invite rudeness toward themselves. Reciprocal response patterns have been found in various behaviors, including interpersonal bonding (Berlin, Cassidy, & Belsky, 1995; Bochner, 1984); speech style (Davis & Hathaway, 1982; Giles, 1977; Yingling, 1995); dialogue rhythm (Cappella & Planalp, 1981; Jaffe & Feldstein, 1970; Schaffer, 1992); and parent–child interaction (Bornstein, 1989b; Bruner, 1983; Dore, 1983).

Clark and Clark's Interactional Principles. Without using the term *maxim*, Clark and Clark (1977) suggested that speakers follow several guidelines when determining what they want to say. Speakers consider: (a) knowledge of the listener (i.e., speakers make adjustments in their talk on the basis of their judgments about what listeners know); (b) the Cooperative Principle; (c) the Reality Principle; (d) the Social Context (i.e., different contexts call for different styles of speaking); and (e) the linguistic devices available (i.e., the linguistic features a particular language makes available to speakers of the language). (In this book we focus not only on language features themselves, but also on interactants' abilities to use these features; see chapter 5.)

Clark and Clark (1977) pointed out that, in many cases, speakers use conventional communicative rules but these rules only partly specify what people say at any moment. People may even flout the rules for their own purposes. Speakers always have choices, and they resolve them on the basis of their goals in talking along with the considerations previously mentioned. Listeners also can choose—to confirm, disconfirm, ignore, challenge, or otherwise respond to speaker's utterances.

Evaluating Conversational Maxims. One difficulty in evaluating the utility of various conversational maxims is that they may interact and conflict with one another. For example, Levinson (1983) suggested that one maxim, the Principle of Informativeness, may contradict the maxim of Quantity. The Principle of Informativeness requires that speakers include in their utterances as much as is consistent with what they know about the world (p. 146). The Quantity maxim, in contrast, suggests that speakers present only that information needed for purposes of the interaction. In a somewhat different vein, do people follow the Politeness maxim or the maxim of Quality, if telling the truth will significantly damage another's face? Are there preferences as to what maxim to follow when two conflict with each other? And if so, how do children learn these preferences or guidelines? The interrelationships among maxims and their implications for how we converse with one another clearly need further attention. Cross-cultural communication differences also make it difficult to assess the strength and applicability of various maxims.

Although few scholars have examined the acquisition of maxims, logic dictates that they unfold in a developmental sequence. The maxim of Manner is probably the first to be learned because parents correct children about what they say (e.g., "We don't talk about funny things people wear"). The Politeness maxim may evolve when children learn formulaic expressions like 'please' and 'thank you.' Quality becomes an issue in terms of lying and telling the truth; some children may be punished for violating the Quality maxim by telling a lie. Evidence suggests that children begin to tell lies, engaging in purposeful deception, around the age of 5. Relevance is undoubtedly the last to be learned; children under 5 years of age may not have the reasoning and cognitive skills necessary to determine relevance. For example, "chaining" or jumping from topic to topic is common among young children; it is often difficult to follow their train of thought when they talk about whatever catches their interest. In such a case, connection between topics is purely coincidental!

Although many of the maxims we reviewed are relevant to conversational encounters in the United States and the United Kingdom, their applicability in other societies remains in dispute. Philips (1974, 1976) suggested that conversational maxims provide a basis for ethnographic studies of conversations in other cultures (1976, p. 89). Her study of the Malagasy demonstrated that following the maxim of Quantity depended on the significance of the information, the interactants' relationship, and their sex. Similar situational constraints seem to operate in Western cultures as well. Bad news does not readily travel up the organizational ladder, certain occupations require discretionary use of information, and the like.

Conversation can thus be described as a dialogue between at least two people, in which each participant contributes to the conversational topic. Conversations are jointly produced, relatively informal occasions for talk. Underlying this coordinated communication is a set of maxims that participants assume are being followed unless circumstances suggest otherwise. These conversational maxims provide a basis for the interpretation of utterances and a guideline for the production of utterances. People conversing with others expect them to be relevant, informative, truthful, and so forth: as communicators, people act on these assumptions until they realize that other speakers violate the rules. While these principles seem quite useful in characterizing our communicative expectations, they nevertheless need to be more precisely conceptualized and their interrelationships more carefully examined.

With these assumptions about the nature of conversation in mind, let us now examine how conversations are organized. Organizing conversations requires a set of management strategies that enable speakers and listeners to coordinate their talk. The previous discussion assumes adult like competence and knowledge in conversation. We detailed this because it is important to understand the complexity of the conversational capabilities the young child is developing; it also illuminates the conceptual models researchers use in trying to pinpoint developmental trends in how conversation emerges. Next, we look more specifically at assumptions developmental scholars make when looking at how children acquire conversational and communicative abilities.

DEVELOPMENTAL ASSUMPTIONS ABOUT CONVERSATIONAL COMPETENCE

Several researchers (e.g., Garton, 1992; Weissenborn, 1986) have suggested that conversational competence involves a constellation of different subskills that develop over a long period of time in varied contexts. Forrester (1993) proposed that any model of conversational competence ought to consider conversation as models (of social interaction, of learning), conversation as a medium (information available to participants and awareness of the ongoing process of conversation), and conversation as criteria (used to assess children's social-cognitive skills). The latter two uses of conversation, as a medium and as criteria, are emphasized in this chapter. Overhearing, as Forrester noted, provides children with opportunities to gain information and to interact with others.

Dimitracopoulou (1990) suggested that an effective conversationalist must have an understanding of intentional communication, of the social context of a message, of the hearers' need to make inferences to interpret utterances, of the relevance of messages to the conversation, and of messages' appropriateness for hearers' viewpoints (p. 27).

Of these assumptions, we believe that relevance and intentionality are the most fundamental. Intentionality presupposes the meaningful and purposeful nature of messages; while relevance mandates a search for connectedness with the ongoing behavior and/or conversation. As noted before, an infant's beginning appreciation of intentionality develops at around 9 or 10 months of age. Knowledge of social contexts will emerge as children's social experience grows; typically 3-year-olds begin to have a good sense of social context as they interact and play with peers in different settings. (In chapters 7 and 8, we explore how social-cognitive communication skills mutually influence one another—as well as youngsters' growth and development.) The inferential nature of communication and the recognition of relevance issues develop when youngsters start to monitor their communication, usually around 5 years of age. At this point, they realize that messages can be unclear or not relevant to ongoing activities.

McTear (1984) suggested that children first need to acquire attention-getting and attention-directing strategies. Early response strategies are limited in content and length; children respond contingently to their immediate circumstances. Only later do children develop strategies for maintaining conversation beyond a single turn (i.e., one response only). Throughout the preschool years, children learn how to structure longer exchanges, for example, by linking a response to a previously mentioned topic. Here, children begin to think in terms of continuing the dialogue, rather than just being responsive.

Haslett (1984) proposed that early communication skills develop in four broad stages. In the first stage, Recognizing the Interpersonal Basis of Communication, infants recognize the fundamental role of communication in establishing relationships with others. The second stage, Creating Communicative Effects, from approximately 4 months to 3 years of age, occurs in three substages: (a) preverbal routines in which children acquire an understanding of the requirements of dialogue, such as role reciprocity and turn taking; (b) communicative intentionality in which children begin to intentionally signal their needs; and (c) linguistic communication in which children demonstrate a functional mastery of language in accomplishing social goals. The third stage of development, Using Communicative Strategies, begins at approximately 3 years of age. During this period, children develop an increasingly diverse set of linguistic forms to accomplish a variety of communicative goals. Thus, communication becomes increasingly adapted to different participants in different communicative settings. The final stage, Monitoring Communication, emerges at around 5 years of age. Children now develop the ability to evaluate the adequacy of messages and to repair messages, when needed, in conversing with others. We use Haslett's stages as a framework for integrating the diverse literatures about the skills youngsters need to be competent communicators (see Table 4.1).

Many scholars have also been concerned with characterizing the relevant social knowledge about communication which enables speakers to adjust their messages appropriately in varying social situations. (The next chapter, "Developing Communicative Knowledge," deals with children's developing social knowledge about communication; such knowledge develops gradually throughout early childhood. First, infants develop an Awareness of Self as Distinct from Others during the first year of life; then, Knowledge of Others becomes increasingly differentiated during the second and third years, and finally, Knowledge of Communicative Contexts begins to emerge at the third year. Although communication skills and knowledge develop simultaneously, for purposes of greater clarity and detail, we have chosen to explore each topic in separate chapters.)

TABLE 4.1
Stages in Children's Development of Communicative Skills

Age	Developmental Stages	Communicative Accomplishments
0–60 wks	**Interpersonal Basis of Communications**	
0–10 wks	Primary interpersonal life	Complex expressive exchanges
11–30 wks	Object prehension and games	Cycles of interaction and withdrawal
31–60 wks	Development of cooperative understanding and expression	Substantial cooperative activities and exchanges with others
4 mos–3 yrs	**Creation of Communicative Effects**	
2–12 mos	Preverbal routines	Understands and participates in interactive routines; appreciates turn taking, role reciprocity, and role reversal
begins at 9–10 mos	Communicative intentionality	Purposively uses and alters messages to accomplish goals; later, conventional signals emerge
begins at 12–18 mos	Linguistic communication	Begins with single words and gradually achieves functional mastery of speech acts, and communicative functions
3–5 yrs	**Communicative Strategies**	Wider range of interactions demands communicative strategies that can adapt to different communicative demands; strategies include use of politeness convention, presuppositions, deictic elements, and conversational postulates; initiates and sustains discourse topics
Begins around 5 yrs	**Monitoring Communication**	Treats talk as an object to be commented on; begins to check message accuracy and adequacy

STAGES OF COMMUNICATIVE DEVELOPMENT

Stage I: Interpersonal Bases of Communication

The first stage of development focuses upon the motivation to communicate; babies recognize early on the intrinsic value of communication itself as the way in which humans establish relationships with one another. The work of Colwyn Trevarthen

(1977a, 1977b, 1979a, 1979b, 1979c, 1980a, 1980b, 1982; Trevarthen & Aitken, 1994) has been most prominent in this area. Trevarthen suggested that humans possess an innate ability for intersubjectivity, defined as a natural understanding of and sensitivity to interpersonal interaction. Trevarthen's analysis focused on how infants' motives influence the development of their consciousness and purposive actions. Motives are viewed as internal processes through which individuals anticipate and interpret behavioral consequences. As Trevarthen pointed out, motives need not take into account external circumstances (for example, how likely something is to happen). In addition, motives may be expressed in a variety of ways (1982, p. 79).

According to Trevarthen, intentions *regulate* behavior by anticipating alternatives for action. Intentional behaviors are guided by motives: How individuals behave to satisfy their motives is largely a matter of choice (1982, p. 80). Trevarthen hypothesized that motives and intentions develop in two stages, primary intersubjectivity and secondary intersubjectivity. Each stage reflects infants' growing abilities to express their intentions to act cooperatively with others.

The first stage, primary intersubjectivity, occurs in three stages. In the first substage, primary interpersonal life, from birth to approximately 10 weeks, infants move from an initial negative period of interaction (i.e., frequent withdrawal) to a later period in which lengthy expressive exchanges occur between adult care-takers and children (Bates, 1979). Considerable fine tuning and coordination occur between mothers and their infants; they mutually specialize and match behaviors (Bornstein & Tamis-LeMonda, 1989, 1990). In the next substage, object prehension and games, from approximately 11 to 30 weeks, infants appear motivated to interact in cycles of avoidance and approach: Motives for affectionate and cooperative interaction with others alternate with motives for withdrawal and avoidance. In the final substage, development of cooperative understanding and expression of meaning, from 31 to 60 weeks, infants show strong interest in others' actions, movements, and statements.

By 9 months, Trevarthen believed that infants' communication signals "clearly conceive of others as having interests, purposes and helpful powers" (1982, p. 100). During this period, infants develop skills and motives that enable them to sustain lengthy interactions with others. As noted in chapter 2, attachment develops during this time and nonverbal channels such as eye gaze, body orientation, and touch are important elements of this interactional synchrony.

The second major stage in the development of motives and intentions, secondary intersubjectivity, emerges during the second year and occurs in cycles of little growth followed by enriched growth. During this stage, infants recognize that humans possess the capability for shared intention and awareness; this stage is marked by more varied and creative interactions with familiar others (Trevarthen & Hubley, 1978, p. 216).

Thus by the end of the second year of life, infants understand the basic intersubjective function of language—its communicative use. Trevarthen highlighted the importance of this development when he observed that primary and secondary intersubjectivity enables humans to act collectively, to share information, and to produce distinct cultures. Infants now possess a fundamental motivation for interpersonal communication and the functional social sensitivity necessary for such communication.

Trevarthen's work fits into both Stage I and Stage II of Haslett's proposed developmental account of verbal communication. We are most interested in the development of primary intersubjectivity, especially Substages I and II of primary intersubjectivity, as this period encompasses the developing recognition of the interpersonal nature of human communication.

Stage II. Creating Communicative Effects

The research of Bates, Dore, and Halliday has described the next stage of communicative development: Creating communicative effects. During this stage, children develop increasing complexity in their understanding of the communication process and its effects. This understanding occurs in three substages: (a) preverbal routines, (b) communicative intentionality, and (c) linguistic communication. The most significant development during this time is children's transition from nonverbal to verbal communication. In what follows, our purpose is to illustrate how children use nonverbal routines and language in order to communicate with others, although we refer to many of the developmental processes discussed in chapters 2 and 3.

Preverbal Routines. From approximately 2 to 6 months of age, infants establish interactive routines with adults. Among these early routines are patterned social exchanges during bathing, bedtime, and feeding, which are subsequently embedded in games like peekaboo. Through participating in such routines, infants develop an understanding of the fundamental aspects of communication such as role reciprocity, role reversibility, turn taking, and strategies for gaining and maintaining joint attention (Bates, 1979; Bruner, 1975; Snow, 1977a; Stern, 1977). Nelson (1981) has termed this learning *participatory imitation* as infants' performances complete the social routine.

Bruner (1983) referred to these preverbal routines as formats. Formats are interactions characterized by four conditions: (a) each member of the dyad has a goal and the means to attain that goal; (b) each member's responses are dependent upon a previous response by the other participant; (c) each member's responses are directed toward achieving that goal; and (d) there is a termination point at which the goal has been achieved. Bruner also pointed out that formats themselves change as new goals and strategies develop, as goals become coordinated between participants, and as the surrounding context changes.

These preverbal routines emphasize the interactive aspects of social encounters. Infants develop expectations about how people communicate: They recognize role reciprocity, role reversibility, and a sense of sequence in communication. One important communicative skill emerging during preverbal routines is turn taking. Dialogue implies that there will be an exchange of speaking and listening roles (i.e., turn-taking), and many scholars suggest this appreciation first develops during preverbal routines.

Turn taking is a mechanism used to organize conversations so that interactants smoothly exchange speaking sequences. Through turn taking, participants coordinate their conversational contributions with each other (Sacks, Schegloff, & Jefferson, 1974). Infants appear to have an early appreciation of turn taking. According to Bruner (1975b), role reciprocity (taking turns and assuming the other's role as in, for example, conversational exchanges) develops through participation in give-and-take games. These social exchanges become intentional around 9 or 10 months of age (Bates, 1979), and gradually become more complex and well organized (Bruner, 1977).

Even with young babies, interactions between infant and caretaker have a definite sequence and timing that is structured by the turn taking of vocal exchanges (Bateson, 1975; Mueller & Lucas, 1975). Turn taking appears to reflect the interactive synchrony of a wide range of human behaviors, and thus Schaffer concluded that infants appear to be preadapted for social exchange (1979, p. 283). Turn taking marks the onset of dialogue and is a prerequisite for the later emergence of communicative roles (Halliday, 1979).

Turn taking has also been observed between very young children. Keenan (1974) found that her twin sons took turns, handled interruptions, and made audible and appropriate responses to one another. Studies by Bloom, Rocissano, and Hood (1976) and by Schaffer, Collis, and Parsons (1977) found that 12- and 24-month-old children exchanged talking turns smoothly with their mothers; overlaps were brief and caused equally by mothers and children. Grant (1994) suggested that some individual differences between infant–mother interaction may be a function of differences in mothers' personalities which are then reflected in their interactions. Through object manipulation, games, and interactive routines, Schaffer (1979) claimed that a 12-month-old infant "appears to comprehend, in a practical sense, the notion of reciprocity with its attendant ideas of complementarity, synchrony and role reversal" (p. 294). Schaffer also noted, however, the difficulty of assessing the extent of infants' interactive skills or the degree to which mothers maintain the dialogue.

Turn taking also occurs when infants are not directly addressed in conversation, or are part of a larger interacting group. Barton and Tomasello (1991) observed that 19- to 24-month-olds were able to take turns and participate interactively with a preschool sibling and their mothers. Triadic conversations were longer, and infants took twice as many turns than they took in a dyadic conversation. Infants were more likely to join in a conversation rather than initiate one, and they were more likely to take a turn if they shared joint attention with the current speaker. Dunn and Shatz (1989) found that 2- and 3-year-olds were able to contribute new information to a conversation between their mothers and a sibling and were able to understand conversations even when not directly participating in them. Like Barton and Tomasello (1991), Dunn and Shatz (1989) also observed that infants were more likely to respond if they were in a joint-attention state with the speaker. (The contributions of siblings to young children's communicative development is discussed more thoroughly in chapter 6.)

Turn-taking skills have also been related to being liked by peers. Black and Hazen (1990) found that turn taking was important in establishing and maintaining social status. Liked children had clear, responsive, and relevant turn-taking styles; thus liked children may be able to provide a conversational structure that enables cohesive interaction to take place.

In summary, turn taking appears to develop from biological patterns of temporal sequencing and interactional synchrony; in the context of communication, sequencing and synchrony develop into role reciprocity and role complementarity. As we have seen, many of the rudimentary skills necessary for interpersonal communication, like turn taking and sequencing, begin during preverbal routines. The degree to which these skills come under the intentional control of infants, however, has been a subject of much controversy.

Communicative Intentionality. In discussing the communicative intentionality substage of development, we examine infants' emerging abilities to control their communicative skills. This concept has been extensively discussed as an important precursor to nonverbal communication in chapter 2. Here, we briefly recap its importance for verbal communication as well.

Dore (1983) argued that by using words, babies signal (a) reference to a conceptual domain, (b) intending a particular function like questioning or requesting, and (c) expectations that hearers will do something in response or, at a minimum, acknowledge the utterance. Dore pointed out the necessary role adults play in this development. How adults interpret children's actions is more important than the child's own intention. That is, both infant and adult need to focus on each other's messages, but adults especially need to respond at an appropriate level. Dore observed that adults' contributions to these dialogues provide not only objects for children to attend to, but also negative examples and corrective vocalizations (e.g., "Oh, no, that's not something to play with. That doll might break.").

Intentionality also presupposes that infants are aware that others have feelings, emotions and knowledge distinct from their own (Golinkoff, 1993). Infants alter their communication to others (Tomasello, Conti-Ramsden, & Ewert, 1990) as well as share information without a clear, overt goal (Franco & Butterworth, 1991). Finally, infants' abilities to synchronize their behaviors with significant adult caretakers presuppose their awareness of different emotions as well as different contexts.

Researchers have commonly measured intentionality in terms of altering behavior. This emphasis on infants' ability to alter their communicative behavior also highlights the interactive nature of communicative intentionality. Infants need the responses of others to gain feedback about their own behavior: They rely on others' interpretations of their signals. Infants cannot progress from intentional communication to the use of conventional communicative signals without adults' interpretation of these signals. Thus, intentionality becomes expressed by conventional communicative signals. Researchers generally acknowledge children's increasing control over expressing their intentions and place the earliest behavioral evidence of intentionality at approximately 9 months. Infants continue to develop increasing skills in refining and controlling intentional messages.

Both preceding substages, preverbal routines and communicative intentionality, are prelinguistic stages. The final substage in communicative effects, linguistic communication, develops between 12 and 18 months. During this period, children begin to communicate using language. Two theoretical approaches have been used to account for the emergence of verbal communication: speech act theory and functional theory. Before presenting the results of research for both views, we briefly highlight some differences between them.

Linguistic Communication. As previously noted, language has often been discussed in terms of linguistic form (nouns, verbs, questions, and so forth) and linguistic function (the purpose for which language is being used—to persuade, to warn, to threaten, etc.). The split between form and function reflects a basic difference in emphasis between speech act analyses and functional analyses. Speech act analyses emphasize linguistic form; functional approaches emphasize linguistic functions. Yet speech act analysis may deal not only with linguistic form itself but also with the intentions, presuppositions, and implicatures of a particular linguistic form (usually considered aspects of functional approaches). For example, the different ways of making a request can presuppose different situational conditions.

Functional analyses generally deal with analyzing the purposes for which children use language. Although functional analyses may seem similar to analyzing the illocutionary force of a speech act, there are several points of contrast. First, functional analyses can be viewed as effect, intention, or both. Speech act theory has generally ignored perlocutionary effect (the outcome) altogether, an attitude that has weakened speech act theory by ignoring linkage between intent and effect. People intend to do things to create a desired effect, and concentrating on intent deals with only part of the communicative process. Second, speech act analyses typically focus on a single proposition whereas functional analyses may incorporate more than a single proposition. Finally, functional approaches allow for the multifunctionality of utterances whereas speech act analysis focuses on one function that an utterance could perform. With these differences in mind, let us now look at developmental research from both of these perspectives.

1. Speech Acts. Our discussion of the developmental sequence for speech acts begins with a more thorough overview of speech act theory itself. It has been one of the most influential approaches to understanding the nature of conversation and how conversations are organized. Early work by Austin (1962) and Searle (1969) established speech act theory (hereafter referred to as SA). Subsequent analysis by Levinson and Bach and Harnish have modified the original SA theory.

At the outset, it is important to note that different theorists conceptualize speech acts in varied ways. Here we use the conceptualization of speech acts developed by Austin and Searle, but varying definitions of the concept exist, even among those who claim to be adherents of the Austin and Searle view (see, for example, Levinson, 1983, chap. 5). Linguistic philosophers have long been concerned with the reference and implications of sentences. Both Austin and Searle base their analyses, in part, on earlier work done by Wittgenstein, who, in *Philosophical Investigations* (1958), suggested that utterances can be explained only in terms of the activities and purposes for which language is used.

In his book *How to Do Things With Words*, Austin (1962) further developed the view that meaning is tied to language use. He suggested that a set of words called performatives accomplish action simply by virtue of being uttered. Speech activities like promising, warning, and apologizing are performatives; their purposes are achieved through being spoken. Performatives are not true or false, but are either successful (felicitous) or unsuccessful (infelicitous). For utterances to be **felicitous**, four conditions must be met:

1. Accepted conventional procedures must be followed—certain words must be uttered by specified individuals in a given situation (for example, a marriage ceremony must be correctly followed and performed by an official who has that particular legal authority);
2. An appropriate individual must state the specific utterance (for example, in the U.S., a child could not be married);
3. All participants must execute the procedures properly, and
4. The procedure must be completed.

Austin also suggested that all utterances have certain **forces**—that is, they accomplish certain actions. Thus, any spoken utterance has a locutionary force (the content of what is said); an illocutionary force (the intent or conventional force of what is said); and a perlocutionary force (the effect, both intended and unintended, of the utterance). Any utterance, then, has simultaneously locutionary, illocutionary, and perlocutionary forces.

A. Searle's Speech Act Analysis. Searle (1969) extended the analysis of illocutionary acts. He argued that any speech act (utterance) consists of a proposition and its illocutionary force. Searle's analysis specified the necessary and sufficient conditions for successfully performing an illocutionary act and the rules governing the use of a particular linguistic expression. Searle's analysis can be demonstrated by working through the act of promising. According to Searle,

1. The propositional content must be appropriate—for promises to be effective, the speaker must promise some future action;
2. Preparatory conditions must be satisfied—e.g., the speaker must believe that the future action is important or desirable to do, the future action must not be what is expected, the speaker must believe s/he can perform the act, and the speaker must believe the listener wants the act performed;
3. The speaker must be sincere; and
4. Stating the utterance implies an obligation to perform the action.

These felicity conditions can be roughly organized into four categories—the specification of propositional content, preparatory conditions, sincerity conditions, and the essential condition (respectively illustrated in the promising example). Such felicity conditions—the necessary and sufficient conditions required to perform a speech act—can be specified for any speech act.

In addition to felicity conditions, Searle (1969) discussed rules governing the use of particular linguistic expressions, such as apologies and distinguished between two types of rules, regulative and constitutive. Regulative rules refer to the conditions for performing various speech acts. These rules can be thought of as governing verbal interactions: who can say what kinds of utterances under what circumstances. In contrast, constitutive rules define "what counts" or what can be recognized as a particular speech act. Regulative rules govern who can perform a speech act (a *judge* must sentence a prisoner); constitutive rules govern the format of a speech act (a judge must follow *specified legal procedures* in sentencing).

Several scholars (Austin, 1962; Bach & Harnish, 1979; Hancher, 1979, Searle, 1976) have classified speech acts into a more limited set of basic actions, like making requests or stating factual information. Although these categories reflect basic actions performed by a set of speech acts, they appear to be inexhaustible as well as culturally variable. Little seems to be gained by such classification schemes, even those based on communicative intentions (see Levinson, 1983, pp. 239–241 on this point). Such categories appear to be based on direct, explicit performatives, but the illocutionary force of an utterance is often indirect, such as in hinting or bribing. To account for these inferential speech acts, Searle distinguished between indirect and direct speech acts.

B. Indirect Speech Acts. According to Levinson (1983), citing Gazdar's analysis of speech acts (1979a,b, 1981), speech act theorists are committed to the **literal force hypothesis** (hereafter LFH). Two key assumptions underlie the

LFH. First, it assumes that explicit performatives specify their illocutionary force via the performative verb in the utterance's main clause. For example, when a person says "I apologize," the performative verb (apologize) expresses the illocutionary force of the utterance, namely the intent to apologize. Second, the LFH assumes that the three main sentence types—imperatives, interrogatives, and declaratives—have conventional illocutionary forces associated with them: respectively, ordering or requesting, questioning, and stating. All other speech acts are indirect speech acts; such utterances are characterized by an additional inferred, indirect force. For example, a person could command someone directly, "Close the window" or hint indirectly, "It's really breezy in here." The hint carries with it the implicit request to close the window so that it is no longer breezy in the room. However, as Levinson noted (1983), most language usage is indirect; it is very difficult to derive illocutionary force from the variety of utterances used in interactions. There is, put succinctly, no simple correspondence between utterance form and utterance force.

C. Criticisms of Speech Act Theories. In addition to the problematic connection between an utterance's form and its function, Levinson (1983) detailed other major difficulties with speech act models. First, it is difficult to distinguish between an utterance's illocutionary and perlocutionary force. Illocutionary acts have built-in consequences, some of which depend on uptake by listeners (such as a bet) while others have direct consequences (such as declaring war). The boundaries between perlocutionary and illocutionary force are thus fuzzy, and the role of listeners in determining the force of an utterance has been largely neglected (Levinson, 1983, pp. 236–237).

Second, indirect speech acts are difficult to explain adequately. They often have syntactic features related to their surface structure form and their illocutionary force (Levinson, 1983, p. 265). For example, the restricted placement of "please" in utterances that are direct and indirect requests and the placement of parenthetical clauses like "I believe" are cited as examples of the connection between an utterance's pragmatic force and syntactic processes. Some theorists have suggested that indirect speech acts may be idioms. P. Brown and Levinson (1978) argued, however, that the universality of indirect speech acts suggests they are not idiomatic in nature but rather reflect a fundamental communicative process. Furthermore, other models explaining indirect speech acts through inferences fail to deal with the motivation for using indirect speech acts (Levinson, 1983, p. 274). Levinson concluded:

> There are some compelling reasons to think that speech act theory may be superseded by much more complex multi-faceted pragmatic approaches to the functions that utterances perform. The first set of these have to do with the internal difficulties that any speech act theory faces, of which the most intractable is probably the set of problems posed by ISAs [indirect speech acts]. Note that any theory of speech acts is basically concerned with mapping utterances into speech act categories,

however those are conceived. The problem then is that either this is a trivial enterprise done by fiat [as by LFH], or an attempt is made to predict accurately the functions of sentences in context. But if the latter is attempted, it soon becomes clear that the contextual sources that give rise to the assignment of function or purpose are of such complexity and of such interest in their own right, that little will be left to the theory of speech acts. . . .

In this way, speech act theory is being currently undermined from the outside by the growth of disciplines concerned with the empirical study of natural language use (as Austin indeed foresaw). (1983, pp. 278–279)

Other objections to speech act analyses of utterances center on its neglect of listeners' roles in interaction. Gazdar (1981) noted problems with the assignment of speech acts to utterances and argued that there is no form–force parallel and that utterances alone do not determine illocutionary force. Similarly, Edmondson (1981) claimed that illocutionary acts have been inadequately characterized. More important, he suggested that illocutionary force is a function of its treatment by a hearer: That is, the hearer's uptake is central to the illocutionary force of an utterance (pp. 50ff). In a similar vein, Haslett (1987) noted that speech act analysis is inherently problematic because it focuses only on the speaker's perspective and ignores the negotiation of meaning between speakers and hearers.

Another problem with speech act theory is that the two-stage processing of speech acts has not been confirmed by empirical data for either children or adults. In speech act theory a message is first interpreted literally; if this seems inappropriate, the listener must search for an indirect interpretation. Adults appear to process indirect and literal meanings equally rapidly (Gibbs, 1979). However, children do not appear to process utterances literally and then nonliterally. In contrast to the literature on the literal force hypothesis, H. Clark (1979) suggested that the conventionality, transparency, and obviousness of requests all help listeners interpret a speaker's intention. In light of the limitations of children's knowledge of linguistic form, linguistic meaning, and background contextual information, all these cues may not be available for their understanding of requests. Instead, Shatz (1974) suggested that children use prototypes of different kinds of requests and identify the prototype being used via sentence features like intonation, politeness, and sentence mood. 'Can you please pass the salt?' would be a prototypical request because it contains a modal, 'you' at the beginning and a politeness marker, 'please.'

Other scholars have found that speech act models fail to adequately analyze the complexity of communicative processes. For instance, both Levinson (1983) and Edmondson (1981) suggested that the speaker's motives, beliefs, and intentions are not always clear from his or her utterances and that a variety of intents may be meant. In brief, utterances typically have more than one function and speech act theory does not account for this. In addition, both Haslett (1987) and Levinson (1983) argued that speech acts are not an appropriate unit of analysis for discourse and that speech act theory fails to consider the importance of background, commonsense knowledge possessed by both speakers and listeners. Cook-Gumperz (1986) noted that the linguistic reasoning used by coders to analyze speech acts is probably redundant because children appear to rely on embedded contextual information.

In also seems apparent that children may use linguistic forms without full knowledge of the range of intentions behind utterances (Cook-Gumperz, 1986; Ervin-Tripp, 1981). Cook-Gumperz (1986) pointed out that although speech act analysis provides useful linguistic information, a more fundamental question is "how children draw on their own knowledge of the world to do things with words" (p. 47). Researchers have increasingly used constructivist, interpretive approaches to link children's knowledge of context with their communication in that context.

One speech act model that attempts to incorporate contextual knowledge is Bach and Harnish's (1979) speech act schema. Their model has built upon listeners' identification of the meanings of an utterance to infer what is being referred to in the context. Participants note the intentions behind utterances and the effects they are to accomplish. In addition, these intentions and effects are judged against the rationality and cooperation demonstrated in conversations and behavior. Listeners generally have to identify the utterance, decode its meaning, infer what the speaker may mean by it, and discern what it refers to.

Three assumptions underlie this model. First, both speaker and listener must share a common language which allows them to identify an utterance's meaning based on linguistic meaning and appropriate contextual knowledge. Second, a speaker must make an utterance that has some identifiable illocutionary intent. Finally, if an utterance can be interpreted literally, it should be so interpreted; if a speaker appears to be speaking nonliterally (for example, metaphorically), then the listener searches for the appropriate meaning in context. Several researchers (e.g., Dimitracopoulou, 1990) have suggested that the speech act schema acknowledges the interpretive, contextual basis of human interaction and as such, represents an important advance in speech act theory.

D. The Development of Speech Acts.   In spite of the limitations of speech act theory and its many forms, a considerable research literature has been devoted to understanding the developmental sequence in which children's use of various speech acts unfolds. From approximately 12 to 18 months, children develop single words that more explicitly signal their intentions. Because there is debate as to whether single words can be viewed as propositional utterances, it is not clear that they can be considered speech acts (utterances that have both illocutionary and locutionary force). Dore (1976) argued, however, that single words are primitive speech acts; single words have illocutionary but not locutionary force. These primitive speech acts include labeling, repeating, answering, action requests, answer requests, calling, greeting, protesting, and practicing (Carter, 1975, 1978a, 1978b).

At around 18 months, single words or primitive speech acts develop into speech acts having both an elementary illocutionary force and a propositional content. Single-word utterances become increasingly elaborate and contain both a predicating and a referring expression. Each utterance performs a specific function, such as asserting or making a request. At the same time, children also master the linguistic forms required for producing different utterances (such as mastering the syntactic forms for asking questions and stating imperatives). As children's linguistic and communicative skills become more elaborate, they begin to produce indirect as well as direct speech acts.

Indirect speech acts are important because they reflect children's knowledge of social relationships and contextual cues as well as the nuances of language. In contrast, direct speech acts reflect children's abilities to explicitly signal their desires or needs appropriately in context. Both indirect and direct speech acts reveal considerable communicative competency on the part of youngsters.

1. Indirect Speech Acts. Several studies have explored children's use of indirect and direct speech acts. There is no evidence to support the view that direct speech acts are learned before indirect speech acts (McTear, 1985). Much individual variation is a function of children's developmental opportunities to respond to both direct and indirect requests (Ervin-Tripp, 1981). Bates (1979) suggested that "the ability to predict whether or not the listener shares a given assumption and to plan one's utterances accordingly is one of the highest achievements in pragmatic development" (p. 447). Her research on conversational maxims has centered on politeness judgments. Politeness may be signaled in the linguistic form of an utterance (e.g., an indirect request rather than a command) or non-verbally (e.g., a soft tone rather than a harsh one).

In addition, children also demonstrate their understanding of speech acts through the use of politeness conventions. Three speech acts, imperatives, declaratives, and interrogatives, can be substituted for one another and serve to "soften" utterances (i.e., make utterances polite or more polite). For example, the imperative "Close the door!" can be softened by using the interrogative "Could you close the door?" By 2½ years, children use polite forms to soften requests (e.g., "Please"). At 3, children seem to have a general concept of politeness and correctly judge the degree of politeness of various linguistic forms (Bates, 1979). Bates suggested that at 30 months, speech act usage shifts from an emphasis on efficiency to an emphasis on politeness.

As Bates pointed out, children may be polite to get what they want efficiently; this supposition presumes that children already understand the relationship between politeness and goal achievement and have learned the pragmatic value of various request–politeness forms. By ages 3 to 4, children use indirect commands, the imperfect tense to soften commands, and formal modes of address as politeness strategies. Bates thought that children shift from focusing on utterances' efficiency to their politeness.

Bates (1979) found that children, ages 2 to 4, responded to both direct and indirect speech acts by their mothers. Shatz (1974) observed that 2-year-olds obeyed both indirect and direct requests with equal frequency. Ervin-Tripp (1981) noted that children produced imperatives (i.e., direct speech acts) as well as requests (i.e., indirect speech acts). She systematically investigated direct and indirect speech acts (Ervin-Tripp, 1981; Ervin-Tripp & Gordon, 1980) and found that the situation itself plays an important role in how children respond to direct or indirect requests. In a helping situation, children complied appropriately to explicit, conventional requests; as requests became more indirect, 3-year-olds were less helpful. In all these studies, children appeared to rely on contextual and nonverbal cues in their interpretations of ongoing encounters. Nonliteral understanding seems to increase at around 6 years of age (Dimitracopoulou, 1990).

Requests can also signal relative status. Becker (1984) found that 4- and 5-year-olds recognized when requests were "bossy" and when they were softened. Older children consistently identified status differences in requests over a wide range of contrasting requests ("Give me a penny" vs. "I really like pennies"). Bossy requests contained more threats and more negative semantic choices than nice requests.

2. Directives. Directives are speech acts that function as requests for action; they may be direct (imperatives) or indirect (interrogatives). Garvey (1975) found that young preschoolers produced both direct and indirect requests for action and that older children produced more indirect requests than did younger children. Ervin-Tripp (1981) noted that the earliest directives used by children were accompanied by gestures, the name of the desired object, or linguistic markers like "want." Eventually children produce many indirect forms (Camras, Pristo, & Brown, 1985), although the desired goal or action must be understood by preschoolers. Read and Cherry (1978) concluded that preschoolers possess a flexible array of directive forms that may be alternated and combined in making requests.

3. Interrogatives. Interrogatives have been widely studied across a variety of functions and contexts. These include their use for clarification and information seeking (Garvey, 1975, 1977; Corsaro, 1977; Robinson & Rackstraw, 1967); their use in turn-taking allocation (Snow, 1977a); and their use as an indirect request for action (Bates, 1979; Shatz, 1974). Ervin-Tripp and Miller (1977) reported that preschoolers understand the obligation to answer questions. Children first appear to comprehend yes–no, what, and where questions (Ervin-Tripp, 1970). The remaining wh-questions are understood in the following order: why, who (subject), where from, when, and who (object) (Owens, 1992). Some have argued that *where* questions can be answered nonverbally, but other wh-questions cannot; this may, in part, explain the order in which wh-questions are acquired (Dimitracopoulou, 1990).

With increasing age, children are more successful at answering questions, although even 2-year-olds appear to recognize that questions require responses.

Because questions require replies, children use questions to gain access to conversations (Mishler, 1976a, 1976b). Shatz and McCloskey (1984) found that some semantic responses to questions appear "empty"; children respond inappropriately as if they do not understand the meaning of 'yes' or 'no.' For example, when asked to do something, some would reply "No" as they completed the requested action. Children appear to use intonation to assess what kind of question is being asked (i.e., to distinguish yes–no questions from wh-questions) and to answer wh-questions that are similar to questions asked during games with their mothers (Allen & Shatz, 1983). Veneziano (1985) found that children's earliest responses to questions included lexical items from the question itself; only later do nonimitative, clearly semantic replies emerge.

With regard to interrogatives, then, as early as 1 year of age, children show sensitivity to question form. By age 2, routine ways of responding to wh-questions and yes–no questions emerge (Shatz & McCloskey, 1984). Near the end of the second year, children were using "OK" without a physical response to imperatives and "yes–no" responses to declaratives. The authors found that older 2-year-olds were able to indicate their unwillingness to perform an action and their disagreement with a statement. Children appear to use intonation, first words in utterances, and the context to help them respond verbally to questions, although their responses may be inappropriate semantically or pragmatically.

A series of studies by Dimitracopoulou (1990) traced the developmental stages of acquiring speech acts. On the basis of analyzing utterances of children ranging in age from 2½ to 6½ years, she found that assertives and responsives were the most frequent speech acts; commissives were used least and not found among the 3½-year-olds. The youngest children used substantial amounts of private speech. Responsives decreased with age, and requestives and expressives increased. With age, labeling (an assertive) also decreased, and descriptions of events and statements about internal events increased. Utterance length increased with age; children also moved from giving minimal responses to multiword responses. Indirect or nonliteral speech acts were rare across all age groups. Hinting, as an indirect speech act, first appeared among the 4½-year-olds and increased thereafter. Dimitracopoulou noted that indirectness needs more thorough discussion and testing because some indirectness may be signaled nonverbally (via intonation) and understood immediately.

Children's ability to sustain conversation also improved over time. Young children were "unequal" conversational partners, with mothers typically using several strategies to gain children's attention. By 7, youngsters were able to create interactions in the form of dialogues that reflected an ability to develop a theme or topic. Repetition was used as a cohesive device as well as a response to others. With increasing age, children relied more on verbal messages to successfully convey their thoughts and desires; they were also more successful in gaining cooperation from others.

Other scholars, such as Bates (Bates, Thal, Whitesell, Fenson, & Oakes, 1989) have examined children's comments about various speech acts. These metapragmatic skills develop in three stages during Piaget's preoperational period. First, children refer explicitly to hearers and speakers and use locatives of space and time to specifically identify the participants and location under discussion. Next, children use conjunctions that link utterances together (such as 'and' and 'if'). According to Bates (1976), the third metapragmatic stage depends upon the cognitive capacity to coordinate three or more information units so that "the third unit is coordinated with a relationship established between the other two" (p. 152): for example, coordination across units as in the utterance "John and Mary can go and I want to too."

Throughout the linguistic communication stage, children thus move from "primitive" to fully formed speech acts (multiword utterances with a clear propositional value and illocutionary force). During this time, children develop distinct types of speech acts such as directives and interrogatives and use communicative strategies such as politeness conventions and indirect speech acts.

As children's mastery of verbal communication grows, they recognize that any utterance can convey more than one intended meaning and that there are many ways of expressing the same intent (e.g., indirect versus direct requests). The recognition of message complexity is accompanied by growing complexity in the interpersonal contexts in which children communicate. Increasing interaction with others involves children in a wide range of social relationships and social contexts; children learn they must deal with the intentions of others as well as their own.

Given this communicative complexity, speech act theory seems very limited in its views of intentionality (i.e., illocutionary force) because this view does not acknowledge the interactive nature of intentionality and interpretation. As Dimitracopoulou (1990) argued, speech act theory fails to account for the sociocognitive abilities needed to perform certain speech acts. Despite these flaws, however, speech act theory has contributed significantly to understanding how language is structured and understood and has pinpointed areas in need of further exploration. One such area is the social purposes or functions for which language is used.

Communicative Functions.   Halliday (1975) argued that language plays a key role in socialization and that the structure of language reflects the functions for which language is used. The functional use of language develops in three phases. Phase I develops from 10½ to 18 months, a time when each utterance, whether a sound or an actual utterance, has only one function. According to Halliday, four language functions appear during this time: instrumental (stating desires and demands); regulators (controlling the actions of others); interactional (expressing social or affective bonds); and personal (informing others about a person's own actions). At 18 months, two further functions emerge: the heuristic (explaining actions and events) and the imaginative (imagining events, actions, and objects).

During the transitional Phase II period, from 18 to 24 months of age, language functions become more complex and abstract. The six functions in Phase I merge into three broad functions: the pragmatic function (a blend of the earlier instrumental and regulatory functions); the pathic function (a blend of the earlier personal and heuristic functions); and the interactional function. Another function, the informative function (which expresses information that is not apparent to listeners from the immediate context) also appears at this time. Grammatical structure begins to develop during this period as well. According to Halliday (1975), grammatical structures allow an utterance to perform more than one function. Much of the development during this phase occurs through the opposition of the pragmatic (action) and mathetic (reflective) functions; Halliday pointed out that objects and ideas are both acted upon and thought about.

The final phase, Phase III, marks the onset of the adult functional system. Two basic functions, the ideational function (derived from the mathetic function and used to "talk about the world") and the interpersonal function (derived from the interactional function and used to establish and maintain social relations), emerge during Phase III. A third function, the textual, reflects how language can be organized to serve other functions. These three basic functions enable speakers to accomplish an infinite variety of purposes (Halliday, 1979). Rees (1978) suggested that the ideational and interpersonal functions parallel the noncommunicative and communicative functions of language (in Halliday's [1978] terms, the reflective and action-oriented functions of language). More recently, Ninio, Snow, Pan and Rollins (1994) proposed a coding system, the Inventory of Communicative Acts, to investigate form-function mapping during the single word stage.

Joan Tough's research (1973) has provided an extension and validation of Halliday's functional analysis. Tough's theoretical perspective distinguished four language functions, each expressing a different mode of thinking. Each function of language can be accomplished in different ways; these alternative means are designated uses of language. The four major language functions are to direct action, to interpret events and situations, to imagine, and to relate to others. Tough found that disadvantaged 3-year-olds used language to focus on their present experience and to monitor their own activities. Advantaged 3-year-olds used language for reasoning, anticipating future events, and creating imaginary contexts more than did disadvantaged peers.

Using Tough's hierarchical analysis of language functions, Haslett (1983a) observed developmental differences in the communicative functions and strategies used by preschoolers in their conversations with peers. At 3, children's most used functions were interpretive (mastering information about the environment) and relational (expressing needs and ideas). Seventy-five percent of relational utterances were self-emphasizing strategies (those reflecting children's egocentrism). At 4, a major developmental shift occurred, with the projective function (strategies using imagination in play) becoming most important, followed by the relational function. Both functions were used heavily in social play with others. Generally, girls developed communicative functions earlier than boys and achieved a more advanced level of cognitive complexity and communicative adaptability in the use of relational and projective strategies.

A. The Referential Function.   One function of language, the informative or referential function, has received considerable attention because of its pervasiveness, its importance for education, and its role as a component in more complex communications (S. Asher, 1979). Children do not understand that speakers are obligated to send messages uniquely identifying a referent; this finding is one of the most consistent in referential communication studies (S. Asher, 1979: S. Asher & Wigfield, 1981; Whitehurst & Sonnenschein, 1981). For instance, children may not understand that the utterance "Give me the ball" is ambiguous when there are twelve balls available.

Young children also do not appear to recognize inadequate instructions and are less likely to ask questions for further information than are older children (Flavell, 1981a; E. Robinson & W. Robinson, 1978b, 1978c). In studies conducted by the Robinsons (1976a, 1976b, 1977, 1978a, 1978b, 1978c), children were asked to account for communicative failure or success by blaming either listeners or speakers. Young children (age 5) usually fall into the listener-blaming category; speaker blame becomes common around 7. Generally, referential communication skills increase with age (Glucksberg, Krauss, & Higgins, 1975).

Lloyd and Beveridge's (1981) monograph on referential communication is of particular interest because the subjects were preschoolers; most referential communication studies have tested children 5 or older. Lloyd and Beveridge found that: (1) preschoolers gave messages adequately describing a referent in 45% of their utterances; (2) when asked to modify their message, 70% of the preschoolers were able to do so; (3) marked individual differences were found in preschoolers' listening and speaking strategies; (4) children performed better as speakers than as listeners; (5) children's messages in a spatial task failed to describe the orientation, position, and placement of the referent; and (6) some preschoolers were able recognize message deficiencies. Although preschoolers can provide adequate descriptions and modify their messages when asked, their comparison skills and recognition of message deficiency are generally lacking. Referential communication accuracy for children at 4 years of age was significantly correlated with skill in vocabulary for children at 12 (McDevitt et al., 1987).

Referential communication, because it is concerned with message accuracy and adequacy, also rests upon children's ability to detect truth and lies in messages. Children's world knowledge and social knowledge provide a foundation for their analysis of truth and falsity; in addition, children must understand the meaning of the abstract terms 'lie' or 'truth.' At 4, children can distinguish a factually accurate statement from a lie (Strichartz, 1980). In a further study,

Strichartz and Burton (1990) asked preschoolers through adults to respond to different puppet stories by identifing the truth or falsity of puppets' statements. Components of prototypic lies included (1) the falsity of a statement, (2) the speakers' (in this case, the puppet characters') belief in the falsity of the statement they uttered, and (3) the speakers' intention to deceive listeners. Strichartz and Burton systematically included these prototypic lie elements in or excluded them from the puppet stories. Results indicated that preschoolers and first graders predominantly relied on judgments of the statements' factual inaccuracies to judge lying or truthfulness. Three-year-olds in the study did not appear to prefer any of the prototypic elements (factuality, intent, or belief) in their judgments. In some cases, they had difficulty labeling statements as true or false. By 4 and 5 years of age, children indicated a strong preference for relying on the factuality of statements in determining truth or falsity. They judged a statement as a lie when it "does not match the facts of the situation and shows no additive effect from the intent and belief components" (p. 217). Interestingly, for older subjects, intent was a significant component in their judgments of when someone is lying, whereas in truth telling, belief was a significant factor in their assessments. For young children, truth and lies are polar opposites of a continuum, and children judged the truth or falsity of a statement by its match with the observable reality of a situation. In other words, what you see is the truth.

In summary, the functional uses of language that begin to emerge at around 12 to 18 months are well established by age 3. The three basic functions of language appear to be ideational (informational), interpersonal (relational), and textual (the organization of language itself). Although other functional systems can be much more elaborate depending upon the needs of the researchers (see, for example, Dore, 1974, or Tough, 1977, for more detailed functional schemes), all of these schemes collapse into the three fundamental functions outlined by Halliday (1975).

The tremendous growth achieved during the linguistic communication sub-stage is impressive. At the start of this substage, children were just beginning to use multiword utterances designed to achieve particular social ends. By the end of this period, they can produce both direct and indirect speech acts and use politeness conventions in their interactions with others.

We have used two approaches to characterize communicative development during this period—speech act analysis and the functional models. Although both these approaches detail the complexity of communicative skills children acquire during this time, each reflects only partial understanding of communicative development. For an adequate theory of human communication, we believe that the unfortunate split between linguistic form and linguistic function must be overcome. When people communicate, form and function interact. This interplay between form and function undoubtedly emerges during early childhood, but most developmental research and theory does not reflect this fact. Thus, although scholars understand how linguistic forms and functions emerge, they have yet to develop models explaining their complex interrelationships during communication. Furthermore, such interrelationships also need to be assessed in light of particular social relationships and given social contexts.

During the next stage of developmental pragmatics, **Using Communicative Strategies**, children experience increased interaction with other peers and unfamiliar adults (e.g., preschool teachers, etc.); as a result, youngsters must adapt their messages to a variety of interactants in a diverse range of settings. Children must be able to communicate clearly, to establish and maintain conversational topics, and to accurately interpret the remarks of others. In short, skills that emerged during the previous eighteen months become refined and expanded.

Stage III: Using Communicative Strategies

Communicative strategies enabling children to sustain conversations with others rapidly expand from approximately 3 to 5 years of age. Children can now initiate and maintain conversational topics (Ochs & Schieffelin, 1984), adapt messages to others (O'Neill, 1996; Shatz & Gelman, 1973; Shatz & O'Reilly, 1990), link statements together to pursue a particular line of reasoning (Eisenberg & Garvey, 1981; Haslett, 1983b), creatively role play in free play with peers (Garvey, 1977; Haslett, 1983c), and so forth. Children demonstrate considerable skill in interacting with others in many settings. In what follows, we examine three communicative devices—deixis, topicalization, and use of conversational maxims—support children's dialogues with others.

Deixis. Deixis refers to linguistic devices that clearly identify person, place, and time when communicating and that anchor the utterance to the communicative setting in which it occurs (Rees, 1978, p. 210). The most basic deictic element is the 'I–you' (speaker–listener) distinction in communication. Other linguistic devices, like demonstratives and adverbs, locate discourse referents in place ('here,' 'this') and in time ('now,' 'later') (Tfouni & Klatzky, 1983). Rees suggested that deictic features convey a significant amount of conversational meaning. According to Bruner (1975a), an understanding of reciprocal roles in discourse is necessary for deixis. During the two-word stage, youngsters use pronouns to refer to objects in the present environment but not to nonpresent objects. Charney (1979) noted that children (3½ years old) understand 'here' and 'there' from the speaker's perspective. DeVilliers and deVilliers (1979) reported that appropriate use of pronouns and demonstratives occurs between 4 or 5 years of age. Finally, deictic elements have also been analyzed in light of their role in cohesion and topic maintenance (deVilliers & deVilliers, 1979; Halliday & Hasan, 1983; Haslett, 1983a, 1987).

Topicalization. Topicalization refers to a speaker's ability to establish coherent discourse (i.e., both speaker and listener must be able to maintain the topic). According to Keenan and Schieffelin (1976), children at the one- and two-word stage can establish topics, get others' attention easily, speak clearly and intelligibly, and specify the objects being talked about. Many of these strategies for getting attention and identifying referents are nonverbal (e.g., pointing, touching).

Children also use presuppositions to maintain the topic. The relation between the propositional topic and its presupposition parallels the figure–ground relation: Children encode the new (the topic) against a background of mutually understood information (presupposition) (Bates, 1979). In a cross-cultural study of communicative strategies distinguishing new from given information, Bates and MacWhinney (1982) found that children used ellipsis, pronominalization, stress, and indefinite-definite pronouns to distinguish topics from their comments about topics.

Initiation and Maintenance Skills.

Initiation and Maintenance Skills. Young children need to develop ways to engage others in conversation. As previously noted, youngsters frequently use interruptions or questions to initiate conversations with adults. These devices work well because adults are typically attuned to children's signals and are willing to respond, but conversing with peers poses a more difficult task. The overtures must get attention, invite involvement, and be expressed in an understandable fashion (Ross & Lollis, 1987; Ross, Lollis & Elliot, 1982). Their study revealed that, at the ages of 20 to 22 months, toddlers used several different strategies for engaging unfamiliar others. These strategies included showing, giving, or offering objects to a peer; requesting objects from a peer; making declarative statements; using expressive actions or words; inviting a peer to play, or attempting to join a peer's play. The most frequently employed strategy was a direct attempt to join in the play of others, followed by expressive actions and invitations to play. Ross et al. estimated that approximately 60% of the responses showed some comprehension of the speaker's action. There was considerable individual variation among dyads, and noncompliance appeared to reflect an unwillingness to cooperate rather than a failure to understand the request. The frequency of a specific strategy was unrelated to its success or effectiveness.

Once a topic is established, however, children need to maintain this topic in conversation with others. The evidence appears to imply that children have limited success in maintaining a topic. Keenan and Schieffelin (1976) suggested that a limited attention span, misunderstanding of the preceding utterances, and distractibility may inhibit young children's ability to produce contingent, relevant responses. However, other studies, in a variety of settings (Garvey & Hogan, 1973; Haslett, 1983b; Haslett & Bowen, 1989) found that children can sustain topics during lengthy exchanges. Social interaction of children between 12 and 42 months, with varied partners in a day care setting, increased in effectiveness over time. More positive interactions and more successful initiations with peers occurred with increasing age (Holmberg, 1980). Children's ability to sustain interaction appears to be a function of their interest and involvement in the topic at hand, but sometimes being a good conversationalist requires participation even with boring topics (or partners!).

Contingent queries are another technique that keeps conversations going. Contingent queries have four components: an utterance, a contingent query (asking for clarification about the utterance), a response, and then a move back to the original conversation. For example,

Child: "Wanna ba!"

Mother: "What do you want?"

Child: "Ba!"

Mother: "Here's the ball. Let's go home now."

Children from 2 to 3 years of age understand and use contingent queries (Gallagher, 1981). Interestingly, studies of both preschoolers and school age children demonstrate that responding contingently and connectedly is important for social acceptance and friendship formation (Gottman, 1983; Hazen & Black, 1989). Kemple, Speranza, and Hazen (1992) found that preschoolers' inability to gain responses to social bids may contribute to low social acceptance. As these scholars noted: "The evidence indicates an association between young children's acceptance by peers, and their use of discourse tactics that contribute to . . . cohesive discourse" (p. 366).

Another class of skills important in maintaining conversations involves the ability to insert a comment in the conversation at an appropriate time. Over time, young children become better at conversational turn taking (without excessive overlap); youngsters find turn taking easier in dyadic, rather than triadic conversations. Dorval and Eckerman (1984) found that preschoolers had a difficult time processing conversations. They attribute these difficulties to (1) an inability to recognize when it is appropriate to make a comment (i.e., transition relevant pauses), (2) a failure to understand what is said quickly enough to respond before others do, and (3) a failure to identify when a specific person is expected to respond. Yet other work suggests that children's turn-taking abilities may be more sophisticated than previously thought. For example, Craig and Gallagher (1982) found that 4-year-olds who were acquainted with one another used eye gaze behavior to identify when it was appropriate to respond. In another study, they found that some preschoolers used overlaps and interruptions to dominate talk; as they noted, this strategy reflects considerable conversational competence rather than inadequacy (Gallagher & Craig, 1982).

Proximity to the speaker is also an important determinant of turn taking. Craig and Gallagher (1982) reported that children initially used proximity to indicate the potential for being interrupted. If a listener wishes to comment, then he or she must monitor the conversation; such monitoring is easier when you are close to the current speaker. Intonation can signal a speaker's willingness to be interrupted (like pausing or dropping intonation), but children do not appear to be particularly skilled at switching turns in this manner.

Forrester (1993) conducted a series of studies on how children responded to naming. Naming occurs when youngsters who are not actively participating in a conversation overhear their name or a reference made about them. In these situations, an adult was typically talking to another child (the addressed child) and referring to another child (the referred-to-child). During preschool years, Forrester observed that responsiveness to conversations in which children were named increased. In multiparty conversations, children looked at the children-being-addressed to see how they would respond; this nonverbal looking occurred for children 2½ to 4½ years of age. From 4½ to 5½ years of age, children anticipated a response from an addressed child and preempted it. These preemptive comments were relevant to the ongoing conversation. As Forrester concluded, among all age groups, referred-to-children did not respond immediately upon the mention of their names but rather looked at the addressed children, or made an appropriate remark before the addressed children began to reply. The precision of the timing of responses by referred-to-children, and their remarks, reflect a sophisticated understanding of when and how people can "take a turn in the conversation."

Gaining access to ongoing interaction is often problematic for preschoolers but is important because such interactions provide opportunities for children to develop and polish their social skills. Cosaro (1979) found that preschoolers relied on nonverbal entry (coming up to the play area) and comments (remarks or actions relevant to the ongoing play) in about 80% of their entry attempts. Repeated efforts to gain access increased the likelihood of entry into the play activity. Haslett and Bowen (1989) observed that preschoolers' most frequently used entry strategy was indirect scene setting, in which children made comments that complemented the ongoing activity; these bids were sucessful in initiating play activity 75% of the time. Bids to enter play also varied as a function of the group's composition. In the isolate condition (groups with one boy and three girls, or three boys with one girl), preschoolers' bids were least successful. Significantly more bids were attempted here than in same-sex or mixed-sex groups (two boys and two girls). Girls most often used indirect bids, especially scene-setting bids which elaborated the context in which the play occurred; such strategies help establish a shared basis for play among the youngsters. Boys used more direct play bids, especially direct commands. Haslett and Bowen suggested that three categories of children can be identified on the basis of their interactional skills: **agenda setters**, children with the highest level of skills, who initiate and dominate play; **responders**, children with the next level of interactional skill, who respond appropriately and maintain interaction; and **isolates**, children who do not recognize opportunities to interact with others or who respond inappropriately or too late. Children who successfully enter into a group's play have more opportunities to develop their communicative skills; one important skill they appear to have is the ability to connect, in some way, to the ongoing play.

Fantasy play also provides multiple learning opportunities. Bretherton (1989) noted that fantasy allows children to manage multiple roles and events, to invent their own plots or plans of action, and to gain more control over their emotions as they act out their roles. She found that secure, well-adjusted children displayed more emotional control during fantasy play that did insecure children. Garvey and Kramer (1989) reported that the communicative requirements of fantasy play involve changing meanings, negotiating the play scene, and acting out the "pretend" world while simultaneously being aware of the real world.

Conversational Maxims.   As you will recall, conversational maxims refer to implicit assumptions about the nature of conversational interaction. Grice (1975) formulated these maxims into four general expectations: Be truthful, be relevant, be clear, and be efficient (i.e., avoid redundancy). Grice suggested that these rules are general guidelines, and, when they are violated, this violation provides information that helps the listener interpret the message.

A study by Pellegrini, Brody, and Stoneman (1987) investigated children's violations of maxims in their conversations with their parents. Violations of maxims decreased with age, and fathers, more than mothers, were directive in responding to their children's violations. These violations are interpreted as reflecting younger children's inability to use their knowledge of maxims to govern their speech.

During the communicative strategies stage, the complexity of communication increases substantially, language itself becomes more complex, and children begin to interact with peers as well as adults in diverse settings. To meet these demands, children refine and extend basic skills previously acquired. Joint attention and reference, developed in earlier preverbal routines between mother and infant, are now precisely fine-tuned through children's use of deictic elements. Children also begin to use pronouns, demonstratives, and locatives to specify the relationships between objects, events, and individuals and to focus attention on these relationships. Children's ability to execute these conversational strategies has been found to predict the kinds of friendships they develop as well as the level of acceptance they enjoy among peers. Being a successful and sought-after conversational partner is important because it affords young children multiple opportunities for developing other communication skills characteristic of peer–peer interaction (e.g., prosocial and conflict management). (In chapters 7 and 8, we take a more detailed look at the interrelationships among communication skills and friendship development.)

Development Contexts.   Three specific contexts deserve more detailed attention because of their developmental significance. Conflict management and friendship provide two important communicative and developmental contexts; effective interaction in both provides the foundation for successful interpersonal relationships. Gender differences are established in early infancy and influence subsequent communicative styles. Although friendship is thoroughly covered in chapters 7 and 8, we would like to briefly indicate interactional skills that facilitate the establishment of friendship and underlie later intimate relationships. Our focus on friendship and conflict management in this chapter emphasizes how communication skills are used in these contexts.

A. Friendship. Infants, toddlers, and preschoolers have friends; 75% of preschoolers 5 years of age have a close relationship with another child, and about 30% have more than one close relationship (Howes, 1983, 1988). The friendship network, however, remains limited for both girls and boys.

Most scholars have argued that friendship is defined as a reciprocal, committed relationship between equals. Children, like adults, have strong emotional commitments to friends. According to Hartup (1989b, 1996), the main foundations of friendship, common interests and affiliation, are recognized in early childhood; among preschoolers, common activities and concrete reciprocity (e.g., sharing and exchanging toys, helping when having trouble with something) create friendships. Scholars generally agree that with increasing age, children's concepts of friendship become more flexible, complex, and differentiated (Hartup, 1992).

Hartup (1989a) also noted that infants and toddlers differ in their social interaction skills. Some infants who are deliberately sought after are more active initiators, respond more contingently to overtures by others, and are responded to contingently by others (Lee, 1973). When infants and toddlers create an atmosphere of acceptance through reciprocal and complementary behaviors, friendships follow. Howes (1983) defined dyadic friendship according to the success of children's social overtures to each other, their complementary actions, and mutual positive affect. Other studies demonstrate the importance of friends as sources of support, fun, and security (Azmitia, 1988; Ipsa, 1981). Popularity during ages 4 and 5 is related to prosocial behavior (giving gifts, being accepting), and preschoolers generally display more prosocial behaviors to their friends than to acquaintances (Hartup, Glazer, & Charlesworth, 1967).

Friends also interact differently than do nonfriends. In a study of peer teaching and game playing, 4- to 6-year-old friends and acquaintances interacted with one another (Brachfield-Child & Schiavo, 1990). Results indicated that friends were more involved with each other, more expressive, and more competitive than were acquainted pairs. Partners taught by friends responded in a more playful, friendly manner than did children taught by acquaintances. Interestingly, peers who taught friends were more domineering than peers teaching acquaintances. In a prisoner's dilemma game, preschoolers who were good friends were more likely to seek mutually satisfactory solutions and were more involved and relaxed with one another than were pairs of nonfriends. Friends also tended to have more fantasy in their mutual play than did nonfriends (Roopnarine & Field, 1983).

Expectations and behaviors begin to change as a function of perceptions of friendship, even in rudimentary stages of friendship. Important themes such as commitment, affiliation, and reciprocity play significant roles in preschoolers' friendships and form the basis for more elaborated, complex conceptualizations of friendship. (Chapters 7 and 8 cover friendship development in greater detail.)

B. Conflict Management. Conflict provides a context in which children must negotiate rules, roles, and property rights among equals. Youngsters do not necessarily accommodate to each other in the same way as adults or parents accommodate to them. With peers, the arguments and reasoning are on similar cognitive and social levels as opposed to dealing with an adult's superior status and knowledge. Much attention has been give to factors that contribute to children's predispositions for and resolution of conflict, such as problematic interactions in the home, family stressors, and intergenerational influences on antisocial behavior (Patterson, DeBarsyche, & Ramsey, 1989). As Ross and Conant (1992) pointed out, through conflicts with peers, children confront opposition on issues of importance to them, evaluate and interpret different experiences, and question their own and others' arguments. They also noted that conflict creates its own social structure, sometimes involving third parties, and requires adjustments to maintain social relationships with others. (See Duncan, 1991, for an excellent discussion of the conventional structure in children's arguments.)

Eisenberg and Garvey (1981) defined the stages of young children's arguments; their classic study is used as a benchmark for research on argumentation. According to these scholars, arguments progress through four different stages:

1. Stage 1 is the stage of **initial opposition.** Opposition becomes apparent, as in protests or challenges to another child.
2. Stage 2 reflects **mutual opposition.** Here one child resists or disagrees with the another child's initial action. If a child gives way to the first child's protest, then the issue is resolved. Haslett (1983) argues that the initial protest must be countered for the interaction to be viewed as conflict; a conciliatory response would end the opposition.
3. Stage 3 involves **oppositional strategies.** A wide range of strategies are pursued during the conflict, and these are modified according to the strategies others employ in the conflict.
4. Stage 4 is the **conflict ending.** Conflicts are either resolved, or one or both parties may not continue the opposition.

Initial opposition can occur as a result of almost any behavior, although moves like taking another child's toy or being verbally agressive increase the likelihood of conflict (Caplan, Vespo, Pederson, & Hay, 1991; Laursen & Hartup, 1989). Conflicts are typically triggered by verbal comments, such as arguments, demands, or insults, when children are older (Haslett, 1983b; Phinney, 1986).

With increasing age, youngsters' oppositional strategies move from physical retaliation and verbalizing protests to more differentiated verbal comments, such as denials, refusals, insults, and appeals to third parties (Caplan, Vespo, Pedersen, & Hay, 1991; Eisenberg & Garvey, 1981; Haslett, 1983b). Two-year-olds frequently resolved a conflict by sharing toys, even when toys were scarce; interestingly, groups dominated by boys used prosocial ways to resolve conflict (Caplan, Vespo, Pedersen, & Hay, 1991). By 5, children employ reasoning and moral appeals in their arguments (Haslett, 1983b; Phinney, 1986). Ross and Conant (1992) noted that physical agression is rarely used for initial opposition, and with age, verbal protests are increasingly used.

Facial expressions also signal aggression or opposition. Stares, lowered brows, lips pressed together, grimaces, and other such expressions can convey opposition (Camras, 1977). Camras observed that children who displayed aggressive facial expressions seemed to intimidate their partners; their partners waited longer to try to regain objects taken from them, and the children with aggressive expressions were likely to resist these attempts to regain objects. Zivin (1977a) found that children won conflicts 66% of the time when displaying a *plus* face (raised brows, wide eyes, direct gaze, and raised chin), whereas when displaying a *minus* face (slightly knitted brows, lowered eyes, and chin) children lost conflicts 85% of the time. Gestures, such as pointing and reaching, called forth protective reactions from peers (Conant, 1987).

Toddlers' remarks during conflict frequently consist of negatives and statements of possession (e.g., "That's mine"; Hay & Ross, 1982). During the second year, children increasingly use verbal comments to control conflict episodes (Brownell & Brown, 1985). With increasing age, more elaborate verbal strategies are employed, including multiparty arguments and extended reasoning (Haslett, 1983b; Phinney, 1986). Eisenberg and Garvey (1981) found that compromise, sharing, giving new information, acknowledging others' perspectives, conditional agreements, and suggested alternatives were useful in resolving arguments. As they noted, these strategies give opponents "something to work with" and thus resolution is more likely than if simple denials or counterassertions are used. With increasing age, preschoolers developed active argumentative strategies (Haslett, 1983b). Haslett found that as children developed more cognitive and communicative complexity, they were able to counter and anticipate others' remarks and thus adapt to them. By 5, children engaged in lengthy multiparty arguments. Ross and Conant (1992) suggested that preschoolers are adept at taking into account their opponents' actions and views and respond effectively. Strayer and Strayer (1976) noted that two underlying behavior modes—involved-attractive and aggressive-dominant—shape preschoolers' social adaptation during the preschool years.

Conflict was also settled in different ways depending upon the issue at hand (Ross & Conant, 1992). Factual arguments needed to be agreed upon so that play or other activity could continue. Conflicts over possessions, over including others in play, or over others' behavior had clear winners; a child might be included or excluded, behavior accepted, or apologies given. Some conflicts, especially those involving psychological harm or disruption of behavior, were often unresolved (Killen & Turiel, 1991). Conflict started by aggression ended in compromise more often than did other types of conflict (Laursen & Hartup, 1989). Conciliation has been found to resolve conflict among preschoolers in approximately one third of their conflicts (Laursen & Hartup, 1989; Sacklin & Thelen, 1984).

1. Gender Differences in Conflict. Gender differences also occur in conflict. Boys' negotiation of conflict is usually more direct; girls use more indirect strategies and rely on mitigating strategies that maintain good interpersonal relationships (Miller, Danaher, & Forbes, 1986). Sheldon (1992) found that girls used a double-voice discourse in their conflict talk. That is, they simultaneously address their own agenda while orienting to the other's viewpoint in same-sex conflict episodes. Sheldon suggested that girls are skilled at constructive conflict management, in which mitigation downplays coercive persuasion, facilitates adjustment, and restores group functioning. Although boys as well as girls can use double-voice discourse (Sheldon & Johnson, 1991), girls' use of double voice appears to be a function of their solidarity-based, relationally oriented groups.

Girls used more collaborative speech to manage conflict (e.g., direct and affiliative, such as invitations to play), and boys used more controlling conflict management strategies (e.g., direct and distancing, such as orders or insults) (Leaper, 1991). Some studies have found girls using assertive strategies that are more polite and ingratiating than are boys' strategies (Camras, 1984; Sachs, 1987). Sheldon (1992) suggested that girls handle conflict in a fundamentally different way from boys; girls' assertiveness "requires responsiveness to others, whereas masculine agency does not necessarily do so" (p. 99).

Children also handled anger with regard to their social relationship with their opponent. Popular preschoolers used more active, direct strategies to handle anger and coped in a manner that minimized further conflict and disruption. Girls tended to use more assertive tactics while boys tended to vent more (Fabes & Eisenberg, 1992). Children used more passive strategies when angered by adults (such as ignoring and distancing); more active, coping responses were used to respond to peers (such as yelling) (Karniol & Heinman, 1987).

Conflicts thus provide an opportunity for developing social and communicative skills. Social skills are developed as children negotiate their relationships with others. Children appear to have less hostile conflicts with friends and to depend on them for support (Hartup, Laursen, Stewart, & Eastenson, 1988; Ross & Conant, 1992). Communicative skills develop as peers must deal with opposition, counter arguments, and justify their own actions (Strayer, 1990).

Up to this point, we have focused on how children expand their competencies as speakers. In the final stage of communicative development, **Monitoring Communication,** children begin to shift their attention to the message itself—its accuracy, clarity, and effectiveness. This message orientation rests on children's ability to metacommunicate, to treat the act of communication itself as an object of evaluation and discussion. Metacommunicative ability begins to emerge at around 5 years of age, and by middle childhood, children have a well-established set of metacommunicative strategies that they apply to messages and listeners (see, e.g., Flavell, Speer, Green, & August, 1981; O'Keefe & Delia, 1979, 1982).

Stage IV: Monitoring Communication

Flavell et al. (1981) argued that communication must be analyzed with reference to other cognitive processes. His research suggested that young children may fail at communication because they do not treat "messages as analyzable cognitive objects" (p. 27). Although aspects of metacommunicative monitoring are well established around 5, metacommunicative comments appear earlier. Utterances such as "He said no" are reported by children between 30 and 36 months (Bates, 1979). Although these comments seem to serve as a report or verification of an event, they nevertheless demonstrate that children can treat talk as an object (i.e., talk can be discussed). The use of politeness also reflects monitoring because it indicates that talk is being adjusted appropriately to people, the situation, or both.

Disputes provide an ideal opportunity for studying communicative monitoring because such monitoring appears to be necessary for constructing arguments and gaining one's ends. Many researchers have analyzed the communicative rules and strategies children use in arguments (Benoit, 1981; O'Keefe & Benoit, 1982). This research has generally indicated that with increasing age, children rely more on messages that contain more information (Eisenberg & Garvey, 1981) and that reflect more flexible strategies and more adaptation to listeners (Delia, Kline, & Burleson, 1979). That is, messages become cognitively and communicatively more complex and more coordinated with the messages of others (Haslett, 1983b). Thus children gradually become more attuned to the communicative demands of disputes and more adept at trying to accomplish their goals. Such ability, again, presupposes growing differentiation in children's metacommunicative knowledge about themselves, about others, about their relationships with others, and about task demands (Applegate & Delia, 1980; Bateson, 1976; Glick, 1978; Shatz & O'Reilly, 1990; Strayer, 1986).

Many models of cognitive and communicative monitoring rest on the assumption that children can identify the *literal* meaning of a speaker's statement and can distinguish it from the speaker's *intended* meaning (Bonitatibus, 1988). An utterance's literal meaning sometimes matches the speaker's intended meaning, but at other times there is no match between them. Studies suggest that children who successfully monitor statements are able to understand and focus on the message's literal meaning, whereas nonmonitors do not. In analyzing failed communication, Robinson and Robinson (1976a,b) found that successful monitors relied on literal meaning to help make these assessments. Children appear to rely most on literal meanings of messages to judge their referential adequacy.

Monitoring also implies that children evaluate their messages with respect to their adequacy for listeners. For example, Shatz and Gelman (1973) found that 4-year-olds adapted their speech to 2-year-olds and demonstrated an awareness of their listeners' restricted capacities for understanding. Peterson, Danner and Flavell (1972) found that children could reframe their messages when explicitly asked to do so but did not reframe when only nonverbal signals of noncomprehension were given. Young children were effective in repairing their own messages, but their responses to parental requests for clarification were less clear (Shatz & O'Reilly, 1990). Other types of monitoring include the recognition of discourse conventions such as the need to respond to questions (McShane, 1980).

Message clarity is also a function of *who* is sending the message as well as *what* is being said. Russell (1984) varied types of message sent and asked children to evaluate them. Messages included plausible or implausible solutions to a practical problem and personal statements about the speaker which subjects were to guess were true or false. Speaker characteristics (relative age and social dominance) were also varied. Older children (7- to 9-year-olds) were able to use inferences about speaker characteristics and the truth of statements to judge messages; younger children did not appear to use speaker characteristics to evaluate messages.

Another more subtle aspect of message evaluation and interpretation is the capacity to detect sarcasm. Ackerman (1983) found that first graders could distinguish between sincere and sarcastic messages. A later study (Ackerman, 1986) demonstrated that after undergoing training sessions, 7-year-olds were able to explain what was meant by sarcastic messages by answering a series of yes–no questions. Capelli, Nakagawa, and Madden (1990) contrasted contextual cues with intonation cues in detecting sarcasm and found that children initially depended primarily on intonation cues.

Children generally tend to overestimate the communicative adequacy of messages and to regard them as much more informative than they really are (Dickson, 1981; Whitehurst & Sonnenschein, 1981). For example, children judged a message as informative when they could construct an interpretation of the intended meaning (Beal & Belgrad, 1990); when they could make unwarranted assumptions about the intended meaning (Speer, 1984); or when they were directly told what the intended meaning was (Beal & Flavell, 1984).

Preschoolers' responses to ambiguous messages are quite variable. Older children (second graders) were more accurate at detecting ambiguities than were younger children (Beal & Belgrad, 1990). Sodian (1990, 1991) found that 7- and 8-year-olds know they can deliberately mislead others by producing ambiguous messages. Depending upon their own certainty about the accuracy of their interpretation, children respond differently to ambiguous and unambiguous messages (Robinson & Whittaker, 1985).

In an intriguing test of responses to ambiguous and unambiguous messages, preschoolers watched puppet characters talking in three different conditions. In one condition, puppet listeners responded to clear messages from a puppet speaker by complying with the requested action. In the second condition, puppets listening to an ambiguous message responded by stating that because the message was ambiguous, they did not know what to do. In the third condition, the puppet listening to the ambigous message insisted that one of two possible referents was clearly being referred to. Kindergartners' judgments of message adequacy were influenced by the puppet character's message as well as by the response of the puppet listening to the message. Singer and Flavell (1981) argued that children's developing ability to evaluate messages includes the awareness that a poor message remains a poor message regardless of listeners' responses. When interpreting vague instructions, kindergartners were more confident of their interpretations when the speaker was cooperative and cues to salient referents were present (Speer, 1984). With increasing age, preschoolers could identify an adequate message and locate the problems contained in an inadequate message (children moved from no awareness of the problem, to recognizing a problem, to being able to identify the nature of the problem; Lempers & Elrod, 1983).

Finally, children realize that personal characteristics affect their judgments of messages. For example, preschoolers are aware that their emotions and fatigue influence learning (Hayes, Scott, Chemelski, & Johnson, 1987). Not only do children monitor their own emotional states and understand how this influences their awareness, but they also explicitly monitor their own messages. Kindergartners demonstrated considerable communicative monitoring and used word corrections, repetitions, inserted ideas, and other means to repair their messages. Second graders were more adept at repairing their own messages than were kindergartners (Evans, 1985).

The monitoring communication stage focuses interactants' attention on the message and its addressees (Flavell, 1979). Children begin to evaluate message adequacy, to adapt their messages when conflict with others' goals is recognized, to discuss the communication process explicitly, and to utilize knowledge of others in constructing their communicative strategies. These skills emerge at age 5 and become well established in middle childhood. By monitoring communication, children become increasingly adept at sending socially appropriate messages in a variety of contexts. Monitoring appears to rely on a network of skills ranging from awareness of the literal meaning of a message, to subtle distinctions about sarcasm or manipulations by the speaker, to personal mood states.

SUMMARY

Throughout this chapter, we have explored children's emerging communication skills. Early in infancy, children have a sensitivity to and understanding of communication as a means of establishing relationships and cooperating with others.

We termed this first stage of development *recognizing the interpersonal nature of communication.* The next stage, *creating communicative effects,* extends from approximately 4 months to 3 years; during this stage, children move from pre-verbal routines to well-established linguistic communication. Children intentionally communicate their views using a variety of speech acts to accomplish differing goals, and language is used to express a range of functions (e.g., expressive, directive, informative). In the next stage, *utilizing communicative strategies,* children refine and extend communication skills like turn taking, maintaining topic, using deixis, and coordinating their messages with others to accomplish differing purposes. This stage, from approximately 3 to 5 years, is also marked by increased interaction with peers. Communication strategies may expand because children are not just communicating with adults who often anticipate and fill in the missing gaps in their messages but are also interacting with peers whose knowledge and capacities are roughly equivalent to their own. The final stage of children's pragmatic communicative skills, *monitoring communication,* develops at around 5 years. Youngsters begin to metacommunicate, at times commenting on their own talk, distinguishing ambiguous from non-ambiguous messages, making conversational repairs, and so forth. (For a summary of these stages and their communicative achievements, see Table 4.1.)

Each developmental stage reflects added cognitive and communicative complexity. The process of communication itself becomes more difficult over time, as language is added as a communicative tool, as tasks become more varied and complex, and as interactants and settings become more diverse. As children mature, adults also expect more and thus "up the ante"; communicative demands are correspondingly increased. The increase in peer–peer interaction, at around 3 years of age, also adds considerable complexity to interpersonal interaction. Although adults typically accommodate their communication to children's cognitive levels, no such accommodation is possible by peers. Thus, children must develop communication strategies that enable them to send socially appropriate, adapted messages.

This ability, however, is not just a matter of the pragmatic skills and strategies discussed throughout this chapter. Children also need to acquire social knowledge about communication which enables them to exercise these various skills and strategies in appropriate settings and at appropriate times. The ability to communicate effectively involves a complex cognitive assessment of the communicative task, the interactants, and the social setting.

Before turning to a more thorough discussion of how children acquire the social knowledge necessary for communication, a brief caution is in order. The unfortunate dichotomy between linguistic form and linguistic function is also present in the treatments of communication skills and communication knowledge. In order to communicate effectively, people must possess effective communication skills, but these skills are relatively useless without the communication knowledge that enables one to use the skills appropriately. Most researchers focus on either communication skills or communication knowledge, and it is easy to understand why: Tracing the development of either the communication skills or the knowledge base for interpersonal interaction is in itself tremendously complex. But for theories of communication to develop, such integration is necessary.

The next chapter on communication knowledge details the growth of social-cognitive knowledge that allows children to make appropriate use of their developing communication skills. As we shall see, this knowledge, like communication skills themselves, develops in a myriad of different contexts and with different conversational partners.

5

Developing Communicative
Knowledge

As previously discussed, when we examine the communicative skills children develop in early childhood, we see only one aspect of the child's communicative competence. Communication scholars are also interested in representing the social knowledge that enables children to communicate appropriately. Social-cognitive knowledge develops gradually over time as the youngster's interact with others in diverse contexts. Such knowledge includes knowledge about people, social situations, and common sense or tacit knowledge about how things are done (cultural knowledge) as well as how the world works physically (the knowledge gained from practical experience). By using this knowledge to help interpret what is going on, children are able to adapt their messages to others and to communicate appropriately in context. For example, using politeness strategies depends upon understanding when it is appropriate to be polite (e.g., young children addressing older people). Much of this knowledge is tacit and taken-for-granted; children learn by making mistakes, by being corrected by others and observing others.

The separate research agendas for studying communication skills and communication knowledge may partly reflect the split between linguistic competence and linguistic performance discussed in chapter 3. Communication knowledge and communication skills develop simultaneously during children's interactions. Communication skill enables children to interact with others while communication knowledge enables children to do so effectively; effective interactions, in turn, allow children to gain more knowledge and more skills. These two components mutually interact and influence each other. For purposes of analytic clarity, we have discussed communication skills in chapter 4 and cover the development of communication knowledge in this chapter. At the end of this chapter, we discuss social reasoning and argumentation in some detail; in these two arenas the interplay between knowledge and skill can be clearly seen.

The critical aspects of social-cognitive knowledge underlying communicative competence include distinguishing self from others, increasing differentiation in the knowledge of others, and developing knowledge about relationships with others, such as authority relationships or friendships. Social-cognitive knowledge also reflects growing understanding of social contexts, such as home or classroom contexts.

DEVELOPING SOCIAL KNOWLEDGE ABOUT COMMUNICATION

Children's communicative development relies on social-cognitive knowledge as well as on the communication skills reviewed in the last chapter. This knowledge base develops gradually as young children interact with more people in a wide variety of situations. Dimitracopoulou (1990) suggested that the types of socio-cognitive knowledge required for conversational competence include: (a) the ability to take another's perspective (i.e., role taking); (b) the ability to attribute inner states to others (such as intentions); (c) the realization that others' internal states may differ from a person's own; (d) an understanding of animacy and causality; (e) an understanding of social rules and social contexts; and (f) knowledge of conventional uses of words (such as metaphor) (p. 42).

Hartup (1989b) noted that two relationships, vertical and horizontal, are crucial for children's ongoing social-cognitive development. In the context of close relationships, Hartup argued, "Language emerges; so does a repertoire for coordinating one's actions with those of others, one's knowledge of oneself, and much of one's knowledge about the world" (p. 120). Vertical relationships are those relationships with people, typically with adult caretakers, who have greater knowledge and social power than children and that consist of complementary actions. In contrast, horizontal relationships provide the context for refining and practicing the basic social skills acquired in vertical relationships. Cooperation, competition, and intimacy develop in horizontal relationships.

As noted in the last chapter, Haslett (1984, 1987) has articulated three broad stages in the acquisition of social knowledge relevant to communication. The most fundamental social distinction needed for communication is the I–thou, speaker–listener distinction, which appears to develop during the first year of life. As more interactions occur with a wider variety of interactants, a more finely differentiated knowledge of others is necessary for effective communication (Chandler, 1982; Chandler & Chapman, 1991; Flavell et al., 1981; Shantz, 1981). This increasingly differentiated knowledge of others gradually emerges during early childhood: by age 5, children have internalized interpersonal constructs of others (O'Keefe & Delia, 1982).

As knowledge of others increases, so too does children's knowledge of social situations and their communicative requirements. Knowledge of others and of social situations develops concomitantly; knowledge of others is undoubtedly facilitated by interacting with others in contexts that highlight different aspects of their personalities. Knowledge of the communicative demands in particular settings may be facilitated by observing how different individuals handle these situations. Assessing children's developing social knowledge about communication offers insight into how individuals begin to establish and maintain interpersonal relations with each other as well as the essential role communication plays in this process. Each of these aspects of social knowledge—knowledge of self as distinct from others, knowledge of others and knowledge of social situations—is discussed below. Although knowledge of self as distinct from others appears to precede and be necessary for knowledge of others and of social situations, no other interactions are advocated here. (See Table 5.1 for an overview and time line for these developmental stages.)

TABLE 5.1
Stages in Children's Development of Communicative Knowledge

Age	*Developmental Stages*	*Communicative Accomplishments*
0–12 mos	I. **Self distinguished from others**	Recognizes animacy and independence of actions of others; becomes aware of other's intentions; recognizes potential of others for social interaction
Begins at 12 mos	II. **Differentiated knowledge of others**	Through the processes of person perception and role taking, gradually begins to recognize the dispositional qualities of others, the communicative and personal requisites of certain roles and situational constraints in communication
Begins at 12 mos, marked growth at around 36 mos	III. **Knowledge of communicative context**	
	Relational knowledge	Initially, possesses relational knowledge about interaction with familiar others; with increasing interaction with peers, relational knowledge incorporates knowledge about general social relations (like authority, friendship, etc.) and knowledge about others as unique individuals
	Social situation	Recognizes communicative demands of different social settings; context provides background knowledge about appropriate behavior

Knowledge of Self as Distinct From Others

An infant's interactions with responsive others enable them to develop emotional attachment and communication (Bruner, 1983; Damon, 1981; Stern, 1977). By 8 or 9 months of age, infants appear to have a sense of personal agency and use objects to obtain goals (Wolf, 1981). Wolf argued that from 9 to 15 months, infants realize the separateness of self from others. Attachment to and fear of separation from familiar others also become evident during this time, and infants recognize that others act as independent agents (Gelman & Spelke, 1981; Harding & Golinkoff, 1979). This sense of separate identity is fundamental to the I–thou, speaker–listener distinction in dialogue.

According to Lewis (1991), three levels of the self emerge during the first two years of life. *Sensorimotor affect knowledge*, from birth to eight months, reflects inborn reflexes, such as swallowing and sucking; from four to eight months, reflexes linked to the environment develop, such as the reaching action patterns. The second level of self emerges from 8 to 18 months and adds representational knowledge to infants' existing sensorimotor affect knowledge. Children can remember actions and events; thus new types of knowledge and meaning emerge. The third level, *abstract* or *symbolic knowledge*, enables children to use symbolic processes to learn and acquire knowledge. Categorization and classification, for example, become important tools for knowing. All levels of knowledge, according to Lewis, continue to develop and mature.

Like Lewis, Neisser (1991) developed a rich, multilevel view of infants' growing sense of self. He suggested that the self develops ecologically through perceptual processes, such as locating the self in space and time, as well as through interpersonal processes that emerge as infants interact and perceive the environment with others. Neisser also discussed the extended self, which is based on memory and expressed by narratives and stories. Narrative events, both stories children hear as well as those they tell, contribute to their understanding of the world.

In a longitudinal study of a single child, Wolf (1981) found that the concept of independent agency emerged in three stages. First, others were regarded as instruments; second, others were regarded as equivalent human actors, and finally, others were regarded as independent agents. These stages developed at different times in different content domains. New levels emerged first in goal-directed interaction, then in games, next in language and doll play, and finally, in addressing a co-participant in dramatic play. Wolf pointed out that human interaction is the outcome of several independent actors' contributing to a situation; participants need to coordinate their own self-generated plans with other interactants (p. 299).

Part of children's sense of self is the degree of control they can exert over their own actions as well as the extent to which they can influence the actions of others. Galejs, Hegland, and King (1986) found that preschoolers' perceptions of their control over others varied as a function of *who* the others were. Preschoolers perceived most control over social interactions with teachers and parents and least control over peers and, interestingly, themselves. Results are not surprising because peers are typically less responsive than are adults and represent more difficult interactional partners, as noted in chapter 4. In another study, Hegland and Galejs (1983) observed that children perceived more control over negative rather than positive outcomes; responses of younger children were not primarily egocentric, and perceptions of control did not vary as a function of age. Because many have argued that locus of control develops as a stable personality trait through interactions with parents, the lack of change in perceptions of control with increasing age is not surprising.

Infants' social understanding at the end of the first year incorporates coordinated representations of others' activities and events and representations about their own manipulations of objects (Emde, Biringen, Clyman & Oppenheim, 1991; Moore & Corkum, 1994). When an infant and an adult are paying attention to the same object, the infant is able to recognize the match between his or her own psychological state and that of another's. As Moore and Corkum stated, "these representations would form the foundation for categories of psychological understanding and, presumably, ultimately a full theory of mind" (p. 369). Interestingly, virtually all accounts of how infants develop selfhood, intentionality, and shared knowledge rely on interaction as a catalyst for realization of these mental constructs. (Moore & Corkum, 1994, have provided an excellent overview of alternative developmental explanations for social understanding.)

In an intriguing study, R. Eder (1990) assessed young children's perceptions of their psychological selves. Youngsters, ages 3½ to 7½, were asked to pick a statement that best described themselves; these paired statements represented the high and low end points of various dimensions. For example, to measure sociability, children would choose either "It's more fun to play with other children than by myself" or "It's more fun to play by myself than with others." The nine dimensions measured were achievement, aggression, alienation, harm–avoidance, social closeness, social potency, stress reaction, traditionalism, and general well-being. These dimensions were then factor analyzed, and three factors emerged for each age group. Salient dimensions in the self-concepts for 3½-year-olds included self-control, general self-acceptance, and rejection. For 5½-year-olds, salient concepts involved self-control, self-acceptance via achievement, and self-acceptance via affiliation. For 7½-year-olds, relevant self-concepts focused on emotional stability, extraversion, and determined fearlessness. By age 3½, children had "rudimentary dispositional concepts of themselves" (p. 861). Eder argued that these findings suggest that children have an elaborated sense of self which allows them to identify behaviors and feelings as consistent or inconsistent with their self-concepts. Eder believed that dispositional self-concepts are available for use by children without their being aware of them or able to articulate them.

Attachment and the Concept of Self. As you will recall, attachment refers to the connection between mother and child or between child and primary caretaker, established during the first year of life and measures the accessibility and sensitivity of the caretaker to the child. When caretakers consistently respond with warmth and sensitivity, children are securely attached and view the environment as a supportive one in which they can trust others. In contrast, when caretakers respond inconsistently and indifferently, insecure attachment develops and infants do not feel that the environment is trusting and nurturing. Insecure attachment can be of two types, insecure-avoidant and insecure-resistant. As discussed in chapters 2 and 6, the work of Ainsworth, Bowlby, and others found attachment to be correlated with personality development, interaction skills, and other important variables. Our concern here is the relationship of attachment to the development of the self-concept and self-esteem.

Sroufe (1989) claimed that the self may be viewed as an "inner organization of attitudes, feelings, expectations, and meanings, which arises from an organized caregiving matrix" (p. 71). The attachment between infants and caregivers precedes and supports infants' self-development, which, in turn, influences their adaptation and experience in later life. The self is viewed as a social organization, which develops from interaction with others. Over time, existing capacities and levels of organization in the self are integrated into new, more complex organizational levels.

Because the inner organization of the self evolves as a function of interaction with others, attachment plays a central role in this evolution (Eder, 1990; Emde, 1976, 1982, 1988). Sroufe (1989) and others have detailed a series of phases, which reflect important issues that infants face throughout self-development. These theories are substantially similar to other explanations of development during the first year, especially because the self is viewed as emerging from social interaction. The phases include:

Basic regulation—from birth to 3 months; infants and caretakers establish synchrony around states of relative activity and quiet.

Reciprocal exchange—from 3 to 6 months; infants and caregivers establish interaction sequences. Infants actively participate, but coordination is largely created by the caregiver. Infants enjoy these exchanges, and the repetition of the exchanges lays the groundwork for initiating such exchanges in the next phase.

Initiative—from 6 to 9 months; infants begin to engage in goal-directed activity, aimed both toward and away from caregivers. There is genuine reciprocity and inner-directed behavior.

Focalization—from 9 to 12 months; infants center their explorations around the home base provided by caregivers. Bowlby (1973) argued that "working models" of the world develop during this period and focus on the attachment figures (caregivers) in the environment and their expected responses to infants' activities.

Self-assertion—from 12 to 24 months; toddlers actively pursue their own goals and realize inner goals that may be counter to the wishes of caregivers. Children separate themselves both physically and psychologically from caregivers; attachment provides the basis for children's autonomy and in turn leads to a redefined parent–child attachment.

Recognition and continuity—from 18 to 36 months; with the development of the symbolic capacity of language, children recognize that shared awareness exists, especially between children and caregivers. Children also gain a sense of the constancy and continuity in the parent–child relationship and consolidate their sense of self and their control over their own behaviors.

The common theme of these phases and other explanations of self-development appears to be that infants' emerging patterns of self-organization evolve from the context of early dyadic interactions with caregivers. These patterns of self-organization are related to later social adaptations to the world. As Sroufe (1989) commented, "From dyadic organization built through care giver responsiveness to infant states and signals, to more reciprocal relationship organization in which the infant is an active participant, to a self-organizing child, the inner core of self develops" (p. 83).

The attachment bond in early infancy is important for infants' subsequent development as well. Suess, Grossman, and Sroufe (1992) found that the overall adaptation of children to the challenges of preschool were strongly related to attachment history. Securely attached children functioned competently and had few behavioral problems; insecurely attached children were not as successful. Suess et al. argued that attachment leads to different views of the social world; children with anxious attachments view others as less available and more threatening. These expectations then create an atmosphere that may lead to rejection by teachers and peers. Conflict resolution was also found to vary as a function of attachment style; youngsters with a secure attachment handled conflict personally (i.e., by dealing with the other children), but children with insecure attachment handled problems by running away or by letting a teacher handle the conflicts.

Children's developmental history, particularly their attachment to caregivers, interacts with their genetic background and the current environment to influence children's overall behavior and development (Sroufe, Egeland, & Kruetzer, 1991). They observed that children grouped on the basis of their attachment history reacted very differently in controlled environments like preschool and summer camp. Children who were anxiously attached were socially isolated, had more contact with adults, and were more dependent than were securely attached children (Elicker, Englund, & Sroufe, 1992). Attachment history also predicted children's subsequent adaptation in toddler, preschool, and middle childhood (Sroufe, 1982, 1983, 1989; Sroufe, Egeland, & Kreutzer, 1990).

Quality of attachment during infancy is also related to quality of maternal support as is toddlers' enthusiasm, compliance, and persistence (Matas, Arend, & Sroufe, 1978). Securely attached children are more self-reliant, emphatic, cooperative with adults, and less hostile with peers (Sroufe, 1989). As Sroufe noted, however, attachment is only one aspect of development and must be considered against the contributions of other factors. The most salient effects from attachment influence children's confidence, efficacy, and self-worth. These factors contribute to many other behaviors, such as friendship and peer interaction. (In chapter 6, we look at how the attachment bond and its relationship to children's growing sense of self influence a variety of relational outcomes throughout life.)

Narrated stories help young children develop a sense of self and of others. Narratives are important ways in which children reconceptualize themselves, others, and their relationships in the social world (Bruner, 1986). Co-narrated stories (stories co-told by children and other siblings or adults) were interpersonal in nature and included the experiences of others. Miller, Mintz, Hoogstra, Fung, and Potts (1992) found that stories told by 2½- to 5-year-olds used three basic strategies—joint activity, social comparison, and "other benefits to the self"—to narrate their stories in conjunction with other family members. Older children used longer utterances and more references to peers and needed less help in telling the story. Self–other distinctions were made in the story itself as well as in the narration of the story. In another study, P. Miller, Potts, Fung, Hoogstra, and Mintz (1990) found such storytelling practices to be used in several cultural settings. Thus, narratives offer another venue in which sense of self develops and are important because the self emerges through collaboration with others in joint storytelling. Narratives also offer a different interactional opportunity for youngsters by enabling them to appreciate diverse viewpoints and responses to situations.

In brief, infants' emerging sense of self develops through social interaction with others. Significant understandings during this period include the self–other distinction, locus of control, animacy, and agency. Attachment also profoundly influences children's basic sense of self and confidence, and these effects are experienced throughout life. Another important aspect of self-identity is gender. It is to this issue we now turn.

Selfhood, Gender Identification, and Gender Differences.   Gender is an important part of people's self-concept; it is a fundamental aspect of socio-biological identity and has significant implications for socialization and learning. Children pass through several stages in acquiring an understanding of gender (Kohlberg, 1966). These stages include children's identifying their own sex, understanding that sex is stable over time, and finally, recognizing that sex identification does not change from one situation to another. As children's understanding of gender increases, their sex-typed preferences and knowledge also increase. In studies examining the unfolding of gender-based knowledge, young children are typically asked to (a) identify the sex of men or women in pictures, (b) to identify what sex they were as babies and what sex they will be in the future (gender stability), and (c) to decide whether their sex would change if they wore opposite-sex clothing (gender constancy). Evidence is mixed about whether the concept of gender constancy is a precursor to sex-typed behavior. Some have argued that gender labeling alone is sufficient for gender-based information processing. For example, Hartup (1989b) noted that same-sex friendship preference and play seem based on in-group (same sex) versus out-group (opposite sex) identification and affiliation.

Gender differences in social responsiveness are demonstrated as early as 6 months, with girls being more responsive to their mothers' vocalizations and initiating more interactions (Gunnar & Donahue, 1980). As early as 25 months, both boys and girls show evidence of gender-based information processing. (Huston, 1985, reviewed this material.) Bauer (1993) argued that identification of two gender groups and children's placement of themselves in one of the groups are all that seems to be required to process information via gender schemata. She found girls showed no preference for recall of female-stereotyped, male-stereotyped, or gender-neutral activities, but boys demonstrated superior recall for male-stereotyped and gender-neutral activities. Both boys and girls begin making sex-typed toy selections by 18 to 20 months (Fagot, 1974). By 26 months, they identify adult possessions and tasks on a gender basis (Weinraub et al., 1984), and by 2 to 3 years of age, children have formed stereotypes about gender-related activities (like play) and traits (boys are loud) (Picariello, Greenberg, & Pillemer, 1990). During the preschool years, children have a better memory for consistent sex-role stereotype information (information consistent with sex-role expected behaviors). In fact, 4- to 7-year-olds have been found to distort information that is gender inconsistent to conform to sex-role expectations (Boston & Levy, 1991; C. Martin & Halverson, 1983).

A study of 3- to 5-year-old children by C. Martin and Little (1990) indicated that even the youngest children reliably identified and discriminated the sexes, understood group membership and gender constancy, and identified some sex-typed knowledge of toys and clothing. Gender group membership is also related to same-sex peer preferences and to sex-typed toy preferences (C. Martin & Halverson, 1983). Analysis of preschoolers' and first graders' same-sex and opposite-sex play partners showed that opposite-sex play situations increased the likelihood of children's using sex-typed play (Trautner, 1995). Boys' play tended to be more sex typed than was girls', and children who played in pairs showed more masculine behavioral qualities (e.g., being loud). Girls appeared less influenced by other children's presence in their play activities.

Social-cognitive theory highlights another aspect of gender differences. According to this view, the social environment, children's knowledge and cognitive capabilities, and their behavior result in gender-based standards and actions. From birth, children are treated as girls or as boys according to their sex, and parents are a primary source through which gendered expectations are conveyed through reinforcement of behaviors such as play activities, dress, and demeanor. During development, behavior changes from external regulation (like parental sanctions) to internal sanctions based on personal standards (Bandura, 1986). Bussey and Bandura (1992) found that older preschoolers reacted self-approvingly to their same-sex behavior and criticized themselves for their cross-sex behavior. Older children's reactions predicted their gendered behavior; they performed actions they regarded as gender appropriate and shunned cross-sex behaviors that would lead to self-criticism. Social sanctions for inappropriate gender behavior (by peers or parents) preceded self-sanctioning for preschoolers. Neither gender knowledge nor gender constancy predicted gendered behavior.

Children also learn sex-role schemas or stereotypes from observing models appropriate to their sex; Maccoby (1988) has labeled this process *cognitive categorizing*. Parents, adults, friends, peers, television, videotapes, and stories all serve as models. Lytton and Romney (1991) argued, however, that "knowledge of sex stereotypes and categories is not a necessary prerequisite for sex-appropriate play preferences, and findings such as these are at variance with cognitive-developmental explanations of the development of sex typing" (p. 296). They suggested that sociobiological and other factors influence gender development. Undoubtedly, multiple influences give rise to gender differences, possibly including biological predispositions, family interactional patterns (see chapter 6 for a discussion of parenting differences) and language itself.

Whatever the reasons, boys and girls interact in different ways. Boys' play revolves around competition, dominance, and independence, whereas girls' play appears more collaborative, close, and cooperative (P. Miller, Danaher, & Forbes, 1986). Girls, even when influencing others, strive to preserve interpersonal relationships, whereas boys frequently do not (Sheldon, 1990). Preschool boys use more direct, demanding, ordering statements and try to assert their dominance, whereas preschool girls use supportive, attentive, socially oriented strategies (Black & Hazen, 1990; Haslett, 1983; Sheldon, 1990; Tannen, 1990). In pretend play, girls interact in longer, coherent episodes of play, whereas boys use multiple, short play sessions with more complex, less easily shared topics (Black, 1989, 1992).

Leaper (1991) noted that these differences emerge at the same time that gender identity and preferences for same-sex playmates are established. During the transition to middle childhood, boys' interactional strategies remain relatively unchanged while girls become more adept in using collaborative strategies (Camras, 1984; Tannen, 1990). Girls' behavior is more modifiable than is boys', and they are less strongly sex typed than are boys (Katz, 1986; Katz & Boswell, 1986).

As discussed in the last chapter, pretend play offers a context for mature, skilled social interaction (Connolly, Doyle, & Reznick, 1988). This remarkably complex form of interaction cannot emerge until children have developed several sophisticated conversational skills. Renegotiation of roles takes place frequently, and continued play depends upon children's agreement on the procedures, roles, and activities governing their play. Children must also mutually support each other's activities through their interactions (Bretherton, 1989). Connected discourse is a skill that is required not only for everyday interaction but also for play (Gottman, 1983; Gottman & Parkhurst, 1980). Cosaro (1986) has suggested that children's spontaneous fantasy play allows them to develop complex discourse skills as well as deal with real concerns of their peer culture.

In a study of 5- and 7-year-olds, Leaper (1991) found that collaborative and cooperative exchanges were most used by dyads playing with puppets. Across both age groups, domineering exchanges were most common in male dyads. Same-gender pairs were most likely to have role-prescribed communication patterns (i.e., collaborative and cooperative patterns for girls, domineering and controlling patterns for boys). More cross-gender communication was found in the mixed-sex dyads; girls used more controlling speech acts when interacting with boys, but boys used more obliging, collaborative speech acts when playing with girls. The female gender role, associated with interpersonal harmony, was present at age 7; male dyads displayed more distant and domineering interactional styles. Gender differences were most differentiated in the older dyads

In an investigation analyzing how effective preschoolers were at entering into play with a pair of peers, Black (1992) observed consistent gender and social status differences in entry strategies. Disliked children used more suggestions and demands, and disliked girls used the most suggestions. Disliked children tried to enter play by using their own ideas whereas liked children explained the ongoing play and incorporated peers' ideas into their entry strategies. Girls used more explanations whereas boys were more likely to negotiate their play by using self-referent terms. These results indicate that communication styles of disliked and liked boys and girls vary systematically.

Sheldon and Rohleder (in press) examined how gender-specific communicative practices develop in same-sex groups by analyzing the ways preschool boys and girls developed different co-constructed stories. Girls developed complex, detailed domestic themes whereas boys enacted detailed stories with adventure–fantasy themes. Gender differences have also been found in children's enjoyment (as measured by frequency of smiling and eye contact) of playing with puppets as part of a dyad or a group (Benenson, 1993). Girls appeared to enjoy the dyadic interaction more, and boys enjoyed the group interaction more. These findings reflect a more general pattern of friendship formation in which girls develop in-depth relationships with a few intimates as opposed to boys' membership in larger groups (discussed in chapter 8).

Gender appears to be an important dimension of the self and influences patterns of interaction and relationship development. Gender also appears to be a salient feature in many different discourse settings and family contexts. Such differences appear to be built into the cultural context of childrearing in many ways and are reinforced by the larger social environment experienced in preschool and other settings (Beal, 1994).

The sense of self develops in a myriad of ways during infancy and early childhood. Self-concept is grounded in attachment, gender, locus of control, and representations of actions and their consequences. Children's interactions with others and others' responses to them help to form a sense of self as unique and distinct. From this developing sense of self, youngsters begin to appreciate that others differ from them; each person represents another perspective and reflects a constellation of different skills, abilities, and needs. How children develop a more finely differentiated knowledge of others is the issue to which we now turn.

Knowledge of Others

By the age of 4, children develop "a systematic set of beliefs about the thoughts, feelings, intentions, motives, knowledge, and capacities of other people" (Gelman & Spelke, 1981, p. 51). Researchers have approached the study of social knowledge of others from two general perspectives: the person perception perspective, which focuses upon various cues that others give off which children must accommodate to, and the role-taking perspective, which emphasizes children's ability to take another's viewpoint (Chandler, 1977). Chandler argued that the person perception perspective focuses on children's accommodation and the role-taking perspective emphasizes the process of assimilation.

Researchers have recently attempted to relate perspective taking to children's concepts of mental life. Children's views of how they themselves acquire knowledge are believed to influence how they reason about others' beliefs and knowledge (Taylor, Cartwright, & Bowden, 1991). In a series of experiments, preschoolers were asked to judge whether others could identify an object from displaying an identifiable part, a nondescript part, or no part of an object. Children stated that others could judge what the object was by seeing part of it; the age of the observer (whether infant, preschooler, or adult) did not influence their answers. These results were replicated in a task of general knowledge. Most preschoolers recognize that being exposed to relevant perceptual information influences the knowledge of the observer, but the degree to which preschoolers are aware of diverse interpretations of the same event or action is difficult to assess.

People can have different information available to them but may also weigh information differently. Dixon and Moore (1990) investigated preschoolers', second graders', and fifth graders' use of different information and analyzed how this information was weighted in making moral judgments. Subjects heard stories about a little boy's transgressions and were asked to make judgments about his behavior, from their perspective as well as from the perspective of the boy's mother. In these stories, the amount of knowledge the mother had and the intent and consequences of the little boy's behavior varied across the stories. Children judged actions more harshly when taking the mother's perspective. Different weighting was given to information depending upon what perspective the subjects took. Both the amount and weighting of the information were used in making judgments. These results suggest that perspective-taking assessments should take into account both aspects of information.

Other attempts to understand children's awareness of mental states and of mental causes of behavior have looked at when children can identify emotions (refer to the discussion on facial expressions in chapter 2), on the development of terms reflecting feelings or mental states (see chapter 3 for a discussion of lexical development) or on distinctions between understanding mental as opposed to physical ("natural kind") constructs (see Keil, 1989, for an excellent overview of these issues).

Yet other research has assessed children's developing awareness of actions based on mistaken or false beliefs about what another individual thinks or feels. Dunn, Brown, Slomkowski, Tesla, and Youngblade (1991) tested children (3½ years old) on several tasks involving labeling, perspective taking, and false beliefs. Seven months earlier, they had observed these children at home interacting with their mothers and siblings. The researchers found strong individual differences in children's social understanding. About one third of the children explained behavior in terms of false beliefs, such as believing people were angry when they were not. Girls were more successful than boys at understanding feelings. Differences in understanding were also associated with cooperative interaction with siblings, quality of mother–child interaction, and discussion of feelings and social cognition at earlier observation sessions. Dunn et al. thus concluded that social understanding is influenced by family interaction and discussions about the social world. Another study of 3- and 4-year-old children found that children could anticipate the consequences of their deceptive messages on the beliefs and behaviors of their opponents and could use false (deceptive) information to both help or hinder their opponents (Hala, Chandler, & Fritz, 1991). As Dunn, Brown, Slokomski, et al. (1991) noted, the important issue is not that of individuals' having false beliefs but of children's linking actions to false beliefs.

Person Perception. According to the person perception model, people register cues given off by another, encode these cues, and then draw inferences from them. A substantial amount of research has found that with increasing age, children move from statements describing concrete characteristics of others to describing others' feelings and thoughts (Chandler, 1977). Many regard this as being the most important and reliable finding from the person perception research literature. As they grow older, children rely more on abstract dispositional constructs, and the number and abstractness of these constructs increase. The knowledge of others is particularly relevant to friendship formation. (Friendship is covered in more detail in chapter 7. Our purpose here is to highlight its development.)

Children's questions about why something occurs may signal an awareness of the psychological motives of others (Keasy, 1979). Shields and Padawer (1983) found that young children recognize steady versus upset emotional states as well as more finely differentiated emotional states by 5 years of age. As mentioned previously, children can more readily identify simple happy emotions than negative or blended emotions (such as anger and disgust). Preschool children seldom use these constructs, but they become a regular part of children's vocabulary by 9 or 10 years of age.

Before the age of 5, children have a global notion of psychological force but after 5, begin to distinguish between intentional and accidental events and to attribute blame accordingly. Like Shields (1985), Dimitracopoulou (1990) suggested that children become increasingly accurate about distinguishing different emotional states and their connectedness to concrete behaviors (see also Denham & Couchoud, 1990).

Scholars in the Wernerian tradition have claimed that these attributions (i.e., dispositional constructs) become increasingly differentiated and hierarchically ordered over time. In studying impression formation, Scarlett, Press, and Crockett (1971) found that age was correlated with the number, variety, and differentiation of dispositional constructs. With increasing age, children's judgments of personal characteristics were moderated by situational or temporal factors or by the internal states of the people being judged. These findings have been widely replicated in other studies. Bigner (1974), in a study of kindergartners through eighth graders, found that with increasing age, children's characterizations of others become more abstract and hierarchically organized. Gollin (1958) observed that as they grew older, children used qualitatively different inference models in forming impressions of others; older children were more able to resolve incongruent cues. Chandler (1977) noted that children's increasing sensitivity to potential social stimuli depends, in part, on how they integrate these stimuli with their own perspectives. In other words, it must depend upon the child's capacity to differentiate his or her own view from another's.

Role Taking. Although person perception depends upon children's recognition of the dispositional characteristics of others, role taking reflects children's capacity to place themselves in others' positions. The cliche about not judging another person until you have walked in their shoes reflects the ability to take on another's role. Role taking has been viewed along a continuum of egocentrism (i.e., a person's view is limited to an individual, personalized perspective) to perspectivism (i.e., a person is increasingly able to distinguish between his or her view and others' views; Chandler, 1977, p. 10).

Higgins (1981) has proposed that role taking develops in three phases: First, situational role taking (i.e., what would I do/think in that situation); second, an acknowledgment that people in the same situation may react differently; finally, a comparison and contrast of one's own views with those of another. Higgins pointed out that controlling the intrusion of personal views is critical in the last stage, when comparisons of viewpoints are made. Depending upon the situation, the individuals involved, and other factors, controlling the intrusion of a person's own view may vary in difficulty (Ross, 1981; Selman, 1994; Selman & Schultz, 1989).

Studies of role-taking abilities have generally produced inconsistent and contradictory findings. Shantz (1981) suggested these contradictory results are due to various methodological difficulties (e.g., stimulus objects being selected to give maximum contrasts for alternative perspectives, the difficulty of distinguishing between role taking and stereotypic responses to situations). Others have suggested that contradictory findings may occur because different nonsocial and social dimensions become salient at different ages or depend on different levels of cognitive ability (Chandler, 1977). Furthermore, children may be able to take the role of another but may not be able to encode this understanding (Shantz, 1981). Acredolo (1977) made a similar point that children may understand different perspectives but may not be able to apply them to ongoing interaction. Levine and Hoffman (1975) also found 4-year-olds ineffective at using their inferential skills to empathize with others.

Despite inconsistent findings, at least one important trend can be identified with respect to the development of role-taking skills. With increasing age, egocentrism has been found to decline and role-taking skills increase. Children often fail to distinguish between public and private information and typically assume that others understand more than they do (i.e., children mistakenly assume that private information, known only by them, is also known by others). For example, Greenspan, Barenboim, and Chandler (1974), in a study of first and third graders, found that older children who were sensitive to incongruent cues given by a central character were reluctant to make inferences about the character and were uncertain about their judgments, but younger children appeared to ignore the incongruent cues and expressed confidence in their judgments. This finding has been replicated by a number of other researchers. Although Flavell (1981) has found rudimentary role taking among 2- and 3-year-old children, the coordination of multiple items of information necessary for role taking generally seems to develop in middle childhood.

In summary, infants' distinctions between self and others develop gradually into a finely differentiated knowledge about others. Two approaches, person perception and role taking, have been used to characterize infants' growing social knowledge of others. Person perception models emphasize children's understanding of others' personal characteristics; role-taking models emphasize their ability to take the view of another in a given situation. Thus, person perception models emphasize more enduring dispositional qualities, while role-taking models stress situationally governed dispositional qualities. Both types of social knowledge appear necessary for effective communication, although one type may be more important than the other in a given communicative context. For example, person perception may be most important in deciding whether or not people want to actively pursue friendship with others, and role taking may be of more value in "sizing up" people in initial encounters.

Our ability to interact effectively with others is dependent upon our recognition of them as independent actors, and our knowledge of them as individuals. The final component of social knowledge needed for effective communication is knowledge of context. Contextual knowledge may be sub-divided into two areas: knowledge of social relationships and knowledge of social situations. While we separate relational knowledge from situational knowledge here for heuristic reasons, it is important to remember that these knowledge bases do not develop in isolation, but rather are closely interrelated. As noted elsewhere, what has been termed "world knowledge" (Clark & Clark, 1977) or "tacit knowledge" (Bransford & McCarrell, 1977) appears to be a complex network of relevant social knowledge (of self, of others, and of context) that is activated in given social encounters and that guides our interpretation of "what is going on" in a given encounter (Gergen, 1990).

KNOWLEDGE OF SOCIAL CONTEXT

Social-cognitive knowledge is conceptually distinct from cognitive knowledge (as discussed in chapter 1). Cognitive knowledge refers to general knowledge of the world and how it operates. In contrast, social-cognitive knowledge refers to a small subset of knowledge—knowledge of other people. For example, people's social-cognitive knowledge reflects the understanding that people are animate, independent beings whose actions may contravene our own actions or desires. We also become aware that some behavioral characteristics of individuals are rather enduring, relatively unchanging characteristics. For instance, Uncle Joe is usually cheerful and Uncle Matt is moody. However, our social cognitive knowledge also reflects our awareness of how people's behavior may change as a function of the social context they are in. Uncle Joe's cheerful demeanor changes when he is being criticized by his boss.

Contexts influence how people behave and are often defined differently by people of different ethnicity, social class, culture, or age. To become competent communicators, young children need to understand the context in which communication occurs: What is going on, what does it mean, how do people interact appropriately in this context, and how will it affect their relationships with others? Of course, children also learn that participants may disagree about what is going on, what it means, how to behave appropriately, and what its relational impact might be. For all these reasons, social-cognitive knowledge is enormously complex and varied.

Youngsters acquire this social-cognitive knowledge through hundreds of interactions with others. Through the process of negotiating meanings with those of others—making mistakes, being insulted and being insulting, explaining actions to others, becoming friends—people construct their social reality. This sense of shared social reality makes it possible to communicate and to develop relationships.

Social knowledge of context includes an understanding of social relationships as well as social contexts, of how knowledge of social relationships and social contexts unfolds, and of how social cognitive knowledge is acquired.

Knowledge of Social Relationships

Damon (1981) pointed out that to become interactionally competent, children must construct "their own systematically organized understanding of social relations and of the multiple types of interaction . . . that maintain these relations"

(p. 10). Children, like adults, must recognize that utterances not only establish a propositional content but express a social order as well (Bateson, 1972; Watzlavick, Beavin, & Jackson, 1967). In a study in which researchers asked children to recall final key statements made in a story, young children scanned utterances for their social meanings. Then they differentiated the propositional context of the statement (i.e., were they being asked to assent to the truth value of the statement?) from its illocutionary force (i.e., were they being asked to comply to a request?) (Olson & Hilyard, 1981)

Several investigations have demonstrated that the form of speech acts which regulate others' actions (e.g., directives, questions, requests) is determined by relational issues such as status and politeness. For example, some children give commands to other children just to establish a dominant status relationship (Mitchell-Kernan & Kernan, 1977). Erwin-Tripp (1977) observed that children varied their directives according to the age, familiarity, or dominance of the listener.

A number of studies (Bates, 1976; Dunn, 1992a; Ervin-Tripp, 1977; Haslett, 1989; Shatz & Gelman, 1973) have shown that young children focus on the *social meaning* of the utterance rather than on its *propositional content.* Others (Cicourel, 1972; Cook-Gumperz & Gumperz, 1976) have pointed out that role and status are continually being negotiated in conversation. In face-to-face interaction, "what looks on the surface to be a series of discrete, successive 'turns' is actually a process of continuous, simultaneously reflexive behaving and monitoring by the two players" (Erickson & Shultz, 1982, p. 246). Thus an utterance's social meaning seems to be a focal point in many messages.

Dodge and colleagues (Dodge, Pettit, McClaskey, & Brown, 1986) carried out an in-depth investigation of the relationship between social knowledge and social behavior in preschoolers' play. According to their model, children's social behavior results from their processing of social cues. In a test of their model, relevant social processing of cues occurred in five steps:

1. Children encode the displayed social cues, which involve attention, sensation, and perception of cues.
2. They apply interpretation rules to the social cues and derive an accurate interpretation.
3. They access a set of responses appropriate for their interpretation of the social cues.
4. They evaluate and select the optimal response.
5. They produce the selected response, which requires verbal and motor skills, and thus social behavior occurs.

These steps are thought to occur very rapidly and with frequent repetition at an unconscious level of processing. Processing mistakes can ensue when children skip a step or respond inaccurately at any step. (For example, they may mistakenly interpret a frown as being playful instead of serious.)

To test the efficacy of these steps, 5- and 7-year-old children were asked to complete two tasks. First, they were presented with videotaped scenarios that evaluated a particular setting (i.e., how youngsters tried to enter a play group). Different scenarios demonstrated different strategies for trying to join a group, and the subjects were asked if they thought the children in the videotaped scenarios would be allowed to join the play. Next, subjects' responses were used to analyze how they evaluated a particular setting (i.e., entering a play group). Then children were asked to actually enter a play group on two different occasions. Their attempts were observed and coded. In general, results indicate that processing cues, especially those in Steps 1, 3, and 4, predicted play entry success and ratings of entry competence.

When actually trying to enter an ongoing play group, high status children were rated as more competent and successful. Older children demonstrated a higher rate of entry behaviors, such as asking to join in, than did younger children. Behaviors from the host child (controlling entry into the play group) were related to the behaviors demonstrated by the entry child (child trying to join the group). Requests for information by the host were followed by the giving of information by the entry child; sociable behavior by the host child was followed by the entry child's sociable behavior, and negative behaviors (such as disagreements without any explanation) by the host child were reciprocated by the entry child. Thus, host children's and entry children's behavior appeared to reciprocally mirror each other's. For example, if the host child refused to let the entry child play, then the entry child refused to accept the host child's judgment. If the host child was friendly, then the entry child responded in a friendly manner as well.

Children who succeeded in entering the play groups and were rated by observers as socially competent demonstrated five important behaviors. They displayed synchronous behavior with the group, gave information, did not engage in negative conflict, displayed connectedness and showed positive reciprocity. Three general conclusions concerning socially competent behavior were thus drawn. First, children who were able to demonstrate connectedness, and talked in ways that made sense such as giving information when it was requested, were rated highly by host children. Second, children who engaged in friendly encounters with host children were successful entrants. And finally, children who did not display irritable or disruptive behaviors were successful at entering play groups.

Although it is difficult to link cognitive structures, such as processing cues, with behavioral outcomes, nevertheless this study demonstrates the specificity of children's judgments in a particular social domain, that of gaining entry into a play group. As we have argued many times before, social exchanges like entering play groups are important for children's developing social skills and friendships with others. Children's successes and failures at social tasks, such as interacting and gaining entry in an ongoing play group, enable them to judge which strategies work and which do not. Their experience, as well as their observations of others, informs them about others' evaluations of ongoing activity and allows them to change their own behavior to adapt to others. As Gottman (1986a) pointed out in his commentary on this study, framing social competence as a series of social tasks is a major step forward in trying to link social thought and social behavior.

As already noted, social relationships between interactants tend to guide their interpretations of the ongoing interaction. Knowledge of the relational dimension thus plays a substantial role in communication: Both decoding and encoding of messages are governed by social relationships, but these relationships need to be considered in light of particular social contexts. The context, for example, may govern the set of social relationships possible. In like manner, social relationships may also influence the social context; they may, for example, render a business meeting less formal. Although it is heuristically useful to separate relational from contextual knowledge, both mutually influence each other in complex ways.

Knowledge of Social Situations

Damon (1977) has suggested that 3- and 4-year-olds go through several stages of reasoning about social contexts and rules when governing social contexts. Young children comply with rules when they are compatible with their own personal desires. By 4, children understand "good" as opposed to "bad" rules but do not necessarily recognize the underlying justification for rules. By 6, some social conventions are recognized as arbitrary; people may follow these rules to help coordinate their activities. Conventional violations are judged as less serious than violations of principles. By 7, children acknowledge the social impact of conventional rules as well as rules of principle.

Cook-Gumperz and Gumperz (1976) have proposed an interactive interpretation of context. They mentioned "processes of contextualization," which rely upon linguistic contextualization cues (for example, using a person's first name to indicate familiarity), the content of the utterance, situational cues, and background expectations. Speakers and listeners use these contextualization cues to identify what type of communication they are involved in (formal discussion, informal debates, casual conversation). In this way, interactants make the context a shared cognitive construct and thus actually create context as well as communicate in a given social situation. Thus, Cook-Gumperz and Gumperz viewed context as a creative interpretation of ongoing interaction—an interpretation developed by both interactants.

Children and adults differ in their use of contextualization cues, and thus misunderstandings may arise (Gumperz & Herasimchuk, 1973). Adults focus their attention on the verbal message against a background of constantly monitored nonverbal information, but children appear to "regard all the available information as similarly weighted for the purpose of what is being said" (Cook-Gumperz & Gumperz, 1976, p. 19).

In a study exploring subjects' judgments of personal dispositions and situational constraints in predicting a story character's response to a situation, young children (5 years old) gave most weight to situational constraints and least weight to personal dispositions. Eight-, 11-, and 15-year-old subjects gave more weight to the behavioral information about the story character which reflected his or her stable personality traits rather than to the specific situation the character faced. As Ross (1981) noted, older subjects appear to fall into the "fundamental attribution error," a specific inferential bias that causes individuals to underestimate the power of situational constraints relative to personal predispositions in controlling behavior (Ross, 1981, p. 21).

Finally, Cook-Gumperz and Corsaro (1976) found that preschoolers' interactions are guided by expectations about "what goes on" in various areas in the nursery (e.g., conventionalized role playing in the playhouse, fantasy play in the sandbox) and that different communicative strategies are used to sustain these interactions. Based on these results, they concluded that "specific properties of social context are part of the information children make note of and utilize in . . . interactive episodes" (p. 431). Evidence from another study of children's persuasive talk led Cook-Gumperz (1981) to conclude that children rely on their "accumulated situational knowledge" as much as they rely on their linguistic knowledge in interpreting others' utterances (p. 48). Similarly, Mishler's analysis (1979) of children's trading (i.e., bargaining) talk suggested that speech acts need to be interpreted in context; a subsequent remark could alter a previous interpretation of an utterance. And Schieffelin's (1981) study of sibling relationships in Kaluli society revealed that mothers carefully "school" their children in their sibling relationships through formulaic messages; these messages occur with a specific set of contextualization cues.

As previously discussed, contextual knowledge—both in terms of relational and situational knowledge—provides an important basis for interpreting ongoing interactions. With the increase in research on human communication, attention has also been directed at how humans acquire this contextual knowledge. Especially relevant to development of social knowledge is the research of Katherine Nelson (1981, 1985) in which she suggested that social knowledge, especially that knowledge relevant to interpersonal communication, is acquired via scripts.

Acquiring Social Knowledge

The work of Argyle (1975, 1981) and Cook-Gumperz (1981) has shown that adults interpret messages by analyzing information across various communication modalities (e.g., eye gaze, intonation, stress, posture). Cook-Gumperz and Gumperz (1976) argued that information available in a context is interpreted against "a developed notion of what constitutes a 'normal array' of information in the background and the foreground features" (p. 18). It seems unlikely that this "normal array" of knowledge is learned piecemeal; rather, children appear to learn the "whole routine" first and only later begin to differentiate particular dimensions or subroutines.

Scripts, as defined by Nelson (1981), reflect a concrete, well-specified sequence of actions, located in a spatial and temporal context, which are designed to accomplish a particular goal. Young children possess general script knowledge (e.g., of everyday events such as going to a restaurant) that is consistent over time and socially accurate. Preschoolers can verbalize and act out scripts, but experienced preschoolers have more script knowledge than do newcomers. Scripts became more skeletal in form as activities became more varied. Young children appear to be very skilled at extracting the main idea or purpose of an event; they use sequencing to connect central events in a script.

Nelson (1981) argued that children acquire scripts through experience. Adults usually arrange exchanges with infants (such as Bruner's formats mentioned in chapter 2). Infants acquire their roles through participation in these interactions. With development, children's roles become progressively more differentiated (Bruner, 1977), and eventually they begin acting out scripts (e.g., playing house, playing school). This social knowledge guides routine encounters, and when these encounters become well-established, individuals run through the sequence of actions automatically. According to Nelson, when an individual is freed from attending to the ongoing action, "cognitive space" is gained, and thus attention can be focused upon problematic aspects of an encounter. Her work indicated that although children appear to be competent at conversations organized around shared script knowledge, they are not skilled negotiators in new areas. Finally, Nelson suggested that abstract categorical knowledge is built up from script knowledge; thus some social categories may be formed on the basis of similar roles in several scripts.

Script knowledge appears to be general, structured, consistent, and socially accurate. For example, a study by Lucariello and Nelson (1987) examined temporally displaced talk (i.e., talk about events and activities that the speakers were not currently engaged in). They found that such talk reflects children's knowledge base which is grounded in event schemas, or cognitive representations of routine activities. For example, a study by Katriel (1985) found Israeli children's conflict behavior to be embedded in ritualized communicative activities; *brogez* refers to an interactional state of anger which contains many ritualized scripts for expressing anger and negotiating conflict in this culture.

Although Corsaro (1986) acknowledged the importance of script knowledge for young children, he also argued that scripts are limited in several ways. First, Corsaro argues that we need to go beyond general constructs like scripts and identify how children's social knowledge is recognized and used in their interactions. Second, he suggested that researchers must specify how children link their social knowledge with features in an interactional setting. Finally, he maintained that Nelson's scripts represent an idealized adult version of the social world. According to Corsaro, it is necessary to study what social knowledge *children* typically use in their peer play activities. In his own ethnographic work, Corsaro has identified two major concerns of preschoolers: trying to gain control over their activities and sharing that control with others.

Corsaro and colleagues (Corsaro, 1985, 1990; Corsaro & Eder, 1990) have assessed how peer cultures form through interaction in order to negotiate meanings and share understanding. Shared routines, negotiating pretend play, setting scenes, and settling conflicts all help establish cultural practices. Corsaro also noted that many routines incorporate aspects of adult culture and that peers' culture changes over time. Such a cultural perspective truly unites social knowledge and communicative practice as children do in their everyday interactions.

Thus far we have looked at young children's developing social knowledge of self, of others, and of context and have explored how this knowledge may be acquired as a gestalt via scripts. In our view, it is not possible to clearly separate the growth of knowledge of others from the growth of knowledge about context. Both sources of knowledge are embedded within scripts that children acquire in early childhood; it appears that children begin to separate personal dispositions (i.e., knowledge of others) from situational constraints (i.e., knowledge of context) in middle childhood (Higgins, 1981; Ross, 1981). Indeed, knowledge of social relationships may well reflect both knowledge of others and of social situations. (See Table 5.1 for a summary of the developmental stages of communicative knowledge.)

At a more general level, the same argument has been made with respect to communicative development. Communication skills and social knowledge about communication have been discussed separately, an approach that reflects the fact that researchers have studied one or the other; only rarely have the interrelationships between these two fundamental components of communication been examined. If theories are to accurately capture the dynamic complexity of human communication, researchers must link aspects of social knowledge with the production of communication strategies.

Social Reasoning: The Interaction of Social Cognition and Communication

Social reasoning is an interesting process to study because it offers an opportunity to observe youngsters' understanding of others and of context along with their communicative skill in pursuing a particular goal. With increasing age, children develop more complex cognitive systems for regulating social behavior. This general development is influenced by many factors including motivation, the influence of peer culture, and opportunities for interaction.

Forbes and Lubin (1981) have viewed social reasoning as the planful regulation of social behavior. As such, social reasoning relies on specific social and cognitive skills, such as making inferences and applying script knowledge to everyday encounters. They postulated three levels of social reasoning (i.e., levels of making inferences). Level 1, mechanistic stereotypy, reflects a correspondence between situational effects and individual psychological reactions—in similar situations, others would react the same way. In Level 2, reactive subjectivism, individuals interpret the situation in the same way (e.g., Situation X is an unhappy occasion) but may react differently to it (e.g., Situation X may make Person A sad, but Person B may not be bothered by it). On Level 3, Constructive Subjectivism, individuals recognize that both interpretations of and reactions to events may vary.

In studies examining this developmental progression, children moved from Level 1 to Level 3 social reasoning with increasing age. The progression from Level 1 to Level 2 reasoning appears to move toward increasing decentration, and the shift from Level 2 to Level 3 moves from a passive view of humans to viewing others as active, intentional actors (Forbes & Lubin, 1981). Level 3 also appears similar to reciprocal role taking (Selman & Byrne, 1975) and to meta-cognition (Flavell, 1981a); thus, these skills may develop earlier than previously thought.

Persuasive strategies were found to be significantly related to levels of social reasoning. Ritualistic strategies, like appeals to rules or norms, reflected Level 1 reasoning; affect-oriented strategies reflected Level 2 social reasoning, and construal strategies, focusing upon clarification of the referent and/or intent, reflected Level 3 reasoning. Furthermore, these persuasive strategies were hier-archically stratified, with ritualistic strategies being least complex and construal strategies most complex. Lubin and Forbes (1981) concluded that children regu-late their behavior, in part, by reasoning processes that are linguistically based.

According to Applegate and Delia (1980), research linking social-cognitive and communicative development has produced mixed results because no clear concep-tual ties have been developed between aspects of social cognitive development and aspects of communicative behavior. Consistent with this line of reasoning, re-searchers operating within the constructivist perspective have attempted to address the problem. Jesse Delia and his colleagues (Applegate & Delia, 1980; Benoit, 1981; R. Clark & Delia, 1979; Delia & Clark, 1977; Delia, Kline, & Burleson, 1979; Delia, O'Keefe, & O'Keefe, 1982; O'Keefe & Delia, 1982) have found individual differences in cognitive complexity (number of cognitive constructs) and construct abstractness with level of persuasive strategy across a variety of domains. Children with greater numbers of constructs used more person-centered communication in talking with peers, comforting, and conflict management. Persuasive strategies were classified according to the degree of sensitivity to the target's perspective. These strategies are significantly correlated with cognitive complexity and con-struct abstractness. Significant correlations were also found between level of persuasive strategies and independent assessments of perspective-taking skills and cognitive complexity in elementary school children.

In a similar research vein, a study linking social knowledge and social com-petence, Mize and Cox (1991) found that the number and quality of children's interactional strategies predicted their behavior. Their study is based on the assumption that underlying cognitive, behavioral, and perceptual abilities provide the foundation for socially skilled interaction. One aspect, social strategy knowledge, has been heavily studied. For example, children who are well liked and socially adept, when interviewed, suggested using prosocial, friendly, and conventional interaction strategies in different settings (Mize & Ladd, 1988). Some research has suggested that the more strategies children can suggest to solve an interpersonal dilemma (such as trying to get a toy from another child), the more strategies available for use and thus the greater likelihood of using an appropriate strategy (K. Rubin & Krasnor, 1983; Rubin & Rose-Krasnor, 1992). Weiss and Sachs (1991) found that 4- and 6-year-old children varied in the strategies they used to persuade others. Older children used more positive strategies, such as offers, bargains, or politeness, while younger children relied on forceful assertions. Yet other research has shown that social strategy knowledge could be embedded in scripts and thus enacted as a routine; children's first responses should therefore (because they trigger the routine) predict children's social behavior toward peers (Mize & Ladd, 1988).

Mize and Cox (1991) tried to test these competing explanations for preschoolers' use of social strategy knowledge—whether the number of strategies or the initial response was most critical. Four- and 5-year-old children were given the Preschool Interpersonal Problem-Solving Tests (PIPS) and an enactive assessment of strategy knowledge. The enactive assessment was done through interviews in which children were asked for their responses to one of six hypothetical preschool situations. Children were given puppets to act out their responses. The children's first strategies were scored for their friendliness (i.e., exhibiting prosocial behavior). Both the friendliness of the children's first responses and the number of strategies they suggested were significantly related to some social behaviors with peers. Mize and Cox concluded that training to improve children's social skills might incorporate both alternatives and thus encourage children to think of more alternatives as well as focus on their initial response.

Much of the social reasoning research has examined peer–peer interaction because social-cognitive knowledge and communication skills are roughly comparable between peers and the developmental trends of each aspect can be clearly assessed. However, social reasoning also develops within families as parents and children, brothers and sisters negotiate issues in their everyday lives. For example, Dunn and her colleagues (Dunn, 1988a; Dunn & Munn, 1985) looked at siblings' conflicts and their understanding of feelings, intentions, and social rules. Teasing behaviors are expressed at 18 months, and by 2 years of age, teasing behaviors increase dramatically. Teasing involves an assessment of what comments annoy another and relies on a thorough understanding of the other's feelings. Common understandings about social behavior are often used to excuse or rationalize children's own behaviors. Frequently used justifications for teasing are the instigator's own feelings and needs, rules of possession and sharing, rules about taking turns, and damage to their property. In two thirds of sibling conflicts in which an older child initiated the conflict, young children appealed for help from their mothers. As Dunn noted, young children thus anticipate how parents might react and demonstrate an understanding of what constitutes acceptable behavior.

Dunn and her colleagues (Dunn, 1993; Dunn & Slomkowski, 1992; Slomkowski & Dunn, 1992) suggested that three aspects of preschoolers' justifications for their behavior deserve special mention. Justifications are clear exemplars of social reasoning because they present a rationale in support of particular action, reflect a fairly sophisticated assessment of social-cognitive knowledge, and link reasons to behaviors. At 3, children are able to question rules and understand that they can be applied differently to different categories of people. Three-year-olds also understand rules about the rights, needs, or feelings of others as well as their own self-interest. Some justifications appear to focus on whether an act was intentional. (More blame is attached when an action is deliberate rather than accidental. For example, breaking a dish accidentally is less blameworthy than deliberately breaking it. Many believe that a complete understanding of this distinction between deliberate and accidental harm does not occur until a later age.) By 5, children account for their behavior in different ways that depend upon the nature of the transgression (e.g., transgressions involving morals, conventions, school regulations, instructions, or beliefs) (Much & Shweder, 1978). Dunn and Brown (1993) found that preschoolers were able to talk about their inner states and social actions and with increasing age, they discussed their feelings and actions in reflective conversations with their mothers. Generally, moral rules appear to be regarded as valid and unconditional.

Although learned in the family, conflict and reasoning are also validated in terms of their cultural settings. What people argue about, with whom, and when are all socialized behaviors that vary culturally, personally, and relationally. Justifications and reasoning are based on what is acceptable and what can be displayed in conflicts (Scott & Lyman, 1968). Garvey and Shantz (1992) suggest that conflict variation can be analyzed in terms of (a) the characterization of a conflict, (b) the nature of metacommunicative comments about conflict (e.g., 'I was just joking,' etc.), (c) communicative markers such as formality or tonal quality and (d) differing interpretations by participants. These elements all vary contextually and culturally.

Discounting.   Others have investigated social reasoning and social knowledge by investigating discounting, the process by which individuals discount a cause for behavior if other, equally plausible reasons can be given for the behavior. For example, one person might discount (not believe) another's account of enjoying a movie after learning that the other was paid to say so. Extrinsic motivation (like money) lessens belief in intrinsic motivation (i.e., personal reasons for doing something). Discounting is of interest because it reveals how children conceptualize causes for behavior (e.g., some believe that people are less motivated to do something when they are offered an external reward for doing it) and judge the effectiveness of disciplinary actions (e.g., are threats of punishment more effective than promises of a reward?) (P. Miller & Aloise, 1990).

Generally, 5- and 6-year-old children think that an external reward increases intrinsic (or internal) motivation—the so-called additive rule (Miller & Aloise, 1990). A social development model explains discounting by arguing that children, through their social experiences, observe that unpleasant activities usually are accompanied by external pressure to comply (Kassin & Ellis, 1988; Kassin & Lepper, 1984).

In addition to such social knowledge, P. Miller and Aloise (1990) suggested that knowledge of another's manipulative intent (i.e., an ulterior motive) and knowledge about the rewards involved are important influences on discounting. They found that sometimes people manipulate others (make them do things they do not want to do). However, young children may regard this manipulation as a bonus (the additive rule) or recognize the ulterior motive (and invoke the discounting rule). A mother's manipulation to get her child to play with a particular toy is not discounted by 6-year-olds when they also are told that the mother wants the child to play with the toy because she knows the child likes the toy (P. Miller, Aloise, & Davis, 1989). Children invoke the additive rule because the child's desire for the toy is matched by the mother's encouragement to play with it. If a manipulative intent is made explicit (a bribe to get someone to do something), 6-year-olds demonstrate more discounting. The individual revealing the manipulative intent is also judged (discounted or not discounted) on the basis of who they are. Mothers, for example, may be perceived as a helpful rather than manipulative authority figure (Costanzo, Grumet, & Brehm, 1974; Laupa & Turiel, 1986). This judgment rests on knowing how punishments and rewards are given. As P. Miller and Aloise (1990) concluded, "Although pre-schoolers and kindergartners can discount under certain conditions, they need to acquire more social knowledge in order to discriminate when to use a discounting rule and when to use an additive rule" (p. 285). (Surber, 1985, discusses this point as well.)

P. Miller and Aloise (1990) noted several factors that cause young children to make errors in discounting. Such factors include not making a comprehensive search of causes, a lack of relevant social knowledge, and limited attention and memory. Thus, the literature on discounting reveals the complex web of social reasoning children use in making judgments, offering justifications, and being persuasive. This process illustrates the connections between children's social-cognitive knowledge and their subsequent behaviors.

SUMMARY

Over time, the growth of children's social knowledge about communication reflects increasing cognitive and communicative complexity. In the first stage of this knowledge, infants separate the self from others; this separation depends on the recognition of people as independent agents and as animate beings. Bruner (1983) and Damon (1981) suggested that this understanding enables infants to recognize other people as having a unique potential for social interaction. In the next stage of developing communicative knowledge, knowledge of others becomes more finely differentiated by person perception and role taking, and knowledge of context also develops. Contextual knowledge incorporates knowledge about social relationships as well as social situations. Social reasoning research has examined the linkages between social-cognitive knowledge and subsequent behavior. A number of investigations have linked cognitive complexity with person-centered persuasive and comforting strategies. Discounting research has also demonstrated the link between people's assessments of motivation (and its sociocultural base) with blame.

We have reviewed the communicative skills and knowledge acquired during the preschool years. Although this overview is of value in itself—because there have been few previous attempts to integrate the diversity of communicative accomplishments outlined here—nevertheless, a developmental perspective implies a concern for how the accomplishments are achieved, not merely a concern for what those accomplishments happen to be.

Communicative development rests on innate biological predispositions for communication as well as on considerable environmental influences. In chapter 6, we analyze the relational influences on communication development, in particular the role of significant adult caretakers, families, and peers. Interactions with others provide unique developmental opportunities for children and influence their ways of acquiring communicative skills. Developing communication knowledge and skill is inextricably interwoven with the development of social relationships.

Chapters 6 through 9 reflect a shift in emphasis from the development of skills to their exercise in particular contexts. This next chapter, on relational influences on communicative development, focuses on the interaction of children within their families and the ways this context provides both a model of interaction as well as a laboratory in which to exercise communicative skills. Chapters 7 and 8, dealing with friendship, analyze both the learning environment provided by friends as well as the exercise of these communicative skills in furthering friendship.

6

Family Influences on Communicative and Social Development

The critical role of family in children's nonverbal, linguistic, communicative, and social development should by now be obvious. The family is the primary context for forming fundamental relationships, which, as has been discussed, not only teach young children important lessons about attachment and authority but instill in them the self-esteem and confidence they need to flourish in the larger social world. The family is also the context in which children are introduced to language and learn the significant functions that communication serves in their lives. Finally, the family is society's most important agent of socialization; as Bernstein (1971, 1973, 1977) has noted, the linguistic and communicative practices parents employ with youngsters both reflect and sustain larger cultural values.

This chapter is designed to more thoroughly overview some of the many ways in which family relationships influence children's development. Thus, we will elaborate on some of the ideas already touched upon in previous chapters as well as introduce some new ways in which the family shapes a child's ability to use communication effectively. Obviously, one of the most significant relationships a child experiences is with his or her primary caretaker (usually the mother). As explained in previous chapters, much research has been devoted to understanding the nature and quality of the attachment bond between mothers and infants as well as the effects of this bond on children's subsequent social development. The following discussion of attachment research focuses on the social consequences associated with various attachment styles across the lifespan.

As the discussion of language development indicated, caretakers influence when and how speech is acquired. In fact, Dunn (1992b) suggested that discourse with any mature member of the culture provides children with great opportunities for language growth. In the second section of this chapter, we explore links between adult–child language (ACL) and youngsters' linguistic and communicative development and between what is known as maternal speech and children's language acquisition.

The third section details more general interaction patterns that occur within the family. We discuss children's linguistic and communicative development in relation to: (a) general parenting styles, (b) social class differences in linguistic and communicative development, (c) behavioral modes characteristic of fathers' interaction with children, and (d) the impact of siblings. In the last part of the chapter, we look at discipline and its effects. Here, we argue that parents' disciplinary efforts not only remediate bad behavior, but also teach children important lessons about the nature of the social world and the role communication plays in it.

ATTACHMENT

Attachment is a theoretical concept that refers to the "special intimacy and closeness" (Sroufe, 1982, p. 95) that develops between infants and their primary caretakers (typically mothers) during the first year of life. The quality of infants' attachments is typically defined in terms of the extent to which they use caregivers as a base for exploring the environment, turn to caregivers as a source of comfort when distressed, and re-establish contact with caregivers after separation.

Bowlby's and Ainsworth's Research

Although most mothers speak of the special bonds they have with their infants, John Bowlby (1969/1982) was the first researcher to examine how these bonds or attachments influence children's social development. Drawing on ethological studies of primates, Bowlby argued that all humans have a fundamental fear of being alone both in infancy and throughout life. Through evolution, Bowlby reasoned, humans developed a complex set of emotions and behaviors that ensure they are not alone. In other words, from Bowlby's perspective, people come into the world prewired to seek and establish close relationships with others (attachment figures) who support and protect them. Bowlby's observations of institutionalized children further led him to believe that the absence of a primary attachment figure had far-reaching detrimental consequences.

Bowlby's work suggested that humans have a common need for attachment, but Mary Ainsworth was interested in whether different caregiving environments produced different styles or forms of attachment (see Ainsworth, Blehar, Waters, & Wall, 1978). To examine this question, she created what is known as the strange situation paradigm where mother–infant dyads are placed in a novel setting (hence the name); how toddlers react to the introduction of interesting toys, a stranger, and temporary separation from their mothers is then observed and recorded. Utilizing this method, Ainsworth identified the three types of mother–infant attachments we have already discussed: secure, anxious-ambivalent, and avoidant (Ainsworth, 1985).

In her early studies, Ainsworth observed that securely attached youngsters were "effective" explorers. They used their mothers as a base for investigating the novel play environment, proceeded on their mothers' encouragement, and heeded their cues for caution. When separated from their mothers, these infants showed marked distress but were quickly soothed on her return. In contrast, anxious-ambivalent children demonstrated little interest in exploring the environment and were extremely wary of adult strangers. Although they cried intensely when separated from their mothers, these youngsters typically threw tantrums upon the mothers' return. Unlike secure infants, anxious-ambivalent children were not comforted by the reintroduction of their mothers who, in fact, seemed to increase their distress and anger. Finally, avoidant infants showed premature independence and paid little attention to their mothers while exploring the play area. Not surprisingly, youngsters with this attachment rarely cried when their mothers left the playroom and actively avoided contact with them when they returned. The attachment styles originally developed by Ainsworth have been replicated in many studies during the nearly two decades since her initial work (for reviews of these studies, see Elicker, Englund, & Sroufe, 1992; Sroufe, 1983, 1989).

What fosters such distinct forms of mother–infant attachment? Studies have suggested that secure, anxious-ambivalent, and avoidant attachments are best predicted by individual differences in maternal responsiveness—a concept that should be familiar from our discussions of nonverbal and linguistic development. As Sroufe (1982) noted, "Good maternal care involves responding to the infant's signals promptly and effectively" (p. 98). Thus, mothers of securely attached infants have been found to react quickly to their children's distress and to engage in warm and affectionate behaviors when their babies seek physical contact. They also strike a balance between responding to infants' signals for stimulation and recognizing when they need time-out to rest and regroup. On the other hand, mothers of anxious-ambivalent children tend to be inconsistent in their availability and responsiveness. Research further indicates that these mothers are anxious and preoccupied with themselves. Finally, avoidant attachments are characteristic of mothers who do not enjoy physical contact and therefore consistently rebuff their infants' signals for closeness.

Hartup (1989a) noted that two people, mother and child, are developing in their relationship with each other. Early-timing mothers (those in their 20s when the first child is born) have more difficulty with discipline and setting limits than do late-timing mothers (first-time mothers in their 30s; Walter, 1986). Mothers at different stages of adult development may thus bring different interpretive frames and social skills when bonding with their children.

As noted in chapter 2, the nonverbal synchrony between caretaker and child appears to be instrumental in establishing attachment between them. Communicative behaviors exchanged between mothers and infants also vary as a function of the attachment they have formed. Thus, communication and attachment reciprocally and mutually influence one another, and the effects of this reciprocal relationship are long lasting and profound.

Recent Research on Attachment

Most recent research on attachment has been directed toward examining the effects of infants' early attachment experiences. This work has confirmed Bowlby's original contention that the absence of a safe and reliable attachment figure has significant long-term consequences. First, attachment patterns remain relatively stable throughout childhood. Studies generally indicate that somewhere between 60% to 80% of children exhibit the same attachment style across development. Even more striking is that the breakdown of adult attachment styles closely parallels the breakdown of attachment styles observed in studies of infants: 55% secure, 20% anxious ambivalent, and 25% avoidant (Shaver & Hazan, 1994; Waters, 1978). Moreover, adults in each attachment group appear to remember relationships with their parents differently. Whereas secure adults have favorable memories of their childhood, adults who are anxious ambivalent remember their parents as inconsistent, intrusive, and unfair. Avoidant adults report their relationships with parents were marked by "coolness and rejection" (see Hazan & Shaver, 1987; Shaver & Hazan, 1994, Shaver, Hazan, & Bradshaw, 1988).

In addition to remaining relatively stable across time, the attachment styles developed as infants influence life experiences both as children and as adults. As we have stated many times in this book, a large and consistent body of literature indicates that secure children fare better than do either anxious-ambivalent or avoidant youngsters. To begin with, secure children have self-esteem, view themselves as lovable (Bowlby, 1988), and tend to approach others with positive expectations. Other positive consequences associated with secure attachments include higher levels of social responsiveness, social competence, and acceptance among peers; better conflict management skills; age-appropriate performance on cognitive tasks; and empathic responses in social situations (for reviews of this work, see Dunn, 1992a; Sroufe, 1983). Elicker and his colleagues reported that friendships are more likely to occur between two securely attached children than between youngsters with other combinations of attachment styles (e.g., Elicker, 1995; Elicker, Englund, & Sroufe, 1992).

In contrast, to secure attachments, insecure attachments (of both types) are related to childhood depression and "exploitative peer relations, especially ones in which an avoidant child victimizes an anxious-ambivalent child" (Shaver & Hazan, 1994, p. 118). Interestingly, gender and insecure attachment appear to mutually influence one another. For example, Turner (1991) found that insecure boys (age 4) were more aggressive, disruptive, controlling, and attention seeking than were secure children. In contrast, insecure girls were more dependent, less assertive, and less controlling and showed more positive expressive behaviors and compliance than did secure children. Finally, teachers' reactions are known to vary as a function of children's attachment styles. Whereas children who are avoidant often elicit anger from teachers, those who are anxious ambivalent typically receive special attention (Rothbard & Shaver, 1994).

In adulthood, attachment affects the nature and stability of relationships that people develop as well as the level of professional success they experience. For instance, anxious-ambivalent adults tend to have an obsessive view of love. Not only do they talk of emotional ups and downs, jealousy, and sexual passion, but they also fear that partners are less committed to relationships than they are. People with this attachment style tend to engage in premature and inappropriate disclosure when forming intimate relationships and, at least for men, marry after a relatively short period of courtship. Adults who are avoidant mistrust intimacy and expect love relationships to fail; they tend to avoid self-disclosure and dislike others who talk about their personal feelings and experiences. In contrast to these two groups, adults with secure attachments see people as good-hearted and well-intentioned and trust their primary relational partners. Like Elicker et al.'s (1992) work with children, studies of adults generally indicate that relationships between two securely attached people stand the best chance of long-term success (see Senchak & Leonard, 1992; Shaver & Brennan, 1992; Weiss, 1982; for a review of these studies, see Shaver & Hazan, 1994).

The effects of attachment can be felt in professional life as well. Secure adults report relatively high levels of satisfaction with their jobs, their co-workers, and their incomes; secure adults also strive to maintain a balance between the demands of career and family. People who are avoidant are much more likely to be workaholics, to find little pleasure in vacations, and to voice dissatisfaction with co-workers. Finally, adults with an anxious-ambivalent attachment style report feeling insecure about their jobs and believe they are neither appreciated nor recognized by co-workers. Moreover, at least one study has found that people who are anxious-ambivalent actually earn less money than either secure or avoidant adults (Hazan & Shaver, 1990).

ADULT–CHILD LANGUAGE

As already discussed, attachment is a fundamental aspect of the mother–infant relationship, and communication is the primary vehicle through which various forms of attachment are established. Considerable research has been devoted to understanding the form and content of early maternal speech aimed at infants and toddlers. As suggested in chapter 3, the characteristics of language directed at infants and toddlers are quite distinctive and, as some argue, appear to be universal across cultures in which language is directed toward young infants. (In some cultures, adults do not talk to their infants because they believe infants incapable of any understanding!) This language is termed adult–child language or ACL, and varied approaches have been used to explore its nature.

Although both the cognitive and social interaction approaches acknowledge that language is acquired in the context of dialogue, the social interaction approach places more emphasis on environmental factors. Early studies claimed that the nature of adult language (as input) determined the subsequent quality of children's language (Newport, Gleitman, & Gleitman, 1977; Snow, 1977a). More recently, it has been recognized that children play an active role in their dialogues with adult caretakers (K. Nelson, 1977).

Linguistic Input

Linguistic input refers to the specific features of language that adults, especially mothers, use to communicate with infants and young children. These features include the types of words employed in maternal utterances, the complexity of maternal utterances, intonation patterns, and the like. For many years, research on linguistic input has aimed to correlate relatively global aspects of mothers' speech (i.e., motherese or baby talk) with various measures of language production and comprehension. In general, this line of research indicates that mothers' speech to their children is simpler, more repetitious, higher pitched, and more focused on immediate events; it contains more questions and imperatives and has more exaggerated emphasis than does adult–adult speech (Sachs, 1977; Snow, 1972, 1977a, 1977b). In addition, mothers' speech to their youngsters varies as a function of the communicative demands of the situation (Snow, 1977a, 1977b). For example, mothers use imperatives ("No!") when telling their infants not to do something and explanatory language when describing an object ("Look. Here's your doggy. See the long fur."). Early research also demonstrated that ACL contained consistent prosodic features. Compared to adults' speech to each other, adult speech to children is characterized by higher pitch, a wider range of pitch levels, shorter utterances, longer pauses, and more simplified speech (e.g., fewer syllables per phrase, fewer phrases per statement, etc.; Grieser & Kuhl, 1988).

Although these early studies highlighted many important aspects of linguistic input, deVilliers and deVilliers (1979) suggested that their tendency to interpret correlations between gross measures of language was "problematic"; thus, many researchers have now turned to assessing more specific measures of linguistic form and production (p. 141). Bates et al. (1979) reached a similar conclusion when they argued that although more linguistic input is related to more and better language in children, specific claims—linking specific types of input to specific outcomes—need to be tested.

An example of more specific testing appears in a study by Barnes, Gutfreund, Satterly, and Wells (1983), in which mothers' use of interrogatives, directives, and extending utterances was positively related to at least one aspect of language development. Toddlers whose mothers used more yes–no questions and deictic statements (pointing out specific objects or their locations) appeared to have more rapid language development (Newport, Gleitman, & Gleitman, 1977). In another study, mothers' use of personal pronouns, especially *we,* was positively related to their own verbal responsiveness to children and to their children's performance on intelligence tests at 5 and 8 years (Laks, Beckwith, & Cohen, 1990).

Studies reporting efforts to use specific types of input (e.g., expansions, recasting sentences, etc.) to enhance language development have reported some success (Brown, 1976; K. Nelson, 1973, 1977). Extensions occur when adults continue the same topic of conversation but do not imitate the child's previous utterance. A child may notice a duck and say "Duck"; the parent replies, "Yes, that's a pretty white duck." In contrast, expansions modify children's initial utterances and expand them into well-formed utterances. A toddler might say, "Want cookie," and the parent might respond, "Do you want a cookie?" Snow (1977b) noted that expansions facilitate language growth because they are ways to provide "relevant, responsive and interesting input to all stages of language development" (p. 39). Although expansions are particularly difficult to assess in spontaneous speech (deVilliers & deVilliers, 1979), several studies have found slightly improved language development when children are tested after being in groups that receive expansions or extensions from adult caretakers as opposed to groups that do not (Cazden, 1972; K. Nelson, Carskaddon, & Bonvillian, 1973).

In a somewhat different vein, Retherford, Schwartz, and Chapman (1980) analyzed mother–child interactions for semantic roles (such as agent or object) and syntactic categories (such as negation). They found that mothers and their children were similar in the relative frequency with which they used different semantic and syntactic categories. Children adapted more to their mothers' standard usage rather than converging (as fine-tuning would suggest). Similarly, Harris (1993) found that children's earliest words were strongly influenced by their mothers' use of words in context. Ninety-three percent of youngsters' first utterances were very close to maternal usage, and 83% were related to the mothers' most frequently used words. Frequent repetition of words in context and repetition of particular routines, were also important for children's learning. Harris thus argued that young children master interactive routines and terms that accompany these routines. Children's subsequent words were less strongly related to maternal use (only 45%).

Because children acquire language in its communicative context, simple behavioral reinforcements are not sufficient for learning. Ninio (1993) believed vocalizing is aimed at trying to learn what the other is attempting to communicate rather than merely pairing words and contexts. Consistent with this line of reasoning, Camaioni (1986) argued that playing games allows children to relate specific actions to specific interactional contexts and to match mothers' linguistic forms to specific actions or objects in the game.

Maternal Speech

Although ACL is concerned with the general features of language directed to children by adults, maternal speech focuses on particular communicative strategies mothers employ when interacting with their young children. Scholars in this area have been especially interested in understanding how mothers and children adapt their speech to one another. Thus, ACL is believed to characterize adults' talk to children generally, but maternal speech refers to the specific developmental opportunities made available to children through interactions with their mothers.

Mothers' internal states as well as their intentions play an important role in the communication opportunities and skills provided for children. For example, maternal levels of stress influence interaction with children. In one study, mothers reported that when "hassles" (defined as daily life stressors) were frequent, they displayed more positive behaviors with their children when they had satisfactory support systems in place (Crnic & Greenberg, 1990). In a somewhat different vein, Olsen-Fulero (1982) found that mothers used language differently when they intended to elicit conversation from children as opposed to direct them. Encouraging conversation with children is believed to facilitate their communicative abilities in a number of important ways, such as providing frequent and multiple turns at talk and fostering the development of a range of skills. L. Bernstein (1981) pointed out, for instance, that certain discourse features, like ellipsis, are only possible via dialogue. In support of this assumption, Hoff-Ginsberg (1986) observed that mothers' communicative goals and structural qualities of speech were positively related to children's language development. More specifically, maternal use of real and verbal-reflective questions was positively related to children's use of auxiliaries. Hoff-Ginsberg (1990) thus argued that maternal speech supports children's development of syntax by modeling structures they are learning.

Several researchers have argued that individual differences in children's initial linguistic orientation are related to early communicative experiences. As we noted earlier, K. Nelson (1973) distinguished between object-oriented (referential) children who acquired vocabulary more rapidly and person-social oriented (expressive) children who developed syntax more quickly. She suggested that these differences were a function of maternal interaction styles; variations in children's language experiences predisposed them to focus on different uses of language (also see K. Nelson, 1976). Similarly, Dore (1974) tracked two children during the initial phases of language acquisition. One child was oriented to word form (i.e., vocabulary), and the other was oriented to intonation (i.e., prosodic features that reflect different language functions). According to Dore, the mothers' relative orientations to the referential (i.e., vocabulary) or expressive (i.e., intonational) aspects of language were reflected in their children's use of language. Maternal verbal stimulation (i.e., using frequent, responsive interaction) has also been related to children's vocabulary progress at 13 and 24 months of age (Olson, Bayles, & Bates, 1986).

In addition, adults tend to keep interaction with children going and often rely on the use of questions and turn-passing devices (e.g., "well," "but"; Bloom, Rocissano, & Hood, 1976; Ervin-Tripp, 1977; Kaye & Charney, 1981; Lieven, 1978). However, Moerk (1974) found that mothers remain quite sensitive to their children's ability to maintain conversation and adapt their messages to appropriate skill levels. As youngsters mature, mothers move from explicit modeling in their interactions to using questions to cue children's responses until, finally, children spontaneously create their own messages by action and talk.

Other studies have also suggested that regardless of their children's ages, mothers modify their speech style as a function of infant behaviors. For example, mothers have been found to fine-tune their interactions to youngsters' ages and tasks. When compared to older youngsters, mothers give more instructions to younger children; these typically incorporate directives, open-ended questions, and nonverbal instructions (Rogoff, Ellis, & Gardner, 1984). However, Penman et al. (1983) found that affect-oriented speech was more sensitive to infant behavior than was informative speech. Kaye and Charney (1981) observed modifications in turnabouts, which both respond to and require a response from another (either verbal or nonverbal). More specifically, these researchers found that mothers produced twice as many turnabouts (which function to keep conversation going) as did their 2-year-old children. Schaffer, Hepburn, and Collis (1983) reported that mothers' directives were more likely to incorporate nonverbal and verbal components when addressed to 10- through 18-month-old infants as opposed to older children.

Specific cultural expectations also appear to be taught during mother–child interaction. Mother–daughter interactions have been studied by P. Miller and her colleagues (1992), who found that mothers offer explicit communicative and behavioral directives to their daughters. During pretend play, mothers initiate, join in, and support their preschool daughters' play attempts (Haight & Miller, 1991). Mothers also teach their daughters explicit rules for responding to interactions (P. Miller & Sperry, 1988). For example, some rules include "When another child hurts you, defend yourself" and "Don't respond aggressively without cause."

Wells and associates (Wells, Montgomery, & MacLure, 1979; Wells, MacLure, & Montgomery, 1981) pointed out that mothers' interactions aid youngsters' communicative development in two distinct ways. First, mothers usually simplify their messages by adopting motherese when speaking with children and thus make it easier for youngsters to understand and respond to utterances. Second, the communicative strategies mothers employ constrain the type and amount of developmental opportunities available to children. In a series of investigations, Wells et al. (1979) found differences between children in their "ability to contribute new and contextually relevant matter to the conversation" (p. 368). The researchers attributed these differences in part to the varying ways in which mothers interpreted their children's conversational abilities and thus shaped their children's possible responses (French & Woll, 1981).

After analyzing videotaped mother–child conversations, Howe (1980) found that "given high motivation . . . children will learn from maternal replies and will be influenced by percentages of minimal and extended replies" (p. 40). According to Howe, previous attempts to look at mother–child interaction have stressed the informational value of the exchange, whereas her findings suggest a motivational value as well. In other words, talking with children not only provides information but encourages them to talk and instills self-esteem and confidence via listening (i.e., it accords children respect by treating their views seriously and paying attention to them).

Maternal Scaffolding.   *Scaffolding* is a term that refers to an adult's structuring of an activity or event to maximize a child's learning. As noted in chapter 1, Vygotsky (1962) used the term when speaking of the "zone of proximal development." For him, the zone of proximal development (ZPD) embodied a set of skills or knowledge children can acquire if aided by an adult or another (e.g., a sibling or peer) who already possesses that skill. In other words, it is other-assisted learning, which youngsters cannot do on their own. As Youniss (1992) noted, the ZPD ranges from children's independent functioning at one end of a continuum to their learning as a junior partner in social interaction at the other end. Youniss argued that the metaphor of scaffolding should imply a flexible shift as parents responds to children's actions; the real issue, according to Youniss, is how a child "becomes self-regulated after a period of other-regulation" (p. 119). Maternal scaffolding in cooperative activities as well as in conflict appears to facilitate children's learning.

Peers also play an important role in youngsters' ongoing development. Recent work with maternal scaffolding has paid close attention to how mothers' input can aid children's communication with peers. As mentioned before, children can negotiate interaction with adults, but they have difficulty accomplishing the same goals with peers. Budwig, Strage, and Bamberg (1986) suggested that adult caretakers can facilitate young children's interaction with peers by helping them learn strategies to initiate and maintain interaction. They argued that this transition from adult–child to child–child interaction provides a "zone of proximal development"; that is, solving peer interactional problems with adult guidance enables youngsters to interact more effectively with peers. In their study, Budwig et al. found that mothers encouraged children to initiate, join in, and maintain interaction through a variety of strategies they suggested while observing the children play. With greater shared playtime, children developed more shared understanding with each other. In addition, mothers of popular children were more likely to encourage their youngsters to follow a group-oriented strategy in engaging others in play. This finding is consistent with other studies (discussed in previous chapters), which suggest that children who are well liked by peers gain access to playgroups by integrating themselves with the group's ongoing activities (as opposed to calling attention to themselves, demanding access, etc.). In contrast, mothers of unpopular children have been found to exhibit a controlling, negative style (Russell & Finnie, 1990).

Although there is some evidence that younger preschoolers benefit more from this type of scaffolding than do older preschoolers (Bhavnagri & Parke, 1991), children of all ages appear to use their parents as interactional models. For example, Putallaz (1987) observed that infants mimic their mothers' behavior; if mothers are demanding, then infants are demanding in return. Similarly, Vandell and Wilson (1987) found that when infants experience turn taking with their mothers, they develop more advanced interactive skills; these skills, in turn, enable them to have better (i.e., smoother, more balanced, less conflictual) interactions with their peers. Interestingly, some work suggests that parents' recollections of their own peer interactions may influence their involvement in children's relationships (Putallaz, Constanzo, & Smith, 1991).

Joint involvement episodes during infancy can be enriched by mothers' direct participation in whatever activity is at hand. Slade (1987a, 1987b) found that higher levels of complexity and longer play were produced when mothers provided specific suggestions to their children and played actively with them. Freund (1990) also found that mothers' direct, active participation facilitated children's learning on a sorting task. When mothers joined in, they provided more fun and more interest and kept infants involved for longer periods of time.

Mothers also provide scaffolding by setting tasks that are slightly more advanced than children's abilities. For instance, mothers may frame or chunk a task into substeps and then guide children's performances. According to Heckhausen (1987), this framing occurs across a variety of tasks throughout the preschool years, from understanding others and their motivations to solving concrete problems. In addition, mothers adapt their speech to the level of inferences they judge their children able to understand. Schneiderman (1983) observed that youngsters who were perceived as most limited in their inferential skills received the most restricted, directive input from mothers.

Maternal scaffolding provides important developmental opportunities for children's conversational style and structure as well. In analyzing naturalistic conversations between mothers and their 30- to 35-month-old children, Fivish and Fromhoff (1988) distinguished between two different maternal conversational styles, elaborative and repetitive. Elaborative mothers talked more, asked more memory questions, and provided more information about an event under discussion than did repetitive mothers. Children of elaborative mothers tended to be more communicative and used more varied speech than children whose mothers typically reiterated comments.

Children can be regulated by others as well as regulate them. In a study of mother–child interaction, Martinez (1987) observed that mothers asymmetrically regulated the conversation, primarily through turnabouts (statements that require a response and then continuation of the conversation). When interacting with peers, 2- and 4-year-old children regulated each other symmetrically by using strategies previously employed by their mothers. In other words, children transferred observations of their mothers' strategies to their own interactions with peers. Mothers thus "scaffolded" regulatory strategies for their children.

Finally, mothers can provide interactional support in pretend play episodes with their children. Haight and Miller (1992) found that mother–child dyads mutually engaged one another; both initiated and responded to pretending, and mothers elaborated and prompted children's pretending. Children played longer with their mothers than when alone and incorporated their mothers' pretend talk into their own subsequent play.

There is thus striking evidence that ACL and maternal speech shape children's linguistic and communicative development. Although maternal sensitivity to children's developmental levels is generally linked to their progress in various domains (Schaffer, 1979; Schaffer & Collis, 1986), the way in which these effects are transmitted is not clear. For example, Bornstein and Tamis-LeMonda (1989) suggested that maternal sensitivity is undoubtedly embedded in a range of caretaking activities, many of which encourage children's growth and development. The other aspects of caretaking covered in the present chapter—and their complex interactions—support this view as well. Children themselves are also skilled at selecting what is and is not relevant to them. O'Connell and Bretherton (1984) noted that even if maternal input is at an inappropriate level, children may realize what is important to the task at hand. Youniss (1992) mentioned that directness may be called for in some tasks, although on others it is not helpful. Explanations of the effects associated with different maternal interaction styles are thus subject to many qualifications. What remains clear, however, is that mother–child interaction has significant, long-lasting effects.

The nature and effects of linguistic input as well as maternal speech continue to occupy researchers' interests, but evidence indicates that studies in these areas must utilize more specific variables and link them to more specific communicative effects (deVilliers & deVilliers, 1979). Theorists such as Snow (1977b) and K. Nelson (1985) have further argued that studies must also account for children's cognitive ability as well as for contextual factors.

In the next section of the chapter, we examine some contextual factors that influence communicative development. For instance, general patterns of parenting create different interactional and developmental opportunities for parents as well as children, and social class differences in styles of parent–child interaction have been of particular interest to researchers. Bernstein (1971) has suggested that the language used by children in lower socioeconomic groups is not well suited to current educational systems and thus limits their future opportunities. In addition, the question of how fathers and siblings shape young children's development has also received a great deal of attention. We now turn to a discussion of these interactional dynamics and their developmental effects.

INTERACTIONAL PATTERNS BETWEEN ADULTS AND CHILDREN

Interpersonal interaction facilitates communicative development in several ways. As indicated in prior discussions, children must participate in interactions with others to develop a concept of self and of their social roles (Wolf, 1981). By 12 months, children have well established communicative schemes that grow through such interactions. We have already reviewed the rich synchrony that exists between mother and child in early infancy. Next, we investigate some of the patterns characteristic of parent–child interaction in later years as well as those in which young children interact with their siblings.

General Styles of Parenting

Perhaps one of the most widely recognized schemes for classifying general styles of parenting was developed by Baumrind (1967, 1971). She distinguished three main styles of parenting: authoritarian, authoritative, and permissive. Others have added a fourth style called neglecting (Maccoby & Martin, 1983). Ervin (1993) suggested there are parallels between these parenting styles and the types of attachment mothers and children develop. Other studies indicate that such styles are systematically related to children's behavior.

The authoritarian style is characterized by detached, controlling parental behaviors; there is little warmth, and behavioral rules are strict. Individuals who exhibit this style emphasize power differences in the parent–child relationship, and compliance appears to be a major goal. As a consequence, children often have low self-esteem and difficulty interacting with peers; they may also demonstrate aggressive behavior (Hart, Ladd, & Burleson, 1990).

In contrast, the authoritative parenting style is responsive, supportive, and flexible. Parents are demanding and firm but also display warmth and receptivity to children's views. Limits and rules are explained, and transgressions discussed. Children whose parents engage in this style have high self-esteem and learn to be critical but also supportive, responsible, and sociable (Roopnarine, 1987).

The permissive style involves indulgent, nondemanding, and warm parenting. Impulsive and uncontrolled behavior is not sanctioned. As a result, children may be sociable but too dependent on parents; their aggressiveness may also be negatively evaluated by peers. Finally, the neglecting style reflects a parental lack of concern for children and, in exceptional cases, leads to neglect and abuse. This style is frequently linked to negative psychological functioning.

Bernstein's Social Class Differences: Codes and Social Control.
Social class differences in parental interaction styles—and their implications for children's development—have received widespread attention (Cook-Gumperz, 1973). Much of this literature is based on Basil Bernstein's groundbreaking work.

A well-known sociolinguist, Bernstein (1970, 1971, 1977) emphasized the role of communication in his theories of socialization and drew a sharp distinction between elaborated and restricted codes. Elaborated communication codes are more complex and more flexible than restricted codes; they permit more explicit, individualized meanings to be expressed. In contrast, restricted communication codes are more stereotyped, condensed, and reliant on nonverbal means; they embody commonly shared social meanings. Bernstein (1977) suggested that these codes at once reflect and sustain particular ways of "being" in the social world. Moreover, he argued that whereas members of middle-class socioeconomic groups typically employ both codes, members of lower-class socioeconomic groups mainly use the restricted code.

In support of Bernstein's ideas, Cook-Gumperz (1973) found that middle-class mothers tend to use an elaborated, personal mode of communication to control their children (i.e., a focus on individual motivations and needs). In contrast, lower-class mothers tend to use a restricted, positional mode of communication (i.e., a focus on the status and role the individual possesses). Along similar lines, Turner (1973) observed that middle-class children are more likely to employ "positional" communication strategies (e.g., based on status obligations, etc.), while lower-class children are more likely to use imperative strategies (e.g., commands, directives, etc.).

A series of studies by Hess and colleagues (Hess & Shipman, 1968; Hess, Shipman, Bear, & Brophy, 1968) reveal that three modes of maternal communication could be linked to complementary styles in children: (a) children whose mothers used an imperative mode tended to acknowledge and obey authority; (b) children whose mothers employed a subjective mode tended to acknowledge personal considerations; and (c) children whose mothers used a cognitive-rational mode tended to focus on tasks and rational principles. In a related vein, W. Robinson and Rackstraw (1972) analyzed maternal strategies in answering questions and examined the influence of these strategies on their children's communication. Middle-class mothers were more likely to answer questions, give more factual and accurate information, and use more analogies and cause–effect relationships in their responses than were lower-class mothers. Lower-class mothers were more likely to rephrase a question as a statement or to respond that things were "always done" in a particular way; in other words, their responses appealed to authority. When answering questions, middle-class children gave more information; this information was more accurate and relevant than that generally given by lower-class children. Lower-class children typically replied by appealing to authority or to general behavioral rules (e.g., "You can't do that because it's naughty"). Middle-class mothers asked more questions of their children, regardless of the objects being discussed; their answers referred to children's experiences and used more referential comparisons. Middle-class children tended to give more appropriate responses to their mothers' questions. Both lower-class mothers and their children used language predominantly to inform.

Bernstein's earliest work examined the transmission of social class differences via communication rather than on language acquisition per se (Turner, 1973). He focused primarily on the interaction between mother and child and covered discipline and explanatory contexts. Over the years since Bernstein's initial publications in the 1970s, his work has been reformulated. Today, codes are not viewed as reflecting linguistic competence but rather as socially constituted practices that occur in particular contexts. These codes not only orient individuals to certain meanings but also dictate what is considered appropriate (and inappropriate) communicative behavior. As Turner (1993) pointed out, part of language (and communication) acquisition involves understanding a particular group's orientation toward meaning.

In an effort to explore this issue, Turner and colleagues (Turner, 1973, 1987) conducted a series of studies examining the consistency of children's meaning orientation over contexts and linkages in language use between mothers and their children. Several findings are worth noting. First, middle-class children initially refused to answer some questions but would answer when the questions were reformulated. Second, in role-play speech questions, lower-class children role-played without difficulty whereas middle-class children were very concerned about the truth or falsity of their responses. Finally, mothers who gave lengthier responses and "altered" the interviewer's questions, especially using denials and imposing multiple situational constraints, had children with more varied communicative responses. This pattern was stronger in the working-class subsample than in the middle-class subsample.

Similar results have been obtained by Hoff-Ginsberg (1991), who observed significant social class differences in mothers' speech to their children across a variety of contexts. In her study, middle-class mothers used more topic-continuing replies and fewer directives with their children than did lower-class mothers. Hoff-Ginsberg also found, however, that reading tended to minimize social class differences in interaction between mothers and their children. Other studies indicate that lower-class mothers generally have less time for mutual play, talk less to their children, use more directives, and are less contingent in their speech than are middle-class mothers (Heath, 1983).

Bernstein suggested that these mothers—and their children—operate under different interpretive rules (now reconceptualized as recognition and realization rules). According to Bernstein, code determines the way in which an individual interprets and behaves in a certain context; interpretation involves recognition rules, and interaction frames involve realization rules. In other words, recognition and realization are tacit rules for interpreting meanings and practices in particular social contexts. Contexts can be strongly (+C) or weakly (–C) classified and strongly (+F) or weakly framed (–F). Thus, cultural codes can define, strongly or weakly (i.e., ambiguously), contexts and their appropriate interactional activities. Bernstein's previous research suggests that middle-class families have relatively ambiguous definitions of contexts and their interactions and leave room for flexible, individualized responses. In contrast, lower-class families tend to interact in very specifically defined contexts and are guided by behaviors that are fairly well understood. In these circumstances, people fit into pre-existing patterns; patterns are not tailored to individuals (behavior more possible in a less structured, well-defined framing common among middle-class people).

Social class thus exerts a clear effect on children's communicative development. Labeling, question asking, analogies, and appeals to authority are only some of the linguistic devices that differ as a function of the social group to which parents belong. Variations in these and other behaviors impart to children appropriate interpretive rules for defining and communicating in different situations.

Paternal Styles of Interaction

Researchers have now begun to investigate how fathers interact with their children and what differences exist between maternal and paternal patterns of interaction. Variations in these interactional patterns have raised questions about the unique contributions of mothers and fathers to their children's development.

Fathers' Competence. As Glen Collins (1982) noted, "Fathers haven't always been a fashionable research subject for social scientists" (p. 181). Until relatively recently, most studies examining the role fathers play in children's social and emotional development focused on the effects of his *absence*. The mother–infant relationship was given preeminent status in developmental research; it was seen as distinct from—and vastly more important than—the bond that develops between a father and his child. For several years, this unfortunate viewpoint in the scientific community fueled the common misperception that men simply are not as capable as women when it comes to rearing children. In the late 1970s, however, researchers such as Collins began to look at the validity of this assumption and, as we know today, found very little evidence to support it.

In a series of important studies, Parke and Sawin (1981) investigated four cultural myths about fathers: Fathers were uninterested in and uninvolved with newborn infants; they were less nurturant towards infants than were mothers; they preferred "non-active" caretaking roles and, therefore, left major responsibilities to mothers; and they were less able to meet the needs of newborn infants. Comparisons of mother–infant and father–infant interactions, however, revealed few differences. Fathers were found to be highly involved with their newborns: They looked at, touched, kissed, and vocalized to their babies as often as mothers did. Fathers also showed as much sensitivity and responsiveness to children's cues as mothers, and babies drank just as much formula when their fathers fed them as when their mothers did. Caretaking emerged as the one dimension on which parents differed. When left alone, fathers were found to feed their infants significantly less than did mothers. Although Parke and Sawin argued that this finding suggests there may be some truth to the assumption that fathers prefer less active caretaking roles than do mothers, Lamb offered an alternative interpretation.

Lamb's work indicated that during the newborn period, both mothers and fathers are equally competent in caretaking activities (Lamb, 1977a, 1977b, 1978, 1987a, 1987b), but because mothers spend more time in child care, they become more attuned to their infants and thus more aware of their individual qualities. Lamb suggested that fathers may come to feel less competent over time and, therefore, decrease their involvement in caretaking responsibilities. Lamb pointed out, however, that when fathers must assume primary care responsibility, they do so with great skill. Clearly, when given the chance, fathers are interested in and involved with their children. Moreover, they are as competent as mothers when it comes to caring for babies. While few differences in the ability to provide sensitive, nurturing child care have been observed, there are striking variations in the modal patterns of interaction that mothers and fathers exhibit with their children (Volling & Belsky, 1992a, 1992b).

Characteristic Modes of Father Interaction. Several studies (Kotelchuck, 1975; Lamb, 1977a, 1977b, 1978; Parke & O'Leary, 1975) of early parent–child interaction have indicated that fathers typically hold their babies to play with them whereas mothers typically hold their infants during caretaking activities (e.g., when feeding, bathing, or burping them). These investigations have also suggested that fathers initiate more physical and idiosyncratic games with their babies, and mothers initiate more verbal play routines. Finally, graphs of parent–child behavior show that mothers tend to interact in modulated and controlled ways. In contrast, fathers interact in a somewhat more playful and exciting manner. As the well-known pediatrician T. Berry Brazelton has explained, both forms of interaction serve important functions for the infant:

> Mother has more of a tendency to teach the baby about inner control, and about how to keep the homeostatic system going; she then builds her stimulation on top of that system in a very smooth, regulated sort of way. The father adds a different dimension, teaching the baby about some of the ups and downs—and also teaching the baby another very important thing: how to get back in control. (cited in Collins, 1982, p. 183)

A similar set of findings has been observed with respect to language development. Kavanaugh and Jirkovsky (1982) followed four parent–infant triads from birth to the children's first words. Both mothers and fathers were found to use simple, redundant, and clear language when talking to their infants. This suggests that throughout infancy, both parents are capable of adapting their speech—especially its semantic content—to children. But other work indicated that with development there are distinctions in the types of speech acts mothers and fathers direct toward children.

Some studies have suggested that on both cognitive and motor tasks, mothers encourage more problem solving and fathers give more directions. For example,

Masur (1982) assessed the cognitive content in parents' speech and found that mothers produced more strategies encouraging and modeling problem-solving approaches than did fathers. In their observations of parent–child play interactions, Bellinger and Gleason (1982) also found that fathers were more directive than were mothers.

In an extensive investigation, Fagot and Hagan (1991) examined the socialization practices of mothers and fathers with children between the ages of 1 and 5. Consistent with expectations, fathers were found to spend more positive playtime with youngsters than mothers; however, mothers were found to give more instructions than fathers. The frequency with which both parents instructed their children increased with age. Interestingly, though, fathers not only started later than mothers, but also gave more positive responses to children engaged in large motor behaviors.

In a related vein, Tomasello, Conti-Ramsden, and Ewert (1990) reported that children experience more communicative breakdowns with their fathers than with their mothers. In their study, fathers requested more clarification from children and used more nonspecific queries, such as "What?" Mothers, on the other hand, not only employed more specific queries but also repeated them. Interestingly, children tended to persist if they did not receive maternal acknowledgment but gave up in the face of their fathers' nonresponses. Some researchers have suggested that this type of interaction with fathers helps prepare children for communicating with less familiar adults; this theory is referred to as the bridge hypothesis. Because mothers generally play a more substantial role in children's earliest development, it is believed that fathers are like "less familiar adults" who help their youngsters learn how to handle the communicative breakdowns that inevitably occur with unfamiliar others.

In many ways, these interaction and speech styles are consistent with cultural stereotypes suggesting that men are more physical, more activity oriented, and less communicative than women. Another stereotype that has received some empirical support concerns parental preferences. Researchers such as Parke and O'Leary (1975) and Pederson (1975) have observed that fathers touch and vocalize to firstborn boys more than to later-born boys or to girls born in any ordinal position. Apparently this pattern continues throughout childhood. Lamb (1987b) found that even among older children, fathers spent more time with their sons than with their daughters. These findings indicate there may be some validity to the notion that fathers prefer boys.

Regardless of whether they actually prefer one gender over the other, research indicates that when compared to mothers, fathers are more concerned with appropriate sex-role behavior in their children—particularly their boys. Indeed, as Henshall and McGuire (1986) noted, one of the strongest trends emerging from research on fathers' interactions with children is their greater concern for the appropriateness of children's sex-role behaviors and the greater pressure on conformity for boys. For instance, Snow, Jacklin, and Maccoby (1983) found that even with children as young as 12 months, fathers encouraged more sex-stereotyped behavior than mothers. Fathers were also found to be "harder" on boys in their discipline and more accepting of dependent behavior by daughters. Similarly, in a study of parental reactions to youngsters' play, Lytton and Romney (1991) observed differences in mothers' and fathers' responses only in the encouragement of sex-typed behaviors, with fathers showing more concern for appropriateness than mothers did. These and other studies have led researchers to conclude that fathers not only tend to play more physically with sons than with daughters but that they are also more consistent in their reinforcement of boys' use of sex-typed behavior and sex-typed toys (Sigel, 1987).

It is important to note that differences between parents in the extent of sex-typing are relative: Both mothers and fathers reinforce sex-appropriate behavior in their children, but fathers do so more frequently than do mothers and appear to be more concerned that their sons (as opposed to their daughters) adopt appropriate sex roles. Mothers, however, clearly share some responsibility for teaching their children to act as little boys or little girls.

For instance, in the Fagot and Hagan study (1991) discussed earlier, both mothers and fathers were found to make sex-determined responses; interestingly, these responses were most likely to occur when youngsters were around 18 months of age. As the authors explained, this pattern may reflect both parents' implicit knowledge that children need to adopt appropriate behaviors as they enter the larger social world. Studies have also suggested that both mothers and fathers structure dialogues with their children so that they approximate conversational practices of adults—practices that some believe perpetuate traditional sex roles.

In a study contrasting mothers' and fathers' conversations with their preschoolers, Grief (1980) found that both parents interrupted daughters more than they did sons and fathers interrupted more than mothers. Fathers had simultaneous talk with their children more than did mothers, and fathers had more simultaneous talk with their daughters than with their sons. Parents were consistent in their styles as either high or low interrupters and high or low simultaneous speakers. Grief (1980) suggested these conversational practices show children that boys and girls are treated differently and that boys are dominant. She further suggested that fathers may use interruptions and simultaneous talk to control conversations and that both parents control daughters more than they do sons.

Other researchers have noted that the qualities mothers and fathers encourage vary according to children's gender. Work by May (1980), Block (1979), and Barry, Bacon, and Child (1957) has indicated that both parents encourage boys to be more self-reliant, independent, emotionally in control, and responsible than girls. Consistent with these studies, both mothers and fathers have been found to reward boys for showing independence and adopting a strategy orientation. In contrast, parents typically reward girls for seeking help and for being concrete in their thinking. Henshall and McGuire (1986) suggested that these patterns are strikingly similar to elementary school teachers' expectations about boys' and girls' cognitive styles. Not surprisingly, parents also influence the people with whom children identify. McGuire (1982) found that when compared to daughters, sons are more likely to share interests with their fathers in physical activities such as sports. Along similar lines, Lynn and Cross (1974) asked children at ages 2, 3, and 4 to choose with which parent they would prefer to play. At all ages, boys preferred their fathers; 2-year-old girls also preferred their fathers, but by age 4 they favored their mothers. It is quite possible that the shift in girls' preferences reflects both changes in interests and increasing recognition of sex-role expectations.

Effects of Fathers' Interaction and Involvement. As Youniss (1992) persuasively argued, parenting in general and fathering in particular need to be viewed in the sociocultural context in which families live. He pointed out research suggesting that paternal interactional styles vary as a function of occupation and socioeconomic status (Kohn, 1969). Whereas managerial fathers, with a relatively high socioeconomic status (SES), encourage their sons to think in logical, self-directed ways, fathers with lower SES encourage their sons to be orderly and conforming. These patterns of paternal interaction fit well with those described by Bernstein.

Along similar lines, in a collection of essays, Michael Lamb (1987a), citing the work of Pleck (1984), traced four models of fatherhood which have dominated different periods in U.S. history: father as moral teacher, father as breadwinner, father as sex-role model, and father as nurturer. As moral teacher, fathers' role of educator ensured that their children would be able to read the scriptures and follow Christian beliefs; this period extended from the 17th century to the mid 1800s. From approximately 1850 to 1935, fathers' role as breadwinner was emphasized at the same time modern industrialization developed. After World War II, a new model emerged. Although fathers were still seen as breadwinners and moral teachers, there was new interest in fathers as sex-role models, especially for sons. During the 1970s, fathers as nurturing, involved, supportive parents emerged. As Lamb noted, all these roles are important, and different subcultural groups may have different emphases. He suggested that today's fathers are important as breadwinners, as sources of emotional support, and as direct interactional partners for their children.

In another study, Lamb (1987a) examined how family circumstances influence paternal involvement. Three levels of involvement were explored: direct interaction, accessibility (in which fathers were available but not directly involved with children), and responsibility for child care (in which fathers were directly responsible for child care as opposed to "just helping out"). Results indicated that in families where mothers were unemployed, fathers spent approximately 20% to 25% of the time mothers spent in direct interaction, about one third as much time in being accessible, and assumed virtually no responsibility for child care. In families where both parents worked, fathers' direct interaction and accessibility were much higher—33% and 66% respectively—but there was no increase in the amount of time they spent in child care activities! According to Lamb, these findings suggest that paternal involvement is affected by a complex set of factors including fathers' motivation to participate in child rearing, mothers' support for the participation, and family circumstances that either enhance or constrain the need for fathers' participation.

For whatever reasons fathers become more involved, the benefits of their participation are clear. Nurturant behavior from both parents is associated with greater achievement and better psychosocial adjustment in children. Preschoolers with highly involved fathers are more cognitively competent, have fewer sex-stereotyped beliefs, more empathy, and a greater internal locus of control than do children of less involved fathers (Pruett, 1983; Sagi, 1982). Paternal warmth and closeness have also been found to predict better sex-role adjustment, higher levels of competency, and stronger achievement orientations in sons. Lamb argued that the positive consequences resulting from highly involved fathers stem from helping to create a "family context in which parents feel good about their marriages and the arrangements they have been able to work out" (1987b, p. 16). Dunn (1993) concurred. As she noted, research generally supports the idea that healthy marital relationships are associated with healthy parent–child relationships. Father-absent families may have problems because the economic, social, and emotional aspects of fathering are not present.

The Impact of Siblings

Scholars once believed that the presence of siblings invariably limited children's linguistic and communicative development because there was less time for adult caretakers to spend with infants. As we have repeatedly argued, sustained contact with an adult caretaker is a very rich source of attention and stimulation for a developing infant. But the presence of siblings can offer a different set of opportunities for growth and development. An increasing number of studies have thus investigated triadic communication, where parent, sibling, and infant interact.

For instance, Jones and Adamson (1987) analyzed naturally occurring interaction between mother–infant dyads and mother–infant–sibling triads to explore the ways that the number of people and the types of activity influenced language use in children from 18 to 23 months old. Results indicated that later-born infants used more social-regulative speech (e.g., "No, don't do that. No.") than did firstborns and that their mothers used less metalinguistic speech than did mothers with only one child.

Other studies have contrasted infants' interaction with different partners. For example, Vandell and Wilson (1987) analyzed babies' interaction with their mothers, a sibling, or a peer at 6 and 9 months. Infants spent more time in turn-taking interactions with mothers than with siblings or peers; mothers frequently initiated interaction by responding to infants or by eliciting infant responses. Babies' interactions with older siblings were briefer, and the siblings did not respond contingently to the infants. In addition, infants generally spent less time in turn taking when interacting with peers. Infants who had more extensive turn-taking experience with skilled partners, however, engaged in a higher frequency of turn-taking interactions with peers.

Triads tend to have longer conversations than dyads, and infants appear to take more turns during mother–infant–sibling dialogues than during mother–infant or sibling–infant interactions. Barton and Tomasello (1991) found that infants readily participated in triadic interactions. Babies responded to remarks directed to them as well as to others; this reaction indicates that they reliably understood language even when it was addressed to others. Woollett (1986) also observed that children as young as 19 months were able to engage in triadic joint attention episodes. These triadic interactions involved some reciprocity among all participants. Infants not only joined in an ongoing conversation but also contributed to it through their own turn at talk. Woollett thus argued that although the presence of older siblings may lessen adult responsiveness to each individual child, they also provide a more varied, stimulating language environment in which differing communicative styles are evident. In addition, when young children talk to siblings, they must adapt their communication to speakers who are both less able—and perhaps less willing—to take their wishes into consideration (Mannle & Tomasello, 1987). In fact, Dunn and Shatz (1989) observed that 2- and 3-year-olds could readily join in conversations (with siblings and others) and contributed new information, even when they were not being directly addressed. This was easier when their entries were topic relevant than when they were not.

Siblings also mediate the relationship between mothers and other children. For example, Dunn and Kendrick (1982) found that differences in the relationship between a mother and her firstborn child, at the birth of the second child, predicted the siblings' relationship one year later. When mothers and their firstborn daughters had intense relationships, the siblings' relationship was hostile. However, conflict between mothers and firstborns (arising at the birth of a second child) was lessened if firstborns had affectionate relationships with their fathers. Mothers' relationships with their second-born children were also linked to siblings' later relationships, and siblings' relationships were, in turn, associated with the relationship each child had with his or her mother.

Finally, research has suggested that siblings learn quickly about their brothers' and sisters' dispositions. Dunn and Munn (1985) noted that teasing behavior (when one sibling playfully annoys another) occurs as early as 18 months and is well in place by 2 years. Teasing behaviors become more detailed, frequent, and verbal during the second year. Children also tease their mothers and are accurate at anticipating their reactions. By age 2, youngsters display a keen understanding of the emotional reactions of other family members; they can engage in supporting and comforting acts as well as exhibit hostile behavior to an opponent when taking sides in a conflict. Dunn (1991) noted that some siblings are interesting, fun companions while others are hostile and aggressive toward one another. In fact, preschoolers often accuse their sibling of "hurting them," and "tattling" on brothers and sisters is common. As the following example from Dunn and Slomkowski (1992, p. 73) indicates, parents frequently become involved:

Child and sibling in an argument.

Father to child: Sort him out.

Sibling to child: Oh, no!

Child to sibling: Len! [Hits him]

Sibling to child: Oh, no!

Child to sibling: Biff him now. [Hits him again]

Child to mother: Hitting it. Mum look. Do Len fight.
                         Enough. Got headache. [Takes boxing gloves off]
                         Len hurt me. Len hurt me. He biff me.

Dunn's work further indicated that siblings are sensitive to the different ways in which mothers treat them (Dunn, 1988b). She believed that maternal behaviors may differentially influence children as a function of age and their particular relationship. Clearly, studies of sibling interaction and its effects need to account for children's developmental level and temperament.

Summary. Reviewing the complex patterns of interaction occurring within families demonstrates the major shifts in developmental research since the 1970s. In the 1970s, researchers focused on how adults talked to young children and analyzed whether this talk (ACL and motherese) simplified language in ways that made it easier for young children to learn. Attention also focused on the nature of mother–infant and mother–child interaction as these were believed to constitute the primary contexts in which attachment bonds developed. The more scholars studied such interaction patterns, however, the clearer it became that families are composed of many members and influenced by many factors. Thus, the complexity of relational and developmental issues within families emerged.

Concern then turned to more global family patterns, such as overall parenting styles, social class differences in family interaction, paternal involvement in child rearing, and the influence of siblings. General parenting styles offer different communicative and relational messages for children. The authoritative style, characterized by firm but supportive and responsive parenting, fosters an atmosphere of trust and respect where communication can flourish and children's self-esteem is enhanced. Class differences in communication suggest that flexible, not rigidly defined interactional contexts maximize children's opportunities for language growth and offer more occasions for communication. The importance of paternal involvement is evident; when compared to mothers, fathers' interactional styles provide different but complementary experiences for children, and the emotional support fathers can give to the entire family is important.

Siblings constitute another interactional environment. Infants and toddlers appear to participate more, not less, when interacting in a family triad of mother–sibling–child. The relationships between siblings are also affected by the relationship of each sibling to the parents, a further illustration of the complexity of family interactions. Siblings also afford communicative opportunities for practicing teasing, conflict management, and comforting and reasoning messages. In this way, they may provide a useful training ground for peer–peer interaction.

DISCIPLINE

Traditional Conceptualizations of Discipline and Its Effects

Discipline is an important part of parenting. Through discipline, children's behavior is monitored and changed if necessary; children learn about cultural and family values as well as about self-control and dealing with others. The patience and tolerance of both children and parents is tested! This is especially true during the "terrible twos" when even the friendliest requests for children to join in a favorite activity receive an emphatic "No!"

In what follows, we discuss different aspects of discipline, paying particular attention to its effects on children's cognitive, motivational, communicative, and social development. "Traditional" conceptualizations of discipline—and methods for studying its effects—are presented first. These traditional conceptualizations are then critiqued and compared with a more current approach to assessing discipline and its influence on children's development. Grounded in constructivist theory, the approach we advocate makes use of Bernstein's social class codes described earlier. More specifically, it examines how such codes manifest themselves in the disciplinary strategies parents employ and the lessons such strategies teach children about the nature of the social world in which they live.

Before beginning our discussion, we should note that even the best disciplinary efforts are not always met with compliance. In a study of children aged 18 to 30 months, Schneider-Rosen and Wenz-Gross (1990) found no differences in compliance to mothers' or fathers' requests across a wide variety of situations. However, 2-year-olds who were undergoing cognitive reorganization as well as facing increased parental demands, demonstrated more varied noncompliant behavior than did other children. Children's compliance also varied as a function of the situational demands. This suggests that compliance, although increasing with age, apparently does not increase linearly but rather as a function of the specific situation.

Traditional Conceptualizations of Discipline

What strategies do parents use in an effort to get their children to comply? Although several schemes exist for categorizing different types of discipline, probably the most widely recognized are those by Baumrind (1989) and M. L. Hoffman (1977). Both these schemes distinguish between strategies that seek to gain compliance through the use of physical punishment or the exercise of material power over children (authoritarian or power assertive) and strategies that attempt to control behavior via explanation and reasoning (authoritative or inductive). These general styles of discipline have been found to predict a variety of competencies in children including advanced social cognitive abilities, motivational orientations, and peer acceptance.

Discipline and Social Cognition. Several studies have examined the relationship between parental discipline and individual differences in children's social cognition. These studies have generally indicated that youngsters who receive inductive forms of discipline exhibit higher levels of role-taking skill than do youngsters who are reprimanded through power-assertive methods. For example, in a study of 6- and 7-year-olds, Bearison and Cassel (1975) observed a significant association between parental reasoning and children's ability to infer and understand the perspectives of others. Similarly, Dlugokinski and Firestone (1974) found that parents' use of inductive strategies predicted "other-centered" values and orientations in third- and fifth-grade children.

Discipline and Motivational Orientations. Other work has indicated that parental disciplinary styles influence the development of motivational orientations in children such as locus of control (people's belief that they can generally control or affect events in the world), empathy (the tendency to understand and orient toward others' feelings), and self-efficacy (the sense of competence developed with respect to exercising particular social skills). Many of these studies focus on the relationship between motivation and parental attitudes toward discipline or motivation and children's perceptions of parental discipline. Studies exploring the connection between motivational variables and actual disciplinary strategies are rare.

Nowicki and Roundtree (1971) and Nowicki and Segal (1973) examined the relation between children's perceptions of parents and their locus of control orientations. In both studies, internal children (i.e., those who believed they controlled events in their lives) perceived parents to be trusting, nurturing, consistent in their behavior, and likely to encourage autonomy. A similar approach has been employed in investigations of empathy and self-efficacy. Both Fay (1970) and Huckaby (1971) observed associations between children's empathy and mothers' self-reported attitudes toward child rearing. More specifically, mothers who reported they were tolerant, affectionate, and permissive had children marked by relatively high degrees of empathic concern. In an investigation examining the link between maternal discipline and children's self-efficacy, Ladd and Price (1986) found that parents who admitted having difficulty promoting their children's cognitive and social competence (e.g., teaching children how to succeed in school and how to make friends) had youngsters who felt less competent in their ability to inhibit aggression.

In the few studies where actual behavior has been the focus, discipline is categorized in relatively global ways. For example, Gordon, Wichern, and Nowicki (1983) examined the relationship between children's locus of control orientations and the frequency of behaviors mothers exhibited during a problem-solving activity with their children. Results indicated that mothers who were warm and nurturing, encouraged independence, and used minimal physical punishment during the task had children with internal orientations. On the other hand, youngsters with external locus of control orientations (i.e., who believed they had no control over events in their lives) had mothers who were more critical and obtrusive. Nowicki and Duke (1983) obtained similar results. Loeb (1975) also observed parents and their children during a problem-solving situation. This time, parents' communication was coded for the extent to which orders, demands, and "other attempts to control children's behavior" were used. Findings suggested that parents who were more directive and controlling in their communication had children with external orientations.

Discipline and Peer Acceptance. In the next chapters, we review some of the consequences associated with children's peer status; several dramatic outcomes are known to result from being rejected by members of a social group. For example, children who experience chronic rejection are at risk for increased feelings of loneliness, higher rates of drug and alcohol abuse, adult criminality, early school withdrawal, and a variety of mental health problems including schizophrenia among girls (see Kupersmidt, Coie, & Dodge, 1990). In view of these findings, it is not surprising that many researchers have sought to establish a link between the kind of discipline parents employ and the level of acceptance children achieve. In general, this work indicates that parents who exhibit power-assertive disciplinary styles have children who behave toward others in relatively hostile and aggressive ways; apparently, such behavior wins them little approval from peers and often leads to rejection. In contrast, parents enacting more inductive styles have youngsters who are socially competent and accepted by peers.

In their study of sixth through eighth graders, Roff, Sells, and Golden (1972) found that children's perceptions of parental warmth and acceptance were positively related to high levels of status among peers. In contrast, Patterson, Kupersmidt, and Griesler (1990) observed that third and fourth graders' reports of parental rejection correlated with low levels of acceptance. Other studies using an observational methodology have supported the claim that parents influence their youngsters' subsequent social competence and peer acceptance. For example,

Putallaz (1987) coded mothers' interactions for the extent to which they included positive verbal statements (e.g., polite requests, suggestions). Putallaz then compared these assessments to children's sociometric ratings and their observed social behavior with peers. Results indicated that mothers' use of positive verbal statements predicted both prosocial behavior and peer acceptance in children. In contrast, mothers' use of negative and controlling strategies predicted disagreeable, demanding social behavior and low levels of peer acceptance. Similarly, in a study examining the relation between discipline and the development of aggressive behaviors in school-age boys, Dishion (1990) observed that parents who employed negative and punishing styles had children who were marked by aggressive, antisocial behavior and were less accepted by their peers. M. L. Hoffman (1960) also found that mothers who relied on power-assertive techniques had children who were hostile with peers, used direct commands, threats, and physical force as ways of influencing others, and resisted all attempts at influence initiated by both teachers and peers.

Summary. This body of literature thus suggests that parental discipline plays a powerful role in determining children's social-cognitive abilities, motivational orientations, and peer status. When compared to power-assertive methods of discipline, inductive efforts have been associated with more advanced role-taking skills, internal locus of control orientations, and higher levels of empathy and self-efficacy in children. In addition, youngsters of inductively oriented parents tend to behave in socially competent ways and enjoy a greater degree of accpetance among peers than do children of power-assertive parents.

Research comparing inductive versus power-assertive styles significantly contributes to understanding how discipline affects children's social development, but this body of work is limited in several ways. First, studies of attitudes toward discipline fail to account for the communicative processes through which these attitudes are transmitted to children. As a result, we are left with little understanding of how (and why) parental beliefs about tolerance, permissiveness, and affection influence the cognitive, motivational, and social outcomes children experience. Second, although behavioral investigations obviously consider communication an important link between parental attitudes and children's development, they tend to take a relatively global approach when categorizing discipline. It is difficult to discern, for example, precisely what constitutes a "warm" or "nurturing" message or the verbal means by which "independence is encouraged."

We believe studies not only need to specify the types of messages characteristic of different disciplinary styles but should also articulate the important features of these messages so that linkages between parental communication and children's development can be understood. In other words, precisely because they are treated as general styles of interaction, current conceptualizations of discipline fail to identify features of messages that affect children's developing logic about the social world or the processes through which this logic is imparted.

The constructivist analysis provides one avenue for identifying important components of disciplinary messages and the processes through which these components influence children's development. We believe that this approach provides a more complete and promising explanation for the role discipline plays in the growth of children's social-cognitive and motivational orientations and their subsequent effects than do other views.

A Constructivist Analysis of Discipline

Our approach grows out of constructivism, a perspective that emphasizes complexity "as a construct for differentiating messages and cognitive systems" (Burleson, Delia, & Applegate, 1995, p. 35) and relates it to the functional pursuit of social goals such as discipline. The constructivist conceptualization of discipline differs from previous approaches in terms of (a) the components of parental messages that are of interest, (b) the structures in children which are affected by these messages, and (c) the process through which parental communication influences children (Applegate, Burleson, & Delia, 1992).

Important Components of Disciplinary Messages. The constructivist analysis of message complexity is grounded in B. Bernstein's (1973) distinction between elaborated and restricted codes. As mentioned, Bernstein suggested that different modes of interaction simultaneously "express and are organized by the assumption of similarity or uniqueness in the psychological experiences underlying social relations" (Applegate et al., 1992, p. 5). The elaborated code both reflects and encourages the assumption that individuals are, to a large extent, unique in their feelings, intentions, and psychological perspectives. In contrast, the restricted code is based on (and perpetuates) the belief that identities and actions are defined by social convention and the positions individuals occupy.

Constructivists have extended Bernstein's analysis by suggesting that, in terms of the goals they seek to accomplish, messages characteristic of the elaborated code are actually more complex than are messages associated with the restricted code (see, for example, Burleson, 1987; O'Keefe & Delia, 1982). Within the constructivist framework, communication is seen as a functional, goal-driven activity directed toward accomplishing some fundamental instrumental aim (Delia, O'Keefe, & O'Keefe, 1982). From this perspective, individuals engage in communication with the purpose of persuading, comforting, telling a story, disciplining, and so forth.

However, in addition to pursuing these primary instrumental goals, individuals may also seek to accomplish other subsidiary aims; for example, they may attend to people's identities, face needs, and relational concerns. Restricted code users are less likely to address these subsidiary goals because they operate in a world defined by rules, a world in which information about people and relationships is contained in a person's position. In contrast, because of their assumption of psychological uniqueness, elaborated code users are more likely to pursue a variety of goals in interaction; their messages must serve instrumental aims as well as attend to people's identities, face needs, and relational concerns. In constructivist language, messages reflecting relatively simple goal configurations are termed *position centered*, whereas messages reflecting more complex goal configurations are called *person centered*.

Obviously, the specific goals pursued in any context vary according to the demands of the situation. Thus, the manner in which person-centeredness manifests itself also varies according to the situation. Within disciplinary contexts, person-centeredness is evident when parents promote children's reflection on the nature of their wrongdoing, the consequences of their actions, and how their transgression might affect the feelings and perspectives of others (Applegate, Burke, Burleson, Delia, & Kline, 1985). As Burleson (1987) wrote, person-centered disciplinary strategies seek to remediate behavior by encouraging the child to "reason through the consequences—especially the interpersonal or social consequences—of his or her actions rather than invoking rules, threatening punitive actions, or using force" (p. 317). These strategies are typically referred to as reflection enhancing.

Structures and Processes Affected in Children. According to Burleson et al. (1995), in view of the variety of circumstances youngsters encounter, parental discipline cannot present children with a set of ready-made behavioral routines for all situations but can direct children's attention to particular features of situations. Discipline imparts a logic about aspects of the social world to be considered when choosing what to do. In the case of reflection-enhancing messages, children's attention is focused on the implications actions have for people's psychological and emotional states. Children are led to see that a complex set of factors (e.g., multiple perspectives, multiple affective states, multiple desires, etc.) defines situations and should be taken into account when enacting behavior. The complexity of these messages thus poses a greater accommodative challenge to children (cf. Applegate, Burleson, et al., 1992; Burleson et al., 1995). Reflection-enhancing messages create a more complex social world for youngsters to evaluate and respond to.

Constructivists have maintained that exposure to complex forms of parental behavior is most likely to influence children's cognitive structures rather than their behavior. As parents direct attention to multiple features of situations, children naturally acquire increasingly sophisticated ways for representing and making inferences about these features. Through the repeated challenge of accommodating to complex, reflection-enhancing messages, children develop more structures for viewing and interpreting the social world.

Within constructivism, the structures through which individuals perceive and interpret the social world are called constructs. Systems of interpersonal constructs can be more or less complex in terms of the number of elements they contain (differentiation) as well as the psychological nature of these elements (abstractness). Researchers have argued that disciplinary strategies embodying the pursuit of multiple goals (i.e., reflection-enhancing strategies) should promote the development of more complex systems of interpersonal constructs in children. Complex systems of interpersonal constructs should, in turn, enable children to engage in more person-centered forms of communication across a variety of functional domains. Importantly, person-centered messages are preferred by peers. Several studies indicate that youngsters who comfort, persuade, inform, and manage conflict in more person-centered ways enjoy a greater degree of acceptance among peers than do youngsters who communicate in more position-centered ways (see Burleson, 1986; Burleson, Applegate, et al., 1986).

From this perspective, communicative competencies and their related outcomes are at least partially determined by the social-cognitive abilities children develop in response to the nature of parental discipline they receive. The constructivist model thus suggests that parental communication affects children's social cognition, and children's social cognition, in turn, influences their interactional skills and associated outcomes. Although limited in number, empirical tests of this model indicate that it is a promising way of conceptualizing the indirect effects of parental discipline.

For example, Applegate, Burke, et al. (1985) found that mothers who used reflection-enhancing discipline had children who were more cognitively complex and exhibited more person-centered comforting and persuasive skills than children whose parents did not use reflection-enhancing discipline. However, associations between mothers' discipline and children's communication became nonsignificant when the effects of complexity were partialled out statistically. Applegate, Burleson, and Delia (1992), Burleson et al. (1995), and Burleson and Kunkel (1996) reported similar findings.

Although not directly informed by constructivist thinking, other work has also suggested that the relationship between parental discipline and children's behavior may be indirect. Petit, Dodge, and Brown (1988) observed that children's problem-solving skills (defined as an index of social cognition) mediated the relationship between early family experience and children's social competence. These researchers examined mothers' responses to interview questions assessing children's levels of exposure to aggressive behavior, the harshness of discipline directed toward children, and the mothers' endorsement of aggression as a disciplinary technique. Results indicated that mothers' endorsement of aggression predicted lower levels of children's cognitive reasoning which, in turn, was related to lower sociometric ratings by peers. Similarly, Putallaz (1987) found that mothers who used polite requests and suggestions as a means of discipline (rather than threats and demands) had children with advanced social problem-solving skills; these children also earned high sociometric ratings from peers. Whiting and Edwards' (1988) investigations of maternal child-rearing strategies found three broad patterns—teaching, controlling, and liberal. Each pattern was associated with different interactional styles and disciplinary practices.

In sum, the few indirect studies of discipline conducted by constructivists and others provide consistent evidence for the assumption that parental communication maintains its strongest and most direct relationship with children's social-cognitive abilities. The strength of the constructivist analysis lies in its ability to explain why different forms of discipline lead to various outcomes in children. Although more traditional analyses of disciplinary effects have provided useful and relevant information, they fail to specify the communicative mechanisms through which these effects occur. By identifying important features of parental messages—as well as the structures in children which are influenced by these message features—constructivists have provided a foundation on which to build an understanding of the *whys* and *hows* of disciplinary effects.

Although it may not seem revolutionary, the indirect effects model posited by constructivists represents an important advance in the study of discipline. Before this work, most studies examined only a piece of the model. Thus, we knew that discipline was related to social-cognitive and motivational development as well as to peer success. But the magnitudes of these relationships and their interconnections were not clear. Today, however, we can say with confidence that disciplinary strategies exert their most powerful effect on children's social cognition and motivation. The ways in which parents remediate children's behavior directly influence the ways in which youngsters think about the social world. This logic then shapes how children communicate as well as the subsequent social outcomes they enjoy. Thus, the effects of discipline on children's communicative competence—and the consequences predicted by such competence— appear to be mediated by the logic parental disciplinary strategies impart to children about the social world and the people in it.

SUMMARY

In this chapter, we have explored the richly varied developmental context provided by families; a context surrounded by a cultural milieu in which cognitive, motivational, communicative, and relational skills emerge. From early research focusing on single variables such as ACL and maternal speech, researchers have moved toward studies examining more complex interactions among a variety of relational variables known to influence children's development.

The studies of attachment reviewed in this chapter (as well as others) indicate that the bonds children develop with primary caretakers have a profound and lasting effect on their sense of self, the way they approach and interact in the social world, and the types of relationships they enjoy. When compared to children with insecure attachments, those with secure attachments (approximately 55% of the population) have higher levels of esteem, social responsiveness, and empathy and demonstrate better conflict management skills. As adults, securely attached individuals fare better in relationships with friends, romantic partners, spouses, and co-workers. A similar set of findings has been observed by researchers investigating the effects of more general styles of parenting. This body of work suggests that authoritative parenting is strongly associated with positive self-concepts and peer success among children. Firm but responsive communication is the hallmark of parents who develop secure attachments with their children and who exhibit the authoritative style.

Bernstein's work showed that parenting styles and their related codes both reflect and sustain the communicative norms of particular cultural groups. Drawing on Bernstein's distinction between elaborated and restricted codes, constructivists have further suggested that parental discipline exerts its most powerful and direct effect on children's social cognition and motivation; these, in turn, shape the way in which youngsters communicate with others and the subsequent social outcomes they experience. From this perspective, disciplinary strategies not only function to correct youngsters' transgressions but also profoundly influence the logic they develop about the social world.

Recent research has also underscored the importance of fathers in children's growth and development. Although fathers are just as competent as mothers at child rearing, they appear to exhibit somewhat different styles when interacting with children These styles offer unique lessons about communication and its role in structuring interpersonal relationships. Sibling relationships constitute another part of family life that influences how children learn to communicate as well as the particular skills they develop. Siblings offer opportunities for practicing turn taking, conflict management, and comforting and thus provide a useful training ground for peer–peer interaction.

These studies have demonstrated that to maximize children's communicative and social development, families must strive to provide a nurturing and supportive environment and at the same time must set limits. On a theoretical level, it is evident that researchers investigating communicative and social development must continue to account for the complex array of factors known to affect children's unfolding interactional skills.

In the next two chapters, we discuss friendship, another context that contributes to children's social-cognitive and communicative development. This context is of special significance because it is an arena of competition and cooperation among equals; here, youngsters must manage their relationships largely on their own, without recourse to adult support or intervention.

7

Conceptions of Friendship:
A Developmental Perspective

When asked how she would feel if she did not have any friends, Julie, 8 years old, replied, "I'd feel like killing myself. I'd be lonely. Nobody to be nice to me. I'd even make friends with King Kong." Five-year-old Matthew was somewhat perplexed by the question of what he would do without his friends. "I guess I'd stay in the house," he said, "because I'd have nothing to do."[1] Danny, a shy 4-year-old, seemed to be having trouble making friends at preschool. Repeated attempts to enter the ongoing games of his peers were thwarted, and Danny often found himself playing alone. When asked who was his best friend in school, Danny told the interviewer it was Caleb, one of the most popular boys in the class. When asked why Caleb was his best friend, Danny sadly replied, "Because I want him to be."[2]

Julie, Matthew, and Danny are real children—and their need to belong, to feel attached, to have someone they call "friend" is clear. Children begin to use the word *friend* somewhere around the age of 4 (Hartup, 1983) and, over the course of development, spend increasing amounts of time with friends. Whereas only 10% of a 2-year-old's interactions involve other peers, by age 11 nearly 50% of social activities are conducted with friends (Barker & Wright, 1955; Hartup, 1983). Although the meanings and behaviors associated with the term vary with age, friends play no less a significant role in children's lives than they do in adults'. As any parent or teacher knows, friendships can be a tremendous source of pleasure and excitement for children—or an ongoing source of pain and frustration.

Empirical evidence confirms the intuitive importance of friendship. A long, well-established line of research has indicated that youngsters who are rejected by their peers (i.e., who do not have any friends) suffer negative life consequences, not the least of which include increased feelings of loneliness as well as higher rates of drug and alcohol abuse, juvenile delinquency, dropping out of school, and suicide attempts (for a review of this work, see Asher & Coie, 1990). Among adults, the presence of one close and enduring friendship has been found to reduce depression after a traumatic event such as divorce or the death of a loved one, to lower the probability of health problems, to speed recovery from severe illness, including cancer and cardiovascular disease, and to increase the lifespan (for reviews of these studies, see Cobb, 1976; Ginsberg, 1980; Gottlieb, 1994).

In addition to its impact on psychological well-being and adjustment, friendship imparts lessons about the social world that are distinct from those learned in the context of parent–child relationships. As Z. Rubin (1980) noted, psychoanalytic theory dominated research on child development throughout much of the 20th century, and for a long time, parents—and in particular, mothers—were seen as having the most profound influence on children's lives. In the mid-1970s, however, social scientists turned their attention toward children's peer relationships and soon discovered that friends make unique and important contributions to each other's development. For one thing, children approach each other as equals; thus, unlike exchanges with authority figures, interactions with friends provide a unique opportunity to learn about mutuality, reciprocity, and negotiation—concepts believed to be the foundation on which successful adult relationships are built. In this sense, then, friends shape children's social and emotional growth in ways parents cannot.

The next two chapters summarize current knowledge about children's friendships. Our intent here is not to provide an exhaustive review of the literature but rather to include areas of research that have received a great deal of attention, that are fundamental to understanding the nature of children's friendships, and that we hope are illuminating to readers, both as students of communicative development and as prospective parents.

In this chapter, we pay particular attention to the question of how children's understanding of friendship changes with development. Studies concerned with this general issue have typically proceeded along one of three lines: examining how youngsters conceptualize or define friendship, exploring the activities children believe are indicative of friendship, and investigating what youngsters expect from real as well as ideal friends. Before the review of this literature, we explore some of the unique functions friendship serves in children's lives, and sketch a picture of what a child's earliest friendships look like.

In many ways, the current chapter focuses on the psychological components that underlie a child's ability to develop and maintain significant relationships with peers; it answers the question of what it means to be a friend for children at various stages of development. We believe that the type of communicative activities in which children engage with friends is intimately intertwined with their conceptualization of friendship. In other words, understanding how young children think about friends ought to make clear what children actually do with friends and why they do it. Chapter 8 focuses on the "doing" of friendship. Here, we address such questions as: What factors predict the initiation and maintenance of actual friendships? Do children behave differently with friends versus non-friends? and Are there identifiable gender differences in children's friendships?

SOME IMPORTANT FUNCTIONS OF FRIENDSHIP

As noted in the previous chapter, socialization is generally defined as the "process by which [individuals] learn the ways of a given society or social group so that [they] can function within it" (Elkin & Handel, 1989). For many years, traditional theories of socialization assumed that much of what children learned about "how to function in society" came from parents. Within these theories, adults were seen as the primary socializing agents whose twofold purpose was to promote children's social and emotional adjustment and to preserve the norms and values associated with society. In 1980, however, James Youniss convincingly argued that peers may be equally influential as socializing agents. Youniss drew heavily on the work of Jean Piaget (1959, 1965) and Harry Stack Sullivan (1953), both of whom suggested two processes by which children are socialized—one occurring in the context of parent–child relationships and one occurring in the context of peer relationships, particularly friendships. For Piaget and Sullivan, each context was uniquely suited to teach children important—but very different—lessons about the social world.

In the first process, parents act as "society's agents" who attempt to bring their youngsters' idiosyncratic (and often egocentric) behavior in line with accepted standards (Youniss, 1980). To accomplish this, parents gradually intrude on children's private desires by offering them a set of social meanings consistent with societal norms and expectations. Through a variety of tactics that may include praise, punishment, cajoling, reinforcement, etc., parents ultimately lead their youngsters to internalize these norms as if they were their own. Youniss labeled this process *conformity* because children must adopt (or conform to) social meanings provided by outside agents. Conformity is well suited to teach children important lessons about cultural expectations as well as the nature and demands of authority relations; on a pragmatic level, the process of conformity may facilitate interaction by imparting basic rules about how to get along with others. But Youniss also believed this form of socialization to be severely limited because children are the *recipients* of externally constructed social meaning rather than *co-creators* of meaning. Thus, there is a risk that they will adopt what is expected of them without understanding why it is important to do so.

The second type of socialization, *reciprocity*, corrects for this potential limitation. In this process, children themselves act as socializing agents who bring to their interactions with one another individual meanings and desires. Neither person's meaning is necessarily better, nor can it be unilaterally imposed (as in the case of conformity). Rather, as Youniss (1980) described it, "Both parties must engage in a joint search to discover which meaning—one's own, the other's, or a new meaning—is most workable" (p. 7). Within this context, there is a focus on interaction; views must be presented, objections must be heeded, and a compromise must be worked out. Reciprocity thus leads to what is called a "cooperative production of meaning," which teaches children significant lessons about equality, mutual understanding, and negotiation—lessons that the hierarchical structure of a parent–child relationship precludes.

In addition to the ideas just outlined, Sullivan (1953) saw children's friendships as correcting some of the "harmful views" of social life that youngsters acquire in their early experiences with parents. Sullivan suggested that, in the home, children learn certain patterns of dealing with authority; they may, for example, learn how to rule parents as "petty tyrants," to exhibit complete obedience in the face of authority, or to expect the "smallest wish to be of the utmost importance" (p. 228). Sullivan referred to these views as "handicapping conditions," which, if left unchecked, would make youngsters intolerable and insensitive as adults. Fortunately, such unhealthy patterns of coping with authority are unlearned through interaction with peers. In fact, according to Sullivan, friends are the only people who stand between the "harmful views of social life" imparted by parents and a child's maladjustment in later years.

Many more current efforts to describe the functions associated with children's friendship are rooted in—and include some of—Sullivan's ideas. For example, several researchers (e.g., Duck, Miell, & Gaebler, 1980; Gottman & Parker, 1986) have argued that friends are an important source of social comparison for children. Friends provide a standard against which children measure their beliefs, attitudes, and abilities. In this way, friends help one another develop a sense of identity. Research suggests that parents simply cannot provide as meaningful a comparison as other children—in large part because the most useful standards for comparative judgments (for any age group) are people with whom one is most similar. As Katherine Read (1976) explained:

> We must measure ourselves against others who are like us, finding our strengths and facing our weaknesses, winning some acceptance and meeting some rejection. . . . A favorable family situation helps us to feel secure, but experiences with our own age group help to develop an awareness of ourselves and of social reality which family experience alone cannot give. (p. 340)

Perhaps this is one reason that similarity has been found to predict the formation of actual friendships. Studies show, for example, that whereas young children become friends with others who are the same age, race, and gender, older children develop friendships with those whom they believe possess similar interests and attitudes (see B. H. Schneider, Wiener, & Murphy, 1994, for a review).

Friends also play a distinctive role in teaching children how to communicate successfully (Z. Rubin, 1980). As our discussion of language development suggested, parents often infer a child's desires on the basis of incomplete utterances; they rush to fill a youngster's needs without forcing him or her to speak clearly and thoughtfully. According to Rubin, peers neither have the patience for decoding such cryptic messages nor the "psychic ability" needed to infer what another child wants in the absence of clear communication (p. 4).

Many other researchers have offered taxonomies of the functions associated with children's friendships. For example, Furman and his colleagues (Furman & Buhrmester, 1985; Furman & Robbins, 1985) suggested that friendship enhances self-worth, promotes a sense of "reliable alliance," and provides opportunities for companionship, instrumental aid, nurturing behavior, intimacy, and affection. Hartup and Sancilio (1986) offered a list of three functions: providing emotional support and security, serving as a context in which social competence is learned, and acting as a model or prototype for later relationships. Parker and Gottman (1989) argued that friendship helps children learn how to regulate affective arousal (a topic covered more thoroughly in the next chapter).

Although the range of functions associated with childhood friendship differs according to particular researchers, there is a common assumption that peers constitute important socializing agents in a young child's life. Among other things, friendship is a meeting ground for equals who, together, must negotiate the terms of their interactions and their relationships. Friendship also provides a context in which children can compare themselves with similar others as well as develop and refine important communication skills such as conflict management. Finally, friendship appears to offer an ongoing source of companionship and support for children. Perhaps the most important lesson to remember from this review, however, is that thanks to the work of Youniss, as well as the seminal thinking of Piaget and Sullivan, today's researchers accept the idea that parents and peers play equally important roles in children's development.

THE EARLIEST FRIENDSHIPS

In his book, *Children's Friendships*, Zick Rubin (1980) described an "interaction" between his son, Elihu, and Vanessa, a classmate. Both youngsters were 8 months old:

> Vanessa takes Elihu by surprise by crawling to him, screaming, and pulling his hair. Elihu looks bewildered. Then he starts to cry and crawls to his mother to be comforted. Such episodes of hair pulling, poking, and pawing when the babies were eight and nine months old did not appear to involve hostile intent. Instead, they seemed to reflect the babies' interest in exploring one another as physical objects. (p. 15)

Studies show that in the earliest stages of peer interaction, babies treat one another much as they would any other interesting toy—as an object to be explored. Often, children of this age come into contact by chance; they literally stumble across each other on the way to grabbing an attractive toy that has sparked their mutual interest. Parallel play is also common at this point. In virtually any play group, babies sit side by side and perform similar activities, yet never engage one another.

Not until the early part of the second year do toddlers begin to direct markedly social behaviors toward one another. These behaviors become increasingly complex and organized over the coming months. For example, at first a youngster might look and smile at a peer; next, he or she looks, smiles, vocalizes, and waves a toy at the same time. Eventually, these behaviors combine to form complex routines during which youngsters exchange roles (e.g., throwing and catching a ball, dialing and answering a phone, chasing one another, etc.).

Research indicates that by age 2½, children's interactions with one another contain all the basic features of adult exchanges including sustained attention, an awareness of turn taking, and reciprocity. A series of studies found that toddlers between 18 and 24 months were increasingly able to manage interaction and jointly coordinate their behavior (Brownell, 1989; Ross & Lollis, 1987). Brownell and Carriger (1990) also observed that youngsters between the ages of 24 and 30 months were able to coordinate their behavior quickly and effectively during a simple cooperation problem. Haslett (1984) argued that children's ability to coordinate interaction with each other represents an important step in the development of conversational competence. Earlier, youngsters typically initiated conversations by responding to something in the environment rather than actively formulating independent messages. With the advent of joint interaction, however, children begin to initiate their own topics. Haslett also suggested that although toddlers between the ages of 24 and 30 months use presuppositions to maintain conversation, their ability to sustain interaction depends upon their growing understanding of conversational postulates (discussed in chapter 4). Throughout this time, coordinated play with peers provides a context in which youngsters hone their understanding of the communicative requirements of relevancy, informativeness, clarity, and the like. Finally, the ability to distinguish between familiar and unfamiliar peers also emerges during this period—and with it, comes the tendency for pairs of children to develop distinctive patterns of interaction. It is here that we find the rudiments of friendship.

As Z. Rubin (1980) noted, eliciting desired responses from peers represents a new level of mastery over the environment. In the first two years of life, children learn to master inanimate objects (which respond in predictable ways) and parents (who, as noted in the previous section, can be overly attentive to infants' social cues). Other youngsters, however, are far less predictable; thus, obtaining the social outcomes for which a child hopes is quite a developmental achievement.

What factors predict whether two children will develop "distinctive patterns of interaction" at this time? Mueller and Vandell (1979) argued that toys facilitate social interaction by luring toddlers to the same object. Youngsters can also pick up cues from parents about which peers they should befriend (Mueller & Lucas, 1975). But similarity in developmental levels, temperament, and behavioral styles seem to be the most important factors underlying the formation of early friendships (Bronson, 1975; Z. Rubin, 1980).

Let us return to our playgroup. This time, however, the interaction is between a pair of 2-year-olds:

> Carrying a cookie, Gwen passes by Dwight who is drinking apple juice. She stops, they look at each other. In the subsequent period of exchanges Gwen repeatedly comments "juice," "cookie," "apple"; to each Dwight responds with "huh?" Later in the session, Dwight shows Gwen the fly-swatter with which he has been playing and vocalizes "fly." She smiles broadly and responds "apple?" (Bronson, 1975, p. 149)

Compared to the infants described earlier in this section, Gwen and Dwight have come a long way. Unlike the younger children, these toddlers direct markedly social behaviors toward one another. Although they have some trouble finding precisely the right words, their exchange nevertheless has all of the hallmarks of adult interaction: The children signal interest in one another, make repeated efforts to gain each other's attention, demonstrate an understanding of how reciprocity functions in communication, and are able to sustain a common focus. Through such "primitive" conversation, youngsters develop specialized patterns of interaction that lead to their earliest friendships. In fact, Gwen and Dwight appear to be well on their way to becoming friends.

DEVELOPMENTAL CHANGES IN CHILDREN'S FRIENDSHIP CONCEPTIONS AND EXPECTATIONS

Throughout the late 1970s and early 1980s, researchers paid a great deal of attention to the ways in which children's ideas about friendship changed over the course of development. As noted earlier, this work typically addressed questions about how children conceptualize or define friendship, the activities they believe to be indicative of friendship, and what they expect from real as well as ideal friends. For the most part, studies of friendship conceptions and expectations fall into one of two categories. Some researchers argued that children's ideas about friendship unfold in an invariant sequence of stages. From this perspective, there is a predictable, linear progression in the ways youngsters think about friends. As children advance through these stages, they do not simply gain more of what characterized the previous stage; rather, each new stage is believed to represent a fundamental reorganization in children's understanding of friendship.

In contrast, other researchers argued for a stage-free conceptualization of development. Although proponents of this viewpoint agreed that ideas about friendship undergo systematic change throughout childhood, they suggested that stage models are too rigid and inflexible. In support of such claims, they pointed to problems researchers have had identifying the precise times at which different stages emerge and an invariant sequence in the unfolding of stages. Scholars operating within this perspective also took issue with the idea that changes in children's thinking about friendship occur in an "abrupt, metamorphosis-like manner" characteristic of hierarchical stage models (Mannarino, 1980).

In spite of their different assumptions and methodologies, the two approaches have yielded remarkably similar findings with respect to how friendship conceptions and expectations change over the course of development. Regardless of whether such change unfolds in a series of abrupt stages or in a more gradual, fluid fashion, it is characterized by a progression from relatively concrete, physical definitions of friends as playmates in early childhood to increasingly more abstract and psychological definitions of friends as trusted companions and confidants in mid and late childhood.

What partially drives this progression is children's developing social cognitive abilities. As youngsters gain more complex and sophisticated ways of viewing the social world, they also develop more complex and sophisticated ways of thinking about and orienting toward people in that world—including friends. In line with this assumption, Peevers and Secord (1973) found that older children described friends (or, more specifically, "liked peers") in terms of particular situational and temporal characteristics as opposed to invariant personality traits. Similarly, Livesley and Bromley (1973) observed that the number of constructs in children's descriptions of friends increased with age.

Stage Models of Friendship Conceptions and Expectations

Bigelow and LaGaipa (1975, 1980) presented one of the first stage models to appear in the literature. These researchers asked first through eighth graders to write essays about "what they expect of their best friend that is different from what they expect from people who are not best friends." Responses were then content coded according to inductively derived categories. In two studies employing this procedure (one conducted in Canada and the other in Scotland), 11 categories were found to increase with age, and 2 were found to decrease. Bigelow and LaGaipa then used a statistical procedure known as *cluster analysis* to ascertain whether particular content categories emerged in the essays of children at the same grade levels. The presence of content categories would be evidence for an invariant sequence of stages in the development of children's expectations for friendship. Results of the cluster analysis indicated that there was, in fact, a notable pattern concerning the points at which certain categories were mentioned. During Grades 2 and 3, a "reward/cost" stage emerged in which children indicated they weighed the costs of their efforts in relation to what they gained from friends. Propinquity (living near one another), common activities, and similarity were the key dimensions that distinguished best friends from acquaintances at this stage. The "normative stage" emerged in Grades 4 and 5. It was marked by the expectation that best friends should share with one another—of particular importance to children in this developmental period was the sharing of norms, values, rules, and sanctions. Finally, the categories of self-disclosure, intimacy, and personality dispositions emerged with some synchrony in Grades 5 and 6. These expectations are thought to be indicative of an "empathetic stage" (Hartup, 1978) or a stage in which "internal and psychological attributes" are emphasized (Serafica, 1978).

Robert Selman's (1981) work is perhaps the best known example of a hierarchical stage model. According to this researcher, an individual's understanding of friendship is both dependent on and representative of his or her ability to take another's perspective. Selman hypothesized that developments in friendship conceptions would be closely tied to more general advances in the ways children construe, interpret, and represent others' points of view. Selman used what is called the clinical interview to test this hypothesis. In his initial studies, youngsters ranging in age from 3 to 15 were presented with a hypothetical story portraying some sort of friendship dilemma (e.g., promising to be with different friends at the same time). A series of probing questions about the nature of the characters' relationships, the process through which old friendships are maintained and new ones initiated, the understanding friends ought to have of one another, and how participants might resolve their dilemma were then posed.

Utilizing this technique, Selman identified four stages in the development of children's ideas about friendship; each stage corresponds to a particular level of social perspective-taking skill. At the lowest level of perspective-taking ability (characteristic of ages 3 through 7), children do not understand that others possess thoughts and feelings that differ from their own. Because the subjective nature of friendship eludes them, youngsters of this age fail to recognize that they might choose friends on the basis of personal characteristics and qualities. Consider the following interview excerpt, cited in a study conducted by Zick Rubin (1980, p. 34):

Interviewer: Why is Caleb your friend?

Tony: Because I like him.

Interviewer: And why do you like him?

Tony: Because he's my friend.

Interviewer: And why is he your friend?

Tony [speaking each word distinctly, with a tone of mild disgust at the interviewer's obvious denseness]: Because . . . I choosed . . . him . . . for . . . my . . . friend.

For children at Stage 0, friends are also defined as those with whom they play, those who live in the neighborhood or go to the same school, and/or those who have good toys. These features of early friendship are illustrated in an interview from one of William Damon's (1977, pp. 154–155) studies:

Interviewer:	Who's your best friend?
Matthew:	Larry.
Interviewer:	Why is Larry your best friend?
Matthew:	'Cause he plays with me a lot.
Interviewer:	Are you Larry's best friend?
Matthew:	Yeah.
Interviewer:	How do you know that?
Matthew:	'Cause I'm friends with lots of people but Larry and me are best friends.
Interviewer:	How did you meet Larry?
Matthew:	I saw him and I told him my name and we just became friends.
Interviewer:	How do you know that Larry likes you?
Matthew:	He plays with me and he gives me toys.
Interviewer:	How did you get Larry to like you?
Matthew:	He came to my house and I played with him and he liked me.
Interviewer:	Does everyone who goes to your house like you?
Matthew:	Sometimes when I play with them, but when I don't play with them, they don't like me.

For Matthew, age 5, play and friendship are equated. Anyone with whom he plays would be considered a friend—but the relationship lasts only as long as the interaction. The process of becoming friends is a simple matter of sharing toys and playing together; when these activities are absent, friendship and liking cannot occur. In fact, nonfriends are considered those who do not play, who are not in geographical proximity, and who do not have good toys to share.

Somewhere between the ages of 4 and 9, youngsters begin to understand that others have thoughts and feelings that differ from their own. They recognize that people develop subjective opinions about each other and their actions and that these opinions can be positive or negative. But children of this age cannot simultaneously account for their own and another's perspectives, nor can they understand themselves from another's point of view. As a result, children in Stage 1 define friends as people who help them or who do things for them. In other words, they recognize the subjective basis of friendship but apply it only to *their* evaluations of *others*.

Not until the next stage of development (between ages 6 and 12) do children understand that reciprocal evaluations take place and that they may be judged in the same way they have judged others. Stage 2 friendship is thus marked by an emphasis on what Selman calls "fair weather" cooperation. Although children try to accommodate to one another's preferences, there is no sense of an enduring relationship; instances of noncooperation or conflict often result in the termination of friendship.

Between the ages of 9 and 15, children develop the capacity to step out of any given interaction and take the perspective of a third party. Selman (1981) argued that this ability "leads to the awareness of the mutuality of human perspectives and hence of the self–other relationship" (p. 251). The idea of reciprocal evaluation is thus replaced with the notion of mutuality. Youngsters in Stage 3 see friendship as an intimate relationship built over time on mutual support, concern, and understanding. They recognize that a relationship resting on such a foundation is less easily terminated; thus, there is an understanding that friendships can withstand minor conflicts. Individuals in this stage of development are, however, limited by possessiveness. Precisely because friendships are seen as the result of time and effort, they are often fiercely protected.

From the standpoint of stage theorists, then, children's ideas about friendship develop in a linear and systematic fashion. Each stage represents a fundamental reorganization in youngsters' understanding of what it means to be a friend and is made possible through their developing cognitive capacities. At least three stages in friendship conceptions appear to be consistent among the hierarchical models just reviewed: Whereas young children define friends primarily in terms of concrete, physical characteristics (like having good toys or living close to each other), youngsters in middle childhood emphasize the role of help and assistance—both in terms of offering physical aid (like fixing a bike) and in sharing with one another important rules and norms. In the last stage, emerging in late childhood or early adolescence, friends are seen as confidants who provide for one another a safe environment in which feelings can be exchanged and discussed.

Stage-Free Models of Friendship Conceptions and Expectations

As already noted, although some researchers have uncovered a similar pattern of changes in children's understanding of friendship, they do not believe it necessarily occurs in an invariant sequence of stages. Rather, these researchers have simply suggested a developmental progression, an unfolding of ideas which, with age, is marked by increasingly sophisticated and complex definitions of friendship. Some stage-free conceptualizations identify *levels* of friendship understanding; others report *categories* of beliefs that may or may not remain consistent across development.

Youniss' (1980) work focused on identifying levels of friendship. Youniss was interested in understanding how children establish and maintain social relations in general, and much of his research centered on how children's developing understanding of reciprocity influenced levels of friendship. To investigate the relationship between reciprocity and friendship, Youniss asked youngsters in three different age groups (6-year-olds, 10-year-olds, and 13-year-olds) to tell stories that "show you like someone," "show that you are friends with someone," and "show you're being kind to someone." Actions indicative of liking, friendship, and kindness were then coded.

In general, these questions did not provoke different responses among the youngest group of children. Their stories about liking most frequently included themes of sharing material possessions and playing with one another; they demonstrated friendship by sharing material goods and spending time together playing; being kind to someone meant more sharing and more play. In contrast, there was some divergence in the responses of youngsters in the middle age group. Like the younger children, they mentioned play as a way of showing they like someone but also noted that actual demonstrations of friendship include inviting another child to play and helping one another when in trouble. Help could take a variety of forms, including acts focused on the recipient's welfare (e.g., "He's a person who helps you. Like if I fall down, he helps me" or "Someone who is nice to me. Like when I was sick, she brought me flowers."); help with schoolwork (e.g., "A friend means that they like you and want to help you. Sometimes when you have homework and don't know what the instructions are, they tell you the instructions."); general assistance (e.g., "Someone who really cares about you and doesn't want to betray you . . . a person who would want to help me out if I was in trouble; just to help out when you need his help."); and alleviating loneliness (e.g., "When you're lonely she plays with you. You go places and do things with them" or "You're lonely and your friend on a bike joins you. You feel a lot better because he joined you.").[3]

Although this pattern continued in the oldest group, some children introduced the idea that friends can help one another by sharing feelings. Children told stories in which friendship was demonstrated through acts of confiding, trusting, and sympathizing. For instance, one 12-year-old explained that a friend is "A person who will help you, like if you have problems. Depend on you and won't leave you if you get in trouble . . . tries to console you if you have problems. Tries to relieve you of some of your problems." Another 14-year-old described a friend as "A person that would always be around whenever you needed them and you always could talk to them."[4] Older children also tailored acts of kindness to particular recipients; in other words, material aid was seen as kind only insofar as it met the unique needs of the other. Some youngsters in this age group even spoke of comforting and consoling as ways of showing kindness.

In sum, then, the younger children in Youniss' studies seemed to demonstrate liking, friendship, and kindness by doing something *with* another child; for older children, these relational states were signaled by doing something *for* someone else. Another important conclusion of Youniss' work is that with development children begin to understand the connection between interpersonal actions and psychological states. In other words, they see that demonstrations of liking, friendship, and kindness can make a lonely person feel connected or a sad person feel happy.

Damon (1977) found a similar three-level progression of friendship conceptions. In his studies, young children defined friends primarily as playmates; youngsters in middle childhood conceptualized friends as helpers; and older children saw friends as confidants. Some of Damon's interviews illustrate the importance of talk for friends in the oldest group. The following interview was conducted with Jack, a 13-year-old (pp. 163–164):

Interviewer: Why is Jimmy your best friend?

Jack: I don't know, I guess it's because we talk a lot and stuff.

Interviewer: What do you talk about?

Jack: Secret stuff, you know, what we think of him or her or whoever. And sports, things we both like to do.

Interviewer: How did you meet Jimmy?

Jack: I don't know; hanging around, I guess. We just sort of got friendly after a while.

Interviewer: When did you get friendly?

Jack: After we found out that we didn't have to worry about the other guy blabbing and spreading stuff around.

Interviewer: Why would you worry about that?

Jack: Well, you need someone you can tell anything to, all kinds of things that you don't want to spread around. That's why you're someone's friend.

Interviewer: Is that why Jimmy is your friend?

Jack: Yes, and we like the same kinds of things. We speak that same language. My mother says we're two peas in a pod.

Interviewer: What would you say you like best about Jimmy?

Jack: Well, you know, we can say what we want to around each other, you don't have to act cool around him or anything.

> Some of the other kids are always pretending to be big shots, acting real tough. That kind of stuff, it kind of turns me off.

Interviewer: How do you know who to become friends with and who not to?

Jack: Well, you don't really pick your friends, it just grows on you. You find out that you really can talk to someone, you can tell them your problems, when you understand each other.

Interviewer: Why do some people have friends and others don't?

Jack: Some people are too afraid, they don't want to make friends.

Interviewer: Why do you think they're afraid?

Jack: I don't know, I guess they don't trust anyone.

Jack's comments about friendship exemplify many of the features other researchers have found to characterize the highest level of friendship conceptions: the notion that friendship is a source of psychological and emotional assistance; the significance of trust, reciprocity, and the sharing of confidences in the formation and maintenance of friendship; and the idea that friendships are built over time and can withstand minor transgressions. Jack's comments also suggest that talk is the vehicle through which these goals are accomplished. In Damon's (1977) words, talk is "regarded as important in and of itself," but it is also the mechanism for "psychological assistance, secret sharing and the establishment of mutual understanding" (p. 164). Jack speaks the "same language" as his best friend, Jimmy; as a result, the two boys feel at ease with one another, as though they can be "themselves."

Rather than attempting to specify particular developmental levels in friendship conceptions, other researchers simply code the frequency with which certain features emerge in the descriptions of friends offered by children of various ages. Here, ideas about friendship are typically elicited by asking youngsters "Why is it nice to have friends?" (e.g., Reisman & Shorr, 1978) or "How can you tell someone is a best friend?" (e.g., Berndt, 1981b). Youngsters have also been asked to describe an actual friendship or to tell a story about what someone might do to "want to be friendly" (e.g., see Berndt & Perry, 1986). In some cases (e.g., Furman & Bierman, 1983; Gamer, 1977), children are given a list of statements about a best friend (e.g., "someone who shares," "someone who likes the same things you do," "someone who helps you") and asked to rate the importance of each.

As a whole, this line of research suggests several conclusions, some that correspond to those just reported and some that do not. First, these studies indicate that children in kindergarten through sixth grade most frequently say that a friend is someone who plays with them or does other activities with them; while comments about play decrease with age, references to common activities increase. Second, features such as behaving prosocially toward friends, having intimate conversations with friends, and being loyal to friends are mentioned more frequently in the responses of older children than in those of younger ones. Finally, children of all ages note the importance of attributes that make it pleasant to be friends with someone (e.g., "He's a nice boy"; see Berndt, 1983, for a review).

Clearly, some of these findings contradict propositions put forth by stage theorists. For example, play emerged as a key component of friendship in the descriptions of children across a wide age range; this argues against the idea that each stage of development transforms a child's understanding of friendship. If this were the case, then older children should not have mentioned play as the most salient feature of their friendships. Similarly, the fact that youngsters of all ages noted the importance of a friend's personal attributes indicates that psychological constructs may be employed earlier than stage models indicate.

Other researchers have reported anecdotal evidence that again disagrees with the rigid progression of friendship conceptions suggested by stage models. For example, Gottman (1983) described a pair of 4-year-olds who managed to stay "best friends" even when one of them moved far away. According to stage models, children this young should not recognize that friendship can withstand any temporary physical distance, let alone prolonged separation. But, as Gottman (1983) explained, "The children discussed their impending separation and made plans to write and see each other periodically. They did both regularly in the subsequent seven years. These contacts resulted totally from the children's efforts since their parents were not friends" (p. 3).

In light of such evidence, it is probably best to assume that although children's understanding of friendship undergoes meaningful and systematic change during development, it does not necessarily occur in an invariant sequence of stages. The most important thing to keep in mind is that as children grow older, they demonstrate increasing awareness that friendship is defined by psychological interdependence between people (i.e., friends need one another); built over time on systematic, coherent, and lasting relations between partners (i.e., friends stick together even during conflict); and based on an appreciation of the complex thoughts, feelings, and personalities of both individuals (i.e., friends are attracted to one another because of their unique characteristics and qualities).

One final point is worth mentioning. Given these trends, a logical question is whether older children actually know their friends better than younger children do? In other words, does shared knowledge between friends increase with age? Studies have suggested that the answers to these questions are yes. Diaz and Berndt (1982) compared children's reports about friends with the friend's own self-report; results indicated that by fourth grade, friends accurately represented one another's external characteristics. Similarly, Ladd and Emerson (1984) found that with age, youngsters in reciprocated friendships were more knowledgeable about characteristics common to both partners than were youngsters in nonreciprocated friendships.

SUMMARY

It should be clear that children's friendships are very different from parent–child relationships. Interacting with peers teaches young children lessons about the social world they simply cannot learn through interactions with parents. Friendship enables children to discover that many relationships in which they engage throughout their lives are based on equality, mutuality, and reciprocity (as opposed to inequality, hierarchy, and authority). Friendship also provides children with unique opportunities for social comparison, for learning to rely on themselves when handling interpersonal dilemmas, and for learning to communicate in a clear and appropriate manner. In many ways, it is in the context of friendship that youngsters come to understand the *inter* in interpersonal relationships.

We have also seen that the rudiments of friendship appear at a very early age. During the first year of life, children treat others much as they would any interesting object. But by age 2½, youngsters have mastered the requisite skills that enable them to become true interactional partners; pairs of toddlers begin to favor one another and subsequently develop specialized interaction routines. By age 4, children use the term *friend* to describe liked peers. Why someone is liked, of course, changes with age. What it means to be a friend rests on the level of social-cognitive thought which children are capable of at any given point in development. The meanings associated with friendship seem to undergo at least three important changes; in young childhood, friends are defined as playmates, in middle childhood as helpers, and in late childhood–early adolescence as confidants.

NOTES

1. Taken from interviews cited in W. Damon (1977), *The social world of the child* (San Francisco: Jossey-Bass), pp. 160 and 155.
2. Taken from an interview cited in Z. Rubin (1980), *Children's friendships* (Cambridge, MA: Harvard University Press), p. 2.
3. Taken from interviews cited in J. Youniss (1980), *Parents and peers in social development: A Sullivan-Piaget perspective* (Chicago: University of Chicago Press), pp. 177–178.
4. Taken from interviews cited in J. Youniss (1980), *Parents and peers in social development: A Sullivan-Piaget perspective* (Chicago: University of Chicago Press), p. 179.

8

Doing Friendship

Knowing how children think about and describe friendship provides a basis for understanding why certain characteristics predict who becomes friends and who does not. In this chapter, we survey many of the factors known to contribute to the formation and maintenance of children's friendships.

The chapter begins by reviewing studies that suggest physical attractiveness, race, gender, and proximity exert a great deal of influence on children's friendship choices. We then briefly survey the sociometric literature and argue for the importance of distinguishing between children's sociometric status (i.e., their relative acceptance among a group of peers) and friendship. The next section presents a detailed summary of observational research on the actual communicative processes through which children *do* friendship. Work exploring how youngsters' behavior with friends differs from their behavior with nonfriends is also reviewed. The chapter ends with a brief discussion of gender differences in children's same-sex friendships.

CORRELATES OF CHILDREN'S FRIENDSHIPS

Our summary of friendship correlates is organized around three themes: personal characteristics limiting the array of possible friendship partners, communicative processes through which children initiate and maintain friendships, and behaviors that distinguish friends from nonfriends. The first category includes "objective" correlates, or factors over which youngsters themselves have very little control. Although objective features account for a relatively large amount of variance in who becomes friends, they cannot be altered. The other groups of correlates are more "subjective" in the sense that they include communicative and behavioral routines that are learned and, therefore, amenable to change. These correlates are especially important for helping children without friends. For them, the hope of avoiding a litany of negative life consequences lies in training programs that remediate deficiencies in the interactive skills we know promote friendship development.

Distinctions Between Friendship and Peer Acceptance

Some of the literature cited throughout this chapter—particularly in the section on objective features of friendship development—belongs to the long and venerable tradition of sociometric research. Sociometry is a methodological technique for identifying people's social standing within a larger peer group (e.g., the classroom for children, a fraternity or sorority for college students, a business organization for adults, etc.). Sociometric status is typically obtained by asking members of a social system to nominate peers they like and peers they dislike, or to rate all individuals on some relevant criteria, or both. Groups of popular, average, neglected, and rejected people are then discerned on the basis of this information (see, e.g., Coie & Dodge, 1990; Coie, Dodge, & Coppotelli, 1982).

The goal of sociometric research is to understand the antecedents of peer acceptance. Nearly 7 decades of research provides strong evidence that children who are accepted by their peers enjoy a number of immediate, positive outcomes while those who are rejected suffer a host of negative consequences. Studies also suggest that unless proper intervention occurs, rejection remains stable throughout childhood and adolescence and actually precedes adult criminality, early school withdrawal, and mental health problems including schizophrenia among women (see Kupersmidt, Coie, & Dodge, 1990). As Coie (1990) explained, once a child is consensually viewed as disliked, "even though it may never be explicitly discussed by the peer group, the dynamics of group life change" (p. 379).

For many years, researchers believed that being well liked within a peer group meant that children had many friends, whereas being rejected meant that they did not. Thus, studies examining the antecedents of peer acceptance were thought to describe the antecedents of friendship development as well. More recently, however, the importance of distinguishing between acceptance and friendship has become clear. For one thing, acceptance refers to a group metric; it indexes the consensual judgment of a group about an individual's overall likability (Parker & Gottman, 1989). Friendship, on the other hand, indicates the existence of a dyadic relationship characterized by certain properties (e.g., reciprocated liking, equality, etc.) as well as by a history (Rawlins, 1992). Studies have suggested that some children experience a great deal of popularity while having no close friends (e.g., Parker & Asher, 1988) and, conversely, that some youngsters who experience rejection have at least one close friend (Asher & Parker, 1989; Furman

& Robbins, 1985). It is not surprising, then, that the processes involved in getting along well among a group of people have been found to differ from those necessary for initiating (and maintaining) meaningful friendships.

For example, Asher and Renshaw (1981) observed that children who scored low on measures of acceptance and friendship were less skilled behaviorally than children who were generally well accepted but lacked close friends. These researchers also found that although coaching youngsters in the use of relevant social skills improved their levels of peer acceptance, it did not change the extent to which they were able to develop close friendships. Similarly, Berndt and Das (1987) found that children's perceptions of their friends' prosocial and aggressive behavior did not vary as a function of the target's sociometric standing. They interpreted this finding to suggest that even unpopular children exhibit relationship-enhancing behaviors, but rejected peers also tend to overestimate their behavioral competence (Patterson, Kupersmidt, & Griesler, 1990).

Where, then, does all of this leave us with respect to our discussion of friendship correlates? We believe that although the behavioral and communicative processes associated with acceptance and friendship differ, the personal characteristics related to each do not. Sociometric status indexes the extent to which a group finds someone to be generally attractive or appealing; children cannot form friendships with those to whom they are not attracted. Thus, the same set of objective characteristics that predict children's social standing among peers may also constrain the field of potential partners with whom they can become friends. From this perspective, objective features known to influence youngsters' acceptance should also affect with whom they develop friendships.

Personal Characteristics That Reduce the Field of Eligible Friendship Partners

Physical Attractiveness. People invoke different criteria when judging attractiveness. Some individuals might pay attention to another's eyes, while other individuals might find body type, or the shape of someone's mouth to be attractive. Research indicates, however, that regardless of the particular preferences influencing individual evaluations, most people come to very similar conclusions (Berscheid & Walster, 1978). In other words, there is remarkable consensus among adults about who is and is not attractive, and children are apparently no different. Studies indicate that children as young as 3 have adopted adult stereotypes for judging facial beauty; adult standards for judging body type are evident among children by age 8 (Cavior & Lombardi, 1973; Cross & Cross, 1971; Dion, 1973).

In addition to sharing adult ideas about what is beautiful, children also seem to choose friends on the basis of physical attractiveness. Young and Cooper (1944) studied over 30 variables that predicted the number of times children were nominated as best friends by classmates. Physical attractiveness was by far the strongest predictor of friendship nominations; children who were better liked were better looking. More recently, researchers have found that youngsters judged to be attractive by adults receive more friendship nominations in both preschool (Dion & Berscheid, 1974) and elementary school (Lerner & Lerner, 1977). Children's own ratings of their peers' attractiveness are also correlated with friendship choice throughout childhood (e.g., Dion, Berscheid, & Walster, 1972). Asher, Oden, and Gottman (1981) suggested a possible explanation for the relationship between attractiveness and friendship choice: Attractive children may be responded to more positively than unattractive children and, therefore, develop better social skills. In support of this claim, peers as well as adults have been found to attribute more negative qualities to children who lack physical beauty than to children who do not—especially when the target is not well known.

When compared to their unattractive counterparts, youngsters rate attractive peers as smarter, more prosocial, friendlier, and less aggressive; attractive children are also judged to be better prospects as friends (Adams & Crane, 1980; Cavior & Dokecki, 1973; Dion, 1973; Langlois & Stephan, 1977). These findings are remarkably consistent and have been observed across a wide age range (i.e., preschool through adolescence), even when potentially confounding variables such as ethnicity are examined. Much like adults, children also consider anything different to be unattractive. In one study, researchers (Richardson, Goodman, Hastorf, & Dornbusch, 1961) asked 10- and 11-year-olds to rank pictures of peers with a variety of physical conditions that departed from the norm. Rankings indicated that the picture of a "normal" child was most preferred; this was followed by a picture of a child with crutches and a brace, a child in a wheelchair, and a child with facial disfigurement. The least preferred picture was of an obese child.

The story is a little more complex when children are well acquainted with each other. Styczynski and Langlois (1977) explored whether perceptions of attractive and unattractive children varied according to who was the judge (i.e., a stranger or an acquaintance). Results indicated that strangers saw attractive children of both sexes to be more prosocial and competent. Acquaintances, however, nominated attractive boys as both more prosocial and more antisocial. Other studies have yielded similar results (e.g., Dion & Stein, 1978; Langlois & Styczynski, 1979), suggesting that the relationship between physical attractiveness and social success becomes less predictable for boys as they mature.

Adults' expectations for children also vary according to attractiveness. Adams and Crane (1980) asked parents to compare pictures of attractive and unattractive children and then predict which individuals their own children would find "nicest" and "choose as a playmate." Mothers and fathers expected their youngsters to attribute a pleasing personality to the more attractive peers; they also anticipated that their children would prefer to play with a physically appealing youngster. Interestingly, mothers' beliefs about whom their children would select as play-mates were highly correlated with their youngster's actual choices. In another study, Dion (1973) showed college students pictures of an attractive or an unattractive child; each picture was accompanied by a description of an episode in which the youngster behaved inappropriately. Participants were asked to predict how likely it was that the child would repeat the behavior and to rate him or her on a series of personality characteristics. Students believed the attractive child was not only less likely to repeat the inappropriate behavior but was also more honest and pleasant. As Asher, Oden, and Gottman (1981) noted, "These findings are striking since the behavior being judged was identical; only physical appearance varied" (p. 279).

Teachers are not immune to what some researchers call the "beauty is good" hypothesis (e.g., Adams, 1978; Hartup, 1983). Ample evidence has suggested that throughout elementary school years, teachers' attributions of academic achievement and social competence are influenced by children's levels of physical appeal. Studies have demonstrated that when compared to unattractive pupils, teachers expect attractive students to get better marks (Clifford & Walster, 1973), perceive them to be better achievers, and rate them more highly on classroom adjustment, emotional adjustment, social behavior, and intellectual adjustment (Styczynski & Langlois, 1980). Perhaps most disturbing is the finding that attractive children actually receive higher achievement test scores than do unattractive children—*even though their IQs do not differ* (Algozzine, 1977). This finding provides some evidence of a self-fulfilling prophecy at work: Children may begin to act in accord with the way they are treated.

Another study has suggested that in their interactions with peers, unattractive children may exhibit some of the negative behaviors attributed to them. Langlois and Downs (1979) observed preschoolers during play sessions; dyads were composed of two attractive children, two unattractive children, or one attractive child and one unattractive child. Observational records indicated that, by age 5, unattractive children were more aggressive toward their partners than were attractive children; they also engaged in fewer "low-key" activities.

Race. Racial awareness develops early. By age 3, youngsters know their own group membership and can correctly identify people from other races (K. B. Clark & Clark, 1947; Durrett & Davy, 1970). Like physical attractiveness, race seems to be a criterion children use to narrow the field of potential friendship partners. Results of several different studies indicate that although children make some cross-race selections, they are far more likely to choose individuals from their own race as friends than individuals from other races (Asher, 1973; Shaw, 1973). Youngsters also appear to prefer playing with members of the same race. Singleton (1974) asked third graders in 11 different schools to indicate (on a 1-to-5 scale) the extent to which they liked playing with each of their classmates. She found that both African American and Euro American children assigned higher play ratings to members of their own race than they did to members of other races (3.58 and 3.17, respectively, for African Americans and 2.96 and 2.86 for Euro Americans). By high school, the picture becomes even more bleak.

Silverman and Shaw (1973) observed students' naturally occurring social interaction and found only 3% to be between Blacks and Whites. These authors speculated that the "threat" of interracial dating may encourage more in-group interactions during adolescence.

Although studies have yielded a consistent pattern with respect to race and friendship development, several qualifications should be noted. First, as Schneider, Wiener, and Murphy (1994) pointed out, most researchers have examined the cross-race preferences of only two groups: African Americans and Euro Americans. Perhaps more cross-race friendships would be discovered among members of other groups. Second, many of the studies were conducted not long after court-ordered desegregation; it remains to be seen whether the same pattern of results would be observed today, over 3 decades later. Finally, although racial factors influence friendship choice, other variables—like gender—appear to be far more important determinants. In 1939, Criswell observed hundreds of hours of interactions among young children. Based on these observations, she concluded "The cleavage between the sexes was greater than racial cleavage" and that, if given a choice, "A group of boys or girls nearly always preferred classmates of the same sex but different race to those of the same race but different sex" (p. 18). This trend has not changed in nearly 60 years.

Gender. When asked whether a girl could be his best friend, 6-year-old Paul answered, "Yes, Chrissy is my friend." A further probe about whether there was any difference between having girls and boys as friends prompted this response: "No, all friends are the same." Now, consider the reply of an 11-year-old boy:[1]

Interviewer: Can a girl be your best friend?

Child: Yes. But only your best friend if you're in love with her.

Interviewer: Is it the same having a girl as a friend as it is a boy?

Child: No, 'cause a girl can't play football 'cause if she gets tackled she'll get hurt.

These responses reflect a consistent trend observed in the literature: Whereas preschoolers and adolescents sometimes have friends of the opposite sex, elementary and middle school children rarely do. For example, Asher (1973) asked fourth- and fifth-grade children to list the names of their five best friends. Approximately 95% of the choices were same-sex peers. In another study, children were found to rate opposite-sex classmates as significantly less fun to play with than same-sex classmates (Singleton, 1974). Naturalistic investigations corroborate these findings. O'Mark and Edelman (1973) observed playground interaction and found that kindergartners, first, and second graders played predominantly with members of the same sex. Similarly, Luria and Hertzog (1985) found that nearly two thirds of the play in which nursery schoolers engaged was with same-sex partners, whereas 80% of children's playground activities in grade school was conducted with same-sex peers.

Interestingly, when cross-sex friendships do form, they tend to be relatively unstable. At two different points in time (spaced approximately 4 months apart), Gronlund (1955) asked youngsters to list the names of their best friends. Only 20% of the cross-sex friendship choices made at time one were also made at time two. In contrast, children's same-sex selections were found to be about three times as stable.

As noted in chapter 5, gender differences in play, type of activity, and talk itself develop early in the preschool years. Our discussion here suggests that gender is a powerful determinant of who will and will not become friends. Whether the tendency to prefer members of the same sex as friends is the *result* of these behavioral and communicative differences—or the *cause* of them—remains unclear. Gender differences in children's friendship are discussed later in the chapter; for now, keep in mind that youngsters beyond the age of 3 or 4 rarely select members of the opposite sex as friends.

Proximity.   Proximity refers to the physical distance between people. A good deal of literature suggests that children are most likely to become friends with peers from the same neighborhood or the same classroom (M. L. Clark & Drewry, 1985; Spurgeon, Hicks & Terry, 1983). Obviously, proximity increases the chance that two youngsters will meet; it also makes it easier to accomplish the sustained contact necessary for friendship development and maintenance. Proximity has been found to be especially important for young children because of their limited mobility (Epstein, 1989).

Summary.   One way of summarizing this literature is to say that children become friends with those who are most similar to themselves. They reduce the field of possible friendship partners by invoking the criterion of similarity and tend to select as friends peers of the same race and gender, who share the same physical space. There is even some evidence that people befriend others whom they believe closely match their level of physical attractiveness (see Burgoon, Buller, & Goodall, 1989; Trenholm & Jensen, 1992).

Although similarity remains a basis for choosing friends throughout childhood and adolescence, there appears to be a developmental shift in the dimensions involved. For instance, Ladd and Emerson (1984) found that although similarity on demographic features declined with age, friends in mid-childhood were still more alike than different with respect to characteristics they used to describe themselves. Other researchers have observed that as children mature, similarity in tastes, attitudes, and interests becomes increasingly salient to friendship selection (Berndt, 1982; Furman & Childs, 1981; McGuire & Weisz, 1982).

Similarity, however, cannot be the only factor determining choice of friends. Every day people meet countless others, some of whom are like them, yet close and enduring friendships rarely result. This suggests that something else must drive friendship formation—and we believe that "something" is communication. If demographic qualities reduce the field of potential relational partners, interaction is what propels two similar strangers toward friendship.

Behavioral Correlates of Peer Acceptance: An Aside

Observational studies of friendship interaction are rare because the behavioral correlates of peer acceptance are often mistakenly assumed to be the behavioral correlates of friendship. Consequently, the predictors of whether children will be well liked within a peer group are better known than are the specific interactional routines through which they establish and maintain friendships.

The literature on peer acceptance is formidable, and summarizing it is well beyond our scope. (For a comprehensive review of this literature, see Asher & Coie, 1990.) At the most general level, two broad classes of behavior have been consistently linked to peer status: Friendliness and sociability are associated with children's acceptance, aggression and antisocial behavior to their rejection.

Friendliness, Sociability, and Prosocial Behavior as Predictors of Sociometric Status. Sociability is generally defined as the total number of social contacts a child makes during a given time period (see Hartup, 1983). Prosocial behavior, on the other hand, refers to a more general class of behaviors exhibited during interactions with peers, including cooperation, helping, and responding to others' distress. Strategies for measuring sociability as well as prosocial behavior vary from study to study. With young children, researchers often use direct observation, partly because of children's limited verbal abilities and partly because the relatively unconstrained environment of nursery school and preschool makes it easy to record natural interaction. Paper-and-pencil measures as well as interviews are more typically employed with older children. Regardless of the particular method used, a consistent picture emerges: Compared to their less popular counterparts, well-liked children exhibit friendlier behaviors toward peers, show greater skill in initiating and maintaining social interaction with other youngsters, and engage in more acts of cooperation and helping. Rejected children are not less sociable or less friendly than are the well-liked youngsters, but they exhibit more antisocial, disruptive, and inappropriate behaviors when interacting with peers.

Differences in friendliness and sociability are apparent even among infants. Lee (1973) studied five babies between the ages of 8 and 10 months old. The baby who was consistently approached by others was a "responsive, but nonassertive social partner" (see Hartup, 1983) whereas the baby who was consistently avoided often engaged in "intensive interactions" and almost always terminated exchanges prematurely. In contrast, prosocial behaviors generally do not emerge until the second year of life and increase in frequency between the ages of 24 and 30 months (Hay, 1979). Scholars have suggested that developing verbal abilities and a differentiation of self from others make prosocial acts possible.

A variety of sociable and prosocial behaviors have been identified as antecedents of popularity among nursery school children. These include (among other things) the frequency with which youngsters initiate positive contacts (Abramovitch, 1979), engage in associative behaviors (Marshall & McCandless, 1957), remain socially visible (E. Clifford, 1963), comply with routines (Koch, 1933), and cooperate with group norms (Lippitt, 1941).

Similar results have been documented for elementary school children. Numerous studies indicate that peer acceptance is linked to friendliness and outgoing behavior for youngsters in this age group (Bonney & Powell, 1953). Showing kindness to peers (Smith, 1950), expressing and receiving positive reinforcement, and knowing how to "make friends" also promote acceptance by peers (Gottman, Gonzo, & Rasmussen, 1975). In addition, several researchers have found that responding to others' requests for help is an important antecedent of acceptance in early and mid-childhood. Campbell and Yarrow (1961) observed that youngsters willing to respond positively to the dependent behaviors of others were better liked by their peers than those who were not willing to do so. Similarly, Ladd and Oden (1979) reported that "conventional modes" of help giving were positively related to indices of peer acceptance and friendliness. The work of Burleson and his colleagues (Burleson et al., 1986) indicated that help may also take the form of offering emotional comfort to distressed peers. These researchers found that of four different communication skills assessed among first and third graders, the ability to comfort best discriminated rejected children from those who were accepted. With development, youngsters increasingly define friendship in terms of help and psychological assistance.

Aggression and Antisocial Behavior as Predictors of Sociometric Status.
Associations among aggression, antisocial behavior, and sociometric status are more complex. As Hartup (1983) explains, no consistent relationship has been found between rejection and the extent to which a child physically attacks his/her peers. Thus, the youngster who fights is not necessarily disliked. What seems to make the difference is whether the child both *initiates and receives* "negative interactions." For example, among preschoolers rejection has been found to be positively correlated with the number of "negative reinforcements" children exhibit towards peers (Gottman, 1977) as well as the number of negative reinforcements they receive (Masters & Furman, 1981).

There is some evidence that throughout elementary school, disruptive and deviant behaviors earn children lower sociometric scores than aggressive acts. Wagner and Asarnow (1980) found that the interactions of rejected boys were best classified as hostile/submissive as opposed to hostile/dominant. Other researchers have observed that children differentiate between liked and disliked peers in terms of deviant behaviors (such as being dishonest, irritating, or immature) rather than aggressive behaviors and that positive associations exist between rejection and disruptive or "objectionable" acts (e.g., Davids & Parenti, 1958; Winder & Rau, 1962; for a review of this work, see Hartup, 1983).

Let us end our brief journey into the sociometric literature by saying that these studies call attention to essential features of behavior that may, in part, be related to friendship development. However, they cannot substitute for investigations of actual friendship interaction. As we have argued before, acceptance and friendship, while not unrelated, are best thought of as conceptually and empirically distinct. And although studies of expectations are informative with regard to how children *think* about friendship and its formation, they do not directly answer the question of how children actually *do* friendship. As Hartup (1996) noted, the quality, identity, and number of friendship relationships—the *doing* of friendship—need much more investigation. Moreover, several researchers (e.g., Gottman, 1983) have maintained that procedures used to examine friendship conceptions rely heavily on children's verbal abilities to comment on social processes; thus, developmental shifts in ideas about friendship may actually reflect increasingly sophisticated verbal skills or a greater awareness of cultural rules about friendship. In the next section of this chapter, we review studies examining "real-world" interactions between children on their way to becoming friends as well as those going about the business of sustaining friendships.

COMMUNICATIVE PROCESSES
THROUGH WHICH CHILDREN INITIATE
AND MAINTAIN FRIENDSHIP

Researchers gain knowledge of friendship processes by actually observing children as they attempt to form and maintain meaningful relationships with each other. Such research involves much time and effort. For example, Gottman (1983) spent nearly 6 years developing and refining a coding scheme that captured the important nuances of children's interactions. His purpose was to examine the processes through which unacquainted children became friends. In the first study, 26 dyads ranging in age from 3 to 6 years were observed playing in their homes with either a best friend or a stranger. In the second study, Gottman recorded the interactions of 18 unacquainted dyads (ages 3 to 9) during three play sessions in a home setting. Interactions were then coded and analyzed.

The extent to which children "hit it off" was measured by the ratio of agreements to disagreements each dyad exhibited. (Research has indicated that agreement-to-disagreement ratios are powerful discriminators of satisfied and dissatisfied marriages as well as of distressed and nondistressed families [see Birchler, Weiss, & Vincent, 1975; Riskin & Faunce, 1972].) In general, Gottman's results suggested that children who hit it off exchanged information successfully, interacted in a connected fashion (i.e., were responsive to each other's needs and demands), managed to establish common activities (i.e., found things to do together), and resolved conflict successfully, either by offering reasons for requests or by complying with weak demands. As children progressed toward friendship, these processes became increasingly important as did some others including communicating clearly, exploring similarities and differences, and self-disclosing. For the most part, these results stood up to variations in age and sex composition of the dyad, but there was some evidence that with development youngsters improved in their "acquaintanceship abilities."

More recently, Gottman and his colleague Jeffrey Parker have extended this analysis by examining the communicative processes through which children attempt to initiate and maintain friendships. After many years of research, they realized that specific processes are salient to friendship at different points in development and that these processes helped children negotiate increasingly broad social and emotional tasks. The researchers argued that through interaction with friends, youngsters acquire unique information about their own affective experiences and the probable responses of others in relation to the display of affect. In an important article published in 1989, Parker and Gottman sought to explain this claim by identifying the underlying social concerns driving the interaction of friends, the conversational processes through which such concerns are addressed, and the specific aspects of affective experience mastered during early, middle, and late childhood.

Early Childhood

The primary concern of young children is to maximize the enjoyment, entertainment, and satisfaction experienced in play. Maximizing pleasure depends on the level of coordination they can achieve with their partners or, as Parker and Gottman (1989) stated, "The extent to which the children fit together their separate lines of action into jointly produced, jointly understood discussions or activities" (p. 105). Three types of play can be identified based on their level of coordination or involvement.

At the lowest level, play is coordinated but parallel; it revolves around conversation that is mostly activity-based and relatively conflict free. For example, two children might be conducting a casual conversation while building blocks side by side. If the two youngsters begin to build something together, they are then involved in joint activity, which represents a slightly higher level of play. Here children must manage the tensions that inevitably arise when two people with their own ideas about how to do things work together on a task. Although joint activity play thus carries with it the potential for conflict, it is also more exciting because of the input and creativity of both parties. The highest level of coordination is fantasy play where, as Parker and Gottman (1989) explained, "Two friends transform their crayons into 'daggers' and their coloring paper into 'dragon skin' and begin an adventure. . . . [they] do not simply act like tigers or dragons or ghosts—they become tigers or dragons or ghosts" (p. 105). Other researchers have identified similar levels of play. For instance, Shugar and Bokus (1986) suggested that children move from onlooking, to parallel play (in which they access another's activity), to associative play (in which two participants blend their activities), to cooperative play (in which joint participation is structured and organized).

To a casual observer, such play may seem effortless. One moment a young boy is all alone and the next he has made a pogo stick into a sword and is off—with a band of others—to save a kingdom. In reality, though, episodes of fantasy play are remarkably complex and require several relatively advanced social-cognitive and communicative abilities. First, to integrate their behaviors, youngsters must feel comfortable with their partners, anticipate one another's moves, and share similar concerns, all of which mandate both clear communication and a good measure of role-taking skill.

Second, episodes of fantasy play rarely develop in a smooth and gradual fashion; rather, most unravel in a series of stops and starts that Parker and Gottman (1989) called "escalations." Any number of problems can cause a developing episode to falter. Disagreements can arise over specific ground rules, appropriate props, or even the theme of play (in the earlier discussion of cognitive schemas, we noted that failure to follow the steps of action in a schema may completely derail it).

In the following example, Wendy and Jeffrey fail to negotiate their roles; as a result, the coordination and intensity of the play is de-escalated:[2]

Wendy: I'm the mommy.

Jeffrey: Who am I?

Wendy: Um, the baby.

Jeffrey: Daddy.

Wendy: Sister.

Jeffrey: I wanna be the daddy.

Wendy: You're the sister.

Jeffrey: Daddy.

Wendy: You're the big sister.

Jeffrey: Don't wanna play house. I don't want to play house. Just play eat-eat. We can play eat-eat. We have to play that way.

As this example illustrates, successful conflict management is key to fantasy play. An episode cannot get off the ground if participants squabble over what should happen. Some research (e.g., Gottman & Parkhurst, 1980) has suggested that young children have more difficulty than older children in preventing disagreements from escalating into long, drawn-out fights. Nevertheless, the interactions of young friends are less conflict ridden than are the interactions of older friends. As Parker and Gottman (1989) pointed out, young friends are more successful at avoiding prolonged conflict sequences because episodes of disagreement and conflict interfere with the ability to sustain highly coordinated forms of play. As the importance of play declines, "So too does the need to avoid negative affect and conflict at any cost" (p. 111).

Studies have shown that once children are involved in episodes of fantasy play, they often refuse to let others join in. For example, Corsaro (1985) observed preschoolers over a 1-year period. He found that youngsters rarely played alone, but when they did, they consistently tried to gain entry into ongoing activities of the group. Children involved in the activities, however, often denied others access because, according Corsaro, "They recognized the fragility of interaction" (p. 168). Youngsters frequently referred to friendship as a basis for inclusion in and exclusion from play. In the following excerpt from Corsaro's field notes (p. 132), Glen tries to join Denny and Leah as they play; just a few minutes before, Glen and Denny had been involved in a mutual activity:

Denny [to Glen]:	Grr-grr. We don't like you.
Leah [to Glen]:	Grr-grr.
Glen [to Denny]:	You were my friend a minute ago.
Denny [to Glen]:	Yeah.
Glen [to Denny]:	Well, if you keep going "grr," you can't be my friend anymore.
Denny [to Glen]:	Well, then I'm not your friend.
Leah [to Glen]:	Yeah, Grr-grr.

In chapters 3 and 4, we suggested that peer entry skills were important because they allow children access to group activities in which other skills (like conflict management) can be learned and practiced. The work of Putallaz and her colleagues (e.g., Putallaz & Wasserman, 1990) indicated that entry skills are also important because of their relevance to peer acceptance and friendship formation. These researchers have observed that children who fail to gain access to ongoing group activities typically employ one of four strategies: They disagree, ask questions, say something about themselves, or state opinions and feelings. Putallaz believed these strategies meet with resistance because they divert the group's attention from the fun of the activity. In contrast, youngsters who are more successful at entering peer activities integrate their behavior with the ongoing conversations of the group.

In the next example, taken from a study by Putallaz and Heflin (1986, p. 296), Eric calls attention to a recent playground incident as he tries to join Tom and David's letter game; in the end, both Eric and his efforts are ignored.

Tom:	M. Um . . . um. . . .
Eric:	Oh, you know. . . . *[David makes a face, and they laugh.]* You know I was playing with Glen. I hope you don't get mad at me. We're playing out there and Glen, he started to wrestle. I told him no, so. . . .
Tom:	Monkey, Monkey. Hey, um, Monkey. Monkey, um, "Move ahead three spaces." It's your turn, dum-dum.
David:	Hey, um, M. Monkey.
Eric:	Uh, Glen . . . I poked his eye. I accidentally poked Glen's eye and then he . . . said he wouldn't take my apology, so Brian started getting mad at me so . . . and there I. . . . Glen can see now . . . he said he couldn't see. Now he could see.
David:	I like this game.
Tom:	OK. OK.

What affective task is accomplished via early childhood play episodes? Parker and Gottman (1989) argued that when it is successful, fantasy play teaches children how to manage their emotions. To coordinate actions, children must sometimes suppress their own desires in favor of someone else's. Through fantasy play, then, youngsters learn how to control emotional reactions so that interaction does not break down.

Fantasy play also provides a channel for mastering fear. Very young children suffer many anxieties: They fear abandonment, growing up, powerlessness, and even death (see Gottman, 1986b). In play, youngsters create and rehearse a drama in which they are heroes or heroines who conquer something dreaded and mysterious. Although fantasy play represents the most challenging form of interaction for young friends, it also has the highest potential for reward—both in terms of children's own satisfaction and in the lessons they learn.

Middle Childhood

With the advent of middle childhood comes drastic social change. Not only does a youngster's number of social contacts increase, but so too does the diversity of these contacts: Children are exposed to people representing different religions, races, ethnic backgrounds, and personalities. Groups begin to segregate on the basis of sex and race; hierarchies reflecting various levels of popularity also emerge. Perhaps most notable, however, is the emphasis on peer approval. The attitudes of friends now rival those of parents with respect to self-definition and self-esteem. Youngsters in middle childhood not only evaluate themselves in comparison with peers but also develop self-presentational skills so that they may project a desired image.

According to Parker and Gottman (1989), the strong concern for "fitting in" drives friendship at this age. The need for belonging and acceptance makes youngsters in middle childhood somewhat insecure, both about themselves and their status within the peer group. Friendship provides a context in which rules of the larger social system can be learned, practiced, and reinforced; in this way, it guards against rejection by ensuring children understand what peers expect of them.

Gossip is the conversational process through which this concern is addressed. In Parker and Gottman's (1989) words, gossip "serves at once to reaffirm membership in important same-sex peer social groups and to reveal the core attitudes, beliefs, and behaviors that constitute the basis for inclusion in or exclusion from these groups" (p. 114). Gossip often revolves around discussing someone who has violated important norms and thus reaffirms the values of the group. In the following example, taken from Parker and Gottman's study (1989, p. 114), Katie is the object of Mikaila and Erica's gossip and is being criticized for her bossiness:

Mikaila: She's mean. She beat me up once *[laughs]*. I could hardly breathe, she hit me in the stomach so hard.

Erica: She acts like . . .

Mikaila: she's the boss.

Erica: "Now you do this." *[mimicking Katie]*

Mikaila: "And I'll . . ."

Erica: "And Erica, you do this. And you substitute for people who aren't here, Erica."

Mikaila: "And you do this, Mikaila. And you shouldn't do that, you shouldn't, you have to talk like this. You understand? Here. I'm the teacher here."

Erica: I know. She always acts like she's the boss.

Other common gossip themes include not sharing, being a crybaby, telling lies, and being a tattletale.

At this point in development, children still have not yet mastered how or when to show emotions. Through dialogue with friends and by observing the reactions of friends, children learn the rules for appropriate emotional displays. According to Parker and Gottman (1989), the modus operandi for children of this age is quite simple: Avoid open sentimentality at all costs. Apparently, in the quest to carve out a self acceptable to other peers, children must be cool and unruffled at all times.

Not surprisingly, rules about sentimentality are most clearly expressed in conversations about embarrassment, particularly over issues of sexuality or cross-sex relations. Embarrassment can be a topic of self-disclosure (e.g., "I was so embarrassed when my mom bought me a bra") or the purpose of the conversation (as in the following case cited in Parker and Gottman's study, 1989, p. 117):

Anna: How's Lance? *[Giggles]* Has he taken you to the movie yet?

Barbara: No! Saw him today but I don't care.

Anna: Didn't he say anything to you?

Barbara: Oh . . .

Anna: Lovers! *[tauntingly]*

Barbara: Shut up!

Anna: Lovers at first sight! *[Giggles]*

Barbara: *[Giggles]* Quit it!

Adolescence

The search for acceptance typical of mid-childhood turns into a quest for defining "who I am" and "who I will become" in adolescence. By this time, youngsters have developed advanced perspective-taking skills (recall Selman) that allow them to view themselves, others, and relationships with more objectivity and insight. This newfound ability is applied (with a vengeance) to adolescents' search for self which is, in large part, accomplished through interactions with friends.

Self-disclosure dominates the conversations of adolescent friends. Other processes like humor, gossip, and social comparison serve to initiate or enhance self-disclosure. Unlike younger children, who often respond to self-disclosure with statements of solidarity (e.g., "Oh, I know. Me too!"), adolescents' disclosure sparks lengthy discussion and psychological attributions. They are also more confrontational and honest in their exchanges which, according to Parker and Gottman (1989), is a sign of intimacy. Put simply, adolescents talk a lot about themselves and their relationships (a habit sometimes greatly lamented by parents and teachers).

Most of the difficult, affective work is behind adolescents. They no longer feel compelled to hide emotions, and their understanding of display rules is quite sophisticated; adolescents also recognize that people can have mixed or ambivalent emotions. Their task seems to be one of figuring out the implications of emotions for interpersonal events and relationships. Consequently, adolescents spend a great deal of time discussing relationship changes and analyzing events that caused either themselves or others to act irrationally.

Summary

Thanks to the patience and dedication of scholars like Gottman and Parker, there is a fairly clear and detailed picture of how children use communication to establish and maintain their friendships at various stages of development. The three communicative processes they described not only enable youngsters to accomplish important affective tasks but also reflect the level of friendship understanding of which they are capable. In chapter 7, we noted that young children primarily define friends as playmates; thus, it is not surprising that fantasy play is the key communicative process in which friends of this age engage. Such play is believed to help children overcome fears, regulate emotions, and learn the importance of following scripts.

In mid-childhood, youngsters exhibit a profound concern for rules. Parker and Gottman (1989) argued that gossip is the primary vehicle through which significant rules are ascertained and reinforced. Based on the discussion in chapter 7, we would like to suggest that one of the most important rules gossip serves to teach and reinforce concerns friendship: namely, that friends should help one another. Finally, as youngsters enter adolescence, friends are increasingly defined as confidants. This conceptualization is reflected in the intimate and extended self-disclosure that characterizes friends' interactions at this stage; such forms of communication apparently aid adolescents in their continuing quest to understand the role emotion (and its display) plays in the world of intimate relationships.

CHILDREN'S BEHAVIORS WITH FRIENDS VERSUS NONFRIENDS

Although relatively few studies have examined the actual processes through which children establish and maintain friendships, several investigations have explored whether children behave differently with friends versus nonfriends. The purpose of this research is to identify behaviors that distinguish friends from other peers (e.g., acquaintances, workmates, strangers, etc.). Two different classes of behavior have been found to vary as a function of friendship: cooperation–prosocial behavior and conflict.

Cooperation–Prosocial Behavior

Many times throughout this chapter as well as the last, we have noted the importance of cooperation—and its related concepts of mutuality, reciprocity, and sharing—to children's friendships. For example, scholars like Youniss (1980) and Sullivan (1953) thought that friendship is the primary source through which children learn how to cooperate. Similarly, youngsters' comments have suggested that from very early on, sharing and reciprocity are seen as core features of friendship. The question remains, however, whether children actually cooperate more with friends than they do with nonfriends.

Even for preschoolers, the answer to this question appears to be yes. Several researchers have observed that among preschool children, "positively reinforcing social exchanges" are more frequent between friends than between neutral contacts or between children who dislike one another (e.g., Hymel, Hayruen, & Lollis, 1982). Some cooperative behaviors involved in these exchanges include giving attention and approval, submitting to another's wishes, giving things to another, and expressing affection and personal acceptance (see Asher, Oden, & Gottman, 1981).

Older children have been found to behave differently with friends and non-friends in situations where resources are limited. In one study (Charlesworth & LaFreniere 1983), children worked in four-person groups that required some youngsters to operate an apparatus that kept the lights on so that another youngster could watch a movie. Results indicated that the lights were left on longer (allowing the movie to be seen) when children were friends than when they were not. In another study, Philp (1940) compared performance on a marble-dropping task between kindergartners who were either "preferred peers" or strangers. In contrast to those paired with strangers, children with preferred peers dropped more marbles, were more helpful to one another, and interacted more. Similarly, Matsumoto and his colleagues found that friends searched for more mutually oriented solutions on a simplified version of the prisoner's dilemma game than did nonfriends (Matsumoto, Haan, Yabrove, Theodorou, & Carney, 1986).

Apparently, the tendency toward cooperation between friends increases with age. Berndt (1983) reported that older children offer to help and share with friends more than younger children. This observation suggests that the sheer number of cooperative acts between friends increases throughout development. In another study, Berndt (1985) observed fourth, sixth, and eighth graders as they worked on a costly problem-solving task with either a friend or an acquaintance. He found that older children were more likely to sacrifice for their friends than for acquaintances; younger children, however, did not help friends more than nonfriends. According to Hartup (1989a), this finding suggests that a "special sensitivity" to the needs and wants of friends may emerge in adolescence (p. 54).

Finally, social responsiveness is greater among friends than among nonfriends. Newcomb, Brady, and Hartup (1979) found that while working on a block-building task, friends smiled and laughed with each other more than nonfriends, paid closer attention to equity rules, directed conversation toward mutual as opposed to unilateral goals, and interacted more. Other work indicated that friends are more likely to match each other's responses than are nonfriends (e.g., Foot, Chapman, & Smith, 1977).

Conflict

Most children expect their interactions with friends to be conflict free. When asked why people do not become friends, youngsters between the ages of 6 and 10 mention "disagreements" as the most frequent reason; 12- and 13-year-olds cite "personality differences" as the most common reason for failed friendship attempts (see Smoller & Youniss, 1982). Children's intuitive ideas about the detrimental effects of conflict on friendship development may be right. As discussed in the previous section, Gottman (1983) found that children who "hit it off" gave reasons for disagreements, issued weak (as opposed to strong) demands that were typically complied with, and avoided extended disagreement chains. In other words, they successfully minimized conflict.

Although episodes of disagreement may prevent youngsters from becoming friends, conflict is an inevitable part of established relationships. Even the best of friendships are not conflict free. For example, Houseman (1972) observed 847 fights in 62 hours of videotaped interaction among 37 preschoolers. The number of conflicts per child ranged from 8 to 47. In an earlier study of 2- through 5-year-olds, Dawe (1934) recorded 200 conflict episodes. In this sample, one child quarreled only once with a playmate, while another youngster engaged in 42 fights with 27 other children! From these studies we can deduce that although conflict is a frequent occurrence among young children, there are considerable individual and dyadic differences in the rates of such behavior.

Information about the issues over which children conflict comes from two primary sources: interviews and observational studies of group activities or dyadic interactions in laboratory settings. Both lines of research suggest that as children mature, their topics of conflict change. For instance, Selman's (1981) work indicated that young children see the cause of conflict as unilateral and typically regard the other as the responsible party. Conflicts between toddlers and young preschoolers often revolve around object and social control. A typical object control conflict (cited in Eisenberg & Garvey, 1981, p. 161) follows.

> *A:* I'm gonna play with the camper.
> *B:* I'm gonna play with the camper.
> *A:* I said I'm gonna play with that.
> *B:* We'll share it.

Social control conflicts center around one child not doing something another wants. He or she may, for example, refuse to play, refuse to adopt a particular role in fantasy play, or fail to enact an imaginary part properly (see Corsarso, 1985; Genishi & DiPaolo, 1982; Houseman, 1972; Parker & Gottman, 1989). O'Keefe and Benoit (1982, p. 178) related a conflict over social control:

> *Matt:* Scott, don't bother me any more.
> *Scott:* I didn't bother you.
> *Matt:* You did too. Over at the blocks.
> *Scott:* Oooh. *[Disagreeing]*
> *Matt:* And you hurt me too.

Shantz and Hobart (1989) noted that somewhere around the age of 4 or 5, the proportion of conflict issues shifts from a majority of object control squabbles to an equal split between object and social control fights. These equal proportions continue through age 6 or 7.

As they get older, youngsters increasingly recognize that "conflict exists between parties" and that "acceptable resolution strategies must satisfy both parties" (Hartup, 1989a, p. 60). Older children and adolescents distinguish between relatively minor conflicts and those that threaten the existence of a friendship (see Hartup, 1989a; Selman, 1980; Shantz & Hobart, 1989). They also view conflict as inherent in all close relationships and believe that it can actually strengthen friendships when properly addressed. Whereas youngsters in middle childhood often conflict about the rules and norms associated with particular social groups, adolescents commonly quarrel about personality differences and jealousy (see Bigelow & LaGaipa, 1975, 1980; Parker & Gottman, 1989; Selman, 1980).

The issues over which children argue do not vary as a function of whether they are interacting with friends or acquaintances (Hartup, Laursen, Stewart, & Eastenson, 1988). However, friends and nonfriends can be distinguished by the frequency of their conflicts as well as by the strategies they employ to manage disagreements. For example, Green (1933) compared 10 preschoolers who were best friends with 10 preschoolers who were not. He found that best friends engaged in more friendly interaction and quarreled more often than did nonfriends. More recently, Hartup et al. (1988) observed that nursery school children exhibited more "active hostility" (e.g., threats, assaults) and "reactive hostility" (e.g., refusals, resistance) to strong associates than to nonassociates. These results thus suggest that the relation between friendship and conflict is complex. As Hartup (1989a) explained, "The child's total experience with conflict may be greater with friends than with nonfriends, but only because more time is spent with them" (p. 61).

In addition to quantitative differences in the occurrence of conflict between friends and nonfriends, qualitative differences in resolution strategies have been observed as well. Eisenberg and Garvey (1981) found that the most common resolution tactic young children employed was insistence on their own desires (e.g., strings of "no's" and "yes's"), a tactic that served to keep conflict going. However, Hartup (1989b) observed that when paired with friends (versus neutral associates), children were more likely to use negotiation and disengagement as methods for resolving disputes. This researcher also found that when compared to nonfriends, friends more often arrived at equal (or nearly equal) solutions, exhibited less intensity in their conflicts with one another, and were more likely to continue interaction once conflict was managed. Other researchers (e.g., Sacklin & Thelen, 1984) have also reported that social interaction is more likely to continue when conflict resolution involves "conciliatory exchanges." Thus, friends elect to manage their disputes in ways that keep interaction going—an outcome that is not guaranteed by the management strategies used by nonfriends.

Somewhat surprisingly, aggressive tactics are employed far less frequently by young children than is typically assumed. For instance, in two studies of toddlers' interactions with one another, aggression occurred in less than 25% of the conflicts reported (Hay & Ross, 1982; Maudry & Nekula, 1939). Similarly, of the 835 resolution attempts Eisenberg and Garvey (1981) observed among preschoolers, only 10 involved physical force. Shantz and Shantz (1982) coded 72 hours of videotapes of 6- and 7-year-olds playing in groups and noted little aggression. Only 5% of all tactics during conflict were physical attacks whereas only 4% involved verbal assaults.

Studies examining how older children manage conflict are relatively scarce, but the little evidence that does exist suggests that, once again, the resolution strategies chosen by friends differ from those selected by nonfriends. J. Nelson and Aboud (1985) found that when school-age children disagreed about social rules, friends not only explained themselves more than did nonfriends but also exchanged more criticism and ultimately achieved more "mature" solutions. For older youngsters, then, conflict management involves the discussion of differences as well as the explanation of individual viewpoints. Although not directly related, other work has indicated that when involved in competitive interactions, friends comply with mutual commands (e.g., "Let's do this") more readily than do nonfriends and issue fewer individualistic commands (e.g., "I want to do this"); individualistic commands are also less likely to elicit negative reactions from friends (see Newcomb, Brady, & Hartup, 1979). Taken together, these studies suggest that, like their younger counterparts, older children employ more cooperative strategies and seek more equitable outcomes in their conflicts with friends as opposed to those with acquaintances or strangers.

GENDER DIFFERENCES IN CHILDREN'S FRIENDSHIPS

As shown earlier in the chapter, research has demonstrated that children have strong preferences for same-sex friends. This preference usually begins to emerge in nursery school (somewhere between the ages of 3 and 4) and continues to strengthen throughout childhood. In adolescence, it once again becomes acceptable to interact with members of the opposite sex—at this point, however, they are seen as romantic partners, not friends. Cross-cultural studies generally confirm this pattern of gender segregation (see O'Mark, O'Mark, & Edelman, 1975). In fact, the only exception comes from rural Kenya (Harkness & Super, 1985).

If children choose friends on the basis of gender, do boys and girls behave differently with their same-sex friends? Much evidence suggests that boys' and girls' same-sex friendship patterns differ. We review these differences below. Some of the patterns we touch upon will be familiar from previous chapters, while others are presented for the first time.

Patterns in Boys' and Girls' Same-Sex Friendships

Girls tend to have smaller and more exclusive friendship networks than boys do. Eder and Hallinan (1978) found that, when compared to boys, girls make fewer new friends over the course of a school year. Similarly, Berndt (1983) observed that girls who began the school term with many friends tended to establish few new relationships; the opposite was true for boys. Children's reports on their actual interactions with peers also indicated that girls spend most of their time with a single "best friend" and boys typically play in larger groups (see Savin-Williams, 1979; Waldrop & Halverson, 1975). Given their tendency toward exclusivity, it is not surprising that girls are more protective of the time they actually spend with friends. Feshback and Sones (1971) observed that pairs of boy friends were more likely to acknowledge and include a child who attempted to join their ongoing activities than were pairs of girl friends. In her review of same-sex friendships, Daniels-Bierness (1989) concluded:

> Throughout the literatures, there is clear evidence that boys' and girls' peer relationships are sex-segregated from a very early age and that the structure of these all-boy and all-girl groups differs in terms of intensivity, exclusivity, stability, reciprocity, and hierarchical organization. Boys play in large, hierarchically structured groups; they have dense friendship networks; and they are open to the development of new friendships. Girls, on the other hand, play predominately in dyads; they have one-to-one, closed, reciprocal relationships. Their social networks are structured horizontally and based on equality. (p. 118)

As previously stated, the nature of the activities in which friends engage also varies as a function of gender. Maccoby and Jacklin (1987) conducted a study in which they observed naturally occurring interactions between preschoolers. These interactions were then coded for the extent to which children played with stereotypically male or female toys and acted out stereotypically male or female themes. Feminine toys and themes included playing with dolls, kitchen equipment, or dress-up clothes, and playing house. Trucks, planes, trains, and blocks were considered masculine toys; male themes included war and cowboy games as well as any play involving toys or imaginary guns. Maccoby and Jacklin's results revealed significant sex differences in the types of play youngsters preferred: Girls had more recorded intervals of typically feminine play whereas boys had more recorded intervals of typically masculine play. Interestingly, however, the overall frequency of stereotypical play was low. During the periods they were observed, children spent most of their time in the sandbox and on the jungle gym and swings, or they worked with clay, paints, and puzzles and read books. This suggests that sex typing in the objects and themes characteristic of children's play may be on the decline.

Regardless of the props children use or the imaginary themes they enact, boys engage in far more rough-and-tumble play than girls do (DiPietro, 1981). For boys, even the most gender-neutral activities are characterized by high levels of body contact. Some of this contact is aggressive, but most often it takes the form of playful wrestling and chasing (see Maccoby, 1985; Maccoby & Jacklin, 1987). In addition to rougher forms of play, boys also favor activities that involve unrestrained movement whereas girls commonly choose activities that involve more restrained movement (Sutton-Smith & Rosenberg, 1971). For instance, Thorne (1986) observed that during recess, boys preferred "run and chase" games that required large spaces and more playmates, while girls tended to play closer to the school building in smaller groups.

Several studies also indicated that, when compared to girls, boys exhibit higher rates of conflict behavior in their same-sex interactions. Some work has suggested that this behavior takes the form of more verbal and physical fighting (see Hartup, 1989a; Miller, Danaher, & Forbes, 1986). However, C. U. Shantz (1989) cautioned that this finding may be a methodological artifact. Most naturalistic studies of children's conflict utilize one of two procedures: focal time sampling, in which each child in a group is randomly selected and observed for a predetermined amount of time, or event sampling, in which all episodes of conflict are recorded across the entire group. Shantz warned that when event sampling is used, observers are more likely to notice the loud, physical fights characteristic of boys and are less likely to pay attention to the quieter, verbal conflicts typical of girls. She also suggested that researchers may be more vigilant in their observations of boys because they expect to see more conflict between them than between girls. In support of these claims, the one major study of children's conflict in which focal sampling was used (Houseman, 1972) showed that girls actually engaged in more conflict than did boys. Moreover, Gilligan's (1982) naturalistic observations indicated that, in contrast to stereotypical beliefs, boys actually resolve disputes more effectively than do girls. As she explained:

> During the course of this study, boys were seen quarreling all the time, but not once was a game terminated because of a quarrel and no game was interrupted for more than seven minutes. In the gravest of debates, the final word was always, to "repeat the play," generally followed by a chorus of "cheater's proof." In fact, it seemed as if the boys enjoyed the legal debates as much as they do the game itself, and even marginal players of lesser size or skill participated equally in these recurrent squabbles. In contrast, the eruption of disputes among girls tended to end the game. (p. 9)

Clearly, the issue of how gender affects friends' conflicts requires further exploration.

Some researchers have suggested that gender differences in the activities of same-sex friends reflect fundamental differences in the issues around which girls and boys organize their friendships. Proponents of the so-called gender as culture hypothesis (e.g., Maltz & Borker, 1982; Tannen, 1986, 1990) have argued that girls are taught to organize their same-sex friendships around interdependence, cooperation, and the pursuit of socioemotional concerns, whereas boys are taught to emphasize independence, influence, and the pursuit of shared activities. From this perspective, gender constitutes a culture which imparts to boys and girls different sets of rules for the conduct of friendship and different sets of assumptions about the functions of communication in friendship. For girls, talk is the primary vehicle through which intimacy and connectedness are created and maintained. Boys, on the other hand, view talk as a mechanism for getting things done, for accomplishing instrumental tasks, for conveying information, and for maintaining autonomy.

Several lines of research have supported this reasoning. First, studies have indicated that boys are more competitive with their same-sex friends than girls are. Berndt (1981a) paired school children with friends and nonfriends and observed as they worked on a task in which they could either share a crayon (at a cost to themselves) or not share (at a cost to their partners). Boys monopolized the crayons, were less likely to comply with requests to share, and showed a greater discrepancy in outcomes when paired with friends versus nonfriends. Second, in their social interactions with one another, boys appear to be more concerned with establishing a hierarchy (Freedman, 1977; Thorne, 1986). Leaders are quickly identified and typically issue commands and imperatives to orchestrate the group's activities. In contrast, leadership for girls tends to focus on making suggestions, eliciting participation and input from group members, and ultimately deciding by consensus (Arliss, 1991; Lockheed & Hall, 1976). When compared to boys, girls have also been found to interrupt one another less, express more agreement with each other's ideas, show greater concern for turn taking, and acknowledge what another has just said when beginning to speak (for a review of these studies, see Maccoby, 1985). Finally, studies of friendship conceptions indicate that as girls mature, they mention intimacy, self-disclosure, and affective exchange as key components of friendship more frequently than boys do (e.g., Berndt, 1983).

Taken together, these studies indicate clear and meaningful differences in the ways girls and boys organize and conduct their same-sex friendships. Whether these differences are enough to constitute distinct cultures, however, requires further investigation. Some of the work we cited (e.g., Maccoby & Jacklin, 1987) suggested that certain stereotypical behaviors are less prevalent today than they were even a few years ago. This finding may show a trend toward increasing similarity between the sexes. In addition, many studies employ a between-groups design when investigating gender differences. This procedure not only inflates differences between boys and girls but also masks variations that can emerge among members of the same sex (see Burleson, Kunkel, Samter, & Werking, 1996; Duck & Wright, 1993). In view of these qualifications, perhaps it best to think of boys and girls as members of one culture that, like any other culture, is marked by shared beliefs as well as individual variation.

Explanations for Gender Differences in Children's Same-Sex Friendships

Why do children exhibit such strong preferences for same-sex friends and engage in such markedly different behaviors with these individuals? Researchers have offered several explanations. We have already reviewed evidence suggesting that mothers and fathers utilize distinct styles when interacting with their children and that these styles impart different but complementary lessons about the nature and function of communication. We have also shown that both mothers and fathers direct somewhat different behaviors to boys and girls. Such socialization practices are known to influence youngsters' linguistic and communicative development as well as the activities they prefer to engage in with friends. Yet there is little evidence that adults actually structure settings so that play as well as task activities are differentiated on the basis of sex.

To begin with, some work has suggested that children whose parents encourage gender-appropriate play are less likely to demonstrate strong same-sex friendship preferences and actually engage in less typical forms of masculine or feminine play than children whose parents do not engage in strong sex typing (Maccoby & Jacklin, 1987). Other work has indicated that the presence of an adult reduces children's exclusionary behavior. For example, Lockheed and colleagues found that the amount of cross-sex interaction was greater in classroom groups formed by a teacher than when children were allowed to select their own partners (Lockheed, 1985; Lockheed & Hall, 1976). Similarly, in *Conversations of Friends*, the book of essays edited by them, Gottman and Parker (1986) noted that many preschoolers they observed had a number of close, cross-sex friends either because they were neighbors or because their parents were friends and encouraged interaction. When the children entered elementary school, however, these relationships either dissipated or went "underground."

Maccoby and Jacklin (1987) argued that such evidence suggests children themselves are instigators of gender segregation and speculated that they may do so to avoid being accused of romantic interest. When the group composition is structured by adults (and, consequently, out of their hands), children feel freer to interact with members of the opposite sex in nonstereotypical ways. In a telling response to the question of why she could not play with boys (reported in Maccoby & Jacklin, 1987), an 11-year-old girl said:

> People would not be my friends. They would scorn me. Nobody who had any care of status would sit next to a boy if they could sit next to a girl. This teasing is worse because it lasts longer. It is sort of like being in a lower rank or peeing in your pants. You would be teased for months about this. But if you wore your shoes backwards you'd only be teased for a few days. (p. 245)

Maccoby and Jacklin (1987) suggested that some of the initial impetus for segregated friendship and activity choice lies in cross-sex patterns of dominance and control. A number of studies have indicated that youngsters have difficulty influencing members of the opposite sex. As failures to exert control accumulate, children return to the safety and predictability of same-sex dyads where stereotypical patterns of interaction are then reinforced. In line with this explanation,

Fagot (1985) found that even very young children (i.e., 20 to 25 months) exhibited "asymmetry" in their influence attempts. More specifically, her data indicated that youngsters changed their behavior in response to negative reactions from members of their own sex but not in response to negative reactions from members of the opposite sex. This pattern held for both boys and girls. Similarly, Maccoby and Jacklin (1987) observed unacquainted pairs of 33-month-old toddlers. Once again, all children responded to the vocal prohibitions of same-sex peers. Within mixed-sex dyads, however, girls terminated their actions as a result of boys' demands, but boys did not desist in the face of girls' protests.

During development, the frequency with which children attempt to influence their peers increases and the methods boys and girls use to exert control show more and more divergence (Serbin, Sprafkin, Elman, & Doyle, 1984). For girls, this increase takes the form of offering more polite suggestions; boys, on the other, show an increase in the use of demands. These tendencies thus set up a dynamic in which boys become less responsive to polite suggestions, which are precisely the influence techniques that girls are developing within their same-sex friendships. This pattern has also been found among adults. Several studies have suggested that adult men dominate interaction in mixed-sex groups (e.g., Aries, 1982, 1987; DeFrancisco, 1991; Lockheed & Hall, 1976; Zimmerman & West, 1975; see Haslett, Geis, & Carter, 1992, for a summary).

Other researchers have argued that same-sex friendship selection and its attendant behavioral differences result from a sharp divergence in interests between boys and girls. Children of all ages view common activities as an important feature of friendship, but evidence suggests that boys and girls prefer different activities. For example, Shure (1963) observed that 4-year-old boys spent more time in the block area and 4-year-old girls spent more time in the art, doll, and book areas. In a study of fifth graders, Asher (1975) found that the top five interests of boys were completely different from the top five interests of girls. These interests tended to reflect traditional concepts of masculine and feminine behavior (Markell & Asher, 1974). As earlier noted, having girls as friends is different from having boys as friends—because girls can get hurt playing football. In line with this argument, other work has suggested that boys who prefer rough-and-tumble play—as well as girls who dislike rough-and-tumble play— make the fewest number of cross-sex friend selections (see Bukowski, Gauze, Hoza, & Newcomb, 1993; Maccoby, 1988).

Gottman and Carrere (1994) took this argument one step further and suggested the activities boys prefer—as well as their tendency to behave more aggressively—reflect a fundamental inability to handle negative emotions. In support of this claim, studies have indicated that compared to girls, boys not only have faster arousal times but also reach higher levels of arousal under stressful conditions (for a brief review, see Maccoby, 1988). According to Gottman and Carrere (1994), the rambunctious, large-group games in which boys frequently engage provide an outlet, a vehicle for working through such arousal. Thus, boys may avoid interacting with girls because they find it boring, and girls may avoid interacting with boys because they find their intensity a bit overwhelming. From this perspective, gender segregation in friendship preferences and behaviors is explained in terms of a biological component.

Although somewhat controversial, this explanation is also supported by studies suggesting that infants prefer to look at pictures of same-sex children as opposed pictures of opposite-sex children (e.g., Lewis & Brooks, 1975). This finding has been observed in babies as young as 12 months and remains relatively robust under potentially confounding conditions. For example, Aitken (1977) found that even when children in slides were dressed to look like the opposite sex (i.e., boys wore frilly dresses and girls wore dungarees), babies still preferred pictures of same-sex infants. In another study, Bower (1989) attached lights to models' joints so that only their patterns of movement were detectable. Even under this condition, baby boys looked more at the pattern generated by other boys and baby girls looked more at the pattern generated by other girls. Gottman and Carrere (1994) suggested that the effects of socialization are unlikely to be seen in babies as young as 12 months. Thus to them, the same-sex preferences demonstrated by infants are indicative of a prewired tendency for boys to orient to boys and girls to orient to girls.

Summary

Clearly, there are consistent differences in the ways boys and girls conduct their same-sex friendships. Girls tend to be more exclusive in their friendships than are boys. Given this trend, it is not surprising that when interacting with friends, boys tend to orient toward group games, prefer rough-and-tumble activities, and cover a rather large expanse of territory; girls, on the other hand, favor more intimate settings and engage in somewhat more sedate forms of interaction and play. Some researchers have argued that these differences reflect the core issues around which children organize their same-sex friendships. Whereas boys' relationships emphasize independence, influence, and the pursuit of shared activities, girls' demonstrate interdependence, cooperation, and the pursuit of socioemotional concerns.

Unfortunately, there is no definitive answer to the question of why boys and girls interact in such distinct ways. Some researchers have argued that socialization is the key source of gender differences, while others have suggested that children segregate themselves because of failed attempts to influence opposite-sex peers and to avoid accusations of romantic involvement. Still others have maintained that a fundamental biological component underlies such variation. Clearly, more research is needed to determine whether any single explanation can account for the significant and consistent differences observed in boys' and girls' same-sex friendships.

SUMMARY

Throughout this chapter, we have sought to sketch at least some of the ways in which children *do* friendship. We know, for example, that in addition to gender, a host of other objective factors (like physical attractiveness, race, and proximity) influence children's choices of friends. However, we also know that although demographic features may narrow the field of potential relational partners, communication is the mechanism through which an *attractive other* becomes a friend. As the literature review indicated, fantasy play, gossip, and self-disclosure appear to be particularly important communicative processes through which youngsters of different ages accomplish this goal. We have also seen that children draw sharp distinctions between friends and nonfriends; friends motivate one another to cooperate, to behave prosocially, and to find ways of managing conflict which do not damage the relationship. Friends play an important role in each other's social, emotional, and communicative development, a role that clearly complements but remains distinct from the role of parents.

NOTES

1. Taken from an interview cited in W. Damon (1977), *The social world of the child* (San Francisco: Jossey-Bass), p. 159.
2. Taken from an interview cited in J. G. Parker & J. M. Gottman (1989), Social and emotional developmental in a relational context: Friendship interaction from early childhood to adolescence, that appears in T. J. Berndt & G. W. Ladd (Eds.), *Peer relationships in child development* (pp. 95–131; New York: Wiley).

9

Parenting:
Principles and Practices

Although the idea is obvious, the first, most important issue that people must consider is whether they want to be parents. Most people who have children agree that parenting is a difficult but rewarding job. Parents are on duty 24 hours a day, for the rest of their lives, not always in terms of physical care, but in terms of commitment and love. As Americans it is particularly ironic that, despite the emphasis on education, there are few chances to study parenting. Although courses and self-help parenting books are available, there is no systematic training for parents, and corporate and governmental agencies do not make it easy to be parents. Policies like flex time and family leave are helpful but remain the exception rather than the rule. Moreover, parents are often "punished" for taking time away from work; such punishment can be in the forms of loss of vacation time, more task demands on return, and so forth.

In this chapter, we outline some general principles and practices we believe lie at the heart of good parenting. These principles and practices are distilled from the research reviewed throughout this book. Although this information is geared primarily for parents or future parents, it is also relevant for aunts, uncles, grandparents, day care workers, or anyone who cares about children and their development. Everyone has a vested interest in children's welfare because they represent society's future and help ensure its continued existence.

The assumption underlying all principles and practices we cite is that parenting is built on nurturing. Parents must provide a safe, secure environment for their children, an environment free from psychological as well as physical abuse. Although the particular ways in which safe, secure environments are created may differ both within and across cultures, parents must nevertheless provide as much security, support, and safety as possible in their particular circumstances.

To illustrate how different environments can influence child rearing, we begin this chapter with a brief survey of cultural variations in parenting beliefs and practices. This discussion summarizes some differences in U.S. values on parenting, provides a selective summary of parenting expectations and styles in other countries, and highlights some issues about day care. In the last section of the chapter, we try to distill from the social science information presented throughout this book a set of principles important for parenting. These principles, in our opinion, promote children's healthy communicative and social development.

CULTURE AS A DEVELOPMENTAL CONTEXT

Culture provides the overarching set of values and practices within which people live, communicate, and bring up successive generations. Elements of cross-cultural variation include different languages, customs, patterns of interaction, and lifestyles. Yet despite cultural diversity, all societies apparently: (a) regard communication as an important basic need; (b) recognize communication as a multichannel phenomenon; (c) identify the main communicative functions of expressing thoughts and feelings, establishing connections with others, and sharing knowledge; and (d) use communication to mark status, politeness, social identity, and power (Haslett, 1989). Whiting and Edwards (1988) also noted that same-sex interaction and play among children appears to be a strong cross-cultural value in societies.

Young children essentially acquire that which is valued by a culture. Although a thorough review of cultural differences in communicative development is well beyond the scope of this book, we nevertheless want to point out that culture is the context in which all development occurs and thus is an inescapable backdrop for discussing communicative development. Despite the cultural diversity in child-rearing practices, language and communication seem to thrive effortlessly in children without explicit teaching and to emerge at approximately 2 years of age.

In everyday social life, cultural and communicative practices are interwoven and inseparable; people express culture via their communication. Different cultures have different expectations about what children should do and know. Schieffelin and Ochs (1983) observed: "The capacity to express intentions is human but which intentions can be expressed by whom, when, and how is subject to local expectations concerning the social behavior of members. With respect to the acquisition of competence in language use, this means that societies may very well differ in their expectations of what children can and should communicate" (p. 307).

Schieffelin and Ochs' essays on cultural differences in the development of communication underscore the wide variation in social practices. Some cultures emphasize dyadic mother–child interactions; others favor multiparty interactions. In some cultures, infants are viewed as knowledgeable; in others, they are seen as having no understanding. Somehow, despite their diversity, these cultural practices allow communication to emerge and flourish.

We have already reviewed studies showing how various attitudes toward communication are reflected and sustained in different subgroups *within* particular cultures. In attitudes toward caretaker–child interaction, striking differences reflect distinct socializing patterns *across* different societies as well (Schieffelin & Ochs, 1983). Like Bernstein and the constructivists, Isbell and McKee (1980) suggested that cross-cultural differences in the structure of caretaker relations influence communication patterns; these communication patterns, in turn, contribute to differences in cognitive orientation (p. 340). Thus, Isbell and McKee argued for an interactive view of cognition that results "from the selective attention of the child to the available and salient information in her/his environment" (p. 350). These salient factors differ in various cultures (for a set of representative studies, see, for example, Bril, Zack, & Nkounkou-Hombessa, 1989; Coll, 1990; Frankel & Roer-Bronstein, 1982; Goodnow & Collins, 1990; Kupersmidt, Griesler, & DeRosier, 1995; S. A. Miller, 1988; Pomerleau, Malcuit, & Sabatier, 1991; Sigel, 1985).

Some degree of scaffolding appears to be culturally universal: All caregivers guide children's activities to some extent, although in different areas (Rogoff, 1990). Rogoff suggested, however, that cultures differ with respect to the explicitness and intensity of both nonverbal and verbal communication, the degree of emphasis on face-to-face communication and the interactional roles of adults and children. Schieffelin and Ochs (1983) proposed two different communicative patterns between adults and children: One style adapts to children's abilities (as in the United States), and the other requires children to adapt to adult standards (as in Kaluli and Samoan groups). Whiting's (1963) classic study of childrearing practices in six different cultures showed that there are many pathways to learning and that linguistic and communicative development seems to be greatly "buffered." That is, regardless of the diverse cultural practices of different societies, most children acquire effective communication skills by age 2, even though the means of acquisition vary widely. This well-known finding suggests that communicative development is buffered, or likely to emerge, even despite wide variation in the environment (Roopnarine, Johnson, & Hooper, 1994).

Differences in general parenting styles both across and within cultures are just part of the picture. In what follows, we briefly characterize culture-specific childrearing practices. Our review begins with a brief sketch of differences observed between the United States and other countries. Then we turn our attention to variations among groups within the United States, particularly in the use and effects of preschool and day care facilities. (For an excellent discussion of some theoretical and methodological issues involved in cross-cultural developmental research, see Bornstein, 1989a; a good review of actual research studies can be found in Scheiffelin and Ochs, 1983. For an updated look at cultural contrasts in childrearing, see Whiting and Edwards, 1988 and other representative studies cited earlier.)

Some Cross-Cultural Differences and Similarities

In a series of studies, Bornstein and his colleagues (Bornstein, 1989b; Bornstein et al., 1992) examined similarities and differences in childrearing activities among Japanese and U.S. mothers. Both cultures were similar in their focus on children, but Japanese mothers saw their infants as extensions of themselves and thus strengthened their children's dependence on them. In contrast, U.S. mothers generally promoted autonomy in their infants and facilitated their verbal and physical independence. U.S. children were encouraged to be creative, exploratory, and self-assertive whereas Japanese children were encouraged to be patient, persistent, and accommodating. Japanese mothers expected their preschoolers to be emotionally mature, to exhibit self-control, and to be courteous; U.S. mothers encouraged early mastery of verbal ability and individual action and initiative (Hess, Kashiwagi, Azuma, Price, & Dickson, 1980).

Goodnow (1985, 1988) looked at how parental beliefs about children's development influenced their parenting practices. Parents from different cultures were found to have different beliefs about the ages at which certain developments would appear (such as peer–peer disputes), and the ways children progress through these developmental stages. Differing beliefs about children's development direct parental behaviors. Blicharski, Gravel, and Trudel (1994) found that children's temperaments were shaped by a complex set of factors including parents' expectations, assessment, and responses to their children. As noted in chapter 6, parental behaviors predict children's subsequent actions (Bates, Maslin, & Frankel, 1985; McGillicuddy-DeLisi, 1982; Sabatier, 1994; Siegal, 1991; Strayer & Moss, 1989). Kaluli children, for example, are not regarded as "having sense" and "communicating meaningfully" until around 6 or 7 years and thus are not given the attention a U.S. infant would receive (Schieffelin, 1981). Athabaskan children who remain silent are viewed as being respectful rather than language delayed or communicatively deficient, as they might be in the U.S. middle-class culture (Scollon & Scollon, 1981). Parental beliefs, then, shape the developmental environment in which children mature; parents' beliefs determine their expectations, demands, teaching, and disciplining of children (Belsky, 1993; K. Rubin, Mills, & Rose-Krasnor, 1989).

In contrast to these differences, cross-cultural similarities also occur. For example, Bornstein et al. (1992) observed that in France, the United States, and Japan, infants and mothers demonstrate specificity in their mutual responses and reciprocity in their interactions. In all three cultures, mothers encourage their infants to explore the environment; mothers respond to infants' vocalizations with imitations and quickly react to infants' distress signals. Differences occurred in responses to infants' gaze behavior and in emphasizing dyadic as opposed to extradyadic interactions. Fernald and Morikawa (1993) also found that Japanese and North American mothers use simple, repetitive speech and adapt it to their infants. However, North American mothers employ more object identification, whereas Japanese mothers engage their children in social routines through using objects.

In many cultures, particularly Third World countries, societies are becoming modern and urbanized. As economies, job opportunities, and patterns change, so do families as they attempt to adapt to new circumstances. Parental roles are likely to be in transition as well. For example, fathers' traditional roles in West Africa emphasized their importance in guiding and preparing their children to accept their family responsibilities. Recent trends toward modernization now emphasize fathers' economic roles and tend to separate them from their families (Nsamenang, 1987). As a result, West African families are caught between conflicting expectations for childrearing.

Some Cultural Differences Within the United States

Parental Values. Bronfenbrenner's (1977) pioneering review of historical changes in U.S. childrearing practices provides a backdrop for looking at parental values in this country. Differences between the lower and middle classes reversed themselves from 1930 to 1950. Lower-class parents became more strict, and middle-class parents more lenient, although both socioeconomic groups grew more flexible during the post-World War II years. In the 1980s, researchers began studying the beliefs that parents express about childrearing; these beliefs are seen as a result of parents' own experiences as well as their perceptions of the roles they play in children's development (Sabatier, 1994; Youniss, 1992). This research uncovered significant cultural differences in how children are viewed developmentally and in what are considered appropriate, supportive parental practices. (See Goodnow, 1985, for an excellent review of these studies.)

Ellis and Petersen (1992) investigated cultural patterns about conformity and individualism. In groups that valued conformity more than self-reliance, both corporal punishment and lecturing were used as disciplinary techniques. In contrast, groups valuing self-reliance and autonomy tended to avoid severe, frequent discipline. Ellis and Petersen noted that attitudes toward conformity and individualism extend to the workplace and therefore influence the type of skills children need to suceed later in life. The associations among social class, conformity, and individualism observed by Ellis and Petersen are similar to those found by Bernstein (discussed in chapter 6). In the same vein, a study by Grimm-Thomas and Perry-Jenkins (1994) found that working class fathers who had positive co-worker relationships and good work clarity were less likely to use psychological control and guilt in their parenting. Thus, paternal (as well as maternal) work satisfaction may be an important family issue that influences parenting practices.

Another study explored cultural variations in parenting as a function of Euro American, African American, Hispanic American, and Asian American parents (Julian, McKenry, & McKelvey, 1994). This study is unique in that it controlled for socioeconimic differences. When variations in socioeconomic status were held constant, striking similarities across the groups were observed; culture did not not contribute more than 4% to any variable. Some parents did, however, place greater emphasis on self-control and school success than did others.

As the cost of living rises, many families come to rely on dual wage earners and women working outside the home are seen as making valuable contributions to family security. Under these circumstances, unless one parent can work at home, alternative child care arrangements are necessary. Extended families with aunts, uncles, and grandparents could once care for children, but today's widespread geographic mobility makes extended family care unlikely. Increasingly, child care arrangements occur in organized group settings, like preschools or day care centers. Finding satisfactory child care arrangements is a major problem for families.

Effects of Preschool and Day Care on Children's Language and Communication Development

The topic of day care causes much tension and concern. Models of child development tacitly assume a nuclear family: mother, father, and 1.7 children. Unfortunately, this model fits less than 20% of families living in the United States today and has probably always reflected an ideal, rather than actual, family life. Some public policy debates about how best to provide for children and families are based on this implied model. Another assumption related to the implicit ideal of the nuclear family is that young children suffer developmental setbacks when a parent does not stay at home and care for them. These assumptions have led people to ignore other family structures and the benefits that might flow to children from alternative family systems. For example, in a meta-analysis of studies comparing preschool and home environments, Clarke-Stewart (1991) concluded that children in preschool centers were *more* advanced socially and intellectually than were youngsters who stayed at home. She suggested that preschool environments enrich children's growth by fostering cognitive and intellectual development, providing opportunities to learn skills necessary for interacting with peers, and encouraging independence and self-direction. Children's experiences in day care also vary as a function of their preferred orientation, either to adults or peers (Galluzzo, Matheson, Moore, & Howes, 1988).

With these considerations in mind, we turn to research examining the effects of preschool and day care on children's development, especially their communicative development. An extensive review of research on the effects of maternal employment in two-parent families by L. Hoffman (1989) found the following:

1. There are no significant differences between children of employed and nonemployed mothers on outcome measures such as indices of cognitive and socioemotional development.
2. Children whose mothers work have less restricted views of sex roles.

3. Employed mothers seem to emphasize independence training more than do nonemployed mothers.

4. The dual roles (mother and worker) predict women's happiness if they desire employment; other factors influencing maternal satisfaction include job quality and stability of child care arrangements.

5. Mothers' job satisfaction is positively related to the quality of mother–child interaction and to other aspects of children's development.

6. Some mothers experience stress from worrying about having enough time for their children and about the adequacy of child care arrangements.

7. Part-time employment is associated with more positive outcomes for family life and child development than are no employment or full-time employment.

8. The relationship between fathers' satisfaction and mothers' employment is complex and depends on social class, sex-role attitudes, and fathers' participation in household jobs and child care.

9. Mothers' employment appears to have no significant effect on marital satisfaction.

10. Mothers' employment changes the division of labor in the household. Fathers' participation is needed and desired; some fathers appear to be positively motivated by more involvement, but others are not.

11. Some studies have suggested that employed mothers compensate for their loss of time with children by increased contact and verbal interaction during nonwork and weekends; other studies have found no differences in mother–child interaction between nonemployed and employed mothers.

12. Studies of maternal or paternal attachment and whether mothers are employed remain inconclusive and difficult to interpret.

13. Mothers' employment is related to their daughters enhanced self-esteem and confidence.

As can be seen from these findings, maternal employment, in and of itself, is not strongly related to any child outcome. In fact, the effects of maternal employment appear to be mediated by a host of other family variables including paternal involvement, stability of child care arrangements, and mothers' desire to work. Instead of focusing on single variables, such as maternal employment or father involvement, researchers should perhaps look at the complex interactions between the various factors that constitute family life (Belsky, Crnic, & Gable, 1995).

Day care centers may offer rich interactional opportunities for young children. For instance, adult day care workers typically adapt their speech to children's age and group size (Pellegrino & Scopesi, 1990). Additional interactional opportunities are provided by peers. Thus, the issue about day care is less the situation itself than the quality of the programs offered. Parents must carefully evaluate the available alternatives and select the program they believe best for their child.

They should talk about the school with other parents and with their children and arrange a time to observe the nursery or drop in unexpectedly. Are their facilities safe? What is the ratio of teachers to students? What activities and programs are offered? What training has the staff had? How much time is provided for unstructured free play, where children develop their own play scenarios? Studies show that it is important for both parents and children to feel comfortable with the child care arrangements.

As this brief sketch of some areas of cultural contrast should make clear, substantial variations in childrearing practices exist; how children are viewed, the skills they are assumed to have, and the rights they possess as children all vary cross-culturally. As Parke (1989) pointed out, burgeoning cross-cultural developmental studies have resulted in increasing recognition of the impact of culture and a corresponding modesty about the scope of research claims. One finding has clearly emerged: Language and communication flourish under a wide range of environmental circumstances.

PARENTING PRINCIPLES AND PRACTICES

With these thoughts in mind, we now turn to specific principles and practices that will enhance children's communicative development as well as the social and emotional outcomes they experience. The practices flow from underlying principles central for a child's communicative growth. Each principle will be explained and a set of practices developed which can help implement the principle. The issue here is not that everyone can carry out these practices with excellence at every moment. Rather, the key is consistency—have these goals in mind and try to follow them as much as possible.

Although we have organized our discussion around particular developmental periods, some principles and practices are important throughout childhood and adolescence. For instance, nurturing is key to raising children who are competent communicators and successful social partners, and fathers' involvement seems to benefit children of all ages. In chapter 6 we noted that fathers are as competent as mothers when it comes to caring for children, but there are consistent variations in the modal patterns of interaction mothers and fathers exhibit with their children. When compared to mothers, fathers initiate more physical and idiosyncratic games and interact with children in what has been called "a playful and exciting manner." Researchers have noted that this style teaches youngsters how to manage the ups and downs of interaction and how to get back in control after an extended period of stimulation. In contrast, mothers initiate more verbal play routines than do fathers and behave in more controlled, modulated ways when interacting with children. This pattern of behavior imparts important lessons about inner control and about how to keep interaction going. Children benefit from both forms of interaction; masculine and feminine patterns of behavior clearly teach young children distinct but complementary lessons about the nature of communication.

Perhaps less obvious is the benefit that fathers' involvement gives mothers. All mothers need a break from constant child care responsibilities; even today, mothers still assume most work in this domain. Studies have indicated that in families where women are unemployed, fathers spend 20% to 25% as much time as mothers in direct interaction with children and assume virtually no responsibility for child care. In families where both parents work, fathers' direct interaction with children increases, but the time they spend in routine child care activities does not. Increased involvement of fathers is likely to benefit the whole family. Fathers get to spend more time with their children, children benefit from more frequent and consistent exposure to multiple interactional partners, and mothers get a break. Marital satisfaction generally predicts healthy parent–child relationships, and part of this satisfaction may come from an equitable distribution of routine childrearing activities.

Siblings can also promote children's linguistic and communicative growth during development. Although the presence of older siblings may lessen adult responsiveness to each child, siblings provide a more varied, stimulating language environment. Children who have more extensive turn-taking experience with skilled partners like siblings engage in a higher frequency of turn taking with peers. Interactions with siblings also provide a context in which youngsters learn and practice important communication skills such as comforting, conflict management, peer entry, and social reasoning. In this way, siblings provide a useful training ground for peer–peer interaction. Parents must remember, however, that the quality of sibling relationships is determined by each child's temperament as well as by his or her relationship with the mother and father. Children benefit from forming unique connections with their parents. Thus, throughout all phases of early development, it is useful to try to arrange time alone with individual children to let siblings know they are valued in their own right.

Thus far, we have discussed principles that apply across the developmental span. In what follows, we look more closely at parental practices that are closely associated with particular periods such as infancy or early childhood. As children mature, parental practices must accomodate children's increasing skills, knowledge, and experience. Such parental adaptation enhances children's social-cognitive development as well as their communication skills.

Infancy

Communication is fundamental to survival; young infants' cries signal a need for attention. As they mature, through both nonverbal and verbal means, infants increasingly communicate their thoughts, feelings, and needs. Adults signal the importance of communication to infants by responding to their signals. Nonverbal communication develops first, and people respond to infants partly because they are aware of infants' well-developed perceptual abilities at birth, particularly in terms of visual and auditory systems. Although in early research infants were seen as tabulae rasae to be filled with experience, many studies have shown that young children are born well equipped for communication and with sophisticated nonverbal abilities.

In chapter 2, we noted that infants listen to their mothers' voice in utero for several months before birth. Babies are also born with the capacity to see about eight inches away (the typical distance between child and caretaker during feeding) and prefer the human face to other visual stimuli. Together, these prewired capacities ensure that infants' attention is drawn to the very thing in which they are most interested (i.e., the mother's face). Because body control flows from head to foot and from body trunk to extremities, babies as they mature are able to control their head and orient their gaze and later to coordinate looking with reaching and touching.

Parents' responsiveness also flows from knowing about the importance of stimulating infants and responding contingently (i.e., immediately) to their signals. Parents' modeling of behaviors for infants constitutes a major source of learning for young children. Babies not only mirror their mothers' facial expressions but also react to them. Ultimately, such maternal stimulation teaches infants how to connect internal emotional states with external representations of these states. Similarly, when adults respond to children's pointing and reaching gestures, they reinforce the meaning attached to these gestures.

Perhaps the most important lesson contingent responses teach babies is that their behaviors have meaning. In fact, parents naturally act as if their children's signals are intentional and meaningful. To illustrate this point, we would like to recount a frequent activity shared by one of the authors of this book, Beth Haslett, and her daughter, Heidi. When Heidi was 3 months old, Beth engaged her in conversational babbling. Obviously, their interactions had no "meaning," but through varying intonation patterns Beth received different responses from her daughter. When her mother was babbling in a high, excited tone, with a facial expression of interest, Heidi would smile and babble happily in response. When Beth used a rising intonation as is typically done in signaling a question, Heidi would look at her mother and babble in a much less animated way. The important point here is that Beth acted as if the nonsensical monologue was actually a dialogue between the two. Heidi's responses were treated as if they were intentional and meaningful, and from Heidi's point of view, they probably were. By contingently responding to infants' signals, Beth and other parents teach children that their messages matter, that their communicative signals are valued, meaningful, and responded to.

Synchrony, another important element of responsiveness, develops when dyadic partners learn how to focus their attention in coordination with each other. Synchrony thus teaches infants that communication is a joint endeavor that begins when two people attend to the same stimuli and that is sustained when they coordinate their actions. Facial expressiveness and coordination of eye gaze are critical for establishing synchronous interactions during the first few months of life. Later, however, different avenues for establishing synchrony emerge. Much of this development depends on infants' temperaments: Some babies are placid, others very active. Infants also vary in the type of stimulation they prefer: Many infants like touch, others try to avoid it. Some babies are soothed by a lot of environmental activity and sound, others respond to this stimulation with anger or distress. Parents must not only attune themselves to infants' temperaments and preferences, but might also recognize that these factors shape the kind of synchrony they develop with their children.

Finally, time is a critical feature of responsiveness. Parents must take time to be with children and to engage them in activities, whether play, going for a walk, giving a bottle, or taking a bath. Talking to infants during routine activities like these engages their attention and focuses it on the interaction. Infants thus learn the value of interaction for obtaining both instrumental and social goals. They come to understand that communication is functional in nature and can be used to accomplish a variety of aims like initiating play, making requests, and getting help.

Each element of responsiveness—contingency, nonverbal synchrony, and time—is crucial in the development of secure attachment or bonding. As earlier mentioned, there are three types of attachment: secure, insecure anxious, and insecure avoidant. Approximately 55% of children experience secure attachment, but 45% experience some form of insecure attachment. Insecure attachments carry negative, long-lasting consequences such as poor peer friendships, turbulent dating and marital relationships, dissatisfaction with co-workers, and low earning potential. Secure attachments, on the other hand, foster self-esteem, confidence, and skill in interacting with others. Consistent, contingent, caring communication with infants is the foundation on which secure attachments are built. Parents can control responsiveness to their children.

The first year is often stressful, especially for first-time parents. Adults should try to keep in mind that they are the only parents their child knows, especially whenever they feel overwhelmed by the responsibility of caring for a baby who depends entirely on them. A new baby impacts the parents' relationship with one another as well as other relationships that exist within the family. For first-time parents, baby makes three. But baby brings four new relationships into existence: mother infant, father infant, mother father infant, and changes in spousal relationships. Some research has suggested that marital satisfaction actually declines after the birth of a first child, partly because of fatigue, stress, and lack of time. If an infant creates four new relationships, relationships multiply greatly when siblings are introduced into the picture. Parents must *expect* changes in relationships and be open and flexible.

Toddlers

When infants become toddlers, typically by their first birthdays, they are able to get around by themselves and consequently show a tremendous interest in exploring the environment. They begin to use language, especially naming, to identify favorite people and objects. Benchmark accomplishments for infants at the end of the first year include a well-developed sense of self as distinct from others, the emergence of intentionality, and a realization that other people may have differing goals and desires. In addition, children's first words typically emerge at around 9 to 12 months. All of these are important prelinguistic accomplishments that pave the way for further language growth.

Young children are prewired for language. Their skills in speech perception and their visual acuity enable youngsters to listen to others and visually inspect the environment. As discussed in chapter 3, adults adapt their language to young children. Adult–child language (ACL) is simpler and has shorter sentence length, more varied stress, and a higher-pitched vocal level than does adult–adult language. These adaptations appear to occur naturally and across cultures. Although innate capacities are critical for language to emerge, most scholars agree that environmental stimulation (i.e., linguistic input from adults or other children) is also necessary. The sheer presence of talk is important; youngsters benefit from communication directed to them and from overhearing conversations aimed at others.

Parents should be aware that children use different strategies to acquire their first words. Some children focus on naming and emphasize the referential nature of language. Other youngsters focus on actions and emphasize the functional nature of language. There is strong evidence that different styles of word acquisition result from different types of adult input. Parents tend to pick out and comment on particular features of the environment, and children in turn adopt these preferences. In general, children understand more than they are able to produce. That is, language comprehension typically precedes language production.

Adult caretakers can enrich word acquisition and language growth through a variety of techniques. For example, naming or labeling objects in the environment is important. Not only does this strategy increase children's vocabulary, it also gives them new terms and concepts to reason with. In addition, labeling increases toddlers' mastery over the environment because they can become more specific in stating their requests, desires, and needs. Whenever possible, labeling should be accompanied by a description of other attributes an object possesses. Some studies have suggested that using more varied language (describing an object in more than one way) is effective in increasing children's recognition of those objects. For example, a book can also be described as a red book, the book about clowns, or the big book; its placement relative to the larger context can also be explained as in "Here are some more books" (referring to other books nearby). Varied descriptions still define the core concept, that of a book, but also draw children's attention to other attributes like size, color, or content.

Scaffolding is another useful technique for promoting linguistic and communicative development (as discussed in chapters 1 and 6). Scaffolding occurs when adults use language and present tasks that are slightly beyond children's capabilities. Underlying scaffolding, of course, is the inescapable fact that children imitate parents' behavior. Modeling slightly advanced skills or suggesting strategies to use when interacting with peers are instances of scaffolding that have been linked to increased interpersonal effectiveness and enhanced cognitive and linguistic skills among children.

Throughout this period, youngsters develop intuitive understandings about the nature of conversations. Maxims, such as relevance or politeness, play an important role in regulating the conduct of interactions with others. These maxims are not explicitly taught, although violations are commented on. Children frequently hear parents or others say "That's rude" when someone has been impolite or "That's stupid" when someone has made an irrelevant remark. Young children are sensitive to conversational maxims, and parents' commentary often confirms children's understandings of the implicit, taken-for-granted conversational expectations.

To illustrate how children gain an understanding of these implicit rules, we return to Beth and her daughter, Heidi. Now Heidi is 2½ years old, and she and her mother are talking to one another on their way back from preschool. Heidi describes her day, but Beth only partly listens and responds "Uh-huh" in acknowledgment of her daughter's comments. Suddenly, Heidi slides out of the car seat, stands on the floor in the back of the car, and stamps her feet, saying "No, Mom. Not okay! Uhm-hm not okay! You not listen! Uhm-hm, not okay!" Heidi is absolutely correct. Beth had not been listening, and when she discovered what her daughter was talking about, "uhm-hm" was definitely not an "okay" response. As it turned out, two youngsters had gotten into a fight at the preschool and created quite a disruption. Mom definitely would not have approved! Heidi knew this and quite rightly confronted her mother about her violation of the manner maxim.

Mastering conversational maxims can be confusing for young children precisely because they are implicit, taken-for-granted rules. For example, the politeness norm dictates that people can comment that someone is pretty but not that someone is fat. Explanations that accompany sometimes bewildering contradictions in conversational rules help children understand the nuances and subtleties of communication and social relationships.

Children frequently make mistakes when practicing their newly found linguistic skills. Sound substitutions and sound variations are quite common. Moreover, sounds that children can produce correctly at the front of words may be nonexistent in the middle of words. This is all part of the child's growing mastery of the phonetic system. Grammatical errors are also likely to occur when children begin to combine words and experiment with syntax. "Me go," "Me want," and "Me no see" are examples of typical grammatical mistakes. Youngsters master names for concrete objects earlier than they do terms for abstract concepts like freedom or justice or evil. Parents need not worry about these common errors. For the most part, the errors correct themselves as children gain sufficient mastery of the underlying discriminations that produce the proper sounds or acceptable grammatical sequences. Parents can, however, correct children's semantic errors and help them develop more finely tuned categories. At some point, all four-legged small animals are cats, but cats are eventually distinguished from dogs, rabbits, and squirrels.

Children interpret sentences very literally. We once overheard a mother caution her child not to lie because "she had eyes in the back of her head." The child promptly climbed up the back of the chair where his mother was sitting and carefully parted her hair to look for the second pair of eyes! In another instance, a woman waiting in the checkout line at a local grocery store glanced at her watch and commented offhandedly, "My, time flies." Her daughter looked up from the grocery cart with a puzzled expression on her face and asked, "Does time have wings?" Although the tendency to interpret sentences literally is often amusing to adults, it can frighten and confuse young children, especially when adults invoke threats. Parents must remember that children cannot discern the metaphorical meaning in phrases like, "I'm going to flatten you" or "Your dad's going to blow up when he gets home." Parents know that these phrases are not to be taken literally, but children may not.

The second year represents a time of profound change for children in terms of the increasing self-control required of them and their own need for more and more independence. Toward the end of this period, toddlers develop the capacity to sustain extended interactions with peers. Whereas parents often compensate for their children's lack of ability, knowledge, or skill, peers do not. Thus, managing extended exchanges with other children represents an important developmental achievement.

In the earliest stages of peer interaction, toddlers treat one another much like they would any other interesting toy—as an object to be explored. By the early part of the second year, youngsters begin to direct markedly social behaviors toward one another. These behaviors become increasingly differentiated and organized over the next few months until, eventually, they form complex routines during which children jointly attend to the same stimuli, take turns at talk, and exchange roles. The ability to distinguish between familiar and unfamiliar peers also emerges around this time. With it, comes the tendency for pairs of children to develop distinctive patterns of interaction that lead to their earliest friendships. Because of the importance of childhood friendship, parents should try to provide opportunities for children to interact with peers. When toddlers begin to play with other children, parents may want to be there to provide some coaching about how to share toys, take turns, resolve disputes, and so forth.

Early Childhood

Communication skills become greatly expanded and refined at around 3 years of age, mostly because peer interaction is significantly increased. The important benchmarks of this developmental period include increased purposive communication and language skills, increasingly differentiated social knowledge, and children's ability to monitor their own communication as well as others'. During this period, children move from the egocentric state of infancy to the sociocentric world of peers.

The transition to the third year is often difficult because children are forced to cope with a variety of demands, such as being expected to exert self-control and independence, to master toilet training, and to interact with peers. For many children, there is the additional challenge of preschool or nursery school, with its own set of rules and procedures.

Increasing social awareness and knowledge enable children to use more varied communicative strategies. They come to appreciate another's viewpoint and to take that viewpoint into account when producing messages. Children's developing language skills also allow them to treat talk objectively and to ask questions if things are not expressed clearly. As illustrated below, language itself is identified as a complex phenomenon worthy of discussion. Here, Haslett's son, Erik, is talking with an English friend, David, and telling him how to "speak American":

Erik: Do you know what *cool* means?

David: Well . . . I know it doesn't mean not hot.

Erik: Well, *cool* means you're bad.

David: *[silence]* Well, I know it's not the kind of word you can look up in the dictionary.

Erik: Do you know what *bad* means?

David: No.

Erik: Well, don't get mad when you come to America, David, but if anybody asks you in America if you're bad, say yes. Cause that means you're cool. And cool is good, ya know. And if they ask if you're good, say you're not. Okay?

David: Okay.

Discipline also becomes more prominent during this period because children explore their social world and meet people with varied backgrounds and behaviors. This exploration helps them deal with the larger cultural milieu but challenges some of the rules and guidelines established at home. Although children test the limits set for them, it is critical that they have some boundaries and guidelines for their own sense of security.

As noted in chapter 6, disciplinary encounters do much more than just mete out punishment: They provide a social logic that helps children interpret their social world. Discipline directly shapes children's social-cognitive and motivational development and indirectly influences their communicative abilities and related social outcomes. Although there are many different disciplinary styles, consistency and reasoning appear to most encourage social development. Explaining why something is dangerous or should not be done models social reasoning processes for children. By giving explanations for their disciplinary practices, parents help children achieve more understanding of their social world.

As research has shown, children most successfully resolve their own conflicts by giving reasons in support of their actions as well as by acknowledging the other person's point of view. Parents can display this reasoning for children when disciplining them. Of course, reasoning has its limits, and parents must learn to use their own judgment about how a particular principle should be established and enforced. Cultural groups vary both in terms of what is tolerated from children and in terms of what methods are considered appropriate for dealing with youngsters' transgressions.

Talking about others' feelings is another important component of discipline. Children need to be aware that others may have different feelings about situations than they do and that people can respond differently to the same situation. In chapter 6 we discussed the "reflection enhancing" disciplinary strategies that encourage children to think about their wrongdoing in terms of its consequences for others' emotional states. Children whose parents consistently employ these strategies have been found to have higher levels of empathy and role-taking skill and to engage in more sensitive, adaptive communication with peers than do other children. Among middle-class Euro Americans, this outcome appears to be desirable.

Recognition of others' feelings and perspectives can also emerge through play with peers. During peer–peer interaction, parents can help children gain an appreciation of another's point of view by discussing reasons for actions (e.g., "Johnny is crying because he's sad his friend is leaving") or for why certain behaviors are required (e.g., "We need to be quiet in the library because people are studying"). These strategies also make children more aware of contextual considerations and the nature of social relationships in general.

There are several other ways in which parents can facilitate their children's interactions with peers. First, parents need to remember that it is through play with peers that interactional skills such as expressing views, arguing with others, articulating ideas and feelings, and resolving disputes emerge. To ensure children ample occasion to develop and practice these skills, parents should plan multiple opportunities for play with a variety of partners. Second, parents can model general prosocial behaviors for children so that children can learn by observing how parents resolve conflicts, cooperate, and engage others in conversation. This latter skill appears to be a particularly important component of friendship formation; children cannot develop close relationships with peers if they cannot access the ongoing group activities where potential friendship partners are found. Research has suggested that successful peer entry involves a person's integrating comments with the ongoing activities of the group, rather than calling attention to him- or herself. Finally, parents can explicitly articulate conversational premises known to promote positive peer interaction; some of these include taking turns, not interrupting, being polite, and asking for things. Each of these very simple strategies provides a way in which adult caretakers can foster their children's social growth.

By 4, children begin to use the term *friend* to refer to peers with whom they have developed close and special relationships. Several factors are related to friendship formation. In early childhood, similarity in demographic features like proximity and gender is a strong predictor of who will and will not become friends. Throughout later childhood and into early adolescence, similar temperaments, dispositions, and attitudes predict children's friendship choices. Research has also shown that parents influence their children's friendship choices through subtle cues; youngsters notice these cues and tend to form close relationships with those children parents prefer. Unfortunately, these preferences are sometimes grounded in external criteria such as race and physical attractiveness.

As children mature, their conceptions of friendship change. The meanings associated with friendship seem to undergo at least three important changes. In young childhood, friends are defined as playmates, in middle childhood as helpers, and in late childhood–early adolescence as confidants. At each stage, these conceptions shape the communicative activities in which friends engage; these activities, in turn, are believed to help children master important affective tasks. For example, fantasy play is the key activity that occupies the time young friends spend together. Fantasy play helps children overcome fears, regulate emotions, and learn the importance of following scripts in their interactions with one another. In contrast, adolescents' concept of friends as confidants is reflected in the intimate and extended self-disclosure that characterizes their interactions during this period. Such forms of communication aid adolescents in their quest for self-understanding and self-identity.

Children's friendships can be a constant source of worry for parents. For one thing, caretakers often complain about the things children do with their friends. Episodes of fantasy play can become boisterous and physical, and adolescents' long phone conversations are tedious and disruptive. Caretakers also fret about the sheer volume of conflict their children seem to experience with friends. But these behaviors are normal and serve important developmental functions in youngsters' lives—functions that parents simply cannot serve because of the hierarchical, authority-based nature of the parent–child relationship. Aside from enabling children to master particular affective tasks (like overcoming fear or understanding themselves), friendship also teaches more general lessons about equality, mutuality, and reciprocity. And although children do, in fact, engage in more conflict with friends than with nonfriends, they also manage these disputes in more cooperative, prosocial ways. Peers make unique contributions to children's development; the lessons youngsters learn in the context of their friendships with others provide the foundation on which they will eventually build successful adult relationships.

Parents also voice concern over whether their children are popular. There seems to be a common misperception that the more friends children have, the better they will do. As discussed earlier, popularity and friendship are conceptually and empirically distinct. Popularity is a group measure, indexing how many peers consider a child to be their "best friend" or the person they "most like." Friendship, on the other hand, indicates that a reciprocal relationship exists between one child and another. Evidence suggests that the presence of one close and enduring friendship is all a youngster needs to avoid the negative consequences associated with peer rejection. Some studies have even found that children who are well liked by their peer group (i.e., who are popular) sometimes lack close friends and therefore may experience some of the same outcomes as rejected children. Parents need to understand not only that popularity and friendship are different but that each carries with it its own unique consequences for children's social development.

While parents should not worry about how many friends children have, they must make sure that children are not actively rejected by a peer group. Youngsters who are consistently rejected by their peers encounter many detrimental consequences including criminality, early school withdrawal, loneliness, and depression. When parents observe how their children interact with peers, they should note that rejected youngsters are not necessarily less sociable or less friendly, but rather engage in more antisocial, disruptive, and inappropriate behavior than do children who are accepted. When this pattern characterizes youngsters' interactions with peers, parents must intervene quickly.

Finally, parents should not anticipate that their sons and daughters will engage in similar friendship behaviors. Gender appears to make a difference in how children communicate, the types of activities they prefer, and the kinds of social relationships they form. Boys engage in more rough-and-tumble play and have a wider circle of friends and more competitive relationships, whereas girls tend to pursue quieter, collaborative play and more exclusive friendships. Although the explanations for these differences remain controversial (i.e., socialization, sociobiological influences, children's own norms), the differences themselves are fairly clear and consistent.

As we have noted throughout this chapter, parenting practices need to be adapted to children's developing skills. Parenting practices range from direct teaching, as in scaffolding or modeling behavior, to providing opportunities for growth and development, such as creating time for peer–peer interaction or for travel opportunities. Parents have a unique role to play in their children's development, and parenting practices are under parental control. Parents' impact on their children has lifelong consequences and provides great challenges as well as great rewards. Parental awareness, sensitivity, and responsiveness help ensure that these consequences are positive for children's development.

SUMMARY

As we suggested at the beginning of this chapter, parenting is one of the most rewarding and difficult jobs many people face—especially in the present increasingly turbulent social environment. All people do things they regret as parents.

Perhaps they respond with anger instead of reason or do not always spend enough time with their children. The time spent with children may be times when parents are tired, stressed, and not at their best in coping with children's demands. Nevertheless, the developmental principles seem fairly clear: Consistent, nurturing responses to children have significant benefits. Consistent, nurturing responses occur in daily interactions with children. Even during the most mundane activities, people not only talk to their children but serve as role models for them as well. To a great extent, as people are, so too are their children.

References

Abramovitch, R. (1979). *Proximity, prosocial and agnostic behaviors of preschool children: An observational study.* Unpublished manuscript, University of Toronto, Ontario.

Ackerman, B. (1983). Form and function in children's understanding of ironic utterances. *Journal of Experimental Child Psychology, 35,* 487–508.

Ackerman, B. (1986). Children's sensitivity to comprehension failure in interpreting a nonliteral use of an utterance. *Child Development, 57,* 485–497.

Acredolo, L. (1977). Developmental changes in the ability to coordinate perspectives of a large-scale space. *Developmental Psychology, 13,* 1–8.

Acredolo, L., & Goodwyn, S. (1988). Symbolic gesturing in normal infants. *Child Development, 59,* 450–466.

Adams, G. R. (1978). Racial membership and physical attractiveness effects on preschool teachers' expectations. *Child Study Journal, 8,* 29–41.

Adams, G. R., & Crane, P. (1980). An assessment of parents' and teachers' expectations of preschool children's social preference for attractive or unattractive children and adults. *Child Development, 51,* 224–231.

Ainsworth, M. (1973). The development of infant–mother attachment. In B. Caldwell & H. Riccuiti (Eds.), *Review of child development research* (Vol. 3, pp. 1–94). Chicago: University of Chicago Press.

Ainsworth, M. (1985). Patterns of attachment. *Clinical Psychologist, 38,* 27–29.

Ainsworth, M., Bell, S., & Stayton, D. (1971). Individual differences in the strange situation behavior of one-year-olds. In H. Schaffer (Ed.), *The origins of human social relations.* New York: Academic Press.

Ainsworth, M., Blehar, M., Waters, E., & Wall, S. (1978). *Patterns of attachment: A psychological study of the strange situation.* Hillsdale, NJ: Lawrence Erlbaum Associates.

Aitken, S. (1977). *Gender preference in infancy.* Unpublished master's thesis, University of Edinburgh.

Algozzine, O. (1977). Perceived attractiveness and classroom interaction. *Journal of Experimental Education, 46,* 63–66.

Allen, R., & Shatz, M. (1983). "What say meow?" The role of context and linguistic experience in very young children's responses to what-questions. *Journal of Child Language, 10,* 321–335.

Amady, N., & Rosenthal, R. (1992). Thin slices of expressive behavior as predictors of interpersonal consequences: A meta-analysis. *Psychological Bulletin, 11,* 256–274.

Applegate, J. L., Burke, J. A., Burleson, B. R., Delia, J. G., & Kline, S. L. (1985). Reflection-enhancing parental communication. In I. E. Sigel (Ed.), *Parental belief systems: The psychological consequences for children* (Vol. 1, pp. 107–142). Hillsdale, NJ: Lawrence Erlbaum Associates.

Applegate, J. L., Burleson, B. R., & Delia, J. G. (1992). Reflection-enhancing parenting as an antecedent to children's social-cognitive and communicative development. In I. E. Sigel, A. V. McGillicuddy-Delisi, & J. J. Goodnow (Eds.), *Parental belief systems: The psychological consequences for children* (Vol. 2, pp. 3–39). Hillsdale, NJ: Lawrence Erlbaum Associates.

Applegate, J., & Delia, J. (1980). Person-centered speech, psychological development, and the contexts of language usage. In R. St. Clair & H. Giles (Eds.), *The social and psychological contexts of language.* Hillsdale, NJ: Lawrence Erlbaum Associates.

Argyle, M. (1975). *Bodily communication.* London: Methuen.

Argyle, M. (1981). The experimental study of the basic features of situations. In D. Magnuson (Ed.), *Toward a psychology of situations.* Hillsdale, NJ: Lawrence Erlbaum Associates.

Aries, E. J. (1982). Verbal and nonverbal behavior in single-sex and mixed-sex groups: Are traditional sex roles changing? *Psychological Reports, 51,* 127–134.

Aries, E. J. (1987). Gender and communication. In P. Shaver & C. Henricks (Eds.), *Sex and gender.* Newbury Park, CA: Sage.

Arliss, L. P. (1991). *Gender communication.* Englewood Cliffs, NJ: Prentice-Hall.

Asher, S. R. (1973). *The influence of race and sex on children's sociometric choices across the school year.* Unpublished manuscript, University of Illinois, Champaign–Urbana.

Asher, S. R. (1975). *The effect of interest on reading comprehension of black children and white children.* Unpublished manuscript, University of Illinois, Champaign–Urbana.

Asher, S. R. (1979). Referential communication. In G. Whitehurst & B. Zimmerman (Eds.), *The functions of language and cognition.* New York: Academic Press.

Asher, S. R., & Coie, J. D. (Eds.) (1990). *Peer rejection in childhood.* New York: Cambridge University Press.

Asher, S. R., Oden, S. L., & Gottman, J. M. (1981). Children's friendships in school settings. In E. M. Hetherington & R. D. Parke (Eds.), *Contemporary readings in child psychology* (2nd ed., pp. 277–294). New York: McGraw-Hill.

Asher, S. R., & Parker, J. G. (1989). The significance of peer relationship problems in childhood. In B. H. Schneider, G. Attili, J. Nadel, & R. P. Weissberg (Eds.), *Social competence in developmental perspective* (pp. 5–24). Dordrecht, The Netherlands: Kluwer.

Asher, S. R., & Renshaw, P. D. (1981). Children without friends: Social knowledge and social skill training. In S. R. Asher & J. M. Gottman (Eds.), *The development of children's friendships.* New York: Cambridge University Press.

Asher, S., & Wigfield, A. (1981). Training referential communication skills. In W. Dickson (Ed.), *Children's oral communication skills.* New York: Academic Press.

Austin, J. L. (1962). *How to do things with words.* Oxford: Clarendon Press.

Azmitia, M. (1988). Peer interaction and problem-solving: When are two heads better than one? *Child Development, 59,* 87–96.

Bach, K., & Harnish, R. (1979). *Linguistic communication and speech acts.* Cambridge, MA: MIT Press.

Backscheider, A., Shatz, M., & Gelman, S. (1993). Preschoolers' ability to distinguish living kinds as a function of regrowth. *Child Development, 64,* 1242–1257.

Baldwin, D., & Markman, E. (1989). Establishing word–object relations: A first step. *Child Development, 60,* 331–398.

Bandura, A. (1986). *Social foundations of thought and action: A social cognitive theory.* Englewood Cliffs, NJ: Prentice-Hall.

Barker, R. A., & Wright, H. F. (1955). *Midwest and its children.* New York: Harper & Row.

Barnes, S., Gutfreund, M., Satterly, D., & Wells, G. (1983). Characteristics of adult speech which predict children's language development. *Journal of Child Language, 10,* 65–84.

Barrera, M., & Maurer, D. (1981). The perception of facial expressions by the three-month-old. *Child Development, 52,* 203–206.

Barrett, K. (1993). The development of nonverbal communication of emotion: A functionalist perspective. *Journal of Nonverbal Behavior, 17,* 145–169.

Barry, H., Bacon, M., & Child, I. (1957). A cross cultural survey of some sex differences in socialization. *Journal of Abnormal and Social Psychology, 55,* 327–332.

Barton, M., & Tomasello, M. (1991). Joint attention and conversation in mother–infant–sibling triads. *Child Development, 62,* 517–529.

Bates, E. (1976). *Language and context: The acquisition of pragmatics.* New York: Academic Press.

Bates, E. (1979). The emergence of symbols: Ontogeny and phylogeny. In W. Collins (Ed.), *Children's language and communication: The Minnesota symposia on child psychology* (Vol. 12). New York: Academic Press.

Bates, E., Benigni, L., Bretherton, I., Camaioni, L., & Volterra, V. (1979). *The emergence of symbols: Cognition and communication in infancy.* New York: Academic Press.

Bates, E., Bretherton, I., Shore, C., & McNew, S. (1983). Names, gestures, and objects: Symbolization in infancy and aphasia. In K. Nelson (Ed.), *Children's language* (Vol. 4). Hillsdale, NJ: Lawrence Erlbaum Associates.

Bates, E., Bretherton, I., & Snyder, L. (1988). *From first words to grammar.* Cambridge, England: Cambridge University Press.

Bates, E., & MacWhinney, B. (1982). Second-language acquisition from a functionalist perspective: Pragmatic, semantic and perceptual strategies. *Annals of the New York Academy of Sciences, 379,* 190–214.

Bates, E., Maslin, C., & Frankel, K. (1985). Attachment security, mother–child interaction, and temperament as predictors of behavior problem ratings at age three years. In I. Bretherton & E. Waters (Eds.), Growing points in attachment theory and research. *Monographs for the Society for Research in Child Development, 209,* 167–193.

Bates, E., Thal, D., Whitesell, K., Fenson, L., & Oakes, L. (1989). Integrating language and gesture in infancy. *Developmental Psychology, 25,* 1004–1019.

Bateson, G. (1972). *Steps to an ecology of mind.* New York: Ballantine.

Bateson, G. (1976). A theory of play and fantasy. In J. Bruner, A. Jolly, & K. Sylva (Eds.), *Play: Its role in evolution and development.* London: Penguin.

Bateson, M. C. (1975). Mother–infant exchanges: The epigenesis of conversation interaction. *Annals of New York Academy of Science, 263,* 101–113.

Bauer, P. (1993). Memory for gender-consistent and gender-inconsistent event sequences by twenty-five-month-old children. *Child Development, 64,* 285–297.

Baumrind, D. (1967). Child care practices anteceding three patterns of preschool behavior. *Genetic Psychology Monographs, 75,* 43–88.

Baumrind, D. (1971). Current patterns of parental authority. *Developmental Psychology Monographs, 4* (1, Pt. 2).

Baumrind, D. (1989). Rearing competent children. In W. Damon (Ed.), *Child development today and tomorrow* (pp. 349–378). San Francisco: Jossey Bass.

Bavelas, J., Black, A., Chovil, N., & Mullett, J. (1990). *Equivocal communication.* Newbury Park, CA: Sage Publications.

Beal, C. (1994). *Boys and girls: The development of gender roles.* New York: McGraw-Hill.

Beal, C., & Belgrad, S. (1990). The development of message evaluation skills in young children. *Child Development, 61,* 705–712.

Beal, C., & Flavell, J. (1984). Development of the ability to distinguish communicative intention and literal message meaning. *Child Development, 55,* 920–928.

Bearison, D. J., & Cassel, T. Z. (1975). Cognitive decentration and social codes: Communicative effectiveness in young children from differing family contexts. *Developmental Psychology, 11,* 29–36.

Becker, J. (1984). Implication of ethology for the study of pragmatic development. In S. Kuczaj (Ed.), *Discourse development.* New York: Springer-Verlag.

Beebe, B., Alson, D., Jaffe, J., Feldstein, S., & Crown, C. (1988). Vocal congruence in mother–infant play. *Journal of Psycholinguistic Research, 17,* 245–253.

Behrend, D., Rosengren, K., & Perlmutter, M. (1989). A new look at children's private speech: The effects of age, task difficulty, and parent presence. *International Journal of Behavioral Development, 12,* 305–320.

Bellinger, D., & Gleason, J. (1982). Sex differences in parental directives to young children. *Sex Roles, 8,* 1123–1139.

Belsky, J. (1979). Mother–father–infant interaction: A naturalistic observational study. *Developmental Psychology, 15,* 601–607.

Belsky, J. (1993). *Promoting father involvement: An analysis and critique* (Comment on Silverstein, 1993).

Belsky, J., Crnic, K., & Gable, S. (1995). The determinants of coparenting in families with toddler boys: Spousal differences and daily hassles. *Child Development, 66,* 629–642.

Benenson, J. (1993). Greater preference among females than males for dyadic interaction in early childhood. *Child Development, 64,* 544–555.

Benoit, P. (1981). *The use of argument by preschool children: The emergent production of rules for winning argument.* Unpublished manuscript.

Berger, C., & Bradac, J. (1982). *Language and social knowledge: Uncertainty in interpersonal relationships.* London: Edward Arnold.

Berk, L. (1986). Relationship of elementary school children's private speech to behavioral accompaniment to task, attention, and task performance. *Developmental Psychology, 22,* 671–680.

Berk, L., & Garvin, R. (1984). Development of private speech among low-income Appalachian children. *Developmental Psychology, 20,* 271–286.

Berk, S., Doehring, D., & Bryans, B. (1983). Judgments of vocal affect by language-delayed children. *Journal of Communication Disorders, 16,* 49–56.

Berlin, L., Cassidy, J., & Belsky, J. (1995). Loneliness in young children and infant–mother attachment: A longitudinal study. *Merrill–Palmer Quarterly, 41,* 91–103.

Berndt, T. J. (1981a). Relations between social cognition, nonsocial cognition, and social behavior: The case of friendship. In J. H. Flavell & L. D. Ross (Eds.), *Social cognitive development: Frontiers and possible futures.* New York: Cambridge University Press.

Berndt, T. J. (1981b). The effects of friendship on prosocial intentions and behavior. *Child Development, 52,* 636–643.

Berndt, T. J. (1982). Fairness and friendship. In K. H. Rubin & H. S. Ross (Eds.), *Peer relationships and social skills in childhood* (pp. 253–278). New York: Springer-Verlag.

Berndt, T. J. (1983). Social cognition, social behavior, and children's friendships. In E. T. Higgins, D. N. Ruble, & W. W. Hartup (Eds.), *Social cognition and social development* (pp. 158–189). New York: Cambridge University Press.

Berndt, T. J. (1985). Prosocial behavior between friends in middle childhood and early adolescence. *Journal of Early Adolescence, 5,* 307–318.

Berndt, T. J., & Das, R. (1987). Effects of popularity and friendship on perceptions of the personality and social behavior of peers. *Journal of Early Adolescence, 7,* 429–439.

Berndt, T. J., & Perry, T. B. (1986). Children's perceptions of friendships as supportive relationships. *Developmental Psychology, 22,* 640–648.

Bernstein, B. (1970). Language and socialization with some reference to educability. In F. Williams (Ed.), *Language and poverty.* Chicago: Markham Press.

Bernstein, B. (1971). *Class, codes and control* (Vol. 1). London: Routledge & Kegan Paul.

Bernstein, B. (1973). *Class, codes and control* (Vol. 2). London: Routledge & Kegan Paul.

Bernstein, B. (1977). *Class, codes and control: Vol. 3.* (2nd ed.). London: Routledge & Kegan Paul.

Bernstein, L. (1981). Language as a product of dialogue. *Discourse Processes, 4,* 117–147.

Berscheid, E., & Walster, E. H. (1978). *Interpersonal attraction* (2nd ed.). Reading, MA: Addison-Wesley.

Bertoncini, J., Bijeljac-Babic, R., Jusczyk, P., Kennedy, L., & Mehler, J. (1988). An investigation of young infants' perceptual representations of speech sounds. *Journal of Experimental Psychology, 117,* 21–33.

Bhavnagri, N., & Parke, R. (1991). Parents as direct facilitators of children's peer relationships: Effects of age of child and sex of parent. *Journal of Social and Personal Relationships, 8,* 423–440.

Bigelow, B. J., & LaGaipa, J. J. (1975). Children's written descriptions of friendship: A multi-dimensional analysis. *Developmental Psychology, 11,* 857–858.

Bigelow, B. J., & LaGaipa, J. J. (1980). The development of friendship values and choice. In H. C. Foot, A. J. Chapman, & H. R. Smith (Eds.), *Friendship and social relations in children* (pp. 15–44). New York: Wiley.

Bigner, J. (1974). A Wernerian developmental analysis of children's descriptions of siblings. *Child Development, 45,* 317–323.

Bijou, S. W. (1993). *Behavior analysis of child development.* (2nd ed., revised). Reno, NV: Context Press.

Birchler, G., Weiss, R., & Vincent, J. (1975). Multimethod analysis of social reinforcement exchange between maritally distressed and nondistressed spouse and stranger dyads. *Journal of Personality and Social Psychology, 31,* 349–360.

Birdwhistell, R. (1970). *Kinesics and context.* Philadelphia: University of Pennsylvania Press.

Biringen, Z. (1987). Infant attention to facial expressions and facial motion. *Journal of Genetic Psychology, 148,* 127–133.

Biringen, Z. (1990). Direct observation of maternal sensitivity and dyadic interactions in the home: Relations to maternal thinking. *Developmental Psychology, 26,* 278–284.

Biringen, Z. (1994a). Infant attention to facial expressions and facial motion. *Journal of Genetic Psychology, 148,* 127–133.

Biringen, Z. (1994b). Attachment theory and research: Application to clinical practice. *American Journal of Orthopsychiatry, 64,* 404–420.

Biringen, Z., Emde, R., Campos, J., & Appelbaum, M. (1995). Affective reorganization in the infant, the mother, and the dyad: The role of upright locomotion and its timing. *Child Development, 66,* 499–514.

Biringen, Z., & Robinson, J. (1991). Emotional availability in mother–child interactions: A reconceptualization for research. *American Journal of Orthopsychiatry, 61,* 258–271.

Biringen, Z., Robinson, J., & Emde, R. (1994). Maternal sensitivity in the second year: Gender-based relations in the dyadic balance of control. *American Journal of Orthopsychiatry, 64,* 78–90.

Black, B. (1989). Interactive pretense: Social and symbolic skills in preschool play groups. *Merrill–Palmer Quarterly, 35,* 379–397.

Black, B. (1992). Negotiating social pretend play: Communication differences related to social status and sex. *Merrill–Palmer Quarterly, 38,* 212–232.

Black, B., & Hazen, N. (1990). Social status and patterns of communication in acquainted and unacquainted preschool children. *Developmental Psychology, 26,* 379–387.

Blake, J., & Dolgoy, S. (1993). Gestural development and its relation to cognition during the transition to language. *Journal of Nonverbal Behavior, 17,* 87–102.

Blake, J., McConnell, S., Horton, G., & Benson, N. (1992). The gestural repertoire and its evolution over the second year. *Early Development and Parenting, 1,* 127–136.

Blicharski, T., Gravel, F., & Trudel, M. (1994). Representational and communicative processes in the social construction of early temperament. In A. Vyt, H. Bloch, & M. Bornstein (Eds.), *Early child development in the French tradition.* Hillsdale, NJ: Lawrence Erlbaum Associates.

Block, J. (1979). Another look at sex differentiation in the socialization behaviors of mothers and fathers. In J. Sherman & F. Denmark (Eds.), *The psychology of women: Future directions of research.* New York: Psychological Dimensions.

Bloom, L. (1970). *Language development: Form and function of emerging grammars.* Cambridge, MA: MIT Press.

Bloom, L. (1973). *One word at a time: The use of single-word utterances before syntax.* The Hague: Mouton.

Bloom, L., Lightbown, P., & Hood, L. (1975). Structure and variation in child language. *Monographs of the Society for Research in Child Development, 40,* 1–97.

Bloom, L., Merkin, S., & Wootten, J. (1982). Wh-questions: Linguistic factors that contribute to the sequence of acquisition. *Child Development, 53,* 1084–1092.

Bloom, L., Rocissano, L., & Hood, L. (1976). Adult–child discourse: Developmental interaction between information processing and linguistic interaction. *Cognitive Psychology, 8,* 521–522.

Bochner, A. (1984). Functions of communication in interpersonal bonding. In C. Arnold & J. Bowers (Eds.), *Handbook of rhetoric and communication.* Boston: Allyn & Bacon.

Bonitatibus, G. (1988). Comprehension monitoring and the apprehension of literal meaning. *Child Development, 59,* 60–70.

Bonney, M. E., & Powell, J. (1953). Differences in social behavior between sociometrically high and sociometrically low children. *Journal of Educational Research, 46,* 481–495.

Booth, C., Rose-Krasnor, L., McKinnon, J., & Rubin, K. (1994). Predicting social adjustment in middle childhood: The role of preschool attachment security and maternal style. Special Issue: From family to peer group: Relations between relationship systems. *Social Development, 3,* 189–204.

Bornstein, M. (1989a). Cross-cultural developmental comparisons: The case of Japanese-American infant and mother activities and interactions: What we know, what we need to know and why we need to know. *Developmental Review, 9,* 171–204.

Bornstein, M. (1989b). Between caretakers and their young: Two modes of interaction and their consequences for cognitive growth. In M. Bornstein & J. Bruner (Eds.), *Interaction in human development* (pp. 197–217). Hillsdale, NJ: Lawrence Erlbaum Associates.

Bornstein, M., & Tamis-LeMonda, C. (1989). Maternal responsiveness and cognitive development in children. *New Directions in Child Development, 43,* 49–61.

Bornstein, M., & Tamis-LeMonda, C. (1990). Activities and interactions of mothers and their firstborn infants in the first six months of life: Covariation, stability, continuity, correspondence, and prediction. *Child Development, 61,* 1206–1217.

Bornstein, M., Tamis-LeMonda, C., Tal, J., Ludemann, P., Toda, S., Rahn, C., Pecheux, M., Azuma, H., & Yardi, D. (1992). Maternal responsiveness to infants in three societies: The United States, France, and Japan. *Child Development, 63,* 808–821.

Boston, M., & Levy, G. (1991). Changes and differences in preschoolers' understanding of gender scripts. *Cognitive Development, 6,* 417–432.

Bower, T. G. R. (1989). *The rational infant: Learning in infancy.* New York: W. H. Freeman.

Bowerman, M. (1978). The acquisition of word meaning: An investigation in some current conflicts. In N. Waterson & C. Snow (Eds.), *Normal and deficient child language.* Baltimore: University Park Press.

Bowlby, J. (1969/1982). *Attachment and loss: Vol 1. Attachment.* London: Basic.

Bowlby, J. (1973). *Attachment and loss: Vol. 2. Separation.* New York: Basic.

Bowlby, J. (1980). *Attachment and loss: Vol. 3. Loss, sadness and depression.* New York: Basic.

Bowlby, J. (1988). *A secure base: Clinical applications of attachment theory.* London: Routledge.

Boyatzis, C., Chazan, E., & Ting, C. (1993). Preschool children's decoding of facial emotions. *Journal of Genetic Psychology, 154,* 375–382.

Boyatzis, C., & Satyaprasad, C. (1994). Children's facial and general decoding and encoding: Relations between skills and with popularity. *Journal of Nonverbal Behavior, 18,* 37–55.

Boyatzis, C., & Watson, M. (1993). Preschool children's symbolic representation of objects through gestures. *Child Development, 64,* 729–735.

Brachfield-Child, S., & Schiavo, R. S. (1990). Interactions of preschool and kindergarten friends and acquaintances. *Journal of Genetic Psychology, 151,* 45–58.

Braine, M. (1976). Children's first word combinations. *Monographs of the Society for Research in Child Development, 41,* 1–104.

Bransford, J., & McCarrell, N. (1977). A sketch of a cognitive approach to comprehension: Some thoughts about understanding what it means to comprehend. In P. Johnson-Laird & P. Wason (Eds.), *Thinking: Readings in cognitive science.* Cambridge, U.K.: Cambridge University Press.

Brazelton, T., Koslowski, B., & Main, M. (1974). The origins of reciprocity: The early mother–infant interaction. In M. Lewis & L. Rosenblum (Eds.), *The effect of the infant on its caregiver.* New York: Wiley.

Bretherton, I. (1985). Attachment theory: Retrospect and prospect. In I. Bretherton & E. Waters (Eds.), Caregiving, cultural, and cognitive perspectives on secure-base behavior and working models: Growing points in attachment theory and research. *Monographs for the Society for Research in Child Development, 44*(60) No. 2–3.

Bretherton, I. (1989). Pretense: The form and function of make-believe play. *Developmental Review, 9,* 383–401.

Bretherton, I., & Bates, E. (1979). The emergence of intentional communication. *New Directions for Child Development, 4,* 81–100.

Bretherton, I., Bates, E., McNew, S., Shore, C., Williamson, C., & Beeghly-Smith, M. (1981). Comprehension and production of symbols in infancy: An experimental study. *Developmental Psychology, 17,* 728–736.

Bril, B., Zack, M., & Nkounkou-Hombessa, E. (1989). Ethnotheories of development and education: A view from different cultures. *European Journal of Psychology of Education, 4,* 307–318.

Brody, L., & Hall, J. (1993). Gender and emotion. In M. Lewis & J. Haviland (Eds.), *Handbook of emotions.* New York: Guilford Press.

Bronfenbrenner, U. (1977). Toward an experimental ecology of human development. *American Psychologist, 32,* 513–531.

Brown, P., & Levinson, S. (1978). Universals in language use: Politeness phenomena. In E. Goody (Ed.), *Questions and politeness: Strategies in social interaction.* Cambridge, U.K.: Cambridge University Press.

Brown, R. (1973). *A first language.* New York: Wiley.

Brown, R. (1976). New paradigm of reference. *Cognition, 4,* 125–153.

Brownell, C. (1989). *Cooperation and social understanding in toddlers.* Unpublished manuscript.

Brownell, C., & Brown, E. (1985, April). *Age differences in object conflicts and possession negotiations during the second year.* Paper presented at the meeting of the Society for Research in Child Development, Toronto.

Brownell, C., & Carriger, M. (1990). Changes in cooperation and self–other differentiation during the second year. *Child Development, 61,* 1164–1174.

Bruner, J. (1975a). The ontogenesis of speech-acts. *Journal of Child Language, 2,* 1–19.

Bruner, J. (1975b). From communication to language—A psychological perspective. *Cognition, 3,* 255–287.

Bruner, J. (1977). Early social interaction and language acquisition. In H. Schaeffer (Ed.), *Studies in mother–infant interaction.* London: Academic Press.

Bruner, J. (1983). The acquisition of pragmatic commitments. In R. Golinkoff (Ed.), *The transition from prelinguistic to linguistic communication.* Hillsdale, NJ: Lawrence Erlbaum Associates.

Bruner, J. (1986). *Actual minds, possible worlds.* Cambridge, U.K.: Cambridge University Press.

Buck, R. (1975). Nonverbal communication of affect in children. *Journal of Personality and Social Psychology, 31,* 644–653.

Buck, R. (1984). *The communication of emotion.* New York: Guilford Press.

Buck, R., Miller, R., & Caul, W. (1974). Sex, personality, and physiological variables in the communication of affect via facial expression. *Journal of Personality and Social Psychology, 23,* 362–371.

Budwig, N., Strage, A., & Bamberg, M. (1986). The construction of joint activities with an age-mate: The transition from caregiver–child to peer play. In J. Cook-Gumperz, W. Corsaro, & J. Streeck (Eds.), *Children's worlds and children's language*. New York: Mouton de Gruyter.

Bukowski, W. M., Gauze, C., Hoza, B., & Newcomb, A. F. (1993). Differences and consistency between same-sex and other-sex peer relationships during early adolescence. *Developmental Psychology, 29,* 255–263.

Bullowa, M. (1976). From nonverbal communication to language. *International Journal of Psycholinguistics, 55,* 5–8.

Burgoon, J., & Baesler, E. J. (1991). Choosing between micro and macro nonverbal measurement: Application to selected vocalic and kinesic indices. *Journal of Nonverbal Behavior, 17,* 57–67.

Burgoon, J., Buller, D., & Goodall, W. (1989). *Nonverbal communication: The unspoken dialogue.* New York: Harper & Row.

Burleson, B. R. (1986). Communication skills and childhood peer relationships: An overview. In M. L. McLaughlin (Ed.), *Communication yearbook* (Vol. 9, pp. 1430–1480). Beverly Hills, CA: Sage.

Burleson, B. R. (1987). Cognitive complexity. In J. C. McCroskey & J. A. Daly (Eds.), *Personality and interpersonal communication* (pp. 305–349). Newbury Park, CA: Sage.

Burleson, B. R., Applegate, J. G., Burke, J. A., Clark, R. A., Delia, J. G., & Kline, S. L. (1986). Communicative correlates of peer acceptance in childhood. *Communication Education, 35,* 349–361.

Burleson, B. R., Delia, J. G., & Applegate, J. L. (1995). The socialization of person-centered communication: Parental contributions to the social-cognitive and communication skills of their children. In M. A. Fitzpatrick & A. L. Vangelisti (Eds.), *Perspectives in family communication* (pp. 34–76). Thousand Oaks, CA: Sage.

Burleson, B. R., & Kunkel, A. W. (1996). The socialization of emotional support skills in childhood. In G. R. Pierce, B. S. Sarason, & I. G. Sarason (Eds.), *Handbook of social support and the family* (pp. 105–140). New York: Plenum Press.

Burleson, B. R., Kunkel, A. W., Samter, W., & Werking, K. J. (1996). Men's and women's evaluations of communication skills in personal relationships: When sex differences make a difference—and when they don't. *Journal of Social and Personal Relationships, 13,* 201–224.

Bussey, K., & Bandura, A. (1992). Self-regulatory mechanisms governing gender development. *Child Development, 63,* 1236–1250.

Calkins, S. (1994). Origins and outcomes of individual differences in emotion regulation. *Monographs of the Society for Research in Child Development, 59,* 53–72, 250–283.

Camaioni, L. (1986). Imitative interactions and development of communication. *Giornale italiano di psicologia, 13,* 297–309.

Campbell, J. D., & Yarrow, M. R. (1961). Perceptual and behavioral correlates of social effectiveness. *Sociometry, 24,* 1–20.

Campos, J. (1981). Human emotions: Their new importance and their role in social referencing. *Research and Clinical Center, Annual Report, 1–7.*

Camras, L. (1977). Facial expressions used by children in conflict situations. *Child Development, 48,* 1431–1435.

Camras, L. (1984). Children's verbal and nonverbal communication in a conflict situation. *Ethology and Sociobiology, 5,* 325–344.

Camras, L., Oster, H., Campos, J., Miyake, K., & Bradshaw, J. (1992). Japanese and American infants' responses to arm restraint. *Developmental Psychology, 28,* 578–583.

Camras, L., Pristo, T., & Brown, M. (1985). Directive choice by children and adults: Affect, situation, and linguistic politeness. *Merrill-Palmer Quarterly, 31,* 19–31.

Camras, L., Sullivan, J., & Michel, G. (1993). Do infants express discrete emotions? Adult judgments of facial, vocal, and body actions. *Journal of Nonverbal Behavior, 17,* 171–185.

Capella, J. N. (1981). Mutual influence in expressive behavior: Adult–adult and infant–adult dyadic interaction. *Psychological Bulletin, 89,* 101–132.

Capella, J., & Planalp, S. (1981). Talk and silence sequences in informal conversations III: Interspeaker influence. *Human Communication Research, 7,* 117–132.

Capelli, C., Nakagawa, N., & Madden, C. (1990). *Child Development, 61,* 1824–1841.

Caplan, D. (1991). Neural structures. In D. Crystal (Ed.), *The international enclyclopedia of linguistics* (pp. 79–83). New York: Oxford University Press.

Caplan, M., Vespo, J., Pederson, J., & Hay, D. (1991). Conflict and its resolution in small groups of one- and two-year-olds. *Child Development, 62,* 1513–1524.

Carpenter, R., Mastergeorge, A., & Coggins, T. (1983). The acquisition on communicative intentions in infants eight to fifteen months of age. *Language and Speech, 26,* 101–109.

Carter, A. (1975). The transformation of sensori-motor morphemes into words: A case study of the development of *more* and *mine. Journal of Child Language, 2,* 233–250.

Carter, A. (1978a). The development of systematic vocalizations prior to words: A case study. In N. Waterson & C. Snow (Eds.), *The development of communication.* New York: Wiley.

Carter, A. (1978b). From sensori-motor vocalization to words: A case study in the evolution of attention directing communication in the second year. In A. Lock (Ed.), *Action, gesture and symbol: The emergence of symbol.* New York: Academic Press.

Carter, A., Mayes, L., & Pajer, K. (1990). The role of dyadic affect in play and infant sex in predicting infant response to the still-face situation. *Child Development, 61,* 764–773.

Casey, R., & Fuller, L. (1994). Maternal regulation of children's emotions. *Journal of Nonverbal Behavior, 18,* 57–88.

Cassidy, J. (1994). Emotion regulation: Influences of attachment relationships. *Monographs of the Society for Research in Child Development, 59,* 228–283.

Cavior, N., & Dokecki, P. R. (1973). Physical attrativeness, perceived attitude similarity, and academic achievement as contributors to interpersonal attraction among adolescents. *Developmental Psychology, 9,* 44–54.

Cavior, N., & Lombardi, D. A. (1973). Developmental aspects of judgments of physical attractiveness in children. *Developmental Psychology, 8,* 67–71.

Cazden, C. (1972). *Child language and education.* New York: Holt, Rinehart & Winston.

Chandler, M. (1977). Social cognition: A selective review of current research. In W. Overton (Ed.), *Knowledge and development.* New York: Plenum Press.

Chandler, M. (1982). Social cognition and social structure. In C. Serafica (Ed.), *Social-cognitive development in context.* New York: Guilford.

Chandler, M., & Chapman, M. (1991). *Criteria for competence.* Hillsdale, NJ: Lawrence Erlbaum Associates.

Charlesworth, W. R., & LaFreniere, P. (1983). Dominance, friendship, and resource utilization in preschool children's groups. *Ethology and Sociobiology, 4,* 175–186.

Charney, R. (1979). The comprehension of "here" and "there." *Journal of Child Language, 6,* 69–80.

Chomsky, C. (1969). *The acquisition of syntax in children from 5 to 10.* Cambridge, MA: MIT Press.

Chomsky, N. (1965). *Aspects of the theory of syntax.* Cambridge, MA: MIT Press.

Chomsky, N. (1980). On cognitive structures and their development: A reply to Piaget. In M. Piattelli-Palmarini (Ed.), *Language and learning: The debate between Jean Piaget and Noam Chomsky.* Cambridge, MA: Harvard University Press.

Chomsky, N. (1981). *Lectures on government and binding.* Dordrecht, Netherlands: Foris.

Cicourel, A. (1970). The acquisition of social structure. In J. Douglas (Ed.), *Understanding everyday life.* Chicago: Aldine.

Cicourel, A. (1972). Basic and normative rules in the negotiation of status and role. In D. Sudnow (Ed.), *Studies in social interaction.* New York: Free Press.

Cicourel, A. (1980). Three models of discourse analysis: The role of social structure. *Discourse Processes, 3,* 101–132.

Clark, E. (1973a). Non-linguistic strategies and the acquisition of word meanings. *Cognition, 2,* 161–182.

Clark, E. (1973b). What's in a word? On the child's acquisition of semantics in his first language. In T. Moore (Ed.), *Cognitive development and the acquisition of language.* New York: Academic Press.

Clark, E. (1980). Here's the top: Nonlinguistic strategies in the acquisition of orientational terms. *Child Development, 51,* 329–338.

Clark, H. (1973). How young children describe events in time. In G. Flores d'Arcais & W. Levelt (Eds.), *Advances in psycholinguistics.* Amsterdam, Netherlands: North-Holland.

Clark, H. (1979). Responding to indirect speech acts. *Cognitive Psychology, 11,* 430–477.

Clark, H., & Clark, E. (1977). *Psychology and language.* New York: Harcourt Brace Jovanovich.

Clark, K. B., & Clark, M. K. (1947). Racial identification and racial preference in Negro children. In T. Newcomb & E. Hartley (Eds.), *Readings in social psychology.* New York: Holt.

Clark, M. L., & Drewry, D. L. (1985). Similarity and reciprocity in the friendships of elementary school children. *Child Study Journal, 15,* 251–263.

Clark, R., & Delia, J. (1979). Topoi and rhetorical competence. *Quarterly Journal of Speech, 65,* 187–206.

Clarke-Stewart, A. (1991) A home is not a school: The effects of environments on development. In M. Lewis & S. Feinman (Eds.), *Social influences and socialization in infancy.* New York: Plenum Press.

Clifford, E. (1963). Social visibility. *Child Development, 34,* 799–808.

Clifford, M. M., & Walster, E. (1973). The effects of physical attractiveness on teacher expectations. *Sociology of Education, 46,* 248–258.

Cobb, S. (1976). Social support as a moderator of life stress. *Psychosomatic Medicine, 38,* 300–315.

Cohn, J., & Tronick, E. (1983). Three-month-old infants' reaction to stimulated maternal depression. *Child Development, 54,* 185–193.

Coie, J. D. (1990). Toward a theory of peer rejection. In S. R. Asher & J. D. Coie (Eds.), *Peer rejection in childhood* (pp. 365–401). New York: Cambridge University Press.

Coie, J. D., & Dodge, K. A. (1990). Peer group behavior and social status. In S. R. Asher & J. D. Coie (Eds.), *Peer rejection in childhood* (pp. 17–59). New York: Cambridge University Press.

Coie, J. D., Dodge, K. A., & Coppotelli, H. (1982). Dimensions and types of social status: A cross-age perspective. *Developmental Psychology, 18,* 557–570.

Coley, J., & Gelman, S. (1989). The effects of object orientation and object type on children's interpretation of the word *big. Child Development, 60,* 372–380.

Coll, G. (1990). Developmental outcome of minority infants: A process-oriented look into our beginnings. In the "Special issue on minority children." In N. Spencer & V. McLoyd (Eds.), *Child Development, 61,* No. 2, 270–290.

Collins, G. (1982). A new look at life with father. In H. E. Fitzgerald & T. H. Carr (Eds.), *Human development 82/83* (pp. 180–186). Guilford, CT: Dushkin.

Colombo, J., Frick, J., Ryther, J., Coldren, J., & Mitchell, D. (1995). Infants' detection of analogs of "motherese" in noise. *Merrill–Palmer Quarterly, 41,* 104–113.

Conant, C. (1987). *Toddler sociability in object conflict with peers.* Unpublished master's thesis, University of Waterloo, Waterloo, Ontario.

Connolly, J., Doyle, A., & Reznick, E. (1988). Social pretend play and social interaction in preschoolers. *Journal of Applied Developmental Psychology, 9,* 301–313.

Cook-Gumperz, J. (1973). *Social control and socialization.* London: Routledge & Kegan Paul.

Cook-Gumperz, J. (1981). Persuasive talk—The social organization of children's talk. In J. Green & C. Wallat (Eds.), *Ethnography and language in educational settings.* Norwood, NJ: Ablex.

Cook-Gumperz, J. (1986). *Children's worlds and children's language.* New York: deGruyter.

Cook-Gumperz, J., & Corsaro, W. (1976). Social-ecological constraints on children's communicative strategies. In J. Cook-Gumperz & J. Gumperz (Eds.), *Papers on language and context.* Berkeley: Language Behavior Research Laboratory.

Cook-Gumperz, J., & Gumperz, J. (1976). Context in children's speech. In J. Cook-Gumperz & J. Gumperz (Eds.), *Papers in language and context.* Berkeley: Language Behavior Research Laboratory.

Corsaro, W. A. (1977). The clarifications request as a feature of adult interactive styles with young children. *Language in Society, 7,* 63–84.

Corsaro, W. A. (1979). "We're friends, right?" Children's use of access rituals in a nursery school. *Language in Society, 8,* 315–336.

Corsaro, W. A. (1985). *Friendship and peer culture in the early years.* Norwood, NJ: Ablex.

Corsaro, W. A. (1986). Discourse processes within peer culture: From a constructivist to an interpretive approach to childhood socialization. In P. A. Adler & P. Adler (Eds.), *Sociological studies of child development.* London: JAI Press.

Corsaro, W. A. (1990). The underlife of the nursery school: Young children's social representations of adult rules. In B. Lloyd & G. Duveen (Eds.), *Social representations and the development of knowledge.* Cambridge, U.K.: Cambridge University Press.

Corsaro, W. A., & Eder, D. (1990). Children's peer cultures. *Annual Review of Sociology, 16,* 197–220.

Costanzo, P., Grumet, J., & Brehm, S. (1974). The effects of choice and source of constraint on children's attributions of preference. *Journal of Experimental Social Psychology, 10,* 352–364.

Craig, H., & Gallagher, R. (1982). Gaze and proximity as turn regulators within three-party and two-party child conversations. *Journal of Speech and Hearing Research, 25,* 65–75.

Criswell, J. H. (1939). A sociometric study of race cleavage in the classroom. *Archives of Psychology, 235,* 1–82.

Crnic, K., & Greenberg, M. (1990). Minor parenting stresses with young children. *Child Development, 61,* 1628–1637.

Cromer, R. F. (1970). "Children are nice to understand": Surface structure clues for the recovery of deep structure. *British Journal of Psychology, 61,* 397–408.

Cross, J. F., & Cross, J. (1971). Age, sex, race, and the perception of racial beauty. *Developmental Psychology, 5,* 433–439.

Damon, W. (1977). *The social world of the child.* San Francisco, CA: Jossey-Bass.

Damon, W. (1981). Exploring children's social cognition on two fronts. In J. Flavell & L. Ross (Eds.), *Social cognitive development.* Cambridge: Cambridge University Press.

Daniels-Beirness, T. (1989). Measuring peer status in boys and girls: A problem of apples and oranges? In B. Schneider, G. Attili, J. Nadel, & R. Weissberg (Eds.), *Social competence in developmental perspective.* London: Kluwer.

Dascal, M. (1981). Contextualism. In H. Parret, M. Sbisa, & J. Verschueren (Eds.), *Possibilities and limitations of pragmatics.* Amsterdam, Netherlands: John Benjamins B.V.

Davids, A., & Parenti, A.N. (1958). Time orientation and interpersonal relations of emotionally disturbed and normal children. *Journal of Abnormal and Social Psychology, 57,* 299–305.

Davis, A., & Hathaway, B. (1982). Reciprocity in parent–child verbal interactions. *Journal of Genetic Psychology, 140,* 169–183.

Dawe, H. C. (1934). An analysis of 200 quarrels of preschool children. *Child Development, 5,* 139–157.

DeFrancisco, V. (1991). The sounds of silence: How men silence women in marital relations. *Discourse and Society, 2,* 413–423.

Delia, J. G., & Clark, R. (1977). Cognitive complexity, social perception, and the development of listener-adapted communication in six-, eight-, ten- and twelve-year-old boys. *Communication Monographs, 44,* 326–345.

Delia, J., Kline, S., & Burleson, B. (1979). The development of persuasive communication strategies in kindergartners through twelfth-graders. *Communication Monographs, 46,* 241–256.

Delia, J. G., O'Keefe, B. J., & O'Keefe, D. J. (1982). The constructivist approach to communication. In F. E. X. Dance (Ed.), *Human communication theory* (pp. 147–191). New York: Harper & Row.

DeLong, A. (1974). Kinesic signals at utterance boundaries in preschool children. *Semiotica, 11,* 43–74.

DeLong, A. (1981). Kinesic signals at utterance boundaries in preschool children. In A. Kendon (Ed.), *Nonverbal communication, interaction and gesture.* The Hague: Mouton.

Denham, S. (1992). *Affective communication between mothers and preschoolers.* Paper presented at the Asilomar Conference on Emotional Development, Pacific Grove, CA.

Denham, S., & Couchoud, E. (1990). Young preschoolers' understanding of emotions. *Child Study Journal, 20,* 171–192.

Denham, S., & Grout, L. (1993). Socialization of emotion: Pathway to preschoolers' emotional and social competence. *Journal of Nonverbal Behavior, 17,* 205–227.

Denham, S., McKinley, M., Couchoud, E., & Holt, R. (1990). Emotional and behavioral predictors of preschool peer ratings. *Child Development, 61,* 1145–1152.

Denzin, N. (1970). Symbolic interactionism and ethnomethodology. In J. Douglas (Ed.), *Understanding everyday life.* Chicago: Aldine.

deVilliers, J., & deVilliers, P. (1979). *Early language.* Cambridge, MA: Harvard University Press.

Diaz, R. (1986). Issues in the empirical study of private speech: A response to Frawley and Lantolf's commentary. *Developmental Psychology, 22,* 709–711.

Diaz, R., & Berk, L. (1992). *Private speech.* Hillsdale, NJ: Lawrence Erlbaum Associates.

Diaz, R. M., & Berndt, T. J. (1982). Children's knowledge of a best friend: Fact or fancy? *Developmental Psychology, 18,* 787–794.

Dickson, W. P. (1981). *Children's oral communication skills.* New York: Academic Press.

Dimitracopoulou, I. (1990). *Conversational competence and social development.* Cambridge: Cambridge University Press.

Dion, K. K. (1973). Young children's stereotyping of facial attractiveness. *Developmental Psychology, 9,* 183–198.

Dion, K. K., & Berscheid, E. (1974). Physical attractiveness and peer perception among children. *Sociometry, 37,* 1–12.

Dion, K. K., Berscheid, E., & Walster, E. (1972). What is beautiful is good. *Journal of Personality and Social Psychology, 24,* 285–290.

Dion, K. K., & Stein, S. (1978). Physical attractiveness and interpersonal influence. *Journal of Experimental and Social Psychology, 14,* 97–108.

DiPietro, J. (1981). Rough and tumble play: A function of gender. *Developmental Psychology, 17,* 50–58.

Dishion, T. (1990). The family ecology of boys' peer relations in middle childhood. *Child Development, 61,* 874–892.

Dixon, J., & Moore, C. (1990). The development of perspective taking: Understanding differences in information and weighting. *Child Development, 61,* 1502–1513.

Dlugokinski, E. L., & Firestone, I. J. (1974). Other centeredness and susceptibility to charitable appeals: Effects of perceived discipline. *Developmental Psychology, 10,* 21–28.

Dodge, K., Pettit, G., McClaskey, C., & Brown, M. (1986). Social competence in children. *Monographs of the Society for Research in Child Development, 51* (Serial No. 213).

Dore, J. (1974). A pragmatic description of early language development. *Journal of Psycholinguistic Research, 3,* 343–350.

Dore, J. (1983). Feeling, form and intention in the baby's transition to language. In R. Golinkoff (Ed.), *The transition from prelinguistic to linguistic communication.* Hillsdale, NJ: Lawrence Erlbaum Associates.

Dore, J. (1985). Cohesion, coherence and context in children's conversations. In T. van Dijk (Ed.), *The handbook of discourse analysis.* New York: Academic Press.

Dorval, B., & Eckerman, C. (1984). Developmental trends in the quality of conversation achieved by small groups of acquainted peers. *Monographs of the Society for Research in Child Development, 49,* 1–72.

Douglas, J. R. (1970). *Understanding everyday life.* Chicago: Aldine.

Duck, S., Miell, D. K., & Gaebler, H. C. (1980). Attraction and communication in children's interactions. In H. C. Foot, A. J. Chapman, & J. R. Smith (Eds.), *Friendships and social relations in children* (pp. 89–115). New York: Wiley.

Duck, S., & Wright, P. H. (1993). Re-examining gender differences in same-gender friendships: A close look at two kinds of data. *Sex Roles, 28,* 709–727.

Duncan, S. (1991). Convention and conflict in the child's interaction with others. *Developmental Review, 11,* 337–367.

Dunn, J. (1988a). *The beginnings of social understanding.* Cambridge: Harvard University Press.

Dunn, J. (1988b). Connections between relationships: Implications of research on mothers and siblings. In R. Hinde & J.Stevenson-Hinde (Eds.), *Relationships within families.* Oxford, U.K.: Clarendon Press.

Dunn, J. (1991). Siblings' influence. In M. Lewis & S. Feinman (Eds.), *Social influences and socialization in infancy.* New York: Plenum Press.

Dunn, J. (1992a). Siblings and development. *Current Directions in Psychological Science, 1,* 6–9.

Dunn, J. (1992b). Lessons from the study of children's conversations: A discussion of the *Quarterly* [Special issue on talk]. *Merrill–Palmer Quarterly, 38,* 139–149.

Dunn, J. (1993). Social interaction, relationships, and the development of causal discourse and conflict management. [Special issue: Everyday life, social meanings, and cognitive functioning]. *European Journal of Psychology of Education, 8,* 391–401.

Dunn, J., & Brown, J. (1993). Early conversations about causality: Content, pragmatics and developmental change. *British Journal of Developmental Psychology, 11,* 107–123.

Dunn, J., Brown, J., & Beardsall, L. (1991). Family talk about feeling states and children's later understanding of others' emotions. *Developmental Psychology, 27,* 448–455.

Dunn, J., Brown, J., Slomkowski, C., Tesla, C., & Youngblade, L. (1991). Young children's understanding of other people's feelings and beliefs: Individual differences and their antecedents. *Child Development, 62,* 1352–1366.

Dunn, J., & Kendrick, C. (1982). *Siblings: Love, envy and understanding .* Cambridge, MA: Harvard University Press.

Dunn, J., & Munn, P. (1985). Becoming a family member: Family conflict and the development of social understanding in the second year. *Child Development, 56,* 480–492.

Dunn, J., & Shatz, M. (1989). Becoming a conversationalist despite (or because of) having an older sibling. *Child Development, 60,* 399–410.

Dunn, J., & Slomkowski, C. (1992). Conflict and the development of social understanding. In C. Shantz & W. Hartup (Eds.), *Conflict in child and adolescent development.* Cambridge, U.K.: Cambridge University Press.

Durkin, K. (1988). Editorial introduction [Special issue on language and social cognition]. *First Language, 8,* 89–101.

Durrett, M. E., & Davy, A. J. (1970). Racial awareness in young Mexican-American, Negro, and Anglo children. *Young Children, 26,* 16–24.

Eder, D., & Hallinan, M. T. (1978). Sex differences in children's friendships. *American Sociological Review, 43,* 237–250.

Eder, R. (1990). Uncovering young children's psychological selves: Individual and developmental differences. *Child Development, 61,* 849–863.

Edmondson, W. (1981). *Spoken discourse: A model for analysis.* London: Longman.

Eisenberg, A. R., & Garvey, C. (1981). Children's use of verbal strategies in resolving conflicts. *Discourse Processes, 4,* 149–170.

Ekman, P. (1977). Biological and cultural contributions to body and facial movements. In J. Blacking (Ed.), *The anthropology of the body.* New York: Academic Press.

Ekman, P. (1982). *Emotion in the human face.* New York: Cambridge University Press.

Ekman, P. (1993). Facial expression of emotion. *American Psychologist, 48,* 384–392.

Ekman, P. (1994). Strong evidence for universals in facial expression: A reply to Russell's mistaken critique. *Psychological Bulletin, 99,* 561–565.

Ekman, P., & Friesen, W. (1969). Nonverbal leakage and clues to deception. *Psychiatry, 32,* 88–106.

Ekman, P., & Friesen, W. (1975). *Unmasking the face: A guide to recognizing emotions from facial clues.* Hillsdale, NJ: Lawrence Erlbaum Associates.

Elicker, J. (1995, June). *From parent–child attachment in infancy to peer relations in middle childhood: Understanding continuities in social development.* Paper presented at the annual conference of the International Network on Personal Relationships, Williamsburg, VA.

Elicker, J., Englund, M., & Sroufe, L. A. (1992). Predicting peer competence and peer relationships in childhood from early parent–child relationships. In R. Parke & G. Ladd (Eds.), *Family–peer relationships: Modes of linkage* (pp. 77–105). Hillsdale, NJ: Lawrence Erlbaum Associates.

Elkin, F., & Handel, G. (1989). *The child and society.* New York: Random House.

Ellis, D., & Donohue, W. (1986). *Contemporary issues in language and discourse processes.* Hillsdale, NJ: Lawrence Erlbaum Associates.

Ellis, G., & Petersen, L. (1992). Socialization values and parental control techniques: A cross-cultural analysis of child-rearing. *Journal of Comparative Family Studies, 23,* 39–54.

Emde, R. (1976). *Emotional expression in infancy.* New York: International University Press.

Emde, R. (1982). *The development of attachment and affiliative systems.* New York: Plenum Press.

Emde, R. (1988). Development terminable and interminable: I: Innate and motivational factors from infancy. *International Journal of Psycho-Analysis, 69,* 23–42.

Emde, R., Biringen, Z., Clyman, R., & Oppenheim, D. (1991). The moral self of infancy: Affective core and procedural knowledge. *Developmental Review, 11,* 251–270.

Emslie, H., & Stevenson, R. (1981). Preschool children's use of the articles in definite and indefinite referring expressions. *Journal of Child Language, 8,* 313–328.

Epstein, J. L. (1989). The selection of friends: Changes across grades and in different classroom environments. In T. J. Berndt & G. W. Ladd (Eds.), *Peer relationships in child development* (pp. 158–187). New York: Wiley.

Erickson, F., & Shultz, J. (1982). *The counselor as gatekeeper: Social interaction in interviews.* New York: Academic Press.

Ervin, P. (1993). *Friendship and peer relations in children.* New York: John Wiley & Sons.

Ervin-Tripp, S. (1970). Discourse agreement: How children answer questions. In J. Hayes (Ed.), *Cognition and the development of language.* New York: Wiley.

Ervin-Tripp, S. (1977). Wait for me roller-skate. In S. Ervin-Tripp & E. Mitchel-Kernan (Eds.), *Child discourse.* New York: Academic Press.

Ervin-Tripp, S. (1981). How to make and understand a request. In H. Parret, M. Sbisa, & J. Verschuren (Eds.), *Possibilities and limitations of pragmatics.* Amsterdam: Benjamins.

Ervin-Tripp, S., & Gordon, D. (1980). The development of requests. In R. Schiefelbusch (Ed.), *Communicative competence: Acquisition and intervention.* Baltimore, MD: Baltimore University Press.

Ervin-Tripp, S., & Miller, W. (1977). Early discourse: Some questions about questions. In M. Lewis & L. Rosenblum (Eds.), *Interaction, conversation, and the development of language.* New York: Wiley.

Evans, M. (1985). Self-initiated speech repairs: A reflection of communicative monitoring in young children. *Developmental Psychology, 21,* 365–371.

Evans, M., & Rubin, K. (1979). Hand gestures as a communicative mode in school-aged children. *Journal of Genetic Psychology, 135,* 189–196.

Fabes, R., & Eisenberg, N. (1992). Young children's coping with interpersonal anger. *Child Development, 62,* 116–128.

Fabes, R., Eisenberg, N., McCormick, S., & Wilson, M. (1988). Preschoolers' attributions of situational determinants of others' naturally occurring emotions. *Developmental Psychology, 23,* 376–385.

Fagot, B. I. (1974). Sex differences in toddlers' behavior and parental reaction. *Developmental Psychology, 10,* 459–465.

Fagot, B. I. (1985). Beyond the reinforcement principle: Another step toward understanding sex-role development. *Developmental Psychology, 21,* 1097–1104.

Fagot, B. I., & Hagan, R. (1991). Observations of parent reactions to sex-stereotyped behaviors: Age and sex effects. *Child Development, 62,* 617–628.

Fantz, R., & Yeh, J. (1979). Configurational selectivities: Critical for development of visual perception and attention. *Canadian Journal of Psychology, 33,* 277–287.

Farren, D., Hirschbiel, P., & Jay, S. (1980). Toward interactive synchrony: The gaze patterns of mothers and children in three age groups. *International Journal of Behavioral Development, 3,* 215–224.

Fay, B. (1970). *The relationships of cognitive moral judgment, generosity, and empathic behavior in six- and eight-year-old children.* Unpublished doctoral dissertation, University of California, Los Angeles.

Fehr, B. J., & Exline, R. (1987). Social visual interaction: A conceptual and literature review. In A. Siegman & S. Feldstein (Eds.), *Nonverbal behavior and communication.* Hillsdale, NJ: Lawrence Erlbaum Associates.

Fenson, L., Dale, P., Reznick, J., Bates, E., Thal, D., & Pethick, S. (1994). Variability in early communicative development. *Monographs of the Society for Research in Child Development, 242, 59.*

Fernald, A. (1984). The perceptual and affective salience of mothers' speech to infants. In L. Feagans, C. Garvey, & R. Golinkoff (Eds.), *The origins and growth of communication.* Norwood, NJ: Ablex.

Fernald, A. (1993). Approval and disapproval: Infant responsiveness to vocal affect in familiar and unfamiliar languages. *Child Development, 64,* 657–674.

Fernald, A., & Morikawa, H. (1993). Common themes and cultural variations in Japanese and American mothers' speech to infants. *Child Development, 64,* 637–656.

Fernald, A., & Simon, T. (1984). Expanded intonation contours in mothers' speech to newborns. *Developmental Psychology, 20,* 104–113.

Feshback, N. D., & Sones, G. (1971). Sex differences in adolescent reactions toward newcomers. *Developmental Psychology, 4,* 381–386.

Feyereisen, P., & deLannoy, J. (1991). *Gestures and speech: Psychological investigations.* Cambridge, U.K.: Cambridge University Press.

Field, J. (1976). Relation of young infants' reaching behavior to stimulus distance and solidity. *Developmental Psychology, 12,* 444–448.

Field, T. (1981). Infant arousal attention and affect during early interactions. *Advances in Infancy Research, 1,* 57–100.

Field, T. (1984). Early interactions between infants and their postpartem depressed mothers. *Infant Behavior and Development, 7,* 517–522.

Field, T. (1994). The effects of mother's physical and emotional unavailability on emotion regulation. In N. Fox (Ed.), *The development of emotion regulation: Biological and behavioral considerations: Monographs of the Society for Research in Child Development, 59.*

Field, T., & Walden, T. (1982). Production and discrimination of facial expressions by preschool children. *Child Development, 53,* 1299–1311.

Field, T., Woodson, R., Greenberg, R., & Cohen, D. (1982). Discrimination and imitation of facial expressions in neonates. *Science, 218,* 179–181.

Fillmore, C. (1968). The case for case. In E. Bach & R. Harmas (Eds.), *Universals in language theory.* New York: Holt, Rinehart & Winston.

Fivish, R., & Fromhoff, F. (1988). Style and structure in mother–child conversations about the past. *Discourse Processes, 11,* 337–355.

Flavell, J. (1979). Metacognition and cognitive monitoring: A new area of psychological inquiry. *American Psychologist, 34,* 906–911.

Flavell, J. (1981). Cognitive monitoring. In W. Dickson (Ed.), *Children's oral communication skills.* New York: Academic Press.

Flavell, J., Speer, J., Green, F., & August, D. (1981). The development of comprehension monitoring and knowledge about communication. *Monographs of the Society for Research in Child Development, 46*, 1–65.

Fogel, A. (1982). Affect dynamics in early infancy: Affective tolerance. In T. Fields & A. Fogel (Eds.), *Emotion and early interaction*. Hillsdale, NJ: Lawrence Erlbaum Associates.

Fogel, A. (1992a). Movement and communication in human infancy: The social dynamics of development. *Human Movement Science, 11*, 387–423.

Fogel, A. (1992b). Origins of the self in early infancy: Is perception sufficient? *Psychological Inquiry, 3*, 115–117.

Fogel, A., Dedo, J., & McEwen, I. (1992). Effect of postural position and reaching on gaze during mother–infant face-to-face interaction. *Infant Behavior and Development, 15*, 231–244.

Fogel, A., & Hannan, T. (1985). Manual actions of nine- to fifteen-week-old human infants during face-to-face interaction with their mothers. *Child Development, 56*, 1271–1279.

Fogel, A., & Reimers, M. (1989). On the psychobiology of emotions and their development. *Monographs of the Society for Research in Child Development, 54*, 1–2 (Commentary, pp. 105–112).

Fogel, A., & Thelen, E. (1987). Development of early expressive and communicative action: Reinterpreting the evidence from a dynamic systems perspective. *Developmental Psychology, 23*, 747–761.

Foot, H. C., Chapman, A. J., & Smith, J. R. (1977). Friendship and social responsiveness in boys and girls. *Journal of Personality and Social Psychology, 20*, 925–931.

Forrester, M. (1993). Affording social-cognitive skills in young children: The overhearing context. In D. Messer & G. Turner (Eds.), *Critical influences on child language acquisition and development*. New York: St. Martin's Press.

Fox, N., Calkins, S., & Bell, M. (1994). Neural plasticity and development in the first two years of life: Evidence from cognitive and socioemotional domains of research. *Development and Psychopathology, 6*, 677–696.

Fox, N., & Davidson, R. (1988). Patterns of brain electrical activity during facial signs of emotion in 10-month-old infants. *Developmental Psychology, 24*, 230–236.

Franck, D. (1981). Seven sins of pragmatics: Theses about speech act theory, conversational analysis, linguistics and rhetoric. In H. Parret, M. Sbisa, & J. Verschuren (Eds.), *Possibilities and limitations of pragmatics*. Amsterdam: John Benjamins B.V.

Franco, F., & Butterworth, G. (1991). *Infant pointing: Prelinguistic reference and co-reference*. Paper presented at the meeting of the Society for Research in Child Development, Seattle.

Frankel, D., & Roer-Bronstein, D. (1982). Traditional and modern contributions to changing infant-rearing ideologies of two ethnic communities. *Monographs of the Society for Research in Child Development, 47*, 4.

Frauenglass, M., & Diaz, R. (1985). Self-regulatory functions of children's private speech: A critical analysis of recent challenges to Vygotsky's theory. *Developmental Psychology, 21*, 357–364.

Frawley, W., & Lantolf, J. (1986). Private speech and self-regulation: A commentary on Frauenglass and Diaz. *Developmental Psychology, 22*, 706–708.

Freedman, D. G. (1977). The development of social hierarachies. In E. M. Hetherington & R. D. Parke (Eds.), *Contemporary readings in child psychology* (1st ed.). New York: McGraw-Hill.

French, L. (1989). Young children's responses to "when" questions: Issues of directionality. *Child Development, 60*, 225–236.

French, P., & Woll, B. (1981). Context, meaning and strategy in parent–child conversation. In G. Wells (Ed.), *Learning through interaction*. Cambridge, U.K.: Cambridge University Press.

Freund, L. (1990). Maternal regulation of children's problem-solving behaviour and its impact on children's performance. *Child Development, 61*, 113–126.

Furman, W., & Bierman, K. (1983). Developmental changes in young children's conceptions of friendship. *Child Development, 54*, 549–556.

Furman, W., & Buhrmester, D. (1985). Children's perceptions of the personal relationships in their social networks. *Developmental Psychology, 21*, 1016–1024.

Furman, W., & Childs, M. K. (1981, April). *A temporal perspective on children's friendships.* Paper presented at the biennial meeting of the Society for Research in Child Development, Boston.

Furman, W., & Robbins, P. (1985). What's the point? Issues in the selection of treatment objectives. In B. H. Schneider, K. H. Rubin, & J. E. Ledingham (Eds.), *Children's peer relations: Issues in assessment and intervention* (pp. 41–54). New York: Springer-Verlag.

Furrow, D. (1984). Social and private speech at two years. *Child Development, 55,* 355–362.

Gajdusek, D., McKhann, G., & Bolis, L. (1994). Evolution and neurology of language. In *Discussions in Neuroscience, 10* (1 & 2, 1–193). Netherlands: Elsevier.

Galejs, I., Hegland, S., & King, A. (1986). Social agents and the development of locus of control in young children. *Journal of Genetic Psychology, 146,* 181–187.

Gallagher, R., & Craig, H. (1982). An investigation of overlap in children's speech. *Journal of Psycholinguistic Research, 11,* 63–75.

Gallagher, T. (1981). Contingent query sequences within adult–child discourse. *Journal of Child Language, 8,* 51–62.

Galligan, R. (1987). Intonation with single words: Purposive and grammatical use. *Journal of Child Language, 14,* 1–21.

Galluzzo, D., Matheson, C., Moore, J., & Howes, C. (1988). Social orientation to adults and peers in infant child care [Special issue: Infant day care: II. Empirical studies]. *Early Childhood Research Quarterly, 3,* 417–426.

Gamer, E. (1977). *Children's reports of friendship criteria.* Paper presented at the meeting of the Massachusetts Psychological Association, Boston.

Garber, J., & Dodge, K. (1991). *The development of emotion regulation and dysregulation.* New York: Cambridge University Press.

Garton, A. (1992). *Social interaction and the development of language and cognition.* Hillsdale, NJ: Lawrence Erlbaum Associates.

Garvey, C. (1975). Requests and responses in children's speech. *Journal of Child Language, 2,* 41–60.

Garvey, C. (1977). Play with language and speech. In S. Ervin-Tripp & E. Mitchell-Kernan (Eds.), *Child discourse.* New York: Academic Press.

Garvey, C., & Hogan, R. (1973). Social speech and social interaction: Egocentrism revisited. *Child Development, 44,* 562–568.

Garvey, C., & Kramer, T. (1989). The language of social pretend play. *Developmental Review, 9,* 364–382.

Garvey, C., & Shantz, C. (1992). Conflict talk: Approaches to adversative discourse. In C. Shantz & W. Hartup (Eds.), *Conflict in child and adolescent development.* Cambridge, U.K.: Cambridge University Press.

Gazdar, G. (1979a). *Pragmatics: Implicatures, presupposition and logical form.* New York: Academic Press.

Gazdar, G. (1979b). A solution to the projection problem. In C. Oh & D. Dinneen (Eds.), *Syntax and semantics II: Presuppositions.* New York: Academic Press.

Gazdar, G. (1981). Speech act assignment. In A. Joshi, B. Webber, & I. Sag (Eds.), *Elements of discourse understanding.* Cambridge: Cambridge University Press.

Gelman, R., & Spelke, E. (1981). The development of thoughts about anaimate and inanimate objects: Implications for research on social cognition. In J. Flavell & L. Ross (Eds.), *Social cognitive development.* Cambridge: Cambridge University Press.

Genishi, C., & DiPaolo, M. (1982). Learning through argument in preschool. In L. C. Wilkinson (Ed.), *Communicating in the classroom* (pp. 49–68). New York: Academic Press.

Gergen, K. (1990). *Everyday understanding: Social and scientific implications.* Newbury Park, CA: Sage.

Gibbs, R. (1979). Contextual effects in understanding indirect requests. *Discourse Processes, 2,* 1–10.

Gibson, J. (1979). *The ecological approach to visual perception.* Boston: Houghton Mifflin.

Giddens, A. (1983). *Central problems in social theory.* Berkeley, Los Angeles: University of California Press.

Giles, H. (1977). *Language, ethnicity and intergroup relations.* London: Academic Press.

Gilligan, C. (1982). *In a different voice: Psychological theory and women's development.* Cambridge, MA: Harvard University Press.

Ginsberg, D. (1980). *Friendship and mental health.* Unpublished manuscript, University of Illinois, Champaign–Urbana.

Gleitman, L., & Wanner, E. (1988). Current issues in language learning. In M. Bornstein & M. Lamb (Eds.), *Developmental psychology: An advanced textbook* (2nd. ed.). Hillsdale, NJ: Lawrence Erlbaum Associates.

Glick, J. (1978). Cognition and social cognition: An introduction. In J. Glick & K. Clarke-Stewart (Eds.), *The development of social understanding.* New York: Gardner Press.

Glucksberg, S., Krauss, R., & Higgins, E. (1975). The development of referential *communication* skills. In F. Horowitz, E. Hetherington, S. Scarr-Salapek, & G. Siegel (Eds.), *Review of child development research* (Vol. 4). Chicago: University of Chicago Press.

Gnepp, J., & Hess, D. (1986). Children's understanding of verbal and facial display rules. *Developmental Psychology, 11,* 103–108.

Goffman, E. (1974). *Frame analysis.* New York: Harper & Row.

Goffman, E. (1976). Replies and responses. *Language in Society, 5,* 257–313.

Golinkoff, R. (1993). When is communication a "meeting of minds"? *Journal of Child Language, 20,* 199–207.

Golinkoff, R., & Hirsh-Pasek, K. (1990). Let the mute speak: What infants can tell us about language acquisition. *Merrill–Palmer Quarterly, 36,* 67–92.

Golinkoff, R., & Hirsh-Pasek, K. (1995). Reinterpreting children's sentence comprehension: Toward a new framework. In P. Fletcher & B. MacWhinney (Eds.), *Handbook of child language.* Oxford, U.K.: Oxford University Press.

Golinkoff, R., Mervis, C., & Hirsh-Pasek, K. (1994). Early object labels: The case for a developmental lexical principles framework. *Journal of Child Language, 21,* 125–155.

Gollin, E. (1958). Organizational characteristics of social judgment: A developmental investigation. *Journal of Personality, 26,* 139–154.

Goodnow, J. (1985). Change and variations in parents' ideas about childhood and parenting. In I. Sigel (Ed.), *Parental belief systems.* Hillsdale, NJ: Lawrence Erlbaum Associates.

Goodnow, J. (1988). Parents' ideas, actions, and feelings: Models and methods from developmental and social psychology. *Child Development, 59,* 286–320.

Goodnow, J., & Collins, W. (1990). *Development according to parents: The nature, sources and consequences of parents' ideas.* Hillsdale, NJ: Lawrence Erlbaum Associates.

Goodsitt, J., Morse, P., VerHoeve, J., & Cowan, N. (1984). Infant speech recognition in multisyllabic contexts. *Child Development, 55,* 903–910.

Goodwin, C. (1979). Language as social activity: Negotiating conversation. *Journal of Pragmatics, 3,* 151–167.

Gopnick, A. (1984). The acquisition of gone and the development of the object concept. *Journal of Child Language, 11,* 273–292.

Gopnick, A., & Meltzoff, A. (1986). Relations between semantic and cognitive development in the one-word stage: The specificity hypothesis. *Child Development, 57,* 1040–1053.

Gopnick, A., & Meltzoff, A. (1987). The development of categorization in the second year and its relation to other cognitive and linguistic developments. *Child Development, 58,* 1523–1531.

Gordon, D. A., Nowicki, S., & Wichern, F. (1981). Observed maternal and child behaviors in a dependency-producing task as a function of children's locus of control orientation. *Merrill–Palmer Quarterly, 27,* 43–51.

Gordon, D. A., Wichern, F., & Nowicki, S. (1983). Observed maternal and child behaviors in a dependency-producing task as a function of children's locus of control orientations. *Merrill–Palmer Quarterly, 29,* 53–67.

Gordon, R., & Yonas, A. (1976). Sensitivity to binocular depth information in infants. *Journal of Experimental Child Psychology, 22,* 413–422.

Gottlieb, B. H. (1994). Social support. In L. A. Weber & J. H. Harvey (Eds.), *Perspectives on close relationships* (pp. 307–324). Needham Heights, MS: Allyn & Bacon.

Gottman, J. M. (1977). Toward a definition of social isolation in children. *Child Development, 48,* 513–517.

Gottman, J. M. (1983). How children become friends. *Monographs of the Society for Research in Child Development, 48* (Serial No. 201).

Gottman, J. M. (1986a). Merging social cognition and social behavior. (Commentary). In K. Dodge, G. Petit, C. McClaskey, & M. M. Brown (Eds.) Social competence in children: *Monographs for the Society for Research in Child Development, 51,* No. 213, 1–88.

Gottman, J. M. (1986b). The observation of social process. In J. M. Gottman & J. G. Parker (Eds.), *Conversations of friends: Speculations on affective development* (pp. 51–102). New York: Cambridge University Press.

Gottman, J. M., & Carrere, S. (1994). Why can't men and women get along? Developmental roots and marital inequities. In D. J. Canary & L. Stafford (Eds.), *Communication and relational maintenance* (pp. 203–229). San Diego, CA: Academic Press.

Gottman, J. M., Gonzo, J., & Rasmussen, B. (1975). Social interaction, social competence, and friendship in children. *Child Development, 45,* 709–718.

Gottman, J. M., & Parker, J. G. (Eds.). (1986). *Conversations of friends: Speculations on affective development.* New York: Cambridge University Press.

Gottman, J., & Parkhurst, J. (1980). A developmental theory of friendship and acquaintanceship processes. In W. Collins (Ed.), *Development of cognition, affect, and social relations.* Hillsdale, NJ: Lawrence Erlbaum Associates.

Grant, V. (1994). Sex of infant differences in mother–infant interaction: A reinterpretation of past findings. *Developmental Review, 14,* 1–26.

Green, E. H. (1933). Friendships and quarrels among preschool children. *Child Development, 4,* 237–252.

Greenspan, S., Barenboim, C., & Chandler, M. (1974). *Children's affective judgments in response to videotaped stories.* Paper presented at the meeting of the Society for Research in Child Development.

Grice, H. (1975). Logic and conversation. In P. Cole & J. Morgan (Eds.), *Syntax and semantics: Vol. 3. Speech acts.* New York: Academic Press.

Grice, H. (1978). Further notes on logic and conversation. In P. Cole (Ed.), *Syntax and semantics: Vol. 9. Pragmatics.* New York: Academic Press.

Grief, E. (1980). Sex differences in parent–child conversations. *Women's Studies Quarterly, 3,* 253–258.

Grieser, D., & Kuhl, P. (1988). Maternal speech to infants in a tonal language: Support for universal prosodic features in motherese. *Developmental Psychology, 24,* 14–20.

Grimm-Thomas, K., & Perry-Jenkins, M. (1994). All in a day's work: Job experiences, self-esteem, and fathering in working-class families. *Family Relations, 43,* 174–181.

Gronlund, N. E. (1955). The relative stability of classroom social status with unweighted and weighted sociometric choices. *Journal of Educational Psychology, 46,* 345–354.

Gross, A., & Ballif, B. (1991). Children's understanding of emotion from facial expressions and situations: A review. *Developmental Review, 11,* 368–398.

Gumperz, J., & Herasimchuk, E. (1973). Conversational analysis of social meaning. In R. Shuy (Ed.), *Sociolinguistics: Current trends and prospects.* Georgetown: Georgetown University Round Table on Linguistics.

Gunnar, M., & Donahue, M. (1980). Sex differences in social responsiveness between six months and twelve months. *Child Development, 51,* 262–265.

Gusella, J., Muir, D., & Tronick, E. (1988). The effect of manipulating maternal behavior during an interaction on three- and six-month-olds' affect and attention. *Child Development, 59,* 1111–1124.

Haight, W., & Miller, P. (1991). *The social nature of early pretend play: Mothers' participation in everyday pretending.* Unpublished manuscript.

Haight, W., & Miller, P. (1992). The development of everyday pretend play: A longitudinal study of mothers' participation. *Merrill–Palmer Quarterly, 38,* 331–349.

Hala, S., Chandler, M., & Fritz, A. (1991). Fledgling theories of mind: Deception as a marker of three-year-olds' understanding of false belief. *Child Development, 62,* 83–97.

Halberstadt, A. (1986). Family socialization of emotional expression and nonverbal communication styles and skills. *Journal of Personality and Social Psychology, 51,* 827–836.

Halberstadt, A. (1991). Toward an ecology of expressiveness: Family socialization in particular and a model in general. In R. Feldman & B. Rime (Eds.), *Fundamentals of nonverbal behavior.* Cambridge, U.K.: Cambridge University Press.

Halberstadt, A. (1993). Emotional experience and expression: An issue overview [Special issue: Development of nonverbal behavior: I. Emotional experience and expression]. *Journal of Nonverbal Behavior, 17,* 139–143.

Halberstadt, A., Grotjohn, D., Johnson, C., Furth, M., & Greig, M. (1992). Children's abilities and strategies in managing the facial display of affect. *Journal of Nonverbal Communication, 16,* 215–230.

Halliday, M. A. K. (1975). *Learning how to mean: Explorations in the functions of language.* London: Edward Arnold.

Halliday, M. A. K. (1978). *Language as a social semiotic.* London: Edward Arnold.

Halliday, M. A. K. (1979). Development of texture in child language. In T. Myers (Ed.), *The development of conversation and discourse.* Edinburgh: Edinburgh University Press.

Halliday, M. A. K., & Hasan, R. (1983). *Cohesion in English.* London: Longman.

Hancher, M. (1979). The classification of co-operative illocutionary acts. *Language in Society, 8,* 1–14.

Harding, C., & Golinkoff, R. (1979). The origins of intentional vocalizations in prelinguistic infants. *Child Development, 49,* 33–40.

Harkness, S., & Super, C. (1985). The cultural context of gender segregation in children's peer groups. *Child Development, 56,* 219–224.

Harris, M. (1993). The relationship of maternal speech to children's first words. In D. Messer & Geoffrey Turner (Eds.), *Critical influences on child language acquisition and development.* New York: St. Martin's Press.

Hart, C., Ladd, G., & Burleson, B. (1990). Children's expectations of the outcomes of social strategies: Relations with sociometric status and maternal disciplinary styles. *Child Development, 61,* 127–137.

Hartup, W. W. (1978). Children and their friends. In H. McGurk (Ed.), *Issues in childhood and social development.* London: Methuen.

Hartup, W. W. (1983). Peer relations. In E. M. Hetherington (Ed.), P. H. Mussen (Series Ed.), *Handbook of child psychology: Vol. 4: Socialization, personality, and social development* (pp. 103–196). New York: Wiley.

Hartup, W. W. (1989a). Social relationships and their developmental significance. *American Psychologist, 89,* 120–126.

Hartup, W.W. (1989b). Behavioral manifestations of children's friendships. In T. J. Berndt & G. W. Ladd (Eds.), *Peer relationships in child development* (pp. 46–70). New York: Wiley.

Hartup, W. W. (1992). Friendships and their developmental significance. In H. McGurk (Ed.), *Childhood social development.* Hillsdale, NJ: Lawrence Erlbaum Associates.

Hartup, W. W. (1996). The company they keep: Friendships and their developmental significance. *Child Development, 67,* 1–13.

Hartup, W. W., Glazer, J., & Charlesworth, R. (1967). Peer reinforcement and sociometric status. *Child Development, 38,* 1017–1024.

Hartup, W. W., Laursen, B., Stewart, M. A., & Eastenson, A. (1988). Conflict and friendship relations of young children. *Child Development, 59,* 1590–1600.

Hartup, W. W., & Scancilio, M. F. (1986). Children's friendships. In E. Schopler & G. B. Mesibov (Eds.), *Social behavior in autism* (pp. 61–80). New York: Plenum Press.

Haslett, B. (1983a). Children's strategies for maintaining cohesion in their oral and written stories. *Communication Education, 32,* 91–106.

Haslett, B. (1983b). Communicative functions and strategies in children's conversations. *Human Communication Research, 48,* 115–124.

Haslett, B. (1983c). Preschoolers' communicative strategies in gaining compliance from peers: A developmental study. *Quarterly Journal of Speech, 69,* 84–99.

Haslett, B. (1984). Communicative development: The state of the art. In R. Bostrom (Ed.), *Communication Yearbook, Vol. 8,* 198–267.

Haslett, B. (1987). *Communication: Strategic action in context.* Hillsdale, NJ: Lawrence Erlbaum Associates.

Haslett, B. (1989). Communication and language acquisition within a cultural context. In S. Ting-Toomey & F. Korzenny (Eds.), *Language, communication, and culture.* Newbury Park, CA: Sage.

Haslett, B., & Bowen, S. (1989). Children's strategies in initiating interaction with peers. In J. Nussbaum (Ed.), *Life-span communication: Normative processes.* Hillsdale, NJ: Lawrence Erlbaum Associates.

Haslett, B., Geis, F. L., & Carter, M. (1992). *The organizational women: Power and paradox.* Norwood, NJ: Ablex.

Hay, D. F. (1979). Cooperative interactions and sharing between very young children and their parents. *Developmental Psychology, 15,* 647–653.

Hay, D. F., & Ross, H. S. (1982). The social nature of early conflict. *Child Development, 53,* 105–113.

Hayes, D., Scott, L., Chemelski, B., & Johnson, J. (1987). Physical and emotional states as memory-relevant factors: Cognitive monitoring by young children. *Merrill–Palmer Quarterly, 33,* 4473–4487.

Hayes, L., & Watson, J. (1981). Facial orientation of parents and elicited smiling by infants. *Infant Behavior and Development, 4,* 333–340.

Hazan, C., & Shaver, P. R. (1987). Romantic love conceptualized as an attachment process. *Journal of Personality and Social Psychology, 52,* 511–524.

Hazan, C., & Shaver, P. R. (1990). Love and work: An attachment-theoretical perspective. *Journal of Personality and Social Psychology, 59,* 270–280.

Hazan, C., & Shaver, P. R. (1994). Attachment as an organizational framework for research on close relationships. *Psychological Inquiry, 5,* 1–22.

Hazen, N., & Black, B. (1989). Preschool peer communication skills: The role of social status and interaction context. *Child Development, 60,* 867–876.

Heath, S. (1983). *Ways with words: Language, life, and work in communities and classrooms.* Cambridge, U.K.: Cambridge University Press.

Heckhausen, J. (1987). Balancing for weaknesses and challenging developmental potential: A longitudinal study of mother–infant dyads in apprenticeship interactions. *Developmental Psychology, 23,* 762–770.

Hegland, S., & Galejs, I. (1983). Developmental aspects of locus of control in preschool children. *Journal of Genetic Psychology, 143,* 229–239.

Heibeck, T., & Markman, E. (1987). Word learning in children: An examination of fast mapping. *Child Development, 58,* 1021–1034.

Henshall, C., & McGuire, J. (1986). Gender development. In M. Richards & P. Light (Eds.), *Children of social worlds.* Cambridge, MA: Harvard University Press.

Heritage, J. (1984). *Garfinkel and ethnomethodology.* Cambridge: Polity Press.

Hess, R., Kashiwagi, K., Azuma, H., Price, G., & Dickson, W. P. (1980). Maternal expectations for mastery of developmental tasks in Japan and in the United States. *International Journal of Psychology, 15,* 259–271.

Hess, R., & Shipman, V. (1968). Maternal influences upon early learning. In R. Hess & R. Bear (Eds.), *Early education*. Chicago: University of Chicago Press.

Hess, R., Shipman, V., Bear, R., & Brophy, J. (1968). *The cognitive environments of urban preschool children*. Chicago: University of Chicago Press.

Higgins, E. T. (1981). Role taking and social judgment: Alternative developmental perspective and processes. In J. Flavell & L. Ross (Eds.), *Social cognitive development*. Cambridge, MA: Cambridge University Press.

Hill, S., & Smith, J. (1984). Neonatal responsiveness as a function of maternal contact and obstetrical drugs. *Perceptual and Motor Skills, 58*, 859–866.

Hirschberg, L. (1990). When infants look to their parents: II: Twelve-month-olds' responses to conflicting parental emotional signals. *Child Development, 61*, 1187–1191.

Hirschberg, L., & Svejda, M. (1990). When infants look to their parents: I: Infants' social referencing of mothers compared to fathers. *Child Development, 61*, 1175–1186.

Hirsh-Pasek, K., & Golinkoff, R. (1993). Skeletal supports for grammatical learning: What the infant brings to the language learning task. In C. K. Rovee-Collier (Ed.), *Advances in infancy research*, Vol. 10. Norwood, NJ: Ablex.

Hittelman, J., & Dickes, R. (1979). Sex differences in neonatal eye contact time. *Merrill–Palmer Quarterly, 25*, 171–184.

Hoff-Ginsberg, E. (1986). Function and structure in maternal speech: Their relation to the child's development of syntax. *Developmental Psychology, 22*, 155–163.

Hoff-Ginsberg, E. (1990). Maternal speech and the child's development of syntax: A further look. *Journal of Child Language, 12*, 85–99.

Hoff-Ginsberg, E. (1991). Mother–child conversation in different social classes and communicative settings. *Child Development, 62*, 782–796.

Hoffman, L. (1989). Effects of maternal employment in the two-parent family. *American Psychologist, 44*, 283–292.

Hoffman, M. L. (1960). Power assertion by the parent and its impact on the child. *Child Development, 31*, 129–143.

Hoffman, M. L. (1977). Moral internalization: Current theory and research. In L. Berkowitz (Ed.), *Advances in experimental and social psychology*. New York: Academic Press.

Hoffner, C., & Badzinski, D. (1989). Children's integration of facial and situational cues to emotion. *Child Development, 60*, 411–422.

Holmberg, M. (1980). The development of social interchange patterns from 12 to 42 months. *Child Development, 51*, 448–456.

Hortacsu, N., & Birsen, E. (1992). Children's reliance on situational and vocal expression of emotions: Consistent and conflicting cues. *Journal of Nonverbal Behavior, 16*, 231–247.

Houseman, J. (1972). *An ecological study of interpersonal conflicts among preschool children*. Unpublished doctoral dissertation, Wayne State University, Detroit, MI.

Howe, C. (1980). Mother–child conversation and semantic development. In H. Giles, W. Robinson, & P. Smith (Eds.), *Language: Social psychological perspectives*. London: Pergamon Press.

Howes, C. (1983). Patterns of friendship. *Child Development, 54*, 1041–1053.

Howes, C. (1988). Peer interaction of young children. *Monographs of the Society for Research in Child Development, 53*, 1–94.

Huckaby, L. M. (1971). *A developmental study of the relationship of negative moral-social behaviors to empathy, to positive social behaviors and to cognitive moral judgment*. Unpublished doctoral dissertation, University of California, Los Angeles.

Huston, A. (1985). The development of sex typing: Themes from recent research. *Developmental Review, 5*, 1–17.

Hymel, S., Hayruen, M., & Lollis, S. (1982, May). *Social behavior and sociometric preferences: Do children really play with peers they like?* Paper presented at the annual meeting of the Canadian Psychological Association, Montreal.

Ingram, D. (1976). *Phonological disability in children*. London: Edward Arnold.

Ingram, D. (1991). *First language acquisition.* Cambridge, U.K.: Cambridge University Press.

Ipsa, J. (1981). Peer support among Soviet day care toddlers. *International Journal of Behavioral Development, 4,* 255–269.

Isabella, R. (1993). Orings of attachment: Maternal interactive behavior across the first year. *Child Development, 64,* 605–621.

Isabella, R., & Belsky, J. (1991). Interactional synchrony and the origins of infant–mother attachment: A replication study. *Child Development, 62,* 373–384.

Isbell, B., & McKee, L. (1980). Society's cradle: An anthropological perspective on the socialisation of cognition. In J. Sant (Ed.), *Developmental psychology and society.* London: Macmillan.

Izard, C. (1971). *The face of emotion.* New York: Appleton-Century-Crofts.

Izard, C. (1991). The substrates and functions of emotion feelings: William James and current emotion theory. *Personality and Social Psychology Bulletin, 16,* 626–635.

Izard, C. (1992). Basic emotions, relations among emotions, and emotion–cognition relations. *Psychological Review, 99,* 561–565.

Izard, C. (1994). Innate and universal facial expressions: Evidence from developmental and crosscultural research. *Psychological Bulletin, 115,* 288–299.

Izard, C., Fantauzzo, C., Castle, J., Haynes, O., Rayias, M., & Putnam, P. (1995). The ontogeny and significance of infants' facial expressions in the first nine months of life. *Developmental Psychology, 31,* 997–1013.

Izard, C., Haynes, O. M., Chisholm, G., & Baak, K. (1991). Emotional determinants of infant–mother attachment. *Child Development, 62,* 906–917.

Izard, C., & Malatesta, C. (1987). Perspectives on emotional development: 1. Differential emotions theory of early emotional development. In J. D. Osofsky (Ed.), *Handbook of infant development* (2nd. ed.). New York: John Wiley & Sons, Inc.

Jaffe, J., & Feldstein, S. (1970). *Rhythms of dialogue.* New York: Academic Press.

Jakobson, R. (1971). *Fundamentals of language.* The Hague: Mouton.

Jakobson, R. (1980). *The framework of language.* Ann Arbor: University of Michigan Press.

Jakobson, R., & Halle, M. (1956). *Fundamentals of language.* s'Gravenhage: Mouton.

Johnson, C., Pick, H., Siegel, G., Cicciarelli, A., & Garber, S. (1981). Effects of interpersonal distance on children's vocal intensity. *Child Development, 52,* 721–723.

Johnston, J. (1979). *A study of spatial thought and expression: "In back" and "in front."* Unpublished doctoral dissertation, University of California, Berkeley.

Johnston, J. (1986). Cognitive prerequisites: The evidence from children learning English. In D. Slobin (Ed.), *Cross-linguistic study of language acquisition.* Hillsdale, NJ: Lawrence Erlbaum Associates.

Johnston, J., & Slobin, D. (1979). The development of locative expressions in English, Italian, Serbo-Croatian, and Turkish. *Journal of Child Language, 6,* 529–545.

Jones, C., & Adamson, L. (1987). Language use in mother–child and mother–child–sibling interactions. *Child Development, 58,* 356–366.

Josephs, I. (1994). Display rule behavior and understanding in preschool children. *Journal of Nonverbal Behavior, 18,* 301–326.

Julian, T., McKenry, P., & McKelvey, M. (1994). Cultural variations in parenting. *Family Relations, 43,* 30–37.

Jusczyk, P., Cutler, A., & Redanz, N. (1993). Infants' preference for the predominant stress patterns of English words. *Child Development, 64,* 675–687.

Kaitz, J., Meschulach-Sarfaty, O., Auerbach, J., & Eidelman, A. (1988). A reexamination of newborns' ability to imitate facial expressions. *Developmental Psychology, 24,* 3–7.

Karniol, R., & Heinman, T. (1987). Situational antecdents of children's anger experiences and subsequent responses to adult versus peer provokers. *Aggressive Behavior, 13,* 689–697.

Kassin, S., & Ellis, S. (1988). On the acquisition of the discounting principle: An experimental test of a social-developmental model. *Child Development, 50,* 463–469.

Kassin, S., & Lepper, M. (1984). Oversufficient and insufficient justification effects: Cognitive and behavioral development. In J. Nicholls (Ed.), *Advances in motivation and achievement: Vol 3. The development of achievement motivation.* Greenwich, CT: JAI Press.

Katriel, T. (1985). Brogez: Ritual and strategy in Israeli children's conflicts. *Language in Society, 14,* 467–490.

Katz, P. (1986). Modification of children's gender-stereotyped behavior: General issues and research considerations. *Sex Roles, 14,* 591–602.

Katz, P., & Boswell, S. (1986). Flexibility and traditionality in children's roles. *Genetic, Social and General Psychology Monographs, 112,* 105–147.

Kavanaugh, R., & Jirkovsky, A. (1982). Parental speech to young children: A longitudinal analysis. *Merrill–Palmer Quarterly, 28,* 297–311.

Kaye, K., & Charney, R. (1981). Conversational asymmetry between mothers and children. *Journal of Child Language, 8,* 35–49.

Kaye, K., & Fogel, A. (1980). The temporal structure of face-to-face communication between mothers and infants. *Developmental Psychology, 16,* 454–464.

Keasy, P. (1979). Children's developing awareness and usage of intentionality and motives. In C. Keasey (Ed.), *Motivation.* Nebraska City, NE: University of Nebraska Press.

Keenan, E. (1974). Conversational competence in children. *Journal of Child Language, 1,* 163–183.

Keenan, E., & Schieffelin, B. (1976). Topic as a discourse notion: A study of topic in the conversation of children and adults. In C. Li (Ed.), *Subject and topic.* New York: Academic Press.

Keil, F. (1989). *Concepts, kinds and cognitive development.* Cambridge, MA: MIT Press.

Kemple, K., Speranza, H., & Hazen, N. (1992). Cohesive discourse and peer acceptance. *Merrill–Palmer Quarterly, 38,* 364–381.

Kendon, A. (1987). On gesture: Its complementary relationship with speech. In A. Siegman & S. Feldstein (Eds.), *Nonverbal behavior and communication.* Hillsdale, NJ: Lawrence Erlbaum Associates.

Killen, M., & Turiel, E. (1991). Conflict resolution in preschool social interactions. *Early Education and Development, 2,* 240–255.

Knapp, M. (1980). *Essentials of nonverbal communication.* New York: Holt, Rinehart & Winston.

Koch, H. L. (1933). Popularity in preschool children: Some related factors and a technique for its measurement. *Child Development, 4,* 164–175.

Kohlberg, L. (1966). A cognitive-developmental analysis of children's sex-role concepts and attitudes. In E. Maccoby (Ed.), *The development of sex differences.* Stanford, CA: Stanford University Press.

Kohn, M. (1969). *Class and conformity.* Homewood, IL: Dorsey.

Korner, A., & Thoman, E. (1972). The relative efficacy of contact and vestibular-proprioceptive stimulation in soothing neonates. *Child Development, 43,* 443–453.

Kotelchuck, M. (1975, September). *Father caretaking characteristics and their influence on infant–father interaction.* Paper presented at the American Psychological Association meeting, Chicago, IL.

Kreckel, M. (1981). *Communicative acts and shared knowledge in natural discourse.* New York: Academic Press.

Kuczaj, S. (1978). Why do children fail to overgeneralize the progressive inflection? *Journal of Child Language, 5,* 167–171.

Kuhl, P. (1987). Perception of speech and sound in early infancy. In P. Salapatek & L. Cohen (Eds.), *Handbook of infant perception: Vol. 2: From perception to cognition.* New York: Academic Press.

Kumin, L., & Lazar, M. (1974). Gestural communication in preschool children. *Perceptual and Motor Skills, 38,* 708–710.

Kupersmidt, J. B., Coie, J. D., & Dodge, K. A. (1990). The role of poor peer relationships in the development of disorder. In S. R. Asher & J. D. Coie (Eds.), *Peer rejection in childhood* (pp. 274–305). New York: Cambridge University Press.

Kupersmidt, J. B., Griesler, P., & DeRosier, M. (1995). Childhood aggression and peer relations in the context of family and neighborhood factors. *Child Development, 66*, 360–375.

Kutter, D., & Durkin, K. (1987). Turn-taking in mother–infant interaction: An examination of vocalizations and gaze. *Developmental Psychology, 29*, 54–61.

Ladd, G. W., & Emerson, E. S. (1984). Shared knowledge in children's friendships. *Developmental Psychology, 20*, 932–940.

Ladd, G. W., & Oden, S. (1979). The relationship between peer acceptance and children's ideas about helpfulness. *Child Development, 50*, 402–408.

Ladd, G. W., & Price, J. M. (1986). Promoting children's cognitive and social competence: The relation between parents' perceptions of task difficulty and children's perceived and actual competence. *Child Development, 57*, 446–460.

Laks, D., Beckwith, L., & Cohen, S. (1990). Mothers' use of personal pronouns when talking with toddlers. *Journal of Genetic Psychology, 151*, 25–32.

Lamb, M. E. (1977a). The development of mother–infant and father–infant attachments in the second year of life. *Developmental Psychology, 13*, 637–648.

Lamb, M. E. (1977b). Father–infant and mother–infant interaction in the first year of life. *Child Development, 48*, 167–181.

Lamb, M. E. (1978). The father's role in the infant's social world. In J. H. Stevens, Jr., & M. Mathews (Eds.), *Mother/child father/child relationships* (pp. 87–108). Washington, DC: National Association for the Education of Young Children.

Lamb, M. E. (1987a). Introduction: The emergent American father. In M. E. Lamb (Ed.), *The father's role*. Hillsdale, NJ: Lawrence Erlbaum Associates.

Lamb, M. E. (1987b). *The father's role*. Hillsdale, NJ: Lawrence Erlbaum Associates.

Lamb, M. E., Morrison, D., & Malkin, C. (1987). The development of infant social expectations in face-to-face interaction: A longitudinal study. *Merrill–Palmer Quarterly, 33*, 241–254.

Langer, E. (1983). *The psychology of control*. Beverly Hills, CA: Sage.

Langlois, J. H., & Downs, A. C. (1979). Peer relations as a function of physical attractiveness: The eye of the beholder or behavioral reality? *Child Development, 50*, 409–418.

Langlois, J. H., & Stephan, C. (1977). The effects of physical attractiveness and ethnicity on children's behavioral attributions and peer preferences. *Child Development, 48*, 1694–1698.

Langlois, J. H., & Styczynski, L. E. (1979). The effects of physical attractiveness on the behavioral attributions and peer preferences of acquainted children. *International Journal of Behavioral Development, 2*, 325–342.

Langsdorf, P., Izard, C., Rayias, M., & Hembree, E. (1983). Interest expression, visual fixation, and heart-rate changes in 2- and 8-month-old infants. *Developmental Psychology, 19*, 375–386.

Laupa, M., & Turiel, E. (1986). Children's conceptions of adult and peer authority. *Child Development, 57*, 405–412.

Laursen, B., & Hartup, W. (1989). The dynamics of preschool children's conflicts. *Merrill–Palmer Quarterly, 35*, 281–297.

Leaper, C. (1991). Influence and involvement in children's discourse: Age, gender and partner effects. *Child Development, 62*, 797–811.

Lee, L. C. (1973). *Social encounters of infants: The beginnings of popularity*. Paper presented at the meeting of the International Society for the Study of Behavioral Development, Ann Arbor, MI.

Legerstee, M., Corter, C., & Kienapple, K. (1990). Hands, arm and facial actions of young infants to a social and nonsocial stimulus. *Child Development, 61*, 774–784.

Lempers, J. (1979). Young children's production and comprehension of nonverbal deictic behaviors. *Journal of Genetic Psychology, 135*, 93–102.

Lempers, J., & Elrod, M. (1983). Children's appraisal of different sources of referential communicative inadequacies. *Child Development, 54*, 509–515.

Lempert, H. (1989). Animacy constraints on preschool children's acquisition of syntax. *Child Development, 60*, 237–245.

Lempert, H., & Kinsbourne, M. (1985). The effect of visual guidance on lateralized vocal-manual interference. *Neuropsychologia, 23,* 691–695.

Lenneberg, E. (1967). *Biological foundations of language.* New York: Wiley.

Lerner, R. M., & Lerner, J. V. (1977). Efects of age, sex, and physical attractiveness on child–peer relations, academic performance, and elementary school adjustment. *Developmental Psychology, 13,* 586–590.

Levine, L., & Hoffman, M. (1975). Empathy and cooperation in 4 year olds. *Developmental Psychology, 11,* 53–54.

LeVine, R. (1977). Child rearing as cultural adaptation. In P. Leiderman, S. Tulkin, & A. Rosenfield (Eds.), *Culture and infancy: Variations in the human experience.* New York: Academic Press.

Levinson, S. (1983). *Pragmatics.* Cambridge: Cambridge University Press.

Levinson, S., & Brown, P. (1987). *Politeness: Some universals in language usage.* Cambridge, U.K.: Cambridge University Press.

Levy, F. (1980). The development of sustained attention (vigilance) in children: Some normative data. *Journal of Child Psychology and Psychiatry and Allied Disciplines, 21,* 77–84.

Lewis, M. (1991). Ways of knowing: Objective self-awareness or consciousness. *Developmental Review, 11,* 231–243.

Lewis, M., & Brooks, J. (1975). Infants' social perception: A constructivist view. In L. B. Cohen & P. Salapetek (Eds.), *Infant perception: From sensation to cognition* (Vol. 2). New York: Academic Press.

Lewis, M., & Michalson, L. (1983). *Children's emotions and moods.* New York: Plenum Press.

Lieberman, P. (1967). *Intonation, perception, and language.* Cambridge, MA: MIT Press.

Lieven, E. (1978). Conversation between mothers and young children: Individual differences and their possible implication for the study of language learning. In N. Waterson & C. Snow (Eds.), *The development of communication.* New York: Wiley.

Lippit, R. (1941). Popularity among preschool children. *Child Development, 12,* 305–322.

Livesley, W. J., & Bromley, D. B. (1973). *Person perception in childhood and adolescence.* London: Wiley.

Lloyd, P., & Beveridge, M. (1981). *Information and meaning in child communication.* London: Academic Press.

Lock, A., Service, V., Brito, A., & Chandler, P. (1989). The social structuring of infant cognition. In A. Slater & G. Bremner (Eds.), *Infant development.* Hillsdale, NJ: Lawrence Erlbaum Associates.

Locke, J. (1993). *The child's path to spoken language.* Cambridge, MA: Harvard University Press.

Lockheed, M. E. (1985). Sex and social influence: A meta-analysis guided by theory. In J. Berger & M. Zelditch (Eds.), *Status, attributions, and rewards* (pp. 406–429). San Francisco: Jossey-Bass.

Lockheed, M. E., & Hall, K. (1976). Conceptualizing sex as a status characteristic: Approach to leadership training strategies. *Journal of Social Issues, 32,* 111–124.

Loeb, R. C. (1975). Concomitants of boys' locus of control examined in parent–child interactions. *Developmental Psychology, 11,* 353–358.

Lubin, D., & Forbes, D. (1981, April). *Understanding sequential aspects of children's social behavior: Conceptual issues in the development of coding schemes.* Paper presented at the biennial meeting of the Society for Research in Child Development, Boston.

Lucariello, J., & Nelson, K. (1987). Remembering and planning talk between mothers and children. *Discourse Processes, 10,* 219–235.

Ludemann, P., & Nelson, C. (1988). Categorical representation of facial expressions by 7-month-old infants. *Developmental Psychology, 24,* 492–501.

Luria, Z., & Hertzog, E. (1985). *Gender segregation across and within settings.* Paper presented at the biennial meeting of the Society for Research in Child Development, Toronto.

Lutkenhaus, P., Grossman, K., & Grossman, K. (1985). Infant–mother attachment at twelve months and style of interaction with stranger at the age of three. *Child Development, 56,* 1538–1542.

Lynn, D., & Cross, A. (1974). Parent preference of preschool children. *Journal of Marriage and the Family, 36,* 555–559.

Lytton, H., & Romney, D. (1991). Parents' sex-related differential socialization of boys and girls: A meta-analysis. *Psychological Bulletin, 109,* 267–296.

Maccoby, E. E. (1985). Social groupings in childhood: Their relationship to prosocial and antisocial behavior in boys and girls. In P. Olweus, J. Block, & M. Radke-Yarrow (Eds.), *Development of antisocial and prosocial behavior: Theories, research, and issues.* San Diego: Academic Press.

Maccoby, E. E. (1988). Gender as a social category. *Developmental Psychology, 26,* 755–765.

Maccoby, E. E., & Jacklin, C. N. (1987). Gender segregation in childhood. In H. W. Reese (Ed.), *Advances in child development and behavior* (Vol. 20, pp. 239–288). Orlando, FL: Academic Press.

Maccoby, E., & Martin, J. (1983). Socialization in the context of the family: Parent–child interaction. In E. M. Hetherington (Ed.), *Handbook of child psychology: Vol. 4. Socialization, personality, and social development* (pp. 1–101). New York: Wiley.

MacWhinney, B. (1987). Applying the competition model to bilingualism. *Applied Psycholinguistics, 8,* 315–327.

Malatesta, C. Z. (1982). The expression and regulation of emotion: A lifespan perspective. In T. Field & A. Fogel (Eds.), *Emotion and early interaction.* Hillsdale, NJ: Lawrence Erlbaum Associates.

Malatesta, C. Z., Culver, C., Tesman, J., & Shepard, B. (1989). Engaging the commentaries: When is an infant affective expression an emotion? *Monographs of the Society for Research in Child Development, 54,* 125–136.

Malatesta, C. Z., & Haviland, J. (1982). Learning display rules: The socialization of emotion expression in infancy. *Child Development, 53,* 991–1003.

Maltz, D. N., & Borker, R. A. (1982). A cultural approach to male–female miscommunication. In J. J. Gumperz (Ed.), *Language and social identity* (pp. 195–216). New York: Cambridge University Press.

Mannarino, A. P. (1980). The development of children's friendships. In H. C. Foot, A. J. Chapman, & H. R. Smith (Eds.), *Friendship and social relations in children* (pp. 43–63). New York: Wiley.

Mannle, S., & Tomasello, M. (1987). Fathers, siblings, and the bridge hypothesis. In K. Nelson & A. Van Kleeck (Eds.), *Children's language* (Vol. 6). Hillsdale, NJ: Lawrence Erlbaum Associates.

Maratsos, M., & Chalkley, M. (1980). The internal language of children's syntax: The ontogenesis and representation of syntactic categories. In K. E. Nelson (Ed.) *Children's language* (Vol. 2). New York: Gardner Press.

Markell, R. A., & Asher, S. R. (1974). *The relationship of children's interests to perceived masculinity and femininity.* Paper presented at the annual meeting of the American Educational Research Association, Chicago, IL.

Markham, R., & Adams, K. (1992). The effect of type of task on children's identification of facial expressions. *Journal of Nonverbal Behavior, 16,* 21–37.

Markman, E., & Wachtel, G. (1988). Children's use of mutual exclusivity to constrain the meaning of words. *Cognitive Psychology, 20,* 121–157.

Marslen-Wilson, W., & Zwitserlood, P. (1989). Accessing spoken words: The importance of word onsets. *Journal of Experimental Psychology, 15,* 576–585.

Marshall, H. R., & McCandless, B. R. (1957). Relationships between dependence on adults and social acceptance by peers. *Child Development, 28,* 413–419.

Martin, C., & Halverson, D. (1983). Gender constancy: A methodological and theoretical analysis. *Sex Roles, 9,* 775–790.

Martin, C., & Little, J. (1990). The relation of gender understanding to children's sex-typed preferences and gender stereotypes. *Child Development, 61,* 1427–1439.

Martin, J., Maccoby, E., & Jacklin, C. (1981). Mother's responsiveness to interactive bidding and nonbidding in boys and girls. *Child Development, 52,* 1064–1067.

Martinez, M. (1987). Dialogues among children and between children and their mothers. *Child Development, 58,* 1035–1043.

Masters, J. C., & Furman, W. (1981). Popularity, individual selections, and specific peer interaction among children. *Developmental Psychology, 17,* 344–350.

Masur, E. (1982). Cognitive content of parents' speech to preschoolers. *Merrill–Palmer Quarterly, 28,* 471–484.

Masur, E. (1983). Gestural development, dual-directional signaling, and the transition to words. *Journal of Psycholinguistic Research, 12,* 93–109.

Matas, L., Arend, R., & Sroufe, L. (1978). Continuity of adaptation in the second year: The relationship between quality of attachment and later competent functioning. *Child Development, 49,* 547–556.

Matsumoto, D., Haan, N., Yabrove, G., Theodorou, P., & Carney, C. C. (1986). Preschoolers' moral actions and emotions in prisoner's dilemma. *Developmental Psychology, 22,* 663–670.

Matsumoto, D., & Kishimoto, H. (1983). Developmental characteristics in judgments of emotion from nonverbal vocal cues. *International Journal of Intercultural Relations, 7,* 415–424.

Maudry, M., & Nekula, M. (1939). Social relations between children of the same age during the first two years of life. *Journal of Genetic Psychology, 54,* 193–215.

May, R. (1980). *Sex and fantasy: Patterns of male and female development.* London: Norton.

Mayes, L., & Carter, A. (1990). Emerging social regulatory capacities as seen in the still-face situation. *Child Development, 61,* 754–763.

McDevitt, T., Hess, R., Kashiwagi, K., Dickson, W. P., Miyake, N., & Azuma, H. (1987). Referential communication accuracy of mother–child pairs and children's later scholastic achievement: A follow-up study. *Merrill–Palmer Quarterly, 33,* 171–185.

McGillicuddy-DeLisi, A. (1982). Parental beliefs about developmental processes. *Human Development, 25,* 192–200.

McGuire, J. (1982). Gender specific differences in early childhood: The impact of the father. In N. Beaill & J. McGuire (Eds.), *Fathers: Psychological perspectives.* London: Junction Books.

McGuire, K. D., & Weisz, J. R. (1982). Social cognition and behavioral correlates of preadolescent chumship. *Child Development, 53,* 1478–1484.

McKenzie, B., Skouteris, H., Day, R., Hartman, B., & Yonas, A. (1993). Effective action by infants to contact objects by reaching and leaning. *Child Development, 64,* 415–429.

McNeill, D. (1985). So you think gestures are nonverbal? *Psychological Review, 92,* 350–371.

McShane, J. (1980). *Learning to talk.* Cambridge, U.K.: Cambridge University Press.

McTear, M. (1984). Structure and process in children's conversational development. In S. Kucjac (Ed.), *Discourse development.* New York: Springer-Verlag.

McTear, M. (1985). *Children's conversation.* Oxford, U.K.: Oxford University Press.

Mehler, J., Jusczyk, P., Lambertz, G., Halsted, N., Bertoncini, J., & Amieltison, C. (1988). A precursor of language acquisition in young infants. *Cognition, 29,* 143–178.

Meltzoff, A., & Moore, M. K. (1977). Imitation of facial and manual gestures by human neonates. *Science, 198,* 75–78.

Menyuk, P. (1977). *Language and maturation.* Cambridge, MA: MIT Press.

Michael, G., & Willis, F. (1968). The development of gestures as a function of social class, education and sex. *Psychological Record, 18,* 515–519.

Miller, P., & Aloise, P. (1990). Discounting in children: The role of social knowledge. *Developmental Review, 10,* 266–298.

Miller, P., Aloise, P., & Davis, T. (1989). *The role of information about manipulative intent in discounting: A comparison of assessment techniques.* Unpublished manuscript, University of Florida, Gainesville.

Miller, P., Danaher, D., & Forbes, D. (1986). Sex-related strategies for coping with interpersonal conflict in children aged five and seven. *Developmental Psychology, 22,* 543–548.

Miller, P., & Sperry, L. (1988). Early talk about the past: The origins of conversational stories of personal experience. *Journal of Child Language, 15,* 293–315.

Miller, P., Mintz, J., Hoogstra, L., Fung, H., & Potts, R. (1992). The narrated self: Young children's construction of self in relation to others in conversational stories of personal experience. *Merrill–Palmer Quarterly, 38,* 45–67.

Miller, P., Potts, R., Fung, H., Hoogstra, L., & Mintz, J. (1990). Narrative practices and the social construction of self in childhood. *American Ethnologist, 17,* 292–311.

Miller, S. A. (1988). Parents' beliefs about children's cognitive development. *Child Development, 59,* 259–285.

Miller, W., & Ervin-Tripp, S. (1964). The development of grammar in child language. In U. Bellugi & R. Brown (Eds.), *The acquisition of language. Monographs of the Society for Research in Child Development, 92.*

Mishler, E. (1976a). Studies in dialogue and discourse: II. Types of discourse initiated and sustained through questioning. *Journal of Psycholinguistic Research, 4,* 99–121.

Mishler, E. (1976b). Studies in dialogue and discourse: III: Utterance structure and utterance function in interrogative sequences. *Journal of Psycholinguistic Research, 5,* 239–305.

Mishler, E. (1979). Would you trade cookies for popcorn: Talk of trade among six-year-old children. In O. Garnica & M. King (Eds.), *Language, children and society.* New York: Pergamon Press.

Mitchell-Kernan, C., & Kernan, K. (1977). Pragmatics of directive choice among children. In S. Ervin-Tripp & C. Mitchell-Kernan (Eds.), *Child discourse.* New York: Academic Press.

Mize, J., & Cox, R. (1991). Social knowledge and social competence: Number and quality of strategies as predictors of peer behavior. *Journal of Genetic Psychology, 151,* 117–127.

Mize, J., & Ladd, G. (1988). Predicting preschoolers' peer behavior and status from their interpersonal strategies: A comparison of hypothetical-reflective and enactive assessments. *Developmental Psychology, 24*(6), 782–788.

Moerk, E. (1974). Changes in verbal child–mother interactions with increasing language skills of the child. *Journal of Psycholinguistic Research, 3,* 101–115.

Moore, C., Bryant, D., & Furrow, D. (1989). Mental terms and the development of certainty. *Child Development, 60,* 167–171.

Moore, C., & Corkum, V. (1994). Social understanding at the end of the first year of life. *Developmental Review, 14,* 349–372.

Moore, C., & Davidge, J. (1989). The development of mental terms: Pragmatics or semantics? *Journal of Child Language, 16,* 633–641.

Morse, P. (1979). The infancy of infant speech perception: The first decade of research. *Brain, Behavior and Evolution, 16,* 351–373.

Much, N., & Shweder, R. (1978). Speaking of rules: The analysis of culture in breach. In W. Damon (Ed.), *Moral development: New directions in child development.* San Francisco: Jossey-Bass.

Mueller, E., & Lucas, T. (1975). A developmental analysis of peer interaction among toddlers. In M. Lewis & L. A. Rosenblum (Eds.), *Friendship and peer relations.* New York: Wiley-Interscience.

Mueller, E., & Vandell, D. (1979). Infant–infant interaction. In J. D. Osofsky (Ed.), *Handbook of infant development.* New York: Wiley.

Murphy, C. (1978). Pointing in a context of a shared activity. *Child Development, 49,* 371–380.

Neisser, U. (1991). Two perceptually given aspects of the self and their development. *Developmental Review, 11,* 197–209.

Nelson, J., & Aboud, F. E. (1985). The resolution of conflict between friends. *Child Development, 56,* 1009–1017.

Nelson, K. (1973). Structure and strategy in learning how to talk. *Monographs of the Society for Research on Child Development, 38* (1–2).

Nelson, K. (1974). Concept, word, and sentence: Interrelations in acquisition and development. *Psychological Review, 81,* 267–285.

Nelson, K. (1976). Some attributes of adjectives used by young children. *Cognition, 4,* 13–80.

Nelson, K. (1977). Facilitating syntax acquisition. *Developmental Psychology, 13,* 101–107.

Nelson, K. (1981). Social cognition in a script framework. In J. Flavell & L. Ross (Eds.), *Social cognitive development*. Cambridge: Cambridge University Press.

Nelson, K. (1985). *Making sense: The acquisition of shared meaning*. New York: Academic Press.

Nelson, K., Carskaddon, G., & Bonvillian, J. (1973). Syntax acquisition: Impact of experimental variation in adult verbal interaction with the child. *Child Development, 44*, 479–504.

Newcomb, A. F., Brady, J. E., & Hartup, W. W. (1979). Friendship and incentive condition as determinants of children's task-oriented social behavior. *Child Development, 50*, 878–881.

Newport, L., Gleitman, L., & Gleitman, H. (1977). Mother, I'd rather do it myself: Some effects and non-effects of maternal speech style. In C. Snow & C. Ferguson (Eds.), *Talking to children*. New York: Cambridge University Press.

Ninio, A. (1985). The meaning of children's first words. *Journal of Pragmatics, 9*, 527–546.

Ninio, A. (1993). Is early speech situational? An examination of some current theories about the relation of early utterances to the context. In D. Messer & G. Turner (Eds.), *Critical influences in child language acquisition and development*. New York: St. Martin's Press.

Ninio, A. (1994). Predicting the order of acquisition of three-word constructions by the complexity of their dependency structure. *First Language, 14*, 119–152.

Ninio, A., Snow, C., Pan, B., & Rollins, P. (1994). Classifying communicative acts in children's interactions. *Journal of Communication Disorders, 27*, 157–187.

Nofsinger, R. (1976). Answering questions indirectly. *Human Communication Research, 2*, 172–181.

Nowicki, S., & Duke, M. P. (1983). The Nowicki–Strickland life-span locus of control scales: Construct validation. In H. M. Lefcourt (Ed.), *Research with the locus of control construct* (pp. 9–51). New York: Academic Press.

Nowicki, S., & Roundtree, J. (1971). Correlates of locus of control in a secondary school population. *Developmental Psychology, 4*, 477–478.

Nowicki, S., & Segal, W. (1973). Perceived parental characteristics, locus of control orientation, and behavior correlates of locus of control. *Developmental Psychology, 10*, 33–37.

Nsamenang, A. (1987). A West African perspective. In M. Lamb (Ed.), *The father's role: Cross-cultural perspectives*. Hillsdale, NJ: Lawrence Erlbaum Associates.

O'Connell, B. J., & Bretherton, I. (1984). Toddlers' play alone and with mother: The role of maternal guidance. In I. Bretherton (Ed.), *Symbolic play: The development of social understanding*. London: Academic Press.

O'Keefe, B. J., & Benoit, P. J. (1982). Children's arguments. In J. R. Cox & C. A. Willard (Eds.), *Advances in argumentation theory and research* (pp. 154–183). Carbondale, IL: Southern Illinois University Press.

O'Keefe, B. J., & Delia, J. (1979). Construct comprehensiveness and cognitive complexity as predictors of the number and strategic adaptation of arguments and appeals in a persuasive message. *Communication Monographs, 46*, 221–240.

O'Keefe, B. J., & Delia, J. G. (1982). Impression formation processes and message production. In M. E. Roloff & C. R. Berger (Eds.), *Social cognition and communication* (pp. 33–72). Beverly Hills, CA: Sage.

Ochs, E., & Schieffelin, B. (1979). *Developmental pragmatics*. New York: Academic Press.

Ochs, E., & Schieffelin, B. (1984). Language acquisition and socialization: Three developmental stories and their implications. In R. Shweder & R. LeVine (Eds.), *Cultural theory*. Cambridge: Cambridge University Press.

Oller, D. (1980). The emergence of the sounds of speech in infancy. In G. Yeni-Komishian, J. Kavanaugh, & C. A. Ferguson (Eds.), *Child phonology: Vol. 1. Production*. New York: Academic Press.

Oller, D., & Eilers, R. (1988). The role of audition in infant babbling. *Child Development, 59*, 441–449.

Olmsted, D. (1971). *Out of the mouth of babes*. The Hague: Mouton.

Olsen-Fulero, L. (1982). Style and stability in mother conversational behavior: A study of individual differences. *Journal of Child Language, 9*, 543–564.

Olson, D., & Hildyard, A. (1981). Assent and compliance in children's language. In W. Dickson (Ed.), *Children's oral communication skills.* New York: Academic Press.

Olson, S., Bayles, K., & Bates, J. (1986). Mother–child interaction and children's speech progress: A longitudinal study of the first two years. *Merrill–Palmer Quarterly, 32,* 1–20.

O'Mark, D. R., & Edelman, M. S. (1973). *A developmental study of group formation in children.* Paper presented at the annual meeting of the American Educational Association, New Orleans, LA.

O'Mark, D. R., O'Mark, M., & Edelman, M. (1975). Formation of dominance hierarchies in young children. In T. R. Willimans (Ed.), *Psychological anthropology.* The Hague: Mouton.

O'Neill, D. (1996). Two-year-old children's sensitivity to parent's knowledge state when making requests. *Child Development, 67,* 659–677.

Owens, R. (1992). *Language development.* New York: Macmillan.

Papousek, M. (1989). Determinants of responsiveness to infant vocal expression of emotional state. *Infant Behavior and Development, 12,* 507–524.

Parisi, D., & Castelfranchi, P. (1981). A goal analysis of some pragmatic aspects of language. In H. Parret, M. Sbisa, & J. Vershueren (Eds.), *Possibilities and limitations of pragmatics.* Amsterdam: John Benjamins B.V.

Parke, R. (1989). Social development in infancy: A 25-year perspective. In H. Reese (Ed.), *Advances in child development and behavior.* New York: Academic Press.

Parke, R. D., & O'Leary, S. (1975). Father–mother–infant interaction in the newborn period: Some findings, some observations, and some unresolved issues. In K. F. Riegel & J. Meacham (Eds.), *The developing individual in a changing world.* The Hague: Mouton.

Parke, R. D., & Sawin, D. B. (1981). Father–infant interaction in the newborn period: A re-evaluation of some current myths. In E. M. Hetherington & R. D. Parke (Eds.), *Contemporary readings in child psychology* (2nd ed., pp. 229–234). New York: McGraw-Hill.

Parker, J. G., & Asher, S. R. (1988, July). *Peer group acceptance and the quality of children's best friendships.* Paper presented at the NATO Advanced Study Institute "Social Competence in Developmental Perspective," Savoy, France.

Parker, J. G., & Gottman, J. M. (1989). Social and emotional development in a relational context: Friendship interaction from early childhood to adolescence. In T. J. Berndt & G. W. Ladd (Eds.), *Peer relationships in child development* (pp. 95–131). New York: Wiley.

Patterson, C., Kupersmidt, J., & Griesler, P. (1990). Children's perceptions of self and of relationships with others as a function of sociometric status. *Child Development, 61,* 1335–1349.

Patterson, C., Vaden, N., Griesler, P., & Kupersmidt, J. (1991). Income level, gender, ethnicity, and household composition as predictors of children's peer companionship outside of school. *Journal of Applied Developmental Psychology, 12,* 447–465.

Patterson, G., DeBarsyche, B., & Ramsey, E. (1989). A developmental perspective on antisocial behavior. *American Psychologist, 44,* 329–335.

Patterson, M. (1983). *Nonverbal behavior: A functional perspective.* New York: Springer-Verlag.

Patterson, M. (1991). A functional approach to nonverbal exchange. In R. Feldman & B. Rime (Eds.), *Fundamentals of nonverbal behavior. Studies in emotion and social interaction* (pp. 458–495). New York: Cambridge University Press.

Pedersen, F. A. (1975, September). *Mother, father and infant as an interactive system.* Paper presented at the meeting of the American Psychological Association, Chicago, IL.

Peevers, H. B., & Secord, P. F. (1973). Developmental changes in attribution of descriptive concepts to persons. *Journal of Personality and Social Psychology, 27,* 120–128.

Pellegrini, A., Brody, G., & Stoneman, Z. (1987). Children's conversational competence with their parents. *Discourse Processes, 10,* 93–106.

Pellegrino, M., & Scopesi, A. (1990). Structure and function of baby talk in a day-care centre. *Journal of Child Language, 17,* 101–114.

Penman, R., Cross, T., Milgrom-Friedman, J., & Meares, R. (1983). Mothers' speech to prelingual infants: A pragmatic analysis. *Journal of Child Language, 10,* 17–34.

Peterson, C., Danner, E., & Flavell, J. (1972). Developmental changes in children's responses to three indications of communicative failure. *Child Development, 43,* 1463–1468.

Pettit, G. S., Dodge, K. A., & Brown, M. M. (1988). Early family experience, social problem solving patterns, and children's social competence. *Child Development, 59,* 107–120.

Philippot, P., & Feldman, R. (1990). Age and social competence in preschoolers' decoding of facial expression. *British Journal of Social Psychology, 20,* 793–796.

Philips, S. (1974). Warm Springs Indian time: How the regulation of participation affects the progression of events. In R. Bauman & J. Sherzer (Eds.), *Exploration in the ethnography of speaking.* Cambridge: Cambridge University Press.

Philips, S. (1976). Some sources of cultural variability in the regulation of talk. *Language in Society, 5,* 81–95.

Philp, A. J. (1940). Strangers and friends as competitors and co-operators. *Journal of Genetic Psychology, 57,* 249–258.

Phinney, J. (1986). The structure of 5-year-olds' verbal quarrels with peers and siblings. *Journal of Genetic Psychology, 147,* 47–60.

Piaget, J. (1936/1952). *The origin of intelligence in the child.* London: Routledge & Kegan Paul.

Piaget, J. (1954). *The construction of reality in the child.* New York: Basic Books.

Piaget, J. (1959). *The language and thought of the child.* London: Routledge & Kegan Paul.

Piaget, J. (1965). *The moral judgment of the child.* New York: Free Press.

Picariello, M., Greenberg, D., & Pillemer, D. (1990). Children's sex-related stereotyping of colors. *Child Development, 61,* 1453–1460.

Pinker, S. (1984). *Language learnability and language development.* Cambridge: Harvard University Press.

Pinker, S. (1995). *The language instinct.* New York: Harper–Collins.

Pleck, J. (1984). *Changing fatherhood.* Unpublished manuscript, Wellesley College.

Pomerleau, A., Malcuit, G., & Sabatier, C. (1991). Child-rearing practices and conceptions in three cultural groups of Montreal: Quebecois, Vietnamese, Haitian. In M. Bornstein (Ed.), *Cultural approaches to parenting.* Hillsdale, NJ: Lawrence Erlbaum Associates.

Post, B., & Hetherington, E. M. (1974). Sex differences in the use of proximity and eye contact in judgments of affiliation in preschool children. *Developmental Psychology, 10,* 881–889.

Pruett, K. (1983). *Two year followup of infants of primary nurturing father in intact families.* Paper presented at the second World Congress on Infant Psychiatry, Cannes, France.

Putallaz, M. (1987). Maternal behavior and children's sociometric status. *Child Development, 58,* 324–340.

Putallaz, M., Costanzo, P., & Smith, R. (1991). Maternal recollections of childhood peer relationships: Implications for their children's social competence. *Journal of Social and Personal Relationships, 8,* 403–422.

Putallaz, M., & Heflin, A. H. (1986). Toward a model of peer acceptance. In J. M. Gottman & J. G. Parker (Eds.), *Conversations of friends* (pp. 292–314). New York: Cambridge University Press.

Putallaz, M., & Wasserman, A. (1990). Children's entry behavior. In S. R. Asher & J. D. Coie (Eds.), *Peer rejection in childhood* (pp. 60–89). New York: Cambridge University Press.

Raffler-Engel, W. von (1977). *The unconscious element in inter-cultural communication.* Unpublished manuscript, Vanderbilt University, Nashville, TN.

Rawlins, W. K. (1992). *Friendship matters: Communication, dialectics, and the life course.* Hawthorne, NY: Aldine de Gruyter.

Read, B., & Cherry, L. (1978). Preschool children's production of directive forms. *Discourse Processes, 1,* 233–245.

Read, K. H. (1976). *The nursery school* (6th ed.). Philadelphia: Saunders.

Rees, N. (1978). Pragmatics of language. In R. Schiefelbusch (Ed.), *The bases of language intervention.* College Park, MD: University Park Press.

Reich, P. (1986). *Language development.* Englewood Cliffs, NJ: Prentice-Hall.

Reisman, J. M., & Shorr, S. I. (1978). Friendship claims and expectations among children and adults. *Child Development, 49,* 913–916.

Retherford, K., Schwartz, B., & Chapman, R. (1980). Semantic roles and residual grammatical categories in mother and child speech: Who tunes into whom? *Journal of Child Language, 8,* 583–608.

Richardson, S. A., Goodman, U., Hastorf, A. H., & Dornbusch, S. A. (1961). Cultural uniformity in reaction to physical disabilities. *American Sociological Review, 26,* 241–247.

Ricouer, P. (1981). The model of the text: Meaningful action considered as a text. *Social Research, 38,* 529–555.

Rime, B., Mesquita, B., Philipott, P., & Boca, S. (1991). Beyond the emotional events: Six studies on the social sharing of emotion. *Cognition and Emotion, 5,* 435–465.

Rinn, W. (1991). Neuropsychology of facial expression. In R. Feldman & B. Rime (Eds.), *Fundamentals of nonverbal behavior.* New York: Cambridge University Press.

Riskin, J., & Faunce, E. E. (1972). An evaluative review of family interaction research. *Family Process, 11,* 365–455.

Robinson, E., & Robinson, W. (1976a). Developmental changes in the child's explanation of communication failure. *Australian Journal of Psychology, 28,* 155–165.

Robinson, E., & Robinson, W. (1976b). The young child's understanding of communication. *Developmental Psychology, 12,* 328–333.

Robinson, E., & Robinson, W. (1977). Development in the understanding of causes of success and failure in verbal communication. *Cognition, 5,* 363–378.

Robinson, E., & Robinson, W. (1978a). Explanations of communication failure and ability to give bad messages. *British Journal of Social and Clinical Psychology, 17,* 219–225.

Robinson, E., & Robinson, W. (1978b). Development of understanding about communication: Message inadequacy and its role in causing communication failure. *Genetic Psychological Monographs, 98,* 233–279.

Robinson, E., & Robinson, W. (1978c). The roles of egocentrism and of weakness in comparing children's explanations of communication failures. *Journal of Experimental Psychology, 26,* 147–160.

Robinson, E., & Whittaker, S. (1985). Children's responses to ambiguous messages and their understanding of ambiguity. *Developmental Psychology, 21,* 446–454.

Robinson, J., & Biringen, Z. (1995). Gender and emerging autonomy in development. *Psychoanalytic Inquiry, 15,* 60–74.

Robinson, J., Little, C., & Biringen, Z. (1993). Emotional communication in mother–toddler relationships: Evidence for early gender differentiation. *Merrill–Palmer Quarterly, 39,* 496–517.

Robinson, W., & Rackstraw, S. (1972). *A question of answers* (Vols. 1 & 2). London: Routledge & Kegan Paul.

Roff, M., Sells, S. B., & Golden, M. M. (1972). *Social adjustment and personality development in children.* Minneapolis, MN: University of Minnesota Press.

Rogers, E. (1983). *Analyzing relational communication: Implications of a pragmatic approach.* Paper presented at the meeting of the Speech Communication Association, Louisville, KY.

Roggman, L., & Woodson, R. (1989). Touch and gaze in parent–infant play. Poster presented at the meeting of the Society for Research in Child Development, Kansas City.

Rogoff, B. (1990). *Apprenticeship in thinking: Cognitive development in social context.* New York: Oxford University Press.

Rogoff, B. (1991). The joint socialization of development by young children and adults. In M. Lewis & S. Feinman, *Social influences and socialization in infancy.* New York: Plenum Press.

Rogoff, B., Ellis, S., & Gardner, W. (1984). Adjustment of adult–child instruction according to child's age and task. *Developmental Psychology, 20,* 193–199.

Roopnarine, J. (1987). Social interaction in the peer group: Relationship to perceptions of parenting and to children's interpersonal awareness and problem-solving ability. *Journal of Applied Developmental Psychology, 8,* 351–362.

Roopnarine, J., & Field, T. (1983). Peer-directed behaviors of infants and toddlers during nursery school play. *Infant Behavior and Development, 6,* 133–138.

Roopnarine, J., Johnson, J., & Hooper, F. (1994). *Children's play in diverse cultures.* Albany, NY: State University of New York Press.

Rosch, E. (1975). Cognitive representations of semantic categories. *Journal of Experimental Psychology General, 104,* 192–233.

Ross, H., & Conant, C. (1992). The social structure of early conflict: Interaction, relationships, and alliances. In C. Shantz & W. Hartup (Eds.), *Conflict in child and adolescent development.* Cambridge: Cambridge University Press.

Ross, H., & Lollis, S. (1987). Communication within infant social games. *Developmental Psychology, 23,* 241–248.

Ross, H., Lollis, S., & Elliott, C. (1982). Toddler–peer communication. In K. Rubin & H. Ross (Eds.), *Peer relationships and social skills in childhood.* New York: Springer-Verlag.

Ross, L. (1981). The "intuitive scientist" formulation and its developmental implication. In J. Flavell & L. Ross (Eds.), *Social cognitive development.* Cambridge: Cambridge University Press.

Rotenberg, K., Simourd, L., & Moore, D. (1989). Children's use of a verbal–nonverbal consistency principle to infer truth and lying. *Child Development, 60,* 309–322.

Rothbard, J. C., & Shaver, P. R. (1994). Continuity of attachment across the lifecourse: An attachment-theoretical perspective on personality. In M. B. Sperling & W. H. Berman (Eds.), *Attachment in adults: Theory, assessment, and treatment.* New York: Guilford.

Roug, L., Landberg, I., & Lundberg, L. (1989). Phonetic development in early infancy: A study of four Swedish children during the first eighteen months of life. *Journal of Child Language, 16,* 19–40.

Rowe, D., & Plomin, R. (1981). The importance of non-shared (EI) environmental influence in behavioural development. *Developmental Psychology, 17,* 517–531.

Rubin, K., Booth, C., Rose-Krasnor, L., & Mills, R. (1995). Social relationships and social skills: A conceptual and empirical analysis. In S. Shulman (Ed.), *Close relationships and socioemotional development.* Norwood, NJ: Ablex.

Rubin, K., Caplan, R., Fox, N. & Calkins, S. (1995). Emotionality, emotion regulation, and preschoolers' social adaptation. *Development and Psychopathology, 7,* 49–62.

Rubin, K., & Krasnor, L. (1983). Age and gender differences in solutions to hypothetical social problems. *Journal of Applied Developmental Psychology, 4,* 263–275.

Rubin, K., & Krasnor, L. (1986). Social-cognitive and social behavioral perspectives on problem solving. In M. Perlmutter (Ed.), *The Minnesota symposia on child psychology, 18,* 1–68.

Rubin, K., Mills, R., & Rose-Krasnor, L. (1989). Maternal beliefs and children's competence. In B. Schneider, G. Attili, I. Nadel, & R. Weissberg (Eds.), *Social competence in developmental perspective.* London: Kluwer Academic Publishers.

Rubin, K., & Rose-Krasnor, L. (1992). Interpersonal problem solving and social competence in children. In V. Van Hasselt & M. Hersen (Eds.), *Handbook of social development: A lifespan perspective. Perspectives in developmental psychology.* New York: Plenum Press.

Rubin, Z. (1980). *Children's friendships.* Cambridge, MA: Harvard University Press.

Russell, A., & Finnie, V. (1990). Preschool children's social status and maternal instructions to assist group entry. *Developmental Psychology, 26,* 603–611.

Russell, J. (1984). Should I believe you, or what you say? Children's beliefs of children's statements. *Developmental Psychology, 20,* 261–270.

Russell, J., & Bullock, M. (1986). On the dimensions preschoolers use to interpret facial expressions of emotion. *Developmental Psychology, 22,* 97–102.

Ryan, J. (1974). Early language development. In M. Richards (Ed.), *The integration of the child into a social world.* Cambridge: Cambridge University Press.

Saarni, C. (1979). Children's understanding of display rules for expressive behavior. *Developmental Psychology, 28,* 424–429.

Saarni, C. (1984). An observational study of children's attempts to monitor their expressive behavior. *Child Development, 55,* 1504–1513.

Saarni, C. (1987). Cultural rules of emotional experience: A commentary on Miller and Sperry's study. *Merrill–Palmer Quarterly, 33,* 535–540.

Saarni, C. (1988). Children's understanding of the interpersonal consequences of dissemblance of nonverbal emotional-expressive behavior. *Journal of Nonverbal Behavior, 12,* 275–294.

Saarni, C. (1989). Children's understanding of strategic control of emotional expression in social transactions. In C. Saarni & P. Harris (Eds.), *Children's understanding of emotions.* New York: Cambridge University Press.

Saarni, C., & Crowley, M. (1990). The development of emotion regulation: Effects on emotional state and expression. In E. Blechman (Ed.), *Emotions and the family: For better or for worse.* Hillsdale, NJ: Lawrence Erlbaum Associates.

Sabatier, C. (1994). Parental conceptions of early development and developmental stimulation. In A. Vyt, H. Bloch, & M. Bornstein (Eds.), *Early child development in the French tradition.* Hillsdale, NJ: Lawrence Erlbaum Associates.

Sachs, J. (1977). The adaptive significance of linguistic input to prelinguistic infants. In C. Snow & C. Ferguson (Eds.), *Talking to children.* London: Cambridge University.

Sachs, J. (1987). Preschool boys' and girls' language use in pretend play. In S. Philips, S. Steele, & C. Tanz (Eds.), *Language, gender and sex in comparative perspective.* New York: Cambridge University Press.

Sacklin, S., & Thelen, E. (1984). An ethological study of peaceful associative outcomes to conflict in preschool children. *Child Development, 55,* 283–306.

Sacks, H., Schegloff, E., & Jefferson, G. (1974). A simplest systematics for the organization of turn taking for conversation. *Language, 50,* 696–735.

Sagi, A. (1982). Antecedents and consequences of various degrees of paternal involvement in child rearing: The Israeli project. In M. Lamb (Ed.), *Nontraditional families: Parenting and child development.* Hillsdale, NJ: Lawrence Erlbaum Associates.

Sander, E. (1972). When are speech sounds learned? *Journal of Speech and Hearing Disorders, 37,* 55–63.

Savin-Williams, R. C. (1979). Dominance hierarchies in groups of early adolescents. *Child Development, 50,* 923–935.

Saxe, G., & Kaplan, R. (1981). Gesture in early counting: A developmental analysis. *Perceptual and Motor Skills, 53,* 851–854.

Scarlett, H., Press, A., & Crockett, W. (1971). Children's descriptions of peers: A Wernerian developmental analysis. *Child Development, 42,* 439–453.

Schacter, F. (1979). *Everyday mother talk to toddlers: Early intervention.* New York: Academic Press.

Schaffer, H. (1979). Acquiring the concept of the dialogue. In M. Bornstein & W. Kessen (Eds.), *Psychological development from infancy: Image and intention.* Hillsdale, NJ: Lawrence Erlbaum Associates.

Schaffer, H. (1992). Joint involvement episodes as context for development. In H. McGurk (Ed.), *Childhood social development.* Hillsdale, NJ: Lawrence Erlbaum Associates.

Schaffer, H., & Collis, G. (1986). Parental responsiveness and child behaviour. In W. Sluckin & M. Herbert (Eds.), *Parental behaviour in animals and humans.* Oxford: Blackwell.

Schaffer, H., Collis, G., & Parsons, G. (1977). Vocal exchange and visual regard in verbal and preverbal children. In H. Schaffer (Ed.), *Studies in mother–infant interaction.* London: Academic Press.

Schaffer, H., Hepburn, A., & Collis, G. (1983). Verbal and nonverbal aspects of mothers' directives. *Journal of Child Language, 10,* 337–355.

Scheflen, A. (1972). *Body language and the social order.* Englewood Cliffs, NJ: Prentice-Hall.

Scheflen, A. (1974). *How behavior means.* New York: Doubleday.

Schieffelin, B. (1981). A sociolinguistic analysis of relationship. *Discourse Processes, 4,* 189–196.

Schieffelin, B., & Ochs, E. (1983). A cultural perspective on the transition from prelinguistic to linguistic communication. In R. Golinkoff (Ed.), *The transition from prelinguistic to linguistic communication*. Hillsdale, NJ: Lawrence Erlbaum Associates.

Schlesinger, I. (1971). Production of utterances and language acquisition. In D. Slobin (Ed.), *The ontogenesis of grammar*. New York: Academic Press.

Schneider, B. H., Attili, G., Nadel, J., & Weisberg, R. (1989). *Social competence in developmental perspective*. New York: Kluwer Academic Publishers.

Schneider, B. H., Wiener, J., & Murphy, K. (1994). Children's friendships: The giant step beyond peer acceptance. *Journal of Social and Personal Relationships, 11*, 323–340.

Schneider, K., & Josephs, I. (1991). The expressive and communicative functions of preschool children's smiles in an achievement situation. *Journal of Nonverbal Behavior, 15*, 185–198.

Schneiderman, M. (1983). "Do what I mean, not what I say!" Changes in mothers' action-directives to young children. *Journal of Child Language, 10*, 357–367.

Schneider-Rosen, K., & Wenz-Gross, M. (1990). Patterns of compliance from eighteen to thirty months of age. *Child Development, 61*, 104–112.

Schnur, E., & Shatz, M. (1984). The role of maternal gesturing in conversations with one-year-olds. *Journal of Child Language, 11*, 29–41.

Schutz, A. (1967). *The phenomenology of the social world* (G. Walshy & F. Lehnert, Trans.). Evanston, IL: Northwestern University Press.

Scollon, R., & Scollon, S. (1981). *Narrative literacy and face in interethnic communication*. Norwood, NJ: Ablex.

Scott, M., & Lyman, S. (1968). Accounts. *American Sociological Review, 33*, 46–62.

Searle, J. (1969). *Speech acts*. Cambridge: Cambridge University Press.

Searle, J. (1976). The classification of illocutionary acts. *Language in Society, 5*, 1–24.

Searle, J. (1983). *Intentionality*. Cambridge: Cambridge University Press.

Selman, R. L. (1980). *The growth of interpersonal understanding*. New York: Academic Press.

Selman, R. L. (1981). The child as a friendship philosopher. In S. R. Asher & J. M. Gottman (Eds.), *The development of children's friendships* (pp. 242–272). New York: Cambridge University Press.

Selman, R. L. (1994). The relation of role taking to the development of moral judgment in children. In B. Puka (Ed.), *Fundamental research in moral development: A compendium* (Vol. 2, pp. 87–99). New York: Garland Publishing.

Selman, R. L., & Byrne, D. (1975). A structural analysis of role-taking levels in middle childhood. *Child Development, 4*, 803–806.

Selman, R. L., & Schultz, L. H. (1989). Children's strategies for interpersonal negotiation with peers: An interpretive/empirical approach to the study of social development. In T. Berndt & G. Ladd (Eds.), *Peer relationships in child development* (pp. 371–406). New York: John Wiley & Sons.

Senchak, M., & Leonard, K. E. (1992). Attachment styles and marital adjustment among newlywed couples. *Journal of Social and Personal Relationships, 9*, 51–64.

Serafica, F. C. (1978). *The development of friendship: An ethological-organismic perspective*. Unpublished manuscript, Ohio State University, Columbus.

Serbin, L. A., Sprafkin, C., Elman, M., & Doyle, A. (1984). The early development of sex differences: Patterns of social influence. *Canadian Journal of Social Science, 14*, 350–363.

Serrano, J., Iglesias, J., & Loeches, A. (1992). Visual discrimination and recognition of facial expressions of anger, fear and surprise in 4-to-6-month-old infants. *Developmental Psychobiology, 25*, 411–425.

Shantz, C. U. (1981). The role of role taking in children's referential communication. In W. Dickson (Ed.), *Children's oral communication skills*. New York: Academic Press.

Shantz, C. U., & Hobart, C. J. (1989). Social conflict and development: Peers and siblings. In T. J. Berndt & G. W. Ladd (Eds.), *Peer relationships in child development* (pp. 71–94). New York: Wiley.

Shantz, D. W., & Shantz, C. U. (1982, August). *Conflicts between children and social cognitive development.* Paper presented at the annual meeting of the American Psychological Association, Washington, DC.

Shatz, M. (1974). *The comprehension of indirect directives: Can two-year-olds shut the door?* Paper presented at the meeting of the Linguistic Society of America, Amherst.

Shatz, M., & Gelman, R. (1973). The development of communicative skills: Modifications in the speech of young children as a function of listener. *Monographs of the Society for Research in Child Development, 38.*

Shatz, M., & McCloskey, L. (1984). Answering appropriately: A developmental perspective on conversational knowledge. In S. Kuczaj (Ed.), *Discourse development.* New York: Springer-Verlag.

Shatz, M., & O'Reilly, A. (1990). Conversational or communicative skill? A reassessment of two-year-olds' behaviour in miscommunication episodes. *Journal of Child Language, 17,* 131–146.

Shaver, P. R., & Brennan, K. A. (1992). Attachment styles and the "big five" personality traits: Their connections with each other and with romantic outcomes. *Personality and Social Psychology Bulletin, 18,* 536–545.

Shaver, P. R., & Hazan, C. (1994). Attachment. In A. L. Weber & J. H. Harvey (Eds.), *Perspectives on close relationships* (pp. 110–130). Needham Heights, MA: Allyn & Bacon.

Shaver, P. R., Hazan, C., & Bradshaw, D. (1988). Love as attachment: The integration of three behavioral systems. In R. J. Sternberg & M. L. Barnes (Eds.), *The psychology of love* (pp. 68–99). New Haven, CT: Yale University Press.

Shaw, M. E. (1973). Changes in sociometric choices following forced integration of an elementary school. *Journal of Social Issues, 29,* 143–157.

Sheilds, M. (1985). *The representation of emotions.* Unpublished manuscript, University of London.

Sheldon, A. (1990). Pickle fights: Gendered talk in preschool dispute. *Discourse Processes, 13,* 5–31.

Sheldon, A. (1992). Conflict talk: Sociolinguistic challenges to self-assertion and how young girls meet them. *Merrill–Palmer Quarterly, 38,* 95–117.

Sheldon, A., & Johnson, D. (1991, March). *Gender differences in double-voice discourse as a conflict talk style in early childhood.* Paper presented at the meeting of the American Association of Applied Linguistics, New York.

Sheldon, A., & Rohleder, L. (in press). Sharing the same world, telling different stories: Gender differences in co-constructed pretend narratives. In D. Slobin, J. Gerhardt, J. Guo, & A. Kyratzis (Eds.), *Social interaction, social context and language.* Hillsdale, NJ: Lawrence Erlbaum Associates.

Sheppard, W., & Lane, H. (1968). Development of the prosodic features of infant vocalizing. *Journal of Speech and Hearing Research, 11,* 94–108.

Shields, S., & Padawer, J. (1983). Children's standards for judging their own facial expressions of emotion. *Journal of Nonverbal Behavior, 8,* 109–125.

Shotter, J. (1993). *Conversational realities: Constructing life through language.* London: Sage.

Shugar, G., & Bokus, B. (1986). Children's discourse and children's activity in the peer situation. In E. Mueller & C. Cooper (Eds.), *Process and outcome in peer relationships.* New York: Academic Press.

Shure, M. B. (1963). Psychological ecology of a nursery school. *Child Development, 34,* 979–992.

Siegal, M. (1991). *Knowing children: Experiments in conversation and cognition.* Hillsdale, NJ: Lawrence Erlbaum Associates.

Siegman, A. (1987). The telltale voice: Nonverbal messages of verbal communication. In A. Siegman & S. Feldman (Eds.), *Nonverbal behavior and communication.* New York: Lawrence Erlbaum Associates.

Siegman, A., & Boyle, S. (1993). Voices of fear and anxiety and sadness and depression: The effects of speech rate and loudness on fear and anxiety and sadness and depression. *Journal of Abnormal Psychology, 102,* 430–437.

Sigel, I. (1985). *Parental belief systems: The psychological consequences for children.* Hillsdale, NJ: Lawrence Erlbaum Associates.

Sigel, I. (1987). Does hothousing rob children of their childhood? *Early Childhood Research Quarterly, 2,* 211–225.

Sigelman, C., & Adams, R. (1990). Family interactions in public: Parent–child distance and touching. *Journal of Nonverbal Behavior, 14,* 63–75.

Silverman, I., & Shaw, M. E. (1973). Effects of sudden mass desegregation on interracial interaction and attitudes in one southern city. *Journal of Social Issues, 29,* 133–142.

Sincoff, J., & Rosenthal, R. (1985). Content-masking methods as determinants of results of nonverbal communication. *Journal of Nonverbal Behavior, 9,* 121–129.

Singer, J. & Flavell, J. (1981). Development of knowledge about communication: Children's evaluations of explicitly ambiguous messages. *Child Development, 52,* 1211–1215.

Singleton, L. (1974). *The effects of sex and race on children's sociometric choices for play and work.* Urbana, IL: University of Illinois.

Slade, A. (1987a). Quality of attachment and early symbolic play. *Developmental Psychology, 23,* 78–85.

Slade, A. (1987b). A longitudinal study of maternal involvement and symbolic play during the toddler period. *Child Development, 58,* 367–375.

Slomkowski, C., & Dunn, J. (1992). Arguments and relationships within the family: Differences in young children's disputes with mother and sibling. *Developmental Psychology, 28,* 919–924.

Smith, G. H. (1950). Sociometric study of best-liked and least-liked children. *Elementary School Journal, 51,* 77–85.

Smoller, J., & Youniss, J. (1982). Social development through friendship. In K. H. Rubin & H. S. Ross (Eds.), *Peer relationships and social skills in childhood* (pp. 277–298). New York: Springer-Verlag.

Smolucha, L., & Smolucha, F. (1992). Vygotskian theory: An emerging paradigm with implications for a synergistic psychology [Special issue: Play, Vygotsky, and imagination]. *Creativity Research Journal, 5,* 87–97.

Smyth, R. (1995). Conceptual perspective-taking and children's interpretation of pronouns in reported speech. *Journal of Child Language, 22,* 171–187.

Snow, C. (1972). Mothers' speech to children learning language. *Child Development, 43,* 543–565.

Snow, C. (1977a). The development of conversation between mothers and babies. *Journal of Child Language, 4,* 1–22.

Snow, C. (1977b). Mothers' speech research: From input to interaction. In C. Snow & C. Ferguson (Eds.), *Talking to children.* Cambridge: Cambridge University Press.

Snow, C. (1978). *The development of communication.* New York: Wiley.

Snow, C., & Gilbreath, B. (1983). Explaining transitions. In R. Golinkoff (Ed.), *The transition from prelinguistic to linguistic communication.* Hillsdale, NJ: Lawrence Erlbaum Associates.

Snow, M., Jacklin, C., & Maccoby, E. (1983). Sex-of-child differences in father–child interaction at one year of age. *Child Development, 54,* 227–232.

Snyder, L., Bates, E., & Bretherton, I. (1981). Content and context in early lexical development. *Journal of Child Language, 8,* 565–582.

Sodian, B. (1990). Understanding verbal communication: Children's ability to deliberately manipulate ambiguity in referential messages. *Cognitive Development, 5,* 209–222.

Sodian, B. (1991). The development of deception in young children [Special issue: Perspectives on the child's theory of mind]. *British Journal of Developmental Psychology, 9,* 173–188.

Sorce, J., Emde, R., Campos, J., & Klinnert, M. (1985). Maternal emotional signaling: Its effect on the visual cliff behavior of 1-year-olds. *Developmental Psychology, 21,* 195–200.

Speer, J. (1984). Two practical strategies young children use to interpret vague instructions. *Child Development, 55,* 1811–1819.

Sperber, D., & Wilson, D. (1986). *Relevance: Communication and cognition.* Cambridge, MA: MIT Press.

Spurgeon, P., Hicks, C., & Terry, R. (1983). A preliminary investigation into sex differences in reported friendship determinants amongst a group of early adolescents. *British Journal of Social Psychology, 22,* 63–64.

Sroufe, L. A. (1982). Attachment and the roots of competence. In H. E. Fitzgerald & T. H. Carr (Eds.), *Human development 82/83* (pp. 94–98). Guilford, CT: Dushkin.

Sroufe, L. A. (1983). Infant–caregiver attachment and patterns of adaptation in preschool: The roots of maladaptation and competence. In M. Perlmutter (Ed.), *Minnesota symposium on child pscyhology* (Vol. 16, pp. 41–81). Hillsdale, NJ: Lawrence Erlbaum Associates.

Sroufe, L. A. (1989). Relationships, self, and individual adaptation. In A. J. Sameroff & R. N. Emde (Eds.), *Relationship disturbances in early childhood: A developmental approach* (pp. 70–96). New York: Basic Books.

Sroufe, L. A., Egelund, B., & Kreutzer, T. (1990). The fate of early experience following developmental change: Longitudinal approaches to individual adaptation in childhood. *Child Development, 61,* 1363–1373.

Sroufe, L. A., Fox, N., & Pancake, V. (1983). Attachment and dependency in developmental perspective. *Child Development, 54,* 1615–1627.

Stack, D., & Muir, D. (1990). Tactile stimulation as a component of social interchange: New interpretations for the still-face effect. *British Journal of Developmental Psychology, 8,* 131–145.

Stack, D., & Muir, D. (1992). Adult tactile stimulation during face-to-face interactions modulates five-month-olds' affect and attention. *Child Development, 63,* 1509–1525.

Stern, D. (1977). *The first relationship.* Cambridge, MA: Harvard University Press.

Stern, D. (1983). The goal and structure of mother–infant play. *Psychiatrie de l'Enfant, 26,* 193–216.

Stern, D. (1985). *The interpersonal world of the infant: A view from psychoanalysis and developmental psychology.* New York: Basic Books.

Stevenson, M., Roach, M., VerHoeve, J., & Leavitt, L. (1990). Rhythms in the dialogue of infant feeding: Preterm and term infants. *Infant Behavior and Development, 13,* 51–70.

Stifter, C., & Grant, W. (1993). Infant responses to frustration: Individual differences in the expression of negative affect. *Journal of Nonverbal Behavior, 17,* 187–204.

Strayer, F. (1990). Co-adaptation within the early peer group: A psychobiological study of social competence. In B. Schneider (Ed.), *Social competence in developmental perspective.* Geneva, Switzerland: Kluwer.

Strayer, F., & Moss, E. (1989). The co-construction of representational activity during social interaction. In M. Bornstein & J. Bruner (Eds.), *Interaction in human development* (pp. 173–193). Hillsdale, NJ: Lawrence Erlbaum Associates.

Strayer, F., & Strayer, J. (1976). An ethological analysis of social agonism and dominance relations among preschool children. *Child Development, 47,* 980–989.

Strayer, J. (1985). Current research in affective development [Special issue: The feeling child: Affective development reconsidered]. *Journal of Children in Contemporary Society, 17,* 37–55.

Strayer, J. (1986). Children's attributions regarding the situational determinants of emotion in self and others. *Developmental Psychology, 22,* 649–654.

Strichartz, A. (1980). *Truth or consequences: The concepts of lies and truth in children three through seven years old.* Undergraduate honors thesis, Cornell University, Ithaca, NY.

Strichartz, A., & Burton, R. (1990). Lies and truth: A study of the development of the concept. *Child Development, 61,* 211–220.

Styczynzki, L. E., & Langlois, J. H. (1977). The effects of familiarity on behavioral stereotypes associated with physical attractiveness in young children. *Child Development, 48,* 1137–1141.

Styczynski, L. E., & Langlois, J. H. (1980). *Judging the book by its cover: Children's attractiveness and achievement.* Unpublished manuscript, University of Texas at Austin.

Suess, G., Grossman, K., & Sroufe, L. A. (1992). Effects of infant attachment to mother and father on quality of adaptation in preschool: From dyadic to individual organisation of self. *International Journal of Behavioral Development, 15,* 43–65.

Sugarman, S. (1973). *Description of communicative development in the prelanguage child.* Unpublished manuscript, Hampshire College, Amherst, MA.

Sugarman, S. (1983). Empirical versus logical issues in the transition from prelinguistic to linguistic communication. In R. Golinkoff (Ed.), *The transition from prelinguistic to linguistic communication.* Hillsdale, NJ: Lawrence Erlbaum Associates.

Sugarman, S. (1984). Why talk? Comment on Savage-Rumbaugh et al. *Journal of Experimental Psychology—General, 112,* 493–497.

Sullivan, H. S. (1953). *The interpersonal theory of psychiatry.* New York: Norton.

Surber, C. (1985). Developmental changes in inverse compensation in social and nonsocial attributions. In S. Yussen (Ed.), *The development of reflection.* New York: Academic Press.

Sutton-Smith, B., & Rosenberg, B. G. (1971). Sixty years of historical change in game references of American children. In R. E. Herron & B. Sutton-Smith (Eds.), *Child's play* (pp. 18–50). New York: Wiley.

Tannen, D. (1986). *That's not what I meant: How conversational style makes or breaks relationships.* New York: Ballantine Books.

Tannen, D. (1990). *You just don't understand.* New York: Morrow.

Tannen, D. (1990). Gender differences in conversational coherence: Physical alignment and topical cohesion. In B. Dorval (Ed.), *Conversational coherence and its development.* Norwood, NJ: Ablex.

Taylor, M., Cartwright, B., & Bowden, T. (1991). Perspective taking and theory of mind: Do children predict interpretive diversity as a function of differences in observers' knowledge? *Child Development, 62,* 1334–1351.

Taylor, M., & Gelman, S. (1988). Adjectives and nouns: Children's strategies for learning new words. *Child Development, 59,* 411–419.

Taylor, M., & Gelman, S. (1989). Incorporating new words into the lexicon: Preliminary evidence for language hierarchies in two-year-old children. *Child Development, 60,* 625–636.

Tennes, K., Emde, R., Kisley, A., & Metcalf, D. (1972). The stimulus barrier in early infancy: An exploration of some formulations of John Benjamin. *Psychoanalysis and Contemporary Science, 1,* 206–234.

Termine, N., & Izard, C. (1988). Infants' responses to their mothers' expressions of joy and sadness. *Developmental Psychology, 24,* 223–229.

Tfouni, L., & Klatzky, R. (1983). A discourse analysis of deixis: Pragmatic, cognitive and semantic factors in the comprehension of "this," "that," "here" and "there." *Journal of Child Language, 10,* 123–133.

Thompson, R. (1990). Emotion and self-regulation. In R. Thompson (Ed.), *Socioemotional development: Nebraska symposium on motivation.* Lincoln: University of Nebraska Press.

Thorne, B. (1986). Girls and boys together, but mostly apart: Gender arrangements in elementary school. In W. W. Hartup & Z. Rubin (Eds.), *Relationships and development.* Hillsdale, NJ: Lawrence Erlbaum Associates.

Tomasello, M., Conti-Ramsden, G., & Ewert, B. (1990). Young children's conversations with their mothers and fathers: Differences in breakdown and repair. *Journal of Child Language, 17,* 115–130.

Tough, J. (1973). *Focus on meaning.* London: Allen & Unwin.

Tough, J. (1977). *The development of meaning.* New York: Wiley .

Tracy, K. (1991). *Understanding face-to-face interaction: Issues linking goals and discourse.* Hillsdale, NJ: Lawrence Erlbaum Associates.

Tracy, K., & Craig, R. (1983). *Conversational coherence.* Newbury Park, CA: Sage.

Trantham, C., & Pedersen, J. (1978). *Normal language development.* Baltimore: Williams & Wilkins.

Trautner, H. (1995). Boys' and girls' play behavior in same-sex and opposite-sex pairs. *Journal of Genetic Psychology, 156,* 5–15.

Trenholm, S., & Jensen, A. (1992). *Interpersonal communication* (2nd ed.). Belmont, CA: Wadsworth.

Trevarthen, C. (1977a). Descriptive analyses of infant communication behavior. In H. Schaffer (Ed.), *Studies in mother–infant interaction.* London: Academic Press.

Trevarthen, C. (1977b). Descriptive analyses of infant communicative behaviour. In H. Schaffer (Ed.), *Studies in mother–infant interaction.* New York: Academic Press.

Trevarthen, C. (1979a). Communication and co-operation in early infancy: A description of primary intersubjectivity. In M. Bullowa (Ed.), *Before speech: The beginnings of human communication.* London: Cambridge University Press.

Trevarthen, C. (1979b). The foundations of intersubjectivity. In M. Bullowa (Ed.,) *Before speech: The beginning of interpersonal communication.* Cambridge: Cambridge University Press.

Trevarthen, C. (1980a). Brain development and the growth of psychological functions. In J. Sants (Ed.), *Development of psychology and society.* London: Macmillan.

Trevarthen, C. (1980b). The foundations of intersubjectivity: Development of interpersonal and cooperative understanding in infants. In D. Olson (Ed.), *The social foundations of language and thought: Essays in honor of J. S. Bruner.* New York: W. Norton.

Trevarthen, C. (1982). The primary motives for cooperative understanding. In G. Butterworth & P. Light (Eds.), *Social cognition.* Chicago: University of Chicago Press.

Trevarthen, C. (1992). An infant's motives for speaking and thinking in the culture. In A. Heen-Wold (Ed.), *The dialogical alternative: Towards a theory of language and mind.* Oslo, Norway: Scandinavian University Press.

Trevarthen, C., & Aitken, K. (1994). Brain development, infant communication, and empathy disorders: Intrinsic factors in child mental health [Special issue: Neural plasticity, sensitive periods, and psychopathology]. *Development and Psychopathology, 6,* 597–633.

Trevarthen, C., & Hubley, P. (1978). Secondary intersubjectivity: Confidence, confiding and acts of meaning in the first year. In A. Lock (Ed.), *Action, gesture and symbol: The emergence of language.* New York: Academic Press.

Tronick, E., Als, H., & Brazelton, T. B. (1977). Mutuality in mother–infant interaction. *Journal of Communication, 27,* 74–79.

Tronick, E., Als, H., & Brazelton, T. B. (1980). Monadic phases: A structural descriptive analysis of infant–mother face to face interaction. *Merrill–Palmer Quarterly, 26,* 3–24.

Tronick, E., & Gianino, A. (1986). The transmission of maternal disturbance to the infant. In E. Tronick & T. Field (Eds.), *Maternal depression and infant disturbance.* New York: Wiley.

Tronick, E., Ricks, M., & Cohn, J. (1982). Maternal and infant affective exchange: Patterns of adaptation. In T. Field & A. Fogel (Eds.), *Emotion and early interaction.* Hillsdale, NJ: Lawrence Erlbaum Associates.

Turner, G. (1973). Social class and children's language of control at ages five and seven. In B. Bernstein (Ed.), *Class, codes and control* (Vol. 2). London: Routledge.

Turner, G. (1993). Social class, maternal speech and the child's semantic orientation. In D. Messer & G. Turner (Eds.), *Critical influences in child language acquisition and development.* New York: St. Martin's Press.

Turner, P. (1991). Relations between attachment, gender, and behavior with peers in preschool. *Child Development, 62,* 1475–1488.

Unzner, L., & Schneider, K. (1990). Facial reactions in preschoolers: A descriptive study. *Journal of Nonverbal Behavior, 14,* 19–25.

Urban, J., Carlson, E., Egelund, B., & Sroufe, A. (1991). Patterns of individual adaptation across childhood [Special issue: Attachment and developmental psychopathology]. *Development and Psychopathology, 199,* 445–460.

van Dijk, T. (1980). *Macrostructures.* Hillsdale, NJ: Lawrence Erlbaum Associates.

van Dijk, T., & Kintsch, W. (1983). *Strategies of discourse comprehension.* New York: Academic Press.

Van Heugten, A., & Van Meel, J. (1980). Hand movements during the intake of information varying in codability and level of difficulty. *Nederlands Tijdschrift voor de Psychologie en haar Grensgebieden, 35,* 23–40.

Vandell, D., & Wilson, K. (1987). Infants' interactions with mother, sibling, and peer: Contrasts and relations between interaction systems. *Child Development, 58,* 176–186.

Vaughn, B., & Waters, E. (1990). Attachment behavior at home and in the laboratory: Q-sort observations and strange situation classifications of one-year-olds. *Child Development, 61,* 1965–1973.

Veneziano, E. (1989). Replying to mothers' questions. *Journal of Pragmatics, 9,* 433–452.

Veneziano, E., Sinclair, H., & Berthoud, I. (1990). From one word to two words: Repitition patterns on the way to structured speech. *Journal of Child Language, 17,* 633–650.

Volling, B., & Belsky, J. (1992a). The contribution of mother–child and father–child relationships to the quality of sibling interaction: A longitudinal study. *Child Development, 63* 1209–1222.

Volling, B., & Belsky, J. (1992b). Infant, father, and marital antecedents of infant–father attachment security in dual-earner and single-earner families. *International Journal of Behavioral Development, 15,* 83–100.

Vygotsky, L. (1962). *Language and thought.* (E. Hanfmann & G. Vaker, Trans.). Cambridge, MA: MIT Press.

Vygotsky, L. (1978). *Mind in society: The development of higher psychological processes.*

Wagner, E., & Asarnow, R. (1980). *The interpersonal behavior of preadolescent boys with high and low peer status.* Unpublished manuscript, University of Waterloo, Waterloo, Ontario.

Waldrop, M. F., & Halverson, C. F., Jr. (1975). Intensive and extensive peer behavior: Longitudinal and cross-sectional analysis. *Child Development, 46,* 19–26.

Wales, R. (1979). Deixis. In P. Fletcher & M. Garman (Eds.), *Language acquisition: Studies in first language development.* Cambridge: Cambridge University Press.

Walter, C. (1986). *The timing of motherhood: Is later better?* New York: Heath.

Waters, E. (1978). The reliability and stability of individual differences in infant–mother attachment. *Child Development, 49,* 483–494.

Waters, E., & Sroufe, A. (1983). Social competence as a developmental construct. *Developmental Review, 3,* 79–97.

Watzlawick, P., Beavin, J., & Jackson, D. (1967). *Pragmatics of human communication: A study of interactional patterns, pathologies, and paradoxes.* New York: Norton.

Weinraub, M., Clemens, L., Sockloff, A., Ethridge, T., Gracely, E., & Myers, B. (1984). The development of sex role stereotypes in the third year: Relationships to gender labeling, gender identity, sex-typed toy preference, and family characteristics. *Child Development, 55,* 1493–1503.

Weiss, D., & Sachs, J. (1991). Persuasive strategies used by preschool children. *Discourse Processes, 14,* 55–72.

Weiss, R. S. (1982). Attachment in adult life. In C. M. Parkes & J. Stevenson-Hinde (Eds.), *The place of attachment in human behavior* (pp. 171–184). New York: Basic Books.

Weissenborn, J. (1986). Learning how to become an interlocutor: The verbal negotiation of common frames of reference and actions in dyads of 7–14 year old children. In J. Cook-Gumperz, W. Cosaro, & J. Streeck (Eds.), *Children's worlds and children's language.* New York: Mouton de Gruyter.

Wellman, H., & Estes, D. (1987). Children's early use of mental verbs and what they mean. *Discourse Processes, 10,* 141–156.

Wells, G. (1979). Learning and using the auxiliary verb in English. In V. Lee (Ed.), *Language development.* New York: Wiley.

Wells, G. (1981). *Learning through interaction.* Cambridge: Cambridge University Press.

Wells, G., MacLure, M., & Montgomery, M. (1981). Some strategies for sustaining conversation. In P. Werth (Ed.), *Conversation and discourse.* New York: St. Martin's Press.

Wells, G., Montgomery, M., & MacLure, M. (1979). Adult–child discourse: Outline of a model of analysis. *Journal of Pragmatics, 3,* 337–380.

Werner, H., & Kaplan, B. (1963). *Symbol formation.* New York: Wiley.

Wertsch, J. (1985). *Vygotsky and the social formation of mind.* Cambridge, MA: Harvard University Press.

Wertsch, J., McNamee, G., McLane, J., & Budwig, N. (1980). The adult–child dyad as a problem-solving system. *Child Development, 51,* 1215–1221.

Whitehurst, G., & Sonnenschein, S. (1981). The development of communication: A functional analysis. *Annals of Child Development, 2,* 1–48.

Whiting, B. (1963). *Six cultures: Studies in child rearing.* New York: Wiley.

Whiting, B., & Edwards, C. (1988). *Children of different worlds.* Cambridge, MA: Harvard University Press.

Wiggers, M., & van Lieshout, T. (1985). Development of recognition of emotions: Children's reliance on situational and facial expressive cues. *Developmental Psychology, 21,* 336–349.

Wilkins, S. J., & Rogers, D. (1987). Possessive pronouns: Why are plurals harder? *Journal of Psycholinguistic Research, 16,* 551–561.

Wilson, T. (1970). Normative and interpretive paradigms in sociology. In J. Douglas (Ed.), *Understanding everyday life.* Chicago: Aldine.

Winder, C. L., & Rau, L. (1962). Parental attitudes associated with social deviance in preadolescent boys. *Journal of Abnormal and Social Psychology, 64,* 337–338.

Wintre, M., & Vallance, D. (1994). A developmental sequence in the comprehension of emotions: Intensity, multiple emotions, and valence. *Developmental Psychology, 30,* 509–514.

Wittgenstein, L. (1958). *Philosophical investigations.* Oxford: Blackwell.

Wolf, D. (1981). Understanding others: A longitudinal case study of the concept of independent agency. In G. Forman (Ed.), *Action and thought.* New York: Academic Press.

Wood, B. S. (1981). *Children and communication: Verbal and nonverbal language development.* Englewood Cliffs, NJ: Prentice-Hall.

Wood, J. (1996). *Gendered relationships.* London: Mayfield Press.

Woollett, A. (1986). The influence of older siblings on the language environment of young children. *British Journal of Developmental Psychology, 4,* 235–245.

Yingling, J. (1995). The first relationship: Infant–parent communication. In T. Socha & G. Stamp (Eds.), *Parents, children and communication* (pp. 23–43). Mahwah, NJ: Lawrence Erlbaum Associates.

Yonas, A., & Hartman, B. (1993). Perceiving the affordance of contact in four- and five-month-old infants. *Child Development, 64,* 298–308.

Young, L. L., & Cooper, D. H. (1944). Some factors associated with popularity. *Journal of Educational Psychology, 35,* 513–535.

Youngblade, L., & Belsky, J. (1992). Parent–child antecedents of 5-year-olds' close friendships: A longitudinal analysis. *Developmental Psychology, 28,* 700–713.

Younger, B. (1992). Developmental change in infant categorization: The perception of correlations among facial features. *Child Development, 63,* 1526–1535.

Youniss, J. (1980). *Parents and peers in social development: A Sullivan–Piaget perspective.* Chicago: University of Chicago Press.

Youniss, J. (1992). Parent and peer relations in the emergence of cultural competence. In H. McGurk (Ed.), *Childhood social development.* Hillsdale, NJ: Lawrence Erlbaum Associates.

Zimmerman, D., & West, C. (1975). Sex roles, interruptions, and silences in conversation. In B. Thorne & N. Henley (Eds.), *Language and sex: Difference and dominance.* Rowley, MA: Newbury House.

Zinober, B., & Martlew, M. (1985). Developmental changes in four types of gestures in relation to acts and vocalizations from 10 to 21 months. *British Journal Developmental Psychology, 3,* 293–306.

Zivin, G. (1977a). Facial gestures predict preschoolers' encounter outcomes. *Social Science Information, 17,* 715–730.

Zivin, G. (1982). Watching the sands shift: Conceptualizing development of nonverbal mastery. In R. Feldman (Ed.), *Development of nonverbal behavior in children.* New York: Springer.

Zivin, G. (1986). Processes of expressive behavior development. *Merrill–Palmer Quarterly, 32,* 103–140.

Zivin, G. (1989). Some basic considerations in the field of expressive behavior development [a commentary]. *Monographs of the Society for Research in Child Development, 54,* 1–2, pp. 114–136.

Author Index

A

Aboud, F. E., 228
Abramovitch, R., 216
Ackerman, B., 129
Acredolo, L., 46, 147
Adams, G. R., 211, 212
Adams, K., 35
Adams, R., 49
Adamson, L., 180
Ainsworth, M., 31, 32, 161, 162
Aitken, K., 102
Aitken, S., 234
Algozzine, O., 212
Allen, R., 114
Aloise, P., 158
Als, H., 41, 54
Alson, D., 23, 51
Amady, N., 43
Amieltison, C., 70
Appelbaum, M., 49
Applegate, J. G., 189, 216
Applegate, J. L., 128, 155, 187, 188, 189
Arend, R., 139
Argyle, M., 152
Aries, E. J., 233
Arliss, L. P., 231
Asarnow, R., 216
Asher, S. R., 117, 193, 209, 210, 211, 212, 213, 215, 225, 233
Auerbach, J., 24
August, D., 128, 134
Austin, J. L., 107, 108
Azmitia, M., 124
Azuma, H., 117, 239

B

Baak, K., 27
Bach, K., 5, 96, 108, 111
Backscheider, A., 79
Bacon, M., 178

Badzinski, D., 37
Baesler, E. J., 56
Baldwin, D., 76
Ballif, B., 37
Bamberg, M., 169
Bandura, A., 141
Barenboim, C., 147
Barker, R. A., 192
Barnes, S., 165
Barrera, M., 48
Barrett, K., 20, 56
Barry, H., 178
Barton, M., 104, 105, 181
Bates, E., 44, 46, 51, 59, 60, 61, 62, 70, 77, 84, 85, 90, 102, 103, 104, 112, 113, 115, 120, 128, 149, 165, 239
Bates, J., 167
Bateson, G., 128, 149
Bateson, M. C., 104
Bauer, P., 141
Baumrind, D., 172, 184
Bavelas, J., 9
Bayles, K., 167
Beal, C., 129, 143
Bear, R., 173
Beardsall, L., 39
Bearison, D. J., 184
Beavin, J., 149
Becker, J., 113
Beckwith, L., 166
Beebe, B., 23, 51
Beeghly-Smith, M., 44, 84
Behrend, D., 76
Belgrad, S., 129
Bell, M., 67
Bell, S., 32
Bellinger, D., 177
Belsky, J., 32, 42, 49, 97, 176, 239, 242
Benenson, J., 143
Benigni, L., 44, 46, 51, 59, 165
Benoit, P. J., 128, 226
Benoit, P., 128, 155
Benson, N., 46

Subject Index